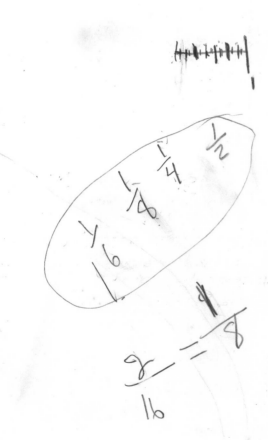

$\frac{1}{2}$

$\frac{1}{4}$

$\frac{1}{8}$

$\frac{1}{6}$

$8 = \frac{8}{16}$

Grade Five
MATHEMATICS

Student Textbook

THE HEAVENS ABOV

Author
Dr. Cal Meyer

Grade Level Editor
Dr. Gary Kimball

Managing Editors
Fran Burdick
Paula Redfield

Senior Content Editor
Dr. James Schwartz

Assistant Managing Editor
JoAnn Keenan

Editing Team
Suzanne Clark
Anita Gordon
Christy Krenek
Mary K. Lirley
Melissa Sheckler

Design Team
Susanna Garmany
Phil Lear
Dan Schultz

Grade 5

1 Place Value of Whole Numbers and Decimals

2 Addition and Subtraction of Whole Numbers and Decimals

3 Multiplication of Whole Numbers

4 Division of Whole Numbers

Table of Contents

5 - Multiplication and Division of Decimals

6 - Geometric Properties

7 - Number Theory and Fractions

Grade 5

Table of Contents

Grade Five

1

Chapter

Lessons 1–11

In the beginning God created the heavens and the earth.

Genesis 1:1

Construct Meaning

Welcome to the neighborhood—not your home and the streets around it, but our neighborhood in the universe! Our solar system consists of the sun, nine planets and their moons, and other objects such as asteroids, meteoroids, and comets.

Our planet, Earth, has one moon. The average distance from Earth to the moon, center to center, is two hundred thirty-nine thousand miles.

thousands period			ones period		
hundred thousands	ten thousands	thousands,	hundreds	tens	ones
2	**3**	**9,**	**0**	**0**	**0**

All whole numbers can be written using only the **digits** 0, 1, 2, 3, 4, 5, 6, 7, 8, and 9. To make large numbers easier to read, commas are used to separate the number into groups of three digits. Each group is called a **period**. The value of each digit is shown by its **place** in a number.

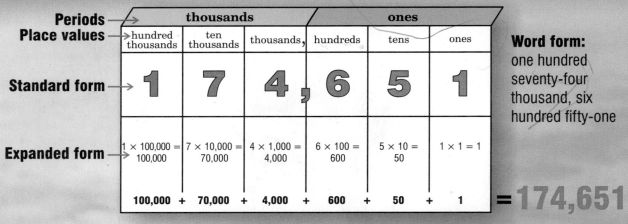

Periods →	thousands			ones		
Place values →	hundred thousands	ten thousands	thousands,	hundreds	tens	ones
Standard form →	**1**	**7**	**4,**	**6**	**5**	**1**
Expanded form →	1 × 100,000 = 100,000	7 × 10,000 = 70,000	4 × 1,000 = 4,000	6 × 100 = 600	5 × 10 = 50	1 × 1 = 1
	100,000 +	70,000 +	4,000 +	600 +	50 +	1

Word form:
one hundred seventy-four thousand, six hundred fifty-one

= 174,651

Check Understanding

a. Write the standard form for 80,000 + 3,000 + 200 + 90 + 4.

b. Write 361,401 in expanded form.

Read each number. Use place value to tell what the orange digit represents.

c. 92,641   d. 89,450   e. 683,526

Place Value to Hundred Thousands

Write the number in expanded form.

thousands			ones		
hundred thousands	ten thousands	thousands	hundreds	tens	ones
1.	6	8 ,	1	9	7
2. 4	2	1 ,	5	7	3
3. 9	3	4 ,	2	0	2

Write the number in standard form.

4. seven hundred fourteen thousand, three hundred sixty-eight
5. four hundred sixty-two thousand, one hundred twelve
6. nine hundred thirty-four thousand, one hundred seventy-nine
7. five hundred nineteen thousand, eight hundred ninety-one
8. 300,000 + 70,000 + 6,000 + 400 + 80 + 2
9. 100,000 + 4,000 + 60
10. 700,000 + 8,000 + 900 + 9
11. 600,000 + 40,000 + 3,000 + 900 + 20 + 5

Use place value to tell what the green digit represents.

12. 89,016
13. 61,721
14. 320,354
15. 754,333

16. Count by tens from 64 to 134. Write each number.
17. Count by hundreds from 827 to 1,427. Write each number.

18. The cashier at First Bank gave Mr. Bennett the following bills: 7 tens, 1 one, and 5 hundreds. What was the amount of the check Mr. Bennett cashed?

Add or subtract.

1. 12 + 3
2. 46 − 9
3. 73 − 8
4. 28 + 14
5. 92 − 6
6. 65 + 37

Multiply or divide.

7. 13 × 2
8. 36 ÷ 6
9. 24 × 4
10. 45 ÷ 9
11. 44 ÷ 4
12. 43 × 8

© Copyright 2001

3

Construct Meaning

The number of people living on planet Earth is over six billion. How would you write this number?

Large numbers are grouped into periods of three digits. **Ones**, **thousands**, **millions**, and **billions** are periods. Commas separate the periods and show you where to use the period name. Six billion is written as 6,000,000,000.

What do you think the following number represents?

billions period			millions period			thousands period			ones period		
hundred billions	ten billions	billions ,	hundred millions	ten millions	millions	hundred thousands	ten thousands	thousands,	hundreds	tens	ones
			2	7	4,	8	7	1,	0	8	4

This was the population of the United States at 5:30 P.M., Eastern Daylight Time, on May 25, 2000.

To read the number, say the number in a period, then the period name: 274 million, 871 thousand, 84.

To write the standard form, use commas to separate the periods: 274,871,084.

To show expanded form, write: 200,000,000 + 70,000,000 + 4,000,000 + 800,000 + 70,000 + 1,000 + 80 + 4.

To use the word form, write: two hundred seventy-four million, eight hundred seventy-one thousand, eighty-four.

Check Understanding

Use the number 274,871,084 to answer each problem.

a. Use place value to write what the 2 represents.

b. Name the period that includes the digits 871.

c. Name the place value position of the digit 0.

d. How can you change the number to 274,971,084?

Write the number shown on the abacus.

1.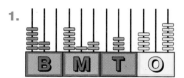

2.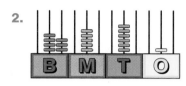

3.

Use place value to tell what the purple digit represents.

4. 338,306,000

5. 870,046,764,597

6. 331,576,832,000

Use the number 585,742,216,147 to write the digits for each period.

7. millions

8. ones

9. billions

10. thousands

Write the word form.

11. 83,175,000

12. 6,453,281,954

13. 2,067,001,905

Write the expanded form.

14. two hundred forty-two million, seven hundred three thousand, seven hundred

15. forty-four billion, three hundred sixteen million, one thousand, two hundred

16. two hundred billion, sixty-seven million, two thousand, eight hundred three

17. Our solar system is part of the vast Milky Way Galaxy. The spiral-shaped Galaxy is about 100,000 light-years across. A light-year is not a measurement of time, but of distance, the distance light travels in one year. Light travels at 186,000 miles per second. One light-year is about 5,879,000,000,000 miles.

In comparison to the Galaxy, our solar system seems small. It is about 12 light-hours across or about 8 billion miles. Write 8 billion in standard form.

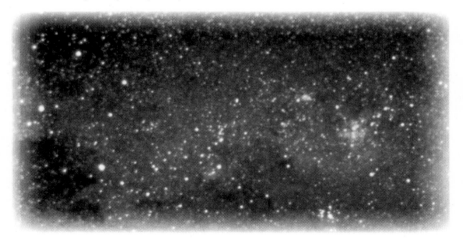

Lesson 3

Construct Meaning

David lives in Ogden, Utah. He is packing for a visit with his aunt and uncle who live in Brainerd, Minnesota. He wants to know which state is larger in area. He learned that Utah has an area of 84,905 square miles and Minnesota has an area of 84,397 square miles. How can David tell which state is larger?

You can <u>compare</u> two numbers by comparing the digits in each place value position.

Minnesota
84,397
square miles

Utah
84,905
square miles

thousands			ones		
hundred thousands	ten thousands	thousands	hundreds	tens	ones
	8	4,	9	0	5
	8	4,	3	9	7

9 > 3, so
84,905 > 84,397

Line up the numbers by place value. Start comparing at the left. Check each place until the digits are different.

In square miles, Utah is slightly larger than Minnesota.

You can <u>order</u> numbers in the same way.

Order the population of these four states from greatest to least:

	millions	hundred thousands	ten thousands	thousands	hundreds	tens	ones
Maryland	5,	1	3	5,	0	0	0
Missouri	5,	4	3	9,	0	0	0
Tennessee	5,	4	3	1,	0	0	0
Wisconsin	5,	2	2	4,	0	0	0

Step 1 The digits in the highest place, millions, are the same, 5 millions.

Step 2 The greatest digit in the hundred thousands place is 4. Both Missouri and Tennessee have a 4.

Step 3 No difference is found between the two greatest populations until the thousands place. 9 > 1, so 5,439,000 > 5,431,000.

Step 4 Compare the remaining numbers: 5,224,000 > 5,135,000.

By population, the four states are ordered: Missouri, Tennessee, Wisconsin, Maryland.

Check Understanding

a. Order from least to greatest. 56,276   56,343   56,145
b. How is comparing 79,617 and 81,823 different from solving the previous problem?
c. Why do you start at the left to compare numbers?

Comparing and Ordering Whole Numbers

Write >, < or = for ⬚.

1. 741 > 471
2. 1,064 < 1,066
3. 6,805 < 6,850
4. 26,765 > 22,886
5. 867,551 > 687,504
6. 503,011 < 503,101

Use the numbers in the chart to answer the following questions.

7. Which numbers are less than 320,000 square kilometers?

8. Which numbers are greater than 335,000 square kilometers?

9. Which numbers come between 310,000 and 325,000 square kilometers?

10. Which number shows a 2 in the ten thousands place?

Areas of Five European Countries	
Finland	338,145 sq km
Germany	357,046 sq km
Italy	301,277 sq km
Norway	324,220 sq km
Poland	312,677 sq km

11. Write the names of the countries in order of their area from the least to the greatest square kilometers.

12. During a mountain hike, Rick walked to the sign marking the elevation as 12,877 feet. His friend Randy reached 14,110 feet. Write a comparison sentence about the hike.

13. Write three numbers greater than 94,329 and less than 95,006.

Review

Use commas to separate the periods in the number.

1. 18264
2. 607352
3. 98954321
4. 100100

Use place value to tell what the blue digit represents.

5. 745,197
6. 3,800,620
7. 6,570,432
8. 102,812

Write in expanded form and word form.

9. 40,800,053
10. 905,632
11. 2,071,300,000
12. 60,497

Construct Meaning

The students of Courageous Christian School recycled soda cans. At the end of the year, 84,352 cans had been collected. To report the total in the "Courageous Chronicle," the school secretary wants to use a rounded number. How would you round 84,352 to the nearest thousand?

You can use a number line.

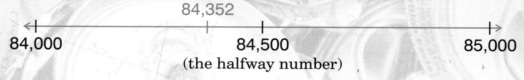

84,352

84,000   84,500   85,000
              (the halfway number)

84,352 is closer to 84,000 than to 85,000.

You can follow these steps to round to any place value position.

Step 1 Locate the digit in the place to which you want to round the number. This is the target digit.

84,352

Step 2 Find the digit to the right of the chosen place. If the digit to the right is 5 or greater than 5, round up. If the digit is less than 5, round down; the target digit stays the same.

84,352

Step 3 Replace the digits to the right of the target place with zeros.

84,000
Rounded to the nearest thousand, 84,352 is 84,000.

Check Understanding

a. Write the number that is halfway between 30,000 and 40,000.

b. Write the thousands that the number 6,520 is between.

c. Round 52,633 to the nearest thousand.

d. Round 184,528 to the nearest ten thousand.

e. Round 8,924,513 to the nearest million.

Rounding Whole Numbers

 ractice

Round the number to the greatest place value.
1. 370,764   2. 26,982   3. 52,344   4. 4,327,600

Round to the nearest ten.
5. 125   6. 11,974   7. 2,689   8. 673

Round to the nearest thousand.
9. 6,660   10. 73,583   11. 9,161   12. 511,482

Round to the nearest hundred thousand.
13. 650,555   14. 8,029,040   15. 1,378,290   16. 216,443

Complete the chart.

Round to →	ten thousands	hundreds	tens
17. 28,634			
18. 4,167,250			
19. 192,329			
20. 304,286			

 pply

21. Trina's assignment was to research the average distance the four inner planets are from the sun, round the numbers to the nearest ten million, then list them from least to greatest. She found these figures: Earth, 92,959,671 miles; Mars, 141,639,220 miles; Mercury, 35,984,589 miles; and Venus, 67,234,201 miles. Write the rounded numbers in the order of the planets' relationship to the sun.

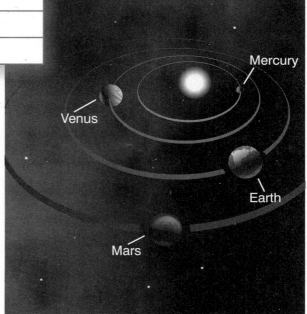

 eview

Write the correct symbol: >, < or =.
1. 45 million ___ 450 thousand   2. 2 billion ___ 2,000,000,000
3. 7,365,049 ___ 7,365,094   4. 2,943,052 ___ 2,953,052

Construct Meaning

space pen — $19.95

key ring — $3.45

Space Station model — $19.90

pin — $3.95

mug — $10.00

sipper cup — $2.95

Mars Pathfinder T-shirt — $12.50

space ice cream — $2.75

Noreen's family is visiting the Johnson Space Center near Houston, Texas. She has $20.00 to spend on items in the gift shop. In addition to buying something for herself, Noreen would like to purchase a gift for her older brother and for her friend Susanna. How would you advise Noreen to spend her money?

Solving a problem is like taking a trip. Noreen's family had to choose the highways to take. Some roads are better than others. Some require more or less time. Some might not even lead to the Johnson Space Center. The Problem-Solving Guide is like a road map to help you move toward your destination.

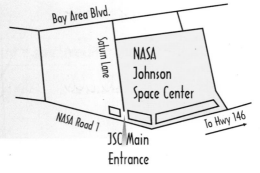

Use the 5-step Problem-Solving Guide to help Noreen make her decisions.

Understand the question.	How can Noreen buy appropriate gifts with $20.00?
Analyze the data.	Noreen has $20.00 to spend. The gifts she is considering range in price from $2.95 to $19.90.
Plan the strategy.	Should Noreen choose her own gift first, or the other two gifts? Should she spend about the same amount for each gift, or unequal amounts? Estimate the total cost.
Solve the problem.	Subtract the total cost of the gifts from $20.00.
Evaluate the result.	Did Noreen make wise purchases? Did she have enough money? If so, she solved her problem in a reasonable way.

Can you think of a different way to solve the problem?

**ractice**

Read the problem in the box. Follow each direction.
1. Rewrite the question in your own words.
2. List the data you were given.
3. Write a plan for solving the problem.
4. Find the solution.
5. Explain how you know your results are reasonable.

Gary sold magazines for a school project. He collected a total of $5.00 in coins. He had 6 nickels, twice as many dimes as nickels, and the rest in quarters. How many of each coin did Gary have?

From the list, choose a strategy for solving the problem. Write the strategy and the answer.

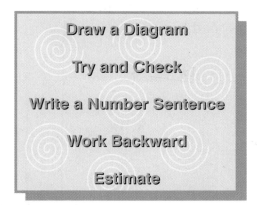

Draw a Diagram

Try and Check

Write a Number Sentence

Work Backward

Estimate

6. Noreen has $0.60 of her $20.00 left. Which three items from the NASA gift shop did she purchase?

7. A best-selling book sold 250,000 copies in the first six months and 100,000 copies in the next six months. How many copies were sold in the first year?

8. The diameter of the planet Jupiter is 142,800 kilometers. About how many hundred thousand kilometers is the diameter of Jupiter?

Use the population chart to solve each problem.

9. The chart shows the 1790 population figures for the first five of the 13 original states of the United States. List the states in order from least to greatest.

Total Population in the Year 1790	
State	**Population**
Delaware	59,096
Pennsylvania	433,611
New Jersey	184,139
Georgia	82,548
Connecticut	237,655

10. Today, the ten-county metropolitan region around Atlanta, Georgia, has over three million people. Round each 1790 state population figure in the chart above to the greatest place value. Round their estimated sum to the nearest million. Is the sum of the rounded numbers more or less than the current population of the Atlanta region? What is the estimated difference?

**eview**

Write the expanded form.
1. 13,574   2. 7,523   3. 3,040,709

Name the number the green digit represents.
4. 26,484   5. 2,379,010   6. 453,228

 **Construct Meaning**

At the 0.5 kilometer marker, Stuart was leading in the 1 kilometer race. How much of the race does Stuart still have to run?

A <u>decimal</u> names part of a whole.

Decimal numbers can be modeled with squares.

      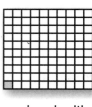

one whole   one tenth   one hundredth
1 or 1.0   0.1 or $\frac{1}{10}$ 0.01 or $\frac{1}{100}$

Stuart has run 0.5 of one kilometer.

He has 0.5 kilometer left to run.

Decimal numbers can be modeled with money.

one whole dollar   one dime   one penny $3.54
100 cents or $1.00   10 cents or $0.10   1 cent or $0.01

Decimal numbers can be written on a place value chart.

hundreds	tens	ones	tenths	hundredths
1	0	2	5	6

One hundred two and fifty-six hundredths is written as 102.56. The whole number part of the number is 102. The decimal part is 0.56.

A <u>decimal point</u> separates the whole number part from the decimal part and is read, "and."

 **Check Understanding**

Copy the place value chart.
Write the numbers.

a. 3 ones, 2 tenths, 4 hundredths
b. 1 ten, 8 ones, 0 tenths, 9 hundredths
c. five and thirty-eight hundredths
d. nine hundred and two tenths
e. fourteen and seventy hundredths

hundreds	tens	ones	tenths	hundredths
		3	2	4
	1	8	0	9

actice

Write the decimal number for the shaded parts.

1.

2.

Use the numbers in the Answer Bank for problems 3 through 7.

3. The digit 9 has a value of 9 tens.
4. The digit 7 has a value of 7 ones.
5. The digit 8 has a value of 8 tenths.
6. The digit 4 has a value of 4 hundredths.
7. The decimal parts of the numbers are equal.

A N S W E R		B A N K	
56.28	24.6	85.19	27.36
80.74	76.89	93.72	62.60

Write a decimal to represent the underlined words.

8. By the time Stuart reached the eight tenths marker in the race, Cody had passed him.
9. The drinking straw measured twenty hundredths of a meter.
10. You can see ninety-nine and ninety-nine hundredths percent of the mass of the solar system with your own eyes, using no instruments whatsoever.

Write as part of one dollar, expressed as hundredths.

11. 6 dimes
12. 2 quarters
13. 47 pennies
14. 3 dimes
15. 25 pennies
16. 3 quarters

pply

17. If Yvonne completed the race in 3.10 minutes and Lacy crossed the finish line in 3.01 minutes, which girl ran faster?

eview

Write >, < or =.

1. 156 < 163
2. 8,600 > 8,588
3. 19,820 = 19,820

Round to the nearest ten thousand.

4. 56,614
5. 127,407
6. 430,917
7. 3,685,000

Construct Meaning

Elizabeth's father works for a company that makes vitamins. He must find the cost of producing various vitamins in order to set the retail price. He made this chart showing the cost of four vitamins.

multiple vitamin	**$0.125 per tablet**
calcium	**$0.053 per tablet**
vitamin C	**$0.116 per tablet**
vitamin E	**$0.129 per capsule**

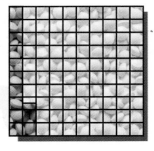

Imagine that each of these one hundred squares was divided into ten smaller squares. Which vitamin pill price would be shown by the shaded parts?

The shaded parts show 0.125, the price ($0.125) of one multiple vitamin pill.

You can use a place value chart to write decimal numbers in expanded form. How would you place the digits to show 4.253?

tens	ones .	tenths	hundredths	thousandths
	4 .	2	5	3
	4×1 . 2×0.1		5×0.01	3×0.001

Write: 4.253

Read: four and two hundred fifty-three thousandths

Expanded form: 4 + 0.2 + 0.05 + 0.003

Check Understanding

a. Write the decimal for one thousandth.

b. How many times greater is the place value of hundredths than thousandths?

Use the number 436.515 for each problem.

c. Write the value of the digit 3.

d. Write the value of the digit 5 in both place value positions.

e. Name the place value position of the digit 1.

f. Write the word form of the number.

Write the decimal.

1. four tenths
2. thirty-five hundredths
3. forty-two thousandths

4. seven hundred fourteen thousandths
5. one and one thousandth

Write the number from the Answer Bank in which 7 has the value of:

Answer Bank	
0.786	4.325
70.122	55.472
2.287	87.324

6. 7 hundredths
7. 7 tenths
8. 7 thousandths
9. 7 ones
10. 7 tens

Write the place value position of each underlined digit.

11. 0.4̲1
12. 1.2̲29
13. 3.0̲17
14. 9.883̲

Write the word form for each decimal number.

15. 0.523
16. 0.374
17. 3.867
18. 8.009

Write the expanded form for each decimal number.

19. 0.813
20. 0.024
21. 0.678
22. 5.43

23. As Allie and Whitney are playing in the ultraviolet rays of the sun, their bodies are making vitamin D. God has designed our bodies so that we can manufacture enough vitamin D in summer to last us through the winter. To prevent sunburn, we use sunblock. If a bottle of sunblock costs $0.179 per ounce, would this be more or less than $0.17 per ounce?

Use mental math and place value to determine how much less A is than B.

1. A 0.27   B 0.28
2. A 4.75   B 4.85
3. A 27.36   B 27.37
4. A 0.8   B 0.81

Write the decimal number in standard form.

5. nineteen and nine hundredths
6. four hundred one and one tenth

 **Construct Meaning**

Radio astronomy is the study of planets, stars, galaxies, and other astronomical objects using radio waves they emit. If the diameters of two dish-shaped reflectors measure 76.2 meters and 76.6 meters, which reflector would be larger?

You can use a number line to compare decimals.

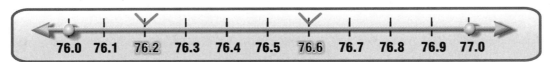

76.0 76.1 76.2 76.3 76.4 76.5 76.6 76.7 76.8 76.9 77.0

The number 76.6 is to the right of 76.2, therefore, 76.6 is greater than 76.2.

The reflector which has a diameter of 76.6 meters would be larger.

As with whole numbers, you can compare two decimals by comparing the digits in each place value position.

Compare 0.883 and 0.892. Start comparing at the left. Check each place until the digits are different.

hundreds	tens	ones	tenths	hundredths	thousandths
		0	8	8	3
		0	8	9	2

8 < 9, so 0.883 < 0.892

You can order decimals the same way.
Order: 3.123, 0.312, and 3.120 from greatest to least.

hundreds	tens	ones	tenths	hundredths	thousandths
		3	1	2	3
		0	3	1	2
		3	1	2	0

- First, line up the numbers by place value.
- Next, compare the numbers two at a time. Because the 3 in the ones place is greater than 0, 3.123 > 0.312 and 3.120 > 0.312.
- Because the 3 in the thousandths place is greater than 0, 3.123 > 3.120.
- Finally, list the numbers from greatest to least: 3.123, 3.120, 0.312.

 **Check Understanding**

Write >, < or =.

a. 2.40 ⬚ 2.04   b. 0.64 ⬚ 0.79   c. 1.55 ⬚ 1.53   d. 4.000 ⬚ 4.001

Order from least to greatest.

e. 66.89 67.91 67.19   f. 88.52 89.78 88.26

Comparing and Ordering Decimals

Practice

Order from greatest to least.

1.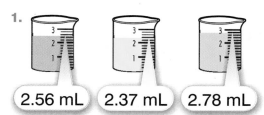

2.56 mL   2.37 mL   2.78 mL

2.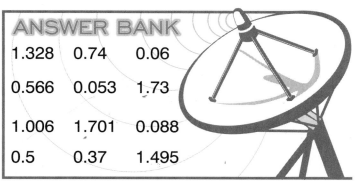

4.3 miles
2.9 miles
2.4 miles
2.1 miles
3.4 miles
NASA Johnson Space Center

Write >, < or =.

3. 3.37 ⬚ 3.39

4. 0.079 ⬚ 0.790

5. 5.510 ⬚ 5.50

6. 28.25 ⬚ 28.250

7. 40.19 ⬚ 40.2

8. 9.06 ⬚ 9.6

Use the numbers in the Answer Bank for questions 9 through 11.

Which numbers are:

9. greater than 1.6?

10. less than 0.074?

11. between 0.3 and 1?

ANSWER BANK		
1.328	0.74	0.06
0.566	0.053	1.73
1.006	1.701	0.088
0.5	0.37	1.495

Apply

12. Dan, Troy, and Aaron have formed a "Future Scientists' Club." Today they plan to listen to a space probe report on the radio. They know that the report will be broadcast on a station near FM station 107.0. There are two local stations, one at 106.5, and another at 106.9. Which do you think they should try first?

Review

Write the word form for each decimal number.

1. 0.034

2. 0.88

3. 304.601

4. 5.007

Write the standard form.

5. one million, two hundred seventy-two thousand

6. three hundred one billion

7. six hundred twenty thousand, sixteen

 **Construct Meaning**

Apply what you know about rounding whole numbers as you round decimals.

Use a number line to locate and round each city's rainfall amount to the nearest inch.

CITY	SEPTEMBER RAINFALL
CHICAGO, ILLINOIS, USA	3.6 INCHES
MILAN, ITALY	3.2 INCHES
ZURICH, SWITZERLAND	3.9 INCHES

3.2   3.6   3.9

3   3.5   4

Which of these decimals is closer to three inches?
Which of these decimals is closer to four inches?
What is the halfway number between 3 inches and 4 inches?

In one year, the total rainfall in Forks, Washington, was 160.88 inches. Simplify this figure by rounding the number to the nearest tenth of an inch. Apply the steps you learned for rounding whole numbers to rounding decimals.

- First, target the digit in the place to which you will round.   160.88

- Look at the digit in the place to the immediate right.   160.88

- If the digit is 5 or more, round up. If it is less than 5, round down, leaving the targeted digit the same. 8 > 5, so the tenths digit increases by 1.

160.88 rounds to 160.9 inches.

 **Check Understanding**

Round each number to the place of the underlined digit.

a. 1<u>2</u>.5   b. 6.<u>3</u>8   c. 4.7<u>3</u>2   d. 8.<u>4</u>6   e. 2.<u>9</u>1

Write the whole numbers between which the decimal falls. Then write the whole number to which it rounds.

f. 0.7   g. 8.2   h. 5.51   i. 9.8   j. 0.04

1. Draw a number line with endpoints of 2 and 3. On the line, locate and label these decimals: 2.1, 2.4, 2.9, 2.2, and 2.7.

2. Which of the decimals round to 3?

3. Which decimals round to 2?

Round to the nearest whole number.

4. 36.4   5. 4.9   6. 13.51   7. 0.7   8. 80.06

Round to the nearest tenth.

9. 61.52   10. 9.763   11. 4.087   12. 55.04   13. 0.11

Round to the nearest hundredth.

14. 23.665   15. 0.942   16. 78.508   17. 39.566   18. 59.610

Round the amount to the nearest dollar.

19. $3.86   20. $9.39   21. $62.73   22. $1.27   23. $40.50

Round the number 12.783 to the nearest:

24. one   25. tenth   26. hundredth   27. ten

28. Katrina is 154.3 centimeters tall. Her brother Chad is 150.6 centimeters tall. Round both figures to the nearest centimeter. Which child's height is closer to 151 centimeters?

29. Write at least five different decimal numbers with digits in the hundredths place that round to 2.1 when rounded to the nearest tenth.

Write the word form.

1. 0.034   2. 0.88   3. 304.601   4. 99.993

Write >, < or =.

5. 31.07 ⬚ 13.70   6. 1.0 ⬚ 0.1   7. 0.56 ⬚ 0.560   8. 0.08 ⬚ 0.80

Write in order from least to greatest.

9. 0.4   0.14   0.142   10. 6.89   6.49   6.09   11. 2.202   2.222   2.212

Lesson 10

A report from Mission Control said $5.25 million was spent for repairs to the Space Shuttle orbiter *Discovery*, and $14.8 million was spent on the orbiter *Columbia*. Round each number to the nearest million dollars. About how much more was spent to repair *Columbia*?

> $5.25 million rounds to $5 million.
>
> $14.8 million rounds to $15 million.
>
> "About" means we can use the rounded figures to estimate the difference:
>
> $15 million − $5 million = $10 million.

Use the steps of the Problem-Solving Guide to solve the problem.

1. Tamara's mother bought gasoline for $1.395 per gallon, while her father filled the tank in his car for $1.399 per gallon. Who got the better buy?

2. Austin checked the prices of four CD players. He found players for $27.95, $43.90, $29.90, and $43.09. Which was the least expensive? Which was the most expensive? Round each amount to the nearest dollar.

3. Kaitlyn is ordering hamburgers and french fries for her friend and herself. Hamburgers cost $3.55 and french fries cost $1.19. Kaitlyn has $11.00. Estimate the total cost. Does Kaitlyn have enough money? Would it be better to overestimate or underestimate the total amount needed?

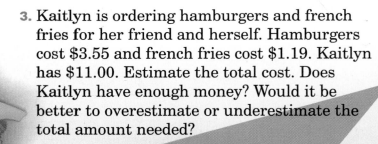

4. Mrs. Snyder is preparing meatloaf for a church dinner. She needs a total of 15 pounds of hamburger. At the supermarket she picks up packages weighing 3.5 pounds, 3.2 pounds, 3.4 pounds, and 3.9 pounds. She rounded the weight of each package to the nearest pound. Did her estimate meet her need? In this situation, would it be better to overestimate or underestimate the total amount she has?

5. The sun contains 99.85 percent of all the matter in the solar system. The planets contain only 0.135 percent of the mass of the solar system. Natural satellites of the planets, comets, asteroids, and meteoroids form the remaining 0.015 percent. Round each decimal number to the nearest tenth.

Times may be given in minutes, seconds, and hundredths of a second. Use the figures in the chart to answer questions 6–8.

6. Who was the first place winner in this event?

7. List the times in order from least to greatest.

8. Round each time to the nearest second.

The XVIII Olympic Winter Games — Women's Downhill		
Athlete	Country	Time
Ertl, Martina	Germany	1:29.76
Goetschl, Renate	Austria	1:29.34
Seizinger, Katja	Germany	1:28.52
Wiberg, Pernilla	Sweden	1:28.86

History Connection

The ancient Romans developed a system for writing numbers that was used throughout Europe until the 1500s. Roman numerals can still be found on clock faces, monuments and public buildings, and introductory pages of books.

The seven symbols are: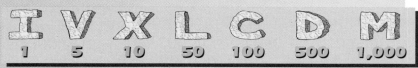

Roman numerals do not have place value. The symbols are combined, usually by addition, and written from left to right.

XXXIII = 33 (10 + 10 + 10 + 1 + 1 + 1)

DCLXVII = 667 (500 + 100 + 50 + 10 + 5 + 1 + 1)

A symbol of lesser value placed before a symbol of greater value means you subtract. This is generally used to represent fours and nines.

IV means 4 (5 – 1)   IX means 9 (10 – 1)

XL means 40 (50 – 10)   XC means 90 (100 – 10)

Write the number in standard form.

9. XIV   10. MDLVIII   11. LXXVI   12. CXC   13. MCMIV

Write the Roman numeral.

14. 48   15. 117   16. 1,730   17. 2,039   18. 504

21

Galaxies to Space Dust: Numbers Great and Small

Write the letter of the correct answer.

1. Which is the standard form for fifteen million, seven?

   a. 15,007   **b.** 15,000,070

   c. 15,000,007   **d.** 15,000,000,007

2. What is the standard form for 200,000 + 20,000 + 3,000 + 200 + 80 + 5?

   a. 2,232,805   **b.** 223,285

   c. 220,325   **d.** 223,205

3. Which is true?

   a. 64.05 > 64.50   **b.** 64.05 = 64.050

   c. 64.05 < 64.050   **d.** 64.05 < 64.00

4. Which number is greater than 781.70?

   a. 781.7   **b.** 781.07

   c. 781.77   **d.** 781.007

Write the number in expanded form.

5. 4,008   6. 4,782.304   7. 19,680   8. 5,001.009

Write the number in word form.

9. 475,069   10. 6,328.5   11. 0.401   12. 134,965,500

Write in order from least to greatest.

13. 1,350,000   1,040,000   1,003,000   1,020,000

14. 2.632   2.326   2.236

15. 70.721   71.272   71.271

Name the place value of the underlined digit.

16. 2<u>3</u>,475   17. 134,<u>8</u>92   18. 0.1<u>3</u>2   19. 89.4<u>5</u>1

Round to the nearest place value given.

20. ten thousand: 75,374   21. million: 163,248,300

22. tenths: 13.01   23. hundredths: 75.374

"For I dipped into the Future, far as human eye could see; saw the vision of the world, and all the wonder that would be." Alfred Lord Tennyson, 1842

"Who is so great a God as our God? You are the God who does wonders." Psalm 77:13–14

Use the chart at the right for problems 24–32.

24. Which items are greater than $1.00 and less than $10.00?

25. The price of which items would round to $24.00?

Alarm Clock $5.78
Baseball Glove $28.98
Mountain Bike $87.00
Calculator $23.86
Car Model $2.69
Chewing Gum $0.26
Toothpaste $0.89

Write >, < or = to compare the prices.

26. toothpaste ⬚ chewing gum

27. car model ⬚ alarm clock

28. baseball glove ⬚ mountain bike

29. Write the prices of the items in order from least to greatest.

30. Make a list of the items. Beside each name, write the price rounded to the nearest dollar.

Calculator Math

31. Add the actual prices to determine the total. Write the exact sum, then round the total to the nearest dime.

32. If the exact total sum from problem 31 was changed into pennies, how many pennies would this be?

33. The inner four planets of the solar system are Earth, Mars, Venus, and Mercury. Of the four planets, the ones that are nearest and farthest from the sun have no moons. Earth, which is the third farthest from the sun has one moon. Venus has two tiny moons. A car has been named for the planet closest to the sun. A candy bar bears the name of the planet fourth from the sun. Write the names of the planets in order, based on their distance from the sun, beginning with the one nearest the sun.

These sentences about place value are missing terms. Write the correct word(s).

34. Each group of three digits in a number is called a ⬚ .

35. In the number 2,415,867,000, the 1 represents ⬚ .

36. The number 2,415,867,000 could be ⬚ to 2,000,000,000.

37. Numbers less than one can be written as ⬚ .

38. In the number 9.016, the value of the 6 is six ⬚ .

39. To the nearest ⬚ , the number 9.016 rounds to 9.02.

40. If you were writing 9.016 in ⬚ , you would write: nine and sixteen thousandths.

Grade Five

2 Chapter

Lessons 12–25

Indeed heaven and the highest heavens belong to the LORD your God, *also* the earth with all that *is* in it.

Deuteronomy 10:14

 **Construct Meaning**

Hot air balloons and airships had already been invented when Wilbur and Orville Wright became convinced there was a better way for people to fly. From examining flying machines that inventors had tried to build, the brothers dealt with problems such as lift, control, and power to push through the air.

The Wright brothers' dream came true on December 17, 1903, at Kitty Hawk, North Carolina. Their aircraft, the *Flyer*, flew 120 feet, 175 feet, 200 feet, and 852 feet in four flights before being damaged by a gust of wind. Today, it holds a place of honor in the National Air and Space Museum in Washington, D.C.

> The symbol ≈ means "is approximately equal to."

- Round the addends.

$$
\begin{array}{rcl}
120 & \rightarrow & 100 \\
175 & \rightarrow & 200 \\
200 & \rightarrow & 200 \\
+\,852 & \rightarrow & 900 \\
\hline
 & & 1{,}400
\end{array}
$$

- Group numbers that are easy to add mentally.

$$
\begin{array}{r}
120 \\
175 \\
200 \\
+\,852
\end{array}
$$

$120 + 175 \approx \mathbf{300}$

$200 + 852 \approx \mathbf{1{,}100}$

$300 + 1{,}100 \approx \mathbf{1{,}400}$

1,400 is a reasonable estimate for the four flights. The exact sum is 1,347.

Rounding to the nearest hundred gives a more precise answer than rounding to the thousands. The process of rounding and estimation is used when you only need an approximate answer.

Choosing the place to which you round depends upon the size of the numbers and how easily you can mentally compute the rounded numbers.

 **Check Understanding**

Estimate the sum by rounding the addends first to the thousands place and then to the hundreds place. Add the rounded numbers.

Example:

$$
\begin{array}{rrr}
8{,}547 & 9{,}000 & 8{,}500 \\
+\,2{,}246 & +\,2{,}000 & +\,2{,}200 \\
\hline
 & 11{,}000 & 10{,}700
\end{array}
$$

a.
$$
\begin{array}{r}
1{,}940 \\
+\,3{,}612 \\
\hline
5052
\end{array}
$$

b.
$$
\begin{array}{r}
2{,}247 \\
+\,1{,}622 \\
\hline
3{,}869
\end{array}
$$

c.
$$
\begin{array}{r}
8{,}735 \\
+\,1{,}056 \\
\hline
9{,}791
\end{array}
$$

Practice

Estimate each sum by rounding to the greatest place value. Find the exact sum.

1. 358
   + 634
   992

2. 8,619
   + 6,322
   14,941

3. 624
   892
   + 147
   1653

4. 12,613
   44,491
   + 26,743
   83747

5. 84,132
   + 25,450
   109,582

Estimate the sum. Compare and write > or < for each ▦ .

6. 823 + 115 ▦ 1,000   7. 5,412 + 4,426 ▦ 10,000   8. 4,426 + 2,158 ▦ 5,000

9. 324 + 298 + 237 ▦ 700   10. 7,239 + 3,916 + 3,463 ▦ 17,000

Apply

11. The first and second flights of the *Flyer* each lasted 12 seconds. The third flight took 15 seconds, and the fourth flight took 59 seconds. Estimate how many total seconds the *Flyer* flew.

12. The weight of the *Flyer* was 605 pounds. The wing surface area was 512 square feet. Estimate how many pounds the *Flyer* weighed. Estimate how many square feet covered the wing area.

Flyer

13. If 1,964 people came to the National Air and Space Museum to see the *Flyer* during the month of July and 2,116 people came during August, about how many visitors came during those two months?

900
200

Review

Write what the **8** represents in each number.
1. 6**8**7,312   2. 43,**8**67   3. 298,**3**94   4. **8**03,469

Write the numbers in order from the least to the greatest.
5. 447 546 232   6. 5,912 5,219 2,519
   546 447 232   *5,912 5,219 2,519*
7. 1,387,248,967 1,837,248,967 1,387,842,967
   1,837,248,967 1,387,842,967 1,387,248,967

Round each number to the nearest ten thousand and to the nearest million.
8. 4,376,152   9. 6,841,793   10. 1,931,220

Round each decimal number to the nearest tenth.
11. 5,176   12. 24.31   13. 1,762.840

Construct Meaning

The production of airplanes increased during World War I (1914–1918). Biplanes, used for spying, traveled in groups called air squadrons.

Aircraft carriers are warships that carry planes. The first time a plane landed on a ship was in 1910.

The airship, also referred to as a dirigible, blimp, or zeppelin, was invented in France. A German inventor, Ferdinand von Zeppelin, made an airship in 1900. He flew in it 17 minutes, traveling 3.7 miles. Germany used zeppelins in World War I.

One zeppelin traveled 3,670 nautical miles and another one traveled 2,794 nautical miles. Estimate the difference between how many miles both zeppelins traveled.

- Use front-end estimation.

  Subtract the front-end digits only.

  $3,670 \rightarrow 3,000$
  $- 2,794 \rightarrow - 2,000$
  _____
  $1,000$

  The front-end estimation strategy uses the digits in the greatest place value and replaces the remaining digits with zeros.

  The difference is 1,000 nautical miles.

- Use rounding to the hundreds place to get an estimate.

  $3,\underline{6}70 \rightarrow 3,700$
  $- 2,\underline{7}94 \rightarrow - 2,800$
  _____
  900

  Round the minuend and the subtrahend to the hundreds place before subtracting.

  The difference is 900 nautical miles.

  1,000 and 900 are estimates. 876 is the exact difference. Which is a rougher estimate? Which is a more precise estimate?

 If the digit to the right of the number being rounded is 5 or more, round that digit up. If the digit is less than 5, the number stays the same.

Check Understanding

Use front-end estimation to find the difference.

a.	b.	c.	d.	e.
375	834	720	4,603	9,134
− 220	− 406	− 570	− 2,706	− 6,032

Round each number to the nearest thousand before subtracting.

f.	g.	h.	i.	j.
5,389	16,535	22,870	8,672	39,271
− 2,272	− 11,213	− 11,232	− 3,457	− 27,042

Estimating Whole-Number Differences

ractice

Use front-end estimation to find the difference.

1. 575	2. 747	3. 652	4. 6,832	5. 22,018
− 384	− 518	− 333	− 3,204	− 10,476

Round each number to the nearest thousand to find the estimated difference.
Then find the exact difference.

6. 7,918	7. 6,230	8. 12,561	9. 47,682	10. 1,632
− 593	− 3,956	− 5,801	− 23,526	− 796

Round to the greatest place value, then write the estimate for each difference.

11. 73 − 37   12. 813 − 584   13. 3,982 − 1,357   14. 62,178 − 38,501

15. 28 − 14   16. 476 − 416   17. 8,731 − 1,875   18. 33,329 − 31,407

pply

19. In a two-week period, out of 766 biplanes, 402 went south. It was estimated in that same period, that about 300 biplanes did not fly south. What estimation strategy was used?

20. Don said that 564 airplanes landed on the aircraft carrier for refueling. 323 airplanes landed for repair. Would an estimate of 400 seem reasonable if you were estimating the difference?

21. The airship stays up because it is filled with lighter-than-air gas and is powered. The *Pilgrim*, a small single-engine airship, had a volume of 51,000 cubic feet. The *Puritan* had two engines and a volume near 86,000 cubic feet. Does an estimate of 40,000 cubic feet seem a reasonable difference in the size of the airships?

eview

Add.

1. 27	2. 518	3. 3,975	4. 3,168	5. 33,881
+ 46	+ 286	+ 389	+ 7,652	+ 67,832

© Copyright 2001

29

Lesson 14

📚 Construct Meaning

As a young boy growing up in Minnesota, Charles Lindbergh became interested in flying airplanes. He went to Nebraska to become a student pilot and found stunt flying a thrilling activity. Raymond Orteig from France offered $25,000 prize money to the first pilot to fly nonstop across the Atlantic Ocean between New York and Paris. Charles accepted the challenge on May 20, 1927. After the 3,600-mile flight which lasted $33\frac{1}{2}$ hours, he landed the *Spirit of St. Louis* in Paris. How many people knew about his feat if 4,273 people saw it and 5,619 people heard the broadcast?

Use regrouping to add the two addends.

$$\begin{array}{r} \overset{1}{4,273} \\ +5,619 \\ \hline 9,892 \end{array}$$

Add the ones. (3 + 9 = 12)
Regroup 12 as 1 ten and 2 ones. The 1 ten is added to the tens column and the 2 ones are recorded.
Add the tens. (1 + 7 + 1 = 9). Add the hundreds, then the thousands.

> **9,892 people knew that Charles Lindbergh made the first solo transatlantic flight.**

Check the answer with your estimate. Is it reasonable?

Compare the number of people who heard about Lindbergh's adventure by radio with the number who watched him land. Find 5,619 – 4,273.

$$\begin{array}{r} \overset{511}{5,\cancel{6}\cancel{1}9} \\ -4,273 \\ \hline 1,346 \end{array}$$

Subtract the ones. (9 – 3 = 6)
Subtract the tens. Since 7 > 1, regroup 6 hundreds as 5 hundreds and 11 tens.
Subtract the tens, hundreds, and thousands.

> **1,346 more people heard the news than saw it.**

Addition and subtraction are **inverse**, or opposite, **operations**. Use the inverse operation to check your work.

Check

$$\begin{array}{r} 4,273 \\ +5,619 \\ \hline 9,892 \end{array} \quad\times\quad \begin{array}{r} 9,892 \\ -4,273 \\ \hline 5,619 \end{array} \checkmark$$

Check

$$\begin{array}{r} 5,619 \\ -4,273 \\ \hline 1,346 \end{array} \quad\times\quad \begin{array}{r} 1,346 \\ +4,273 \\ \hline 5,619 \end{array} \checkmark$$

Regroup to add these three addends. 735 + 696 + 595 = ▓▓▓. Write the addends vertically so the digits in each number are lined up by the same place value.

$$\begin{array}{r} \overset{1}{735} \\ 696 \\ +595 \\ \hline 6 \end{array}$$
Add the ones. Regroup 16 as 1 ten and 6 ones.

$$\begin{array}{r} \overset{2\,1}{735} \\ 696 \\ +595 \\ \hline 26 \end{array}$$
Add the tens. Regroup 22 as 2 hundreds and 2 tens.

$$\begin{array}{r} \overset{2\,1}{735} \\ 696 \\ +595 \\ \hline 2,026 \end{array}$$
Add the hundreds. Regroup 20 as 2 thousands and 0 hundreds. 2,026 is the sum.

Check Understanding

Solve. Check problems a and b.

a. 69
+64

b. 6,872
−2,493

c. 12,705
−10,962

d. 347 + 631 + 595

Practice

Solve. Check problems 1 and 2.

1. 52,467
−13,698

2. 9,876
+ 987

3. 706
−429

4. 4,675
−1,598

5. 37,638
− 4,729

6. 714 + 77 + 561

7. 354 + 523 + 310

8. 1,736 + 14 + 309

Apply

9. Anna's family wants to take a flight from New York to France via London. It takes 5 hours and 45 minutes to travel from New York to London; it takes 2 hours and 15 minutes to travel from London to France. How many hours will the family spend flying one way? How many hours will the round trip take?

10. One airline advertises 10 trips to Europe daily; another airline offers 16 flights daily, another 15 flights daily, and another 8 flights per day. How many flights to Europe do these four airlines promote?

11. Calvin received 3,500 frequent flyer miles for one way from North Carolina to California. He received the same on his return trip. On another trip from Kentucky to Kansas he received 900 frequent flyer miles each way. What is the difference in the number of frequent flyer miles each trip offered?

Review

Write addends that give the <u>estimated</u> sum.

1. ▦ + ▦ ≈ 600
2. ▦ + ▦ ≈ 300
3. ▦ + ▦ ≈ 1,200
4. ▦ + ▦ ≈ 14,000

Write the numbers in order from the greatest to the least.

5. 5,678   5,768   5,876   8,675

6. 12,710   12,723   12,718   12,719

Estimate by rounding to the greatest place value.

7. 614
+386

8. 1,940
−1,242

9. 46,736
+21,579

10. 3,081
+ 974

11. 72,186
−56,349

Construct Meaning

People began to fly helicopters in the 1930s. Helicopters do not have wings; they have rotor blades that spin to create lift. The pilot can fly the helicopter forward, backward, or sideways when there is enough lift. They can hover motionless in the air and they do not need a runway. Helicopters may be used to get an injured person medical help or they may be used to transport an object to a location quickly. They may also be used to give someone a scenic ride. During the summer months a theme park offered 351 tickets for helicopter rides. 162 tickets were sold in 30 days. How many tickets were still available?

Use the Problem-Solving Guide to write an equation.

Step 1 Understand the question. How many tickets were still available?

Step 2 Analyze the data. At the start of summer, 351 tickets were available. Of that number, 162 tickets have been sold. Is the fact that the requests were received in 30 days important for solving this problem? No, we are only concerned with numbers of tickets.

Step 3 Plan the strategy. If we find the difference between the number of tickets available at the beginning of sales and the number of tickets that have been sold, we will know how many tickets were left. Finding the difference is a subtraction problem.

An **equation** is a number sentence written with an equal sign. x is the unknown number.

$$351 - 162 = x$$
$$400 - 200 = 200$$

Use rounding to estimate the answer.

Step 4 Solve the problem.

$$\begin{array}{r} \overset{14}{\underset{2\,\cancel{4}\,11}{\cancel{351}}} \\ -\ 162 \\ \hline 189 \end{array}$$

$$351 - 162 = 189$$
$$x = 189 \text{ tickets}$$

Step 5 Evaluate the result. Check your answer. Compare it to the estimate.

189 tickets still available
+ 162 tickets sold
351 tickets at beginning of sales

Is this a reasonable answer compared to the estimate of 200 tickets?

Problem Solving: Addition and Subtraction

Write an equation. Solve. Check your answer.

1. Miss Shirley earned $540 in two weeks. She bought a VCR for $299. How much money did she have left?

2. Jack gave a total of 79 hours to help the Sunday school class clean the yards of the elderly. Ted gave 23 fewer hours than Jack. How many hours did Ted give?

3. At Forest Christian School, 578 students gave toys for needy children. At Windsor Academy, 756 students gave toys. How many students gave toys at Windsor Academy and at Forest Christian School?

4. A salesman delivered T-shirts to four sporting goods shops. One shop was given 48, another shop was given 60, another received 72, and the last shop received 36. How many T-shirts were taken to the shops to be sold?

5. Ted has put in 1,487 hours toward receiving his helicopter's license. His license requires a total of 2,000 hours. How many more hours does Ted need to get his pilot's license?

6. Jason paid $120 for license fees, $240 for flight-test fees, $265 for course materials, and $1,175 for a new helmet. How much money did he spend at the beginning of his flight training?

7. To get supplies to a remote location, a missionary pilot traveled 1,876 miles on Monday. The next day he traveled 2,003 miles. Everyone rejoiced when the plane circled overhead. How many miles was the trip to the mission station?

8. The most remote village was 225 miles by canoe from the mission station. Len had canoed 143 miles. How much farther did he have to go?

9. Igor I. Sikorsky born in Kiev, Russia, designed the first true production helicopter. His U.S. patent was filed June 27, 1931, and on September 14, 1939, the VS-300 made its first flight successfully. How many years passed between his filing of the patent and the first successful flight?

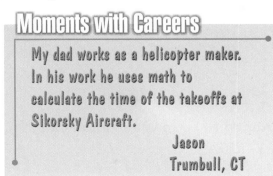

Moments with Careers

My dad works as a helicopter maker. In his work he uses math to calculate the time of the takeoffs at Sikorsky Aircraft.

Jason
Trumbull, CT

Lesson 16

Construct Meaning

Prior to arrival, the pilot may announce the temperature of your destination.

Destination	Temperature
Portland, Oregon	70.1° Fahrenheit
Washington, D.C.	75.8° Fahrenheit
São Paulo, Brazil	87.5° Fahrenheit

Use the number line to round to the nearest whole number.

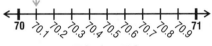 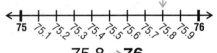 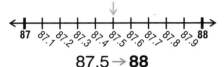

70.1→**70**   75.8→**76**   87.5→**88**

Decimals can be rounded the same way whole numbers are rounded.

- Use the place value chart to round **9.787** to the nearest hundredth.

ones	tenths	hundredths	thousandths
9	7	8	7

Find the target digit in the <u>hundredths</u> place.

Look at the digit in the place to the <u>right</u>.

Because 7 is greater than 5, <u>increase</u> the target digit by 1.   9. 7 9

All digits to the right of the digit in the hundredths place are dropped.

9.787 rounds to 9.79.

- Use front-end estimation to estimate decimal sums.
  Bob saved his money for a new video. The first week he saved $6.45 and the second week he saved $5.32. About how much had he saved?

Step 1	**Step 2**	**Step 3**
Add the front-end digits.	Consider the tenths and hundredths.	Adjust the estimate.
$6.45 + 5.32 11.	$6.45 + 5.32 $0.45 + 0.32 ≈ $1.00	$11.00 + 1.00 $12.00

> Bob saved about $12.00.

Check Understanding

Round to the nearest whole number. Add to estimate the sum.

a. 34.27
   +12.35

b. 7.3
   +5.8

c. 29.80
   +64.76

d. 4.4 + 3.82 + 7.1

34

$2.7 = 3.0$

Round to the nearest tenth, then add. | Round to the nearest hundredth, then add.

e.	8.75	f.	25.16
	+ 4.66		+ 17.29

g.	5.666	h.	43.872
	+ 4.982		+ 11.931

Use front-end estimation to estimate decimal sums.

Step 1	**Step 2**		**Step 3**
$3.51	$3.51	$0.51 + 0.35 \approx \$1.00$	$8.00
+ 5.35	+ 5.35		+ 1.00
8.		i.	

 **Practice**

Round to the nearest whole number to estimate the sum.

1.	45.32	2.	72.6	3.	4.6	4. $21.9 + 46.3 + 82.8$
	+ 17.84		+ 34.8		+ 3.3	

Round to the nearest tenth to estimate the sum.

5.	8.75	6.	23.54	7.	107.42	8.	76.39	9.	2.661
	+ 4.66		+ 60.17		+ 218.55		+ 23.07		+ 3.543

Use front-end estimation to find the sum. Adjust your estimate.

10.	$8.67	11.	$2.06	12.	$3.68	13.	$7.03	14.	$2.12
	+ 4.54		+ 9.78		+ 1.33		+ 1.12		+ 3.05

 Apply

15. Amelia Earhart saw her first airplane at the age of 11. At the age of 25, she had her pilot's license. In 1932, she became the first woman to fly alone across the Atlantic Ocean. Most of the Atlantic Ocean may be seen on a map between 74.8 degrees and 6.4 degrees longitude. Round each decimal to the nearest whole number.

16. Todd ran 1.2 miles, Bill ran 1.4 miles, and Tim ran 1.6 miles in the relay race. Round each number to the nearest whole number to estimate the length of the race.

17. Jake spent $50.95 on new in-line skates. He spent $20.99 on a new helmet. Use front-end estimation to estimate how much he spent.

 Review

Round each number to the place given in parenthesis.

1. 36.06 (nearest ten)
3. 8.39 (nearest whole number)

2. 7.54 (nearest tenth)
4. 58.173 (nearest hundredth)

Lesson 17

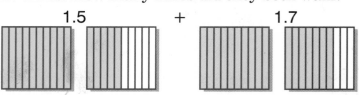Construct Meaning

Mrs. Parker's fifth grade class participated in a walk-a-thon to raise money for a field trip to an air show. Jeff walked 1.5 miles and Rob walked 1.7 miles. How many miles did they both walk?

1.5   +   1.7

```
  1
  1.5
+ 1.7
-----
  3.2
```

Line up the place values and the decimal points.
Add the tenths, regrouping if necessary.
Add the whole numbers.
Write the decimal in the sum between the ones and the tenths.

> **Jeff and Rob walked 3.2 miles.**

The walk-a-thon was successful and the students were excited about the air show. Prior to the outing, the teacher read about Chuck Yeager who flew his Bell X-1 to reach 0.85 Mach, which is more than eight-tenths the speed of sound, in August 1947. Two months later on, October 14, he flew his rocket-powered plane faster than the speed of sound by exceeding Mach 1. The sonic boom was heard all over the Mojave Desert in California! The X-1 had been pushed 0.20 Mach beyond 0.85. How fast did it go?

0.85   +   0.20

```
   1
   0.85
+  0.20
-------
   1.05
```

Line up the place values and the decimal points.
Add the hundredths, then the tenths.
Add the whole numbers.
Write the decimal in the sum.

Chuck Yeager reached the speed of Mach 1.05 that day.

When adding or comparing numbers of different place value, use a zero to make an equivalent decimal.	26.30 +16.85

Check Understanding

Write decimal numbers using the models. Add.

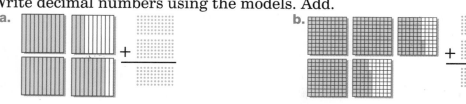

a.   b.

Adding Tenths and Hundredths

Line up the decimals and add.

1. 3.6 + 5.9 + 2.7   2. 6.7 + 3.48   3. 53.89 + 49.65   4. 246.71 + 89.3

Draw and shade models to show the value of the decimal number. Add to find the sum.

5. 1.5 + 2.3   6. 1.25 + 2.67

Add.

7. 3.6   8. 7.48   9. 21.39   10. 113.7   11. 55.38
  + 1.2   + 5.17   + 4.51   + 86.42   + 7.6

12. Drew's model airplane flew 19.7 feet, Chad's airplane flew 21.4 feet, and Jeremy's flew 20.9 feet. What was the combined footage for the three models?

13. Patrick bought several tools before he could build shelves for his model airplanes. He bought a hammer for $9.95, pliers for $8.75, a drill for $24.99, and a set of screwdrivers for $16.49. How much did Patrick spend?

14. Jack's radio-controlled glider flew at a speed of 46.25 miles per hour. This speed doubled the next time he flew the glider. Was the maximum number of miles per hour greater than or less than 95 miles per hour?

Round to the nearest ten. Write the letter of the estimated sum.

1. 46.31 + 25.74   2. 235.1 + 40.8   3. 14.3 + 26.578
   a. 60   a. 280   a. 41
   b. 80   b. 275   b. 40
   c. 70   c. 270   c. 50

Add, then check.

4. 26,531   5. 184   6. 3,241   7. 9,764   8. $65.45
  + 35,479   + 798   + 5,683   + 2,843   + 38.59

Lesson 18

Construct Meaning

Biplanes, jets, rockets, missiles! Aircraft technology had already boomed by the beginning of World War II in 1939. A Soviet military rocket carried the first payload, a 184-pound artificial satellite called Sputnik I, into space in 1957. By 1963 the United States had an X-15 ascend to 354,200 feet, or 67.08 miles, from the earth into space. This achievement involved many people. How many crew members worked on the X-15 if there were 9 technicians and 8 engineers?

• **Commutative (Order) Property of Addition**

$9 + 8 = 17$ or $8 + 9 = 17$ Rearranging the order of addends does not change the sum.

addend addend sum   addend addend sum

17 crew members would be working on the X-15.

• **Associative (Grouping) Property of Addition**

$(1.3 + 2.5) + 43.7 = $ ▦   or $1.3 + (2.5 + 43.7) = $ ▦

$3.8 + 43.7 = 47.5$ $1.3 + 46.2 = 47.5$

Addends can be grouped differently without changing the sum.

• **Zero Property of Addition**

$136 + 0 = 136$ or $0 + 136 = 136$

When zero is added to any addend, the sum is the other addend. Some mathematicians call the Zero Property the Identity Property of Addition because the zero always identifies the other addend as the sum.

These properties use the terms addend and sum. The **sum** is the result of two or more **addends** being added together.

Use your calculator to find the sum.

Check Understanding

Identify the addition property. Write *Commutative Property, Associative Property,* or *Zero Property*.

a. $(2.6 + 5.2) + 4.8 = 2.6 + (5.2 + 4.8)$

b. $17 + 0 = 17$

c. $45.6 + 13.1 = 13.1 + 45.6$

d. $6 + 8 + 7 = 8 + 6 + 7$

 **ractice**

Complete. Identify the property shown.

1. 6.5 + 8.1 = ⬚ + 6.5

2. 46 + (77 + 33) = (⬚ + 77) + 33

3. 156 + ⬚ = 156

4. (57.9 + 3.4) + 23.6 = 57.9 + (3.4 + ⬚)

5. ⬚ + 24.8 = 24.8 + 83.2

6. 14 + 6 + 20 + 9 = 20 + 14 + ⬚ + 6

Use the Commutative Property of Addition to rewrite each equation. Find the sum.

7. 8.1 + 9.4 = n

8. 69 + 37 + 10 = n

9. 376 + 13 = n

10. 14.8 + 26.5 = n

$9.95 $17.45 $15.50

11. Use the Associative Property of Addition to show two different ways to find the sum of the gift prices.

Use the Zero Property of Addition to find the missing addend or sum.

12. 45 + ⬚ = ⬚

13. ⬚ + 0 = 18.3

14. ⬚ + ⬚ = 33.3

Use your calculator to find the sum.

15. 9.7 + 6.4 + 35.8

16. 876 + 115 + 4,703

 pply

Use the Associative Property of Addition to solve the problem two different ways.

17. Test pilots used F-100 and F-104 Starfighter jets to get a sense of flying the X-15. The planes accelerated to 25,000 feet quickly, then 50,000 feet more, and 25,000 additional feet. What was the final altitude the planes reached?

 **eview**

Write the numbers in order from the greatest to the least.

1. 45,791   47,591   41,579   54,179

2. 364,176   365,716   369,617   363,116

Add.

3. 54,971
   + 67,487

4. 89,264
   + 37,825

5. 76,542
   + 13,906

6. 23,476
   + 38,924

7. 54 + 83 + 16

8. 7.46
   + 9.37

9. 14.9
   + 72.3

10. 65.3
    + 8.17

11. 406.1
    + 24.9

12. 25.4 + 6.01

Construct Meaning

In 1969 the Boeing 747, referred to as the Jumbo Jet, made its first flight. The 747 can carry 624 passengers and 57,065 gallons of fuel and can fly 6,495 miles nonstop. That same year the Concorde, a supersonic airliner, was in service. The top speed of 1,450 miles per hour allows it to fly from London to New York in 3 hours; however, the Boeing 747 takes twice that long. Flying at an altitude of 59,000 feet, the Concorde flies almost twice as high as a normal airliner. 1969 was also the year that Neil Armstrong and Buzz Aldrin were the first persons to walk on the moon.

Concorde

Check Understanding

Missionaries, tourists, and business people use different types of airplanes and maps to fly from one destination to another.

Use the map of South America to answer the questions. The red numbers stand for miles between the cities.

a. Stuart and Sheney Salazar traveled from Lima, Peru, to Quito, Ecuador. They visited Alliance Academy and then went to Bogotá, Columbia, where they visited El Camino Academy. How many miles did they travel?

b. Pastor Bob and the youth group flew from São Paulo, Brazil, to Asunción, Paraguay, before landing in Buenos Aires, Argentina. After refueling, they flew on to Santiago, Chile, where they spent the night. The next day they arrived in La Paz, Bolivia. How many miles was their trip?

c. Phil bought an airline ticket to travel from Caracas, Venezuela, to São Paulo, Brazil, for $756.99. A month later his wife Joyce bought a ticket to the same destination for $698.50. How many miles was the round trip? How much did they both spend on tickets?

Did You Know?

A Boeing 747's wingspan is longer than the Wright brothers' first flight.

Practice

1. The president of a copper mining company in Chile needs to travel from Santiago to Caracas, Venezuela. There are two possible routes. Describe both routes and give the total mileage of each one.

2. Charlie lives in Lima, Peru, and plans to make a round trip to Quito which is Ecuador's cultural center as well as its second largest city. How many miles will he travel?

3. Nathaniel is attending college in São Paulo, Brazil. At Christmastime, he goes home to Buenos Aires, Argentina, by way of Asunción, Paraguay. How many miles from home does he attend college?

4. La Paz, Bolivia, is the capital city with the highest elevation in the world. José lives in Lima, Peru, and visits La Paz each year. What is the distance of his round trip?

5. One can find Inca ruins near the city of Cuzco which is about 250 miles southeast of Lima, Peru. Samuel lives in Bogotá, Columbia. How many miles will he travel to get to Cuzco, Peru?

6. Dave received 1,200 frequent flyer miles for his round trip from Asunción, Paraguay, to Caracas by way of São Paulo. How many miles did he travel to earn this award?

7. Use your calculator to find the total number of miles for a tour of South American cities that leaves Caracas, Venezuela, and follows the red lines on the map back to Caracas.

Moments with Careers

My Dad works as an engineer at Boeing. In his work, he uses math to figure things on airplanes and helps me if I have problems in math.

Grace
Seattle, WA

God is omnipresent—present everywhere at all times. Even when you are riding in a plane above the clouds, God is there. Deut. 33:26 says, "*There is* no one like the God of Jeshurun, *Who* rides the heavens to help you, and in His excellency on the clouds."

Lesson 20

The Airbus Industrie A320 is a mid-size airliner that carries between 120 and 180 passengers. The pilot is assisted by five computers when flying.

Commuter airliners, however, are small and carry only a few passengers a short distance. The CBA-123 Vector carries 19 passengers. A radar dish in its nose allows the pilot to avoid bad weather.

Radar detects a thunderstorm 9.25 miles ahead. The pilot's destination is 5.75 miles away. About how many miles is the difference between the destination and the storm?

You can estimate the difference with decimals just as you did with whole numbers.

- Use front-end estimation to estimate decimal differences.

$$\begin{array}{r} 9.25 \\ -5.75 \\ \hline \end{array}$$ Subtract the front-end digits.

4 miles   **The pilot knows the storm is about 4 miles beyond his destination.**

- Another method of estimation is rounding to the nearest whole number. Use mental math to subtract.

$$\begin{array}{r} 9.25 \longrightarrow 9 \\ -5.75 \longrightarrow -6 \\ \hline 3 \text{ miles} \end{array}$$ Round to the nearest whole number before subtracting.

The pilot knows the storm is about 3 miles beyond his destination.

Compare the estimate each method gave you. The front-end method informs the pilot the storm is about 4 miles beyond his destination. The rounding method tells him the storm is about 3 miles beyond his destination. He would be wise to make decisions based on the shorter distance, so the rounding method would be more helpful.

Rounding decimals can give a more precise answer than front-end estimation.

| Front-end estimation | $\begin{array}{r} 3.462 \\ -1.731 \\ \hline 2 \end{array}$ | $\begin{array}{r} 3.462 \longrightarrow \overset{2\ 15}{3.\cancel{5}} \\ -1.731 \longrightarrow -1.7 \\ \hline 1.8 \end{array}$ | Rounding to the nearest tenth |

1.8 is more precise than 2.

Use front-end estimation.

Round to the nearest whole number and subtract.

a. $\begin{array}{r} 6.2 \\ -3.4 \\ \hline \end{array}$

b. $\begin{array}{r} 8.37 \\ -6.25 \\ \hline \end{array}$

c. $\begin{array}{r} 7.54 \\ -2.71 \\ \hline \end{array}$

d. $\begin{array}{r} 37.824 \\ -23.061 \\ \hline \end{array}$

Use front-end estimation to estimate the difference.

1. 6.7	2. 7.8	3. 33.29	4. 24.72	5. 50.61
− 3.9	− 5.2	− 15.72	− 13.86	− 25.14

Use rounding to the nearest whole number to estimate the difference.

6. 2.86	7. 30.25	8. 54.216	9. 81.259	10. 134.29
− 1.48	− 16.52	− 3.890	− 19.715	− 98.52

Estimate by rounding to the nearest tenth.

11. 35.52	12. 88.15	13. 3.227
− 2.35	− 6.76	− 1.827

Estimate by rounding to the nearest ten. Subtract mentally.

14. $34.62	15. $116.98	16. $89.16	17. $475.49	18. $706.84
− 15.17	− 45.62	− 43.62	− 93.21	− 19.35

19. The Rogers family traveled 236.6 miles on an airliner. Their connecting flight took them 232.1 more miles to their final destination in Florida. Mr. Rogers estimated a difference of five miles in traveling the two segments. What method of estimation did he use?

Write what the **2** represents in each number.

1. 6,132   2. 42,576,840   3. 9.2   4. 524   5. 29,073

Use > or < to compare the numbers.

6. 387,461 ⬚ 389,456   7. 4,873 ⬚ 4,983   8. 63,010 ⬚ 60,310

9. 52,107 ⬚ 52,106   10. 1,365,237 ⬚ 1,366,237   11. 708 ⬚ 807

12. 924,429 ⬚ 904,409   13. 5,771 ⬚ 5,762   14. 23,741 ⬚ 23,740

Add or subtract.

15. 185 − 93   16. 1,675 − 388   17. 281 + 4,564 + 67   18. 384 + 76

 Construct Meaning

Writing a zero at the end of a decimal does not change the value of a decimal, even though the decimal is given a new name. This allows for writing equivalent decimals since the zero has no value. **Equivalent decimals** are different names for the same number.

Decimal squares help to model equivalent decimals.

 0.4
4 tenths
4 out of 10

 0.40
40 hundredths
40 out of 100

 0.400
400 thousandths
400 out of 1,000

0.4 is read as "four tenths."
0.40 is read as "forty hundredths" because the zero took the hundredths place.
0.400 is read as "four hundred thousandths" because zeros took the hundredths and thousandths places. The zeros must be placed to the <u>right</u> of the number four in order to form an equivalent decimal.

Place value charts help to form equivalent decimals. Solve $6.7 - 4.13 = n$.

ones	tenths	hundredths
6	7	0 ←
− 4	1	3

Line up the decimals.
Use zero to make an equivalent decimal.
Subtract.

$$\begin{array}{r} \overset{6\ 10}{6.7\cancel{0}} \\ -\ 4.13 \\ \hline 2.57 \end{array}$$

The decimal is read as "and."

The zero renamed 6.7 from six <u>and</u> seven tenths to six <u>and</u> seventy hundredths so four <u>and</u> thirteen hundredths could be subtracted.

Solve $5.148 + 3.26 = n$.

ones	tenths	hundredths	thousandths
5	1	4	8
+ 3	2	6	0 ←

Line up the decimals.
Place a zero. 3.26 is equivalent to 3.260. Add.

$$\begin{array}{r} \overset{1}{}\ \\ 5.148 \\ +\ 3.260 \\ \hline 8.408 \end{array}$$

 Check Understanding

Stuart prepared to do the obstacle course by running 1.3 miles as fast as he could. Mark ran 1.03 miles. Did they run the same distance?

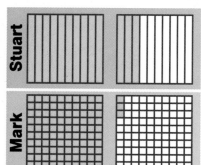

a. ⬚⬚⬚ ran farther than ⬚⬚⬚ .

b. 1.3 and 1.03 are not equivalent decimals. The ⬚⬚⬚ in 1.03 was not placed to the right of the number 3.

c. Write 0.006 in word form.

d. Write two and fifty-three thousandths in standard form.

Make a decimal place value chart as shown in the example.
Write three equivalent decimals for the shaded part of the model.

ones	tenths	hundredths	thousandths
0	7		
0	7	0	
0	7	0	0

1.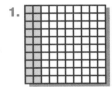

2.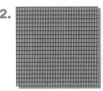

Write an equivalent decimal for each number.

3. 6.3   **4.** 5.10   **5.** 9.800   **6.** 39.6   **7.** 438.57

Write the word form for each decimal.

8. 3.7   **9.** 42.03   **10.** 9.145   **11.** 6.106   **12.** 0.001

Write in standard form.

13. forty-five thousandths   **14.** nine and nine hundred one thousandths

Write what the **7** represents in each number.

15. 3,241.07   **16.** 8.007   **17.** 7.245   **18.** 1.718

Write *yes* or *no* to indicate if the decimals are equivalent.

19. 9.1 and 9.11   **20.** 0.80 and 0.08   **21.** 0.200 and 0.2   **22.** 0.560 and 0.56

Solve.

23. 5.4 – 3.22   **24.** 0.032 + 0.1   **25.** 44.55 – 2.6   **26.** 13.22 + 11.0

27. Warren holds a box. Does it weigh 0.25 pounds or 0.250 pounds? Explain.

28. By deflecting radar signals, a stealth fighter flew 1,450.5 miles before being observed. Write the number in word form.

Write >, < or = to compare.

1. 3.752 ▨ 3.572   **2.** 6.252 ▨ 62.52   **3.** 0.04 ▨ 0.040   **4.** 17.6 ▨ 1.76

Construct Meaning

Aerobatic airplanes are small and light. They are customized to allow the pilot to perform daring twists, turns, loops, and rolls in the air. The Pitts Special S-2A is an aerobatic airplane used in air shows. Weighing only 1,000 pounds, it is a little over 17 feet long and 6 feet high.

Steve and Marsha attended the Sun 'n Fun Fly-In. One plane left a trail of smoke 1.3 miles long. Another trail was 0.15 miles long. Find the difference in the lengths of the trails of smoke.

Solve $1.30 - 0.15 = x$

• Use a number line.

Start here and count back 15 hundredths.

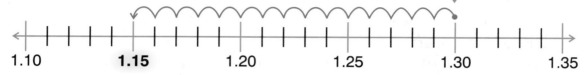

• Use decimal models.

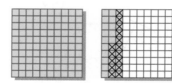

$1.30 - 0.15 = $

• Use base ten blocks.

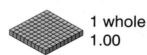 1 whole 1.00

1 tenth 0.10

1 hundredth 0.01

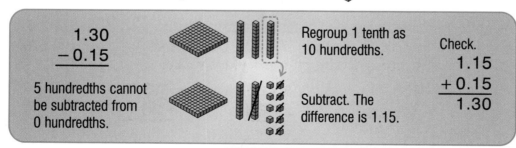

1.30
− 0.15

5 hundredths cannot be subtracted from 0 hundredths.

Regroup 1 tenth as 10 hundredths.

Subtract. The difference is 1.15.

Check.
1.15
+ 0.15
1.30

The trails of smoke differ in length by 1.15 miles.

Check Understanding

a. Draw a number line and number it like the one above. Solve $1.24 - 0.05 = x$.

b. Write an equation for the decimal model.

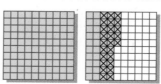

Subtract.

c. $2.7 - 1.4$ d. $5.1 - 3.8$ e. $25.18 - 16.19$ f. $42.91 - 16.37$

 **ractice**

Subtract. Place an extra zero where needed.

1. $45.31 − 23.56	2. 9.3 −2.5	3. 762 − 144.15	4. $6.49 − 1.50	5. 4,362.7 −1,784.9

6. 4.9 − 0.75   7. 9.06 − 8.67   8. 15 − 7.6   9. 24.6 − 9

10. 901.7 − 52.8   11. 37.1 − 29.46   12. $5 − 2.51   13. 479 − 0.3

 pply

14. Steve took $30.00 to the air show. He had $22.50 left after buying tickets. How much money did he spend for the tickets?

15. With the amount of money he had left after purchasing the tickets, he spent $4.75 on refreshments. How much money did Steve take home?

 eview

Estimate the sum by rounding to the greatest place value.

1. 49 + 84	2. 455 + 391	3. 1,466 +2,836	4. 13,781 + 26,147	5. 8,247 +6,679

Write the standard form.

6. 8,000,000,000 + 300,000,000 + 4,000,000 + 900,000 + 20,000 + 1,000 + 600 + 50 + 7

7. Sixty-three billion, three hundred sixty-five million, nine hundred twenty-two thousand, five.

Estimate the difference by rounding to the nearest whole number.

8. 3.4 −1.5	9. 4.9 −2.1	10. 126.8 − 6.7	11. 17.03 −13.39	12. 762.68 − 144.74

Lesson 23

Construct Meaning

The world's fastest and highest-flying production aircraft is the SR-71. It can fly 2,200 miles per hour (mph) or 3 times the speed of sound and at an altitude of over 85,000 feet. One of its uses is to carry out experiments in the area of aerodynamics.

Jane's first airline trip alone was to visit her grandparents in Texas. She was aboard an airplane that cruised at a speed of 427.5 miles per hour and then accelerated to an additional 68.25 miles per hour during the course of the flight. Jane thought to herself, "This is fun; I wonder how much faster the fastest plane in the world can travel."

THINK through the steps of the Problem-Solving Guide to solve the problem.

1. **What do you want to know?**

   What is the difference between the speed of Jane's airplane and the speed of an SR-71, the fastest plane?

2. **What information do you have?**

   The pilot of the aircraft increased its speed 68.25 more miles per hour after reaching 427.5 miles per hour. The SR-71 can travel 2,200 miles per hour.

3. **What is an efficient method to solve this problem?**

   Can the question be answered by doing one operation? No, we must find how fast Jane's aircraft was traveling, then compare it to how fast an SR-71 can travel. This problem requires two operations.

4. **Apply math skills.**

   ```
     427.50              2,200.00
   +  68.25            −   495.75
     495.75 mph         1,704.25 mph
   ```
   (how fast Jane's aircraft travels)   (how much faster the SR-71 travels)

5. **The answer is logical.**

   Since the SR-71 is the world's fastest aircraft, it makes sense that it could travel 1,704.25 miles per hour faster (Wow!) than a commercial aircraft.

Check Understanding

a. Jane arrived safely at the airport where her grandmother was waiting for her. At a snack shop Jane bought a slice of pizza for $2.75, a drink for $1.25, and a cookie for her grandmother that cost $1.00. Jane paid with a $20 bill. How much change did she receive?

Problem Solving: Two-Step Problems

1. When Jane arrived in Avalon, Texas, the morning temperature was 88.9°F. The sun was bright and that afternoon it was 6.7°F warmer. The temperature that evening cooled down 10.4°F. What was the evening low?

2. Grandmother stopped at the grocery store and bought a gallon of milk for $3.29. The cashier also rang up $0.18 tax. How much change did Grandmother receive from a $5 bill?

3. One day at the county fair Jane bought an ice-cream cone that cost $1.45. The waffle cone was an additional $0.25. She had a coupon for $0.75 off the total price. How much did she pay?

4. Jane attended church on Sunday with her grandparents. There was a report that showed the monthly financial support for a missionary family in Ireland. $17.68, $20.95, and $9.40 were the offerings received for three Sundays. What did the fourth offering need to be if the amount pledged to support the missionary family was $60 per month?

5. The average yearly rainfall for Avalon, Texas, is 997.6 mm. The total rainfall for January through March is 212.5 mm. The total for April through June is 359.6 mm. What is the average yearly rainfall for the second half of the year?

6. Jane earned $15 for a job she did for her grandparents. She gave $2.50 to the missionary family. She bought a souvenir for $4.00 and a T-shirt for $7.98. How much money was left?

Find the missing addend.

1. $235 + y = 561$

2. $x + 89 = 101$

3. $z = 4{,}672 + 37$

4. $b + 18.6 = 92.5$

5. $118.32 = t + 38.7$

6. $402.9 + p = 549.2$

7. $1.1 + c = 7.92$

8. $136.93 = 57.13 + f$

9. $42 = m + 3.8$

Lesson 24

🧱 Construct Meaning

In 1998, while playing first base for the St. Louis Cardinals, Mark McGwire hit a record 70 home runs. In July of 2000, Mark McGwire's batting average was 0.301. The record for highest lifetime batting average, 0.366, is held by Ty Cobb, who played for the Detroit Tigers between 1905 and 1928. What is the difference between Ty Cobb's record and Mark McGwire's batting average on the date given?

One decimal place shows
Two decimal places show
Three decimal places show

| ones . tenths | hundredths | thousandths |

Official batting averages are recorded in the thousandths.

When subtracting decimals, it is important to:

- line up each place value and the decimal points.
- subtract the thousandths, the hundredths, then the tenths, regrouping if necessary.
- subtract the whole numbers.
- write the decimal between the ones and the tenths.

$$\begin{array}{r} 0.366 \\ -\ 0.301 \\ \hline 0.065 \end{array}$$

The difference between Ty Cobb's record and Mark McGwire's batting average is 0.065, or sixty-five thousandths.

When adding or subtracting decimals, it is sometimes necessary to place zeros after the decimal point to make an equivalent decimal.

Solve 1.8 + 4.938.

$$\begin{array}{r} 1.800 \\ +\ 4.938 \\ \hline 6.738 \end{array}$$

Read as "six **and** seven hundred thirty-eight thousandths."

✔ Check Understanding

Solve.

a. $\begin{array}{r} 0.234 \\ +\ 1.782 \end{array}$

b. $\begin{array}{r} 2.71 \\ +\ 2.428 \end{array}$

c. $\begin{array}{r} 72.645 \\ -\ 39.427 \end{array}$

d. $1.4 - 0.765$

e. $3.014 + 2.398$

Write the correct word name.

f. 1.654
   one and six hundred fifty-four
   one and six hundred fifty-four thousandths
   one and sixty-five four

g. 0.008
   eight thousands
   eight hundredths
   eight thousandths

50

Adding and Subtracting Thousandths

 **ractice**

Write a word name for each number.

1. 0.8 **2.** 0.016 **3.** 1.72 **4.** 163.52 **5.** 4.004

Solve.

6. 0.425
   + 1.763

7. 2.314
   + 6.8

8. 24.86
   − 18.275

9. 4.567 + 16.32
10. 246.3 − 8.712

CUMULATIVE REVIEW: Chapters 1 and 2

Write the number as directed.

in expanded form	in word form	in standard form
1. 7,009	**2.** 0.301	**3.** nineteen million, three

Write in order from the least to the greatest.

4. 3,570,000   3,050,000   3,007,000   3,060,000

Write >, < or =.

5. 0.35 ▦ 0.350 **6.** 6.381 ▦ 63.81 **7.** 42.7 ▦ 24.7

Estimate by rounding each number to the greatest place value before adding or subtracting. Then find the exact sum or difference.

8. 7,436
   + 2,241

9. 6,807
   − 483

10. 49,231
   − 20,974

11.   874
   + 78

Solve.

12. 98.7 + 1.64
13. 235 + 1,782 + 49
14. 96.52 − 1.782

15. x + 417 = 485
16. 6,114 − y = 5
17. s + 7.9 = 10.386

Estimate the sum or difference by rounding to the nearest tenth.

18. $5.87
   − 1.42

19. 28.168
   + 2.643

20. 0.154
   + 0.097

21. 479.80
   − 35.753

Solve. Check your answer.

22. The driver put 30.536 gallons of gasoline in the bus to take the baseball team to the airport. 14.511 gallons were used for the one-way trip. How many gallons of gasoline remained for the return trip from the airport?

AIRPORT

Adding and Subtracting at the Controls

Estimate the sum by rounding to the greatest place value before adding.

1. 247
  +634

2. 8,517
  +5,322

3. 514
  773
  +276

4. 13,724
  34,582
  +48,031

Round each number to the nearest thousand to find the estimated difference.

5. 8,517
  − 593

6. 5,140
  −2,856

7. 14,651
  − 4,703

8. 86,571
  −23,613

Write the letter of the addition property illustrated by each number sentence.

9. (1.4 + 3.6) + 18.2 = 1.4 + (3.6 + 18.2)

10. 9 + 0 = 9

11. 6 + 7 + 4 = 4 + 7 + 6

12. 76 + 98 = 98 + 76

13. 23 + (45 + 76) = (23 + 45) + 76

a. Commutative Property

b. Associative Property

c. Zero Property

Complete.

14. 7.9 + 6.2 = ▦ + 7.9

15. 32 + (64 + 23) = (▦ + 64) + 23

16. 243 + ▦ = 243

17. 12 + 16 + 18 = 16 + ▦ + 12

Write an equivalent decimal for each number.

18. 5.4

19. 6.10

20. 4.700

21. 562.47

Write *yes* or *no* to indicate if the decimals are equivalent.

22. 8.2 and 8.22

23. 0.300 and 0.3

24. 0.70 and 0.07

25. Draw decimal models and explain in your own words why 0.5 = 0.50.

Estimate the sum by rounding to the nearest whole number before adding.

26. 38.27
+13.42

27. 7.3
+1.8

28. 347.80
+362.74

29. 8.4 + 0.86 + 7.523

Round to the nearest tenth. Write the letter of the estimated sum.

30. 6.71
+3.49

a. 10.2
b. 10.3
c. 1.02

31. 23.74
+71.17

a. 9.49
b. 9.94
c. 94.9

32. 304.22
+219.48

a. 523.7
b. 533.7
c. 52.37

33. 5.671
+3.645

a. 0.93
b. 9.3
c. 9.4

Estimate the difference by rounding to the nearest ten before subtracting.

34. $42.51
− 17.16

35. $113.96
− 35.51

36. 76.135
− 8.617

37. 909.812
−126.742

Solve.

38. 5.2
+3.4

39. $9.31
− 4.75

40. 8,205
−2,167

41. 97.31
−35.094

42. 271 + 576 + 893 + 408

43. 2,716 + 4,892 + 3,947

44. $r + 94 = 123.7$

45. $66 + n = 85$

46. $b + 4,372 = 5,001$

47. $a − 17.06 = 34.12$

48. $104 − z = 37.42$

49. $w − 241 = 421$

50. 3,247 flights arrived on time. 1,124 flights were behind schedule and 1,087 flights arrived a few minutes early. Compare the number of flights that arrived on time with those that did not arrive as scheduled.

God cares about numbers. Luke 12:7 says, "But the very hairs of your head are all numbered. Do not fear therefore; you are of more value than many sparrows."

Grade Five

3

Chapter

Lessons 26 - 40

He counts the number of the stars;
He calls them all by name.

Psalm 147:4

Lesson 26

Giotto space probe

When Mike and Joy visited the Kennedy Space Center, they were amazed at the difference in size of the space shuttle and the various types of probes. During the tour, they were told that the *Giotto* space probe, which flew past Halley's comet in 1986, was only 10 feet long (about the size of a compact car). They learned that today's space shuttles are more than 18 times as long as the *Giotto* space probe. Since they were curious about the length of the space shuttle, Mike and Joy used multiplication to determine its length.

One of the uses of multiplication is to <u>compare sizes or amounts to find information</u>.

length of the Giotto probe × 18 = approximate length of the space shuttle
10 feet × 18 = 180 feet

Multiplication is also used as <u>a shortcut to replace repeated addition</u>.

If a bus that holds 40 people makes 5 trips an hour around the launch pad, how many people take the tour in one hour?

40 + 40 + 40 + 40 + 40 = 200
40 × 5 = 200

REMEMBER

Multiplication is the operation that finds the **product** of two **factors**.

factor × factor = product

Properties of Multiplication

1. Zero Property of Multiplication
Multiplying any factor by 0 results in a product of zero.

$12 \times 0 = 0$
$400 \times 0 = 0$

2. Multiplication Identity Property of One
If one factor is 1, the product will be the other factor.

$1 \times 89 = 89$
$1,000 \times 1 = 1,000$

3. Commutative (Order) Property of Multiplication
The order of the factors may change without changing the product.

$4 \times 5 = 20$
$5 \times 4 = 20$

4. Associative (Grouping) Property of Multiplication
The grouping of factors may change without changing the product.

$6 \times (5 \times 2) = 60$
$(6 \times 5) \times 2 = 60$

5. Distributive Property
The product remains the same whether the factor is multiplied by the sum of the addends or by each addend.

$2 \times (4 + 5) = 18$
$(2 \times 4) + (2 \times 5) = 18$

Mathematics Grade 5

 **Check Understanding**

Name the multiplication property demonstrated by each number sentence.

a. $2 \times 9 = 9 \times 2$

b. $3 \times (7 \times 4) = (3 \times 7) \times 4$

c. $0 \times 9 = 0$

d. $1 \times 32 = 32$

e. $3 \times (4 + 8) = (3 \times 4) + (3 \times 8)$

f. $11 \times 15 = 15 \times 11$

g. $(8 \times 8) \times 3 = 8 \times (8 \times 3)$

h. $10,000 \times 0 = 0$

i. $6 \times (5 + 3) = (6 \times 5) + (6 \times 3)$

 Practice

Write the missing number(s) and identify the property of multiplication.

1. $3 \times \boxed{0} = 0$

2. $7 \times (6 \times \boxed{5}) = (7 \times 6) \times 5 = \boxed{210}$

3. $1 \times \boxed{9} = 9$

4. $6 \times (8 + \boxed{7}) = (6 \times 8) + (\boxed{6} \times 7) = \boxed{90}$

5. $4 \times 5 = \boxed{5} \times 4 = 20$

6. $3 \times (20 + 10) = (3 \times \boxed{20}) + (3 \times \boxed{10}) = \boxed{90}$

7. $15 \times 2 = 2 \times \boxed{15} = 30$

8. $1,245 \times 0 \times 3,626 = \boxed{0}$

Write a number sentence to illustrate each property.

9. Commutative Property of Multiplication

10. Associative Property of Multiplication

11. Zero Property of Multiplication

12. Multiplication Identity Property of One

13. Distributive Property

 **Apply**

14. Describe how the Distributive Property could help you solve 4×23 using only mental math.

 **Review**

Problem Solving WITH A Partner Think fast and state each fact to a partner.

1. 3×9 9×3 4×9 5×9

2. 4×7 3×7 7×7 7×9

3. 7×6 6×6 2×7 7×8

4. 9×8 9×7 9×6 9×5

5. 5×2 5×5 5×8 5×7

6. 6×8 6×7 8×8 5×6

7. 9×2 9×10 9×11 8×9

8. 8×7 7×5 7×10 7×11

Lesson 27

Construct Meaning

In her study of the planets, Melissa learned that Jupiter takes 12 times longer to make one revolution of the sun than the time required for Earth to make one revolution of the sun. She knows that it takes Earth 365 days to complete one revolution of the sun. How can she quickly determine the time it takes for Jupiter to go completely around the sun?

Round 365 days to the nearest hundred, which is 400 days, for Earth's orbit. If Jupiter's orbit is 12 times longer, multiply 400×12.

THINK: If $4 \times 12 = 48$, then $40 \times 12 = 480$, and $400 \times 12 = 4,800$.
It takes Jupiter about 4,800 days to orbit the sun.

> A **multiple** is the product of a select number and another whole number.

Multiples of 10, 100, and 1,000 are easy to remember.

Multiples of 10 ⟶ 10   20   30   40   50   60   70   80   90   100.
Multiples of 100 ⟶ 100   200   300   400   500   600   700   800   900   1,000
Multiples of 1,000 ⟶ 1,000   2,000   3,000   4,000   5,000   6,000   7,000   8,000   9,000   10,000.

Use these multiples to do mental math.

Begin with any two factors and their product.

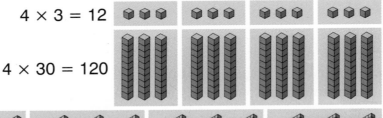

$4 \times 3 = 12$

$4 \times 30 = 120$

$4 \times 300 = 1,200$

$4 \times 3,000 = 12,000$

What pattern do you see when you multiply with multiples of 10, 100, and 1,000?

Tell why you agree or disagree with the following statement.

> The total number of zeros in the factors will equal the total number of zeros in the product. Is there an exception to this rule?

Mathematics Grade 5

80

 **Check Understanding**

Copy and complete the pattern.

a. $5 \times 3 = 15$
$5 \times 30 = 150$
$5 \times 300 = 1,800$
$5 \times 3,000 = 15,000$

b. $7 \times 2 = 14$
$7 \times 20 = 140$
$7 \times 200 = 1,400$
$7 \times 2,000 = 14,000$

c. $11 \times 8 = 88$
$11 \times 80 = 880$
$11 \times 800 = 8,800$
$11 \times 8,000 = 88,000$

d. $12 \times 6 = 72$
$12 \times 60 = 720$
$12 \times 600 = 7,200$
$12 \times 6,000 = 72,000$

 **Practice**

Use mental math to multiply.

1. $60 \times 6 = 360$
2. $400 \times 5 = 2,000$
3. $3,000 \times 4 = 12,000$
4. $8,000 \times 3 = 24,000$
5. $9,000 \times 2 = 18,000$
6. $800 \times 7 = 5,600$
7. $90 \times 5 = 450$
8. $200 \times 8 = 1,600$
9. $700 \times 4 = 2,800$
10. $30 \times 9 = 270$

 Apply

Use mental math.

11. Mark's father works as a scientist for NASA. His monthly salary is $4,000. What does he earn in one year?

12. A telescope magnifies distant objects, enabling astronomers to study the planets and stars. The reflecting telescope actually uses bowl-shaped mirrors to gather light and make objects visible to us. An early reflecting telescope on Mount Wilson in California has a mirror that is 60 inches across. There is a similar telescope in Russia that is about four times wider. Approximately how many inches across is the mirror on the Russian telescope?

13. The children at Faith Christian School decided to recycle newspapers and save the earnings to purchase a telescope for the school. If there are 12 classes and each class collects about 500 pounds of paper, what is the approximate total weight of the newspapers?

14. The W. M. Keck Observatory is located in Hawaii on the summit of the dormant Mauna Kea volcano. Two of the world's largest optical and infrared telescopes, the Keck I and Keck II, are used there to study space. The cost of the telescopes was over $140 million. If four corporations each gave $40 million to the Keck Foundation, would that equal or exceed the amount needed for the telescopes?

Lesson 28

Scott's teacher asked him to complete a chart to show the first ten multiples of 3 and 5. When he had finished, he noticed that some of the numbers were the same.

Multiples of 3	3	6	9	12	15	18	21	24	27	30
Multiples of 5	5	10	15	20	25	30	35	40	45	50

Which multiples are the same?

In the chart above, we see that 15 and 30 are multiples of both 3 and 5. Multiples that are shared by two or more numbers are **common multiples**. What do you notice about the common multiples of 3 and 5?

The smallest common multiple of two or more numbers is the **least common multiple (LCM)**. The least common multiple of 3 and 5 is 15.

USE A CALCULATOR

A calculator is useful for finding the multiples of a number.

Press , then   .

Continue to press for each multiple of 7.

Multiple triangle motif on Ukranian egg

Complete the definition.

a. The multiples of a number are the products of ▦ .

b. A common multiple is a number that ▦ .

c. The least common multiple (or LCM) is ▦ .

d. What is a strategy to find the LCM of two numbers?

e. How would you find the LCM of three numbers?

60

Mathematics Grade 5

 **Practice**

List the first ten multiples of each number.

1. 4   2. 6   3. 2   4. 8   5. 9   6. 7   7. 3   8. 5

Compare the first ten multiples of each pair of numbers. List the common multiples and identify the LCM.

9. 4 and 6   10. 6 and 8   11. 8 and 9   12. 2 and 5

13. 3 and 4   14. 5 and 7   15. 2 and 3   16. 3 and 7

 Apply

17. Cassie and her younger sister have soccer practice after school. Cassie's team practices every other day, and her sister's team practices every third day. Mom said, "I wish you and your sister had practice on the same day once in a while." Cassie said, "We do, Mom!" If both teams begin practice on September 1, how often will the girls have practice on the same day? (Hint: Use the calendar to help you see the dates of each girl's practice.)

18. Complete each analogy using the least common multiple.

   a. 15 is to 3 and 5 as ▦ is to 4 and 5.

   b. 6 is to 2 and 3 as ▦ is to 3 and 4.

   c. 10 is to 2 and 5 as ▦ is to 2 and 9.

SEPTEMBER

Sun	Mon	Tue	Wed	Thu	Fri	Sat
	1	2	3	4	5	6
7	8	9	10	11	12	13
14	15	16	17	18	19	20
21	22	23	24	25	26	27
28	29	30				

Review

Find the product. Use mental math when possible.

1.	2.	3.	4.	5.	6.
300	7,000	500	2,000	80	900
× 4	× 10	× 10	× 9	× 7	× 8
1,200	70,000	5000	18000	56 0	7,200

Copy and complete.

7. $7 \times 8 = 8 \times 7 = 56$

8. $2 \times (8 + 3) = (2 \times 8) + (2 \times 3) = $ ▦

9. $9 \times (2 + 5) = ($ ▦ $\times 2) + ($ ▦ $\times 5) = $ ▦

Lesson 29

Construct Meaning

<u>Multiples</u> of a given number are greater than or equal to that number.
6, 12, 18, 24, and 30 are some multiples of 6.

A <u>factor</u> of a given number is a number that will divide evenly into it.
If 6 is the product, what are the possible equations?

$$1 \times 6 = 6 \qquad\qquad 2 \times 3 = 6$$
$$\text{factor} \times \text{factor} \qquad\qquad \text{factor} \times \text{factor}$$

The factors of 6 are 1, 2, 3, and 6.
Factoring is the process of finding parts of a number by using multiplication and division facts.

Find the factors of 14.

$1 \times 14 = 14$
$2 \times 7 = 14$
Factors of 14 are 1, 2, 7, and 14.

Find the factors of 32.

$1 \times 32 = 32$
$2 \times 16 = 32$
$4 \times 8 = 32$
Factors of 32 are 1, 2, 4, 8, 16, and 32.

Use a Venn diagram to find the **common factors,** those shared by two or more numbers, of 14 and 32.

The largest common factor of two or more numbers is known as the **greatest common factor** (GCF). What is the GCF of 14 and 32?

Strategies for Finding Factors

- Factors of a number will divide evenly into that number.
- Any number is a factor of itself.
- Use multiplication facts.
- 1 is a factor of all whole numbers.
- 2 is a factor of all even numbers.
- 5 and 10 are factors of all numbers that end with a 0.
- Break down larger factors into smaller factors.

Check Understanding

Use a Venn diagram to show the common factors and the greatest common factor of each.

a. 10 and 20

b. 6 and 12

c. 24 and 32

List the factors of each number. Circle the common factors and box the greatest common factor.

1. 9 and 15

2. 8 and 16

3. 12 and 16

4. 9 and 36

5. 30 and 50

6. 15 and 25

7. 18 and 27

8. 7 and 21

9. 7 and 11

10. Drew wants to make ice-cream sundaes. He has 12 scoops of vanilla ice cream and 18 spoons of chocolate chips. He decides to divide the ice cream and chocolate chips into portions of equal size with nothing left over. How many sundaes will he make? What is the amount of ice cream and chocolate chips that will be in each sundae?

11. Tina was listing the factors of a number less than 50. The first five numbers that she wrote were 1, 2, 3, 5, and 6. What is the number she was factoring?

12. Courtney's teacher gave her a piece of poster board that measured 12 inches by 8 inches. She asked her to divide it evenly into squares of the largest size possible. What size will each square be?

Find the LCM (least common multiple) for each pair of numbers.

1. 6 and 9

2. 2 and 6

3. 2 and 7

4. 3 and 6

5. 5 and 6

6. 4 and 10

7. 4 and 5

8. 3 and 11

9. 2 and 9

10. 12 and 30

Lesson 30

Construct Meaning

The pull of gravity on the moon is about $\frac{1}{6}$ of the earth's gravitational pull. This means that your best long jump on Earth would be about 6 times as long on the moon. The men's long jump record is a little more than 29 feet. How far could the world-record holder jump on the moon?

29 feet × 6

Step 1

$$\begin{array}{r} \overset{5}{2}9 \\ \times\ 6 \\ \hline 4 \end{array}$$

Multiply the ones.
6 × 9 ones = 54 ones.
Regroup 54 ones as 5 tens and 4 ones.

Step 2

$$\begin{array}{r} \overset{5}{2}9 \\ \times\ 6 \\ \hline 174 \end{array}$$

Multiply the tens.
6 × 2 tens = 12 tens.
Add the regrouped tens as 12 tens + 5 tens = 17 tens.

On the moon, the record long jump would be more than 174 feet.

We multiply three-digit numbers the same way. Try 6 × 292.

Multiply the ones.
Regroup 12 ones as 1 ten and 2.

$$\begin{array}{r} 2\overset{1}{9}2 \\ \times\ 6 \\ \hline 2 \end{array}$$

Multiply the tens.
6 × 9 tens = 54 tens.
Add the regrouped ten for 55 tens.
Regroup 55 tens as 5 hundreds and 5 tens.

$$\begin{array}{r} 2\overset{5\ 1}{9}2 \\ \times\ 6 \\ \hline 52 \end{array}$$

Multiply the hundreds.
6 × 2 hundreds = 12 hundreds.
Add the regrouped hundreds.
12 + 5 = 1 thousand and 7 hundreds.

$$\begin{array}{r} \overset{5\ 1}{2}92 \\ \times\ 6 \\ \hline 1,752 \end{array}$$

Check Understanding

Multiply to find the product.

a.
$$\begin{array}{r} 92 \\ \times\ 8 \\ \hline 736 \end{array}$$

b.
$$\begin{array}{r} 72 \\ \times\ 4 \\ \hline 288 \end{array}$$

c.
$$\begin{array}{r} \overset{4}{8}07 \\ \times\ 6 \\ \hline 4842 \end{array}$$

$$\begin{array}{r} \overset{23}{6}35 \\ \times\ 7 \\ \hline 4445 \end{array}$$

e. The largest crater on the near side of the moon, Bailey Crater, is 188 miles wide. The Orientale Basin, located on the dark side of the moon, is three times wider than Bailey Crater. How wide is the Orientale Basin?

Multiply to find the product.

1. 36 × 5	2. 68 × 4	3. 241 × 3	4. 52 × 4	5. 72 × 3
6. 84 × 5	7. 432 × 6	8. 67 × 6	9. 98 × 8	10. 157 × 7
11. 317 × 4	12. 657 × 9	13. 958 × 3	14. 25 × 8	15. 401 × 9

16. One of the moons of Mars is 5 miles in diameter. The diameter of Earth's moon is 432 times larger than that moon. What is the diameter of Earth's moon?

17. The maximum recorded speed of a canvasback duck is 72 miles per hour. If it flew at a rate of 63 miles per hour, how far could a canvasback duck fly in 4 hours?

18. A sailfish can swim 68 miles per hour. If it could swim from noon until 6:00 P.M., how many miles would it travel?

19. In 1958, a tornado struck Wichita Falls, Texas, at a speed of 280 miles per hour. On the planet Neptune, the wind blows 4 times faster than a tornado on Earth. Using the speed of the tornado in Wichita Falls for comparison, compute the speed of Neptune's wind.

Find the sum.

3,246 + 4,786	2. 5,785 + 6,941	3. 9,321 + 7,652	4. 18,747 + 2,789
11,539 + 4,600	23,416 + 18,323	7. 46,630 + 33,758	8. 2,235 + 8,221

Construct Meaning

Computing with larger numbers requires solid knowledge of place value. To find multiplication products, pay attention to place value and work in sequence.

3,428 can be written as:

3 thousands
4 hundreds
2 tens
8 ones

OR

Remember, each number has its own "place."

3 thousands, 4 hundreds 2 tens 8 ones

42,759 can be written as:

4 ten thousands
2 thousands
7 hundreds
5 tens
9 ones

OR

4 ten thousands 2 thousands, 7 hundreds 5 tens 9 ones

Use the Distributive Property to find the product of 3,428 × 5.

$$3,000 \times 5 = 15,000$$
$$400 \times 5 = 2,000$$
$$20 \times 5 = 100$$
$$8 \times 5 = +\ \ \ \ 40$$
$$17,140$$

Multiply the number in each place.
Add the products.

Find the product by multiplying ones, tens, hundreds, and thousands. Regroup as needed.

$$\begin{array}{r} {}^{2\ 14} \\ 3,428 \\ \times\ \ \ \ \ 5 \\ \hline 17,140 \end{array}$$

Compare the products of each method.

Check Understanding

a. Copy and complete. Use the Distributive Property to find the product of 42,759 × 6.

$$40,000 \times 6 = \boxed{}$$
$$2,000 \times 6 = \boxed{}$$
$$700 \times 6 = \boxed{}$$
$$50 \times 6 = \boxed{}$$
$$9 \times 6 = +\ \underline{\boxed{}}$$

b. Regroup as needed.

$$\begin{array}{r} 42,759 \\ \times\ \ \ \ \ \ 6 \\ \hline \end{array}$$

c. Compare the products from a and b.

Write the product.

1. 7,961
   × 4

2. 13,563
   × 7

3. 8,124
   × 5

4. 6,082
   × 9

5. 22,935
   × 3

6. 3,136
   × 2

7. 56,207
   × 7

8. 4,927
   × 8

9. 77,898
   × 0

10. 9,601
    × 7

11. 90,999
    × 3

12. 84,611
    × 9

13. 1,707
    × 7

14. 6,526
    × 5

15. 1,888
    × 8

Use mental math and the Distributive Property to solve.

16. 4,200 × 5   17. 7,500 × 2   18. 51,000 × 3   19. 2,200 × 4

20. Flying at supersonic speed, the Concorde is capable of traveling 32,496 miles in a 24-hour period. If you left today on the Concorde, it would take a week to fly to the moon. What is the approximate distance from Earth to the moon?

21. The diameter of the moon is about 2,155 miles. Earth's diameter is about 4 times that of the moon. What is the approximate diameter of the earth?

22. Nicole knows that 9 × 8,200 = 73,800. How can she compute 8 × 8,200 without using multiplication?

Write the word form for each number.

1. 55,020
2. 849,303
3. 3,126,900
4. Put commas in the number 3262988004, then write the number in word form.

Construct Meaning

Mrs. Drake's tenth grade science students want to take a class trip to the Dominion Observatory in Victoria, British Columbia. Since they will take a ferry from Seattle to Vancouver Island and pay for their own meals, the approximate cost per student is $185. If there are 22 students, what is the approximate total cost of the class trip?

Estimate.

1. Round to the highest place value. Multiply.

$185 → $200
× 22 → × 20
$4,000

Or

2. Use front-end digits. Multiply.

$185 → $100
× 22 → × 20
$2,000

Which method of estimation is more accurate in this case? Why?

Check Understanding

If the trip to the Dominion Observatory is successful, Mrs. Drake will estimate the projected cost of returning next year. She believes the cost may increase by about $25 per student and knows she will have 26 students in her class. Use both methods of estimation to estimate the total cost for next year's trip.

cost per student: $185
cost increase: + 25
next year's cost: $210

Estimate, using the projected figures for next year.

a. Round to the greatest place value. Multiply.

$210 → 200
× 26 → × 30
6,000 total cost of the trip

Or

b. Use front-end digits. Multiply.

$210 → 200
× 26 → × 20
400 total cost of the trip

26 students will be on the trip.

Compare your results.

Use front-end digits to estimate the product.

1. 455
   × 62

2. 801
   × 35

3. 1,221
   ×   82

4. 337
   × 50

5. 7,221
   ×   90

6. 718
   × 42

7. 533
   × 74

8. 122
   × 80

9. 635
   × 91

10. 249
    × 21

Round each factor to the greatest place value. Estimate the product.

11. 491
    × 35

12. 862
    × 48

13. 3,200
    ×   61

14. 697
    × 43

15. 998
    × 56

16. 275
    × 68

17. 149
    × 33

18. 5,025
    ×   50

19. 382
    × 76

20. 725
    × 29

Use rounding to the greatest place value to estimate.

21. Mrs. Harrison went to the grocery store to buy fruit for a large salad she was preparing for a church supper. She had only $20, so she estimated the cost as she selected each item. Use mental math to estimate the total cost of the fruit on her list. Is $20 enough to pay for the total cost of the fruit?

22. About how much more do four pounds of grapes cost than five pounds of apples?

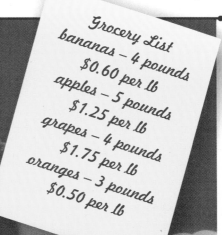

Grocery List
bananas – 4 pounds
$0.60 per lb
apples – 5 pounds
$1.25 per lb
grapes – 4 pounds
$1.75 per lb
oranges – 3 pounds
$0.50 per lb

 **Construct Meaning**

The moon is Earth's only natural satellite, traveling around the earth in an elliptical path called an orbit. One complete trip of the moon around Earth, called a revolution, takes 27 days. How many days does it take for the moon to make 12 revolutions?

Multiply 27 days × 12.

1 Multiply by the digit in the ones place. Regroup if necesary.

$$\begin{array}{r} \overset{1}{27} \\ \times\ 12 \\ \hline 54 \end{array}$$

2 Multiply by the digit in the tens place.

$$\begin{array}{r} 27 \\ \times\ 12 \\ \hline 54 \\ +270 \\ \end{array}$$
◁ Write a zero to show you multiplied by 10.

3 Add the two partial products.

$$\begin{array}{r} 27 \\ \times\ 12 \\ \hline 54 \\ +270 \\ \hline 324 \end{array}$$

It takes 324 days for the moon to make 12 revolutions around Earth.

You know that it takes the earth one year, or 365 days, to make one revolution around the sun. How many days are required for Earth to make 12 revolutions?

Multiply 365 × 12.

$$\begin{array}{r} \overset{1\ 1}{365} \\ \times\ 12 \\ \hline 730 \end{array}$$ Multiply by 2. ← 2 × 365

$$\begin{array}{r} 365 \\ \times\ 12 \\ \hline 730 \\ +3\ 650 \\ \end{array}$$ Multiply by 10. ← 10 × 365

$$\begin{array}{r} 365 \\ \times\ 12 \\ \hline 730 \\ +3\ 650 \\ \hline 4{,}380 \end{array}$$ days
Add the partial products. Regroup to add.

Add three days for the three "leap years" occurring during the 12 revolutions. 4,383 days are required for the earth to make 12 revolutions around the sun.

Find the product.

1.	2.	3.	4.	5.	6.	7.
36 × 25	28 × 17	44 × 56	15 × 32	43 × 21	38 × 19	52 × 20

8.	9.	10.	11.	12.	13.	14.
45 × 37	73 × 33	617 × 18	412 × 70	328 × 75	720 × 24	639 × 83

15.	16.	17.	18.	19.	20.	21.
594 × 62	1,422 × 51	107 × 98	3,266 × 22	590 × 44	6,100 × 39	785 × 63

22. If Earth orbits the sun at an average speed of 18 miles per second, how many miles does Earth travel

    a. in 1 minute?
    b. in 1 hour?
    c. in 1 day?

23. Tell if each statement is a reasonable estimate or not.

    a. The product of 75 and 25 is greater than 10,000.
    b. The product of 122 and 12 is less than 400.

24. Katrina's father promised to buy a computer she could use for math practice and research for school projects. She spent four Saturdays traveling with her father to various stores in the city. If it is 92 miles (round trip) from their home in the country to the city, how many miles did they travel to find the best computer?

List the multiples of 10, 100, and 1,000 for each number.

  1. 7   2. 8   3. 9

Find the estimated product by rounding to the greatest place value before multiplying.

4.	5.	6.	7.	8.
28 × 3	41 × 9	55 × 8	73 × 7	69 × 4

Use front-end digits to find the estimated product.

9.	10.	11.	12.	13.
37 × 4	82 × 11	94 × 7	56 × 2	25 × 6

🧱 Construct Meaning

Mr. Mason's fifth graders formed an Astronomy Club to study planets, stars, and other objects in the universe. They plan to visit an observatory that has several large telescopes to observe the objects in the heavens. If 32 students bring $18 each to cover the cost of the trip, how much money will Mr. Mason collect?

Solar Telescope at Kitt Peak National Observatory, Arizona

Problem-Solving Guide

1. Understand the question.
   How much money is needed for all the students to go on the trip?

2. Analyze the data.
   There are 32 students.
   Each student will pay $18.

3. Plan the strategy.
   Multiply to solve.
       $18 × 32 students
   Estimate by rounding to the greatest place value.
       $20 × 30 = $600
   About $600 is needed.

4. Solve the problem.

$$\begin{array}{r} \$18 \\ \times\ 32 \\ \hline 36 \\ +540 \\ \hline \$576 \end{array}$$

   $576 will be collected for 32 students to go on the trip.

5. Evaluate the result.
   $576 seems reasonable since the estimate was $600.

LOVE TO STUDY SPACE? JOIN THE ASTRONOMY CLUB!

More Hints For Problem Solving:
Read the problem and restate in your own words.
Find the information needed and eliminate the rest.
Decide on the first step and work in order.
Always check to be sure your answer makes sense.

The students in Mr. Mason's class decided to open membership in their Astronomy Club to other classes at school. At the next meeting, the total attendance was 53 students, three teachers, and four parent volunteers! Use the Problem-Solving Guide to solve the following problems.

1. Some of Mr. Mason's students brought cookies for this meeting. Josh and Cara each brought 3 dozen. Kevin and Jamie each brought 4 dozen. Are there enough cookies for each person attending to have two cookies?

2. One of the parent volunteers owns a toy store. He gave the Astronomy Club 35 bags of "glow-in-the-dark" planets and stars to distribute to the members. If each bag contained 19 planets and stars, how many pieces were there altogether?

3. Two of Mr. Mason's students, Jan and Eric, wanted to regroup the planets and stars into small bags so each student at the Astronomy Club meeting would be able to take some home. Eric thought they should put 13 into each bag, but Jan said they had only enough to put 12 into each bag. Who was right?

4. After the meeting, Mr. Mason decided to make copies of information about astronomy for the club members. Each packet required 27 pieces of paper. How many sheets of paper did Mr. Mason need to make an information packet for every child who attended the meeting?

5. A ream of paper contains 500 sheets. If Mr. Mason had three reams, did he have enough for 53 information packets?

 Construct Meaning

There are 374 students enrolled at Hope Academy. This year the school cafeteria staff prepared 297 lunches per day. If the school year was 176 days long, how many lunches were prepared?

$$\begin{array}{r} 297 \\ \times 176 \end{array}$$

$$\begin{array}{r} {}^{5\,4} \\ 297 \\ \times 176 \\ \hline 1\ 782 \end{array}$$ Multiply the ones.

$$\begin{array}{r} {}^{6\,4} \\ 297 \\ \times 176 \\ \hline 1\ 782 \\ 20\ 790 \end{array}$$ Multiply the tens.

$$\begin{array}{r} {}^{5\,4} \\ 297 \\ \times 176 \\ \hline 1\ 782 \\ 20\ 790 \\ +\ 29\ 700 \end{array}$$ Multiply the hundreds. Add the three partial products.

52,272 lunches

Another way to look at 297 × 176 is 297 × (100 + 70 + 6).

$$\begin{array}{r} 297 \\ \times 176 \longrightarrow 100 + 70 + 6 \\ \hline 1\ 782 \longleftarrow 6 \times 297 \\ 20\ 790 \longleftarrow 70 \times 297 \\ +\ 29\ 700 \longleftarrow 100 \times 297 \\ \hline 52,272 \end{array}$$

> Check your answer by multiplying the rounded factors to see if the product is reasonable. The answer 52,272 is reasonable because 300 × 200 = 60,000.

Solve 2,312 × 342.

$$\begin{array}{r} 2,312 \\ \times\ \ 342 \\ \hline 4\ 624 \end{array}$$ Multiply the ones.

$$\begin{array}{r} {}^{1} \\ 2,312 \\ \times\ \ 342 \\ \hline 4\ 624 \\ 92\ 480 \end{array}$$ Multiply the tens.

$$\begin{array}{r} 2,312 \\ \times\ \ 342 \\ \hline 4\ 624 \\ 92\ 480 \\ +\ 693\ 600 \\ \hline 790,704 \end{array}$$ Multiply the hundreds.

Add the partial products.

 Check Understanding

Examine each problem. Write *C* if the problem has been solved correctly. If there is an error, write *I* for incorrect and explain the error.

a.
$$\begin{array}{r} 529 \\ \times\ 384 \\ \hline 2\ 016 \\ 42\ 320 \\ +\ 158\ 700 \\ \hline 203,036 \end{array}$$

b.
$$\begin{array}{r} 6,177 \\ \times\ \ \ 215 \\ \hline 30\ 885 \\ 61\ 770 \\ +\ 123\ 540 \\ \hline 216,195 \end{array}$$

c.
$$\begin{array}{r} 4,000 \\ \times\ \ \ 189 \\ \hline 36\ 999 \\ 320\ 000 \\ +\ 400\ 000 \\ \hline 756,999 \end{array}$$

d.
$$\begin{array}{r} 303 \\ \times\ 504 \\ \hline 1\ 212 \\ 0\ 000 \\ +\ 151\ 500 \\ \hline 152,712 \end{array}$$

Multiplying by a Three-Digit Factor

 ractice

Find the product. Check your answer using estimation.

| 1. 264
×327 | 2. 421
×271 | 3. 612
×494 | 4. 423
×325 | 5. 283
×846 |

| 6. 517
×716 | 7. 745
×281 | 8. 1,485
× 182 | 9. 2,537
× 863 | 10. 7,351
× 545 |

Choose the better estimate.

11. 61 × 340
    1,800 or 18,000

12. 9 × 599
    40,000 or 50,000

13. 308 × 3,000
    90,000 or 900,000

 pply

14. In 1970, the crew of Apollo 13 traveled the farthest distance anyone has ever traveled from Earth. The distance was more than 31 times Earth's diameter, which is 7,926 miles. How far away from Earth was the Apollo 13 crew when they set this record?

 eview

Solve.

| 1. 617
− 543 | 2. 5,492
− 2,843 | 3. 6,918
− 3,859 | 4. 26,437
− 5,766 |

| 5. 493
668
+285 | 6. 4,720
+5,986 | 7. 78,484
+ 32,246 | 8. 153,469
+ 822,383 |

Write > or <.

9. 0.625 ▦ 0.652   10. 49.88 ▦ 498.8   11. 0.03 ▦ 0.003

12. 10,000 × 5 ▦ 5,000 × 12   14. 4,000 × 10 ▦ 400 × 1,000

75

 **Practice**

Problem-Solving Guide

  Understand the question.
    Analyze the data.
      Plan the strategy.
        Solve the problem.
          Evaluate the result.

Solve each problem using the steps in the Problem-Solving Guide.

1. A tiny delicatessen in New Orleans bakes rolls daily for a popular sandwich called a "mufaletto." During the height of the tourist season, they bake 425 rolls per day. How many rolls are baked during this 154-day period of time?

2. The manager of the deli calculated that during the busiest part of the tourist season, 125 pounds of meat were used each day to make mufalettos. Based on 154 days, how many pounds of meats were used?

3. The Amtrak *Crescent* travels from New York City to New Orleans and back. The distance between the two cities is 1,380 miles. What is the total mileage if the Crescent makes 85 round trips?

4. The deli workers frequently donate brownies to a local Christian school. During the most recent school year, the students sold the brownies after school to raise money for a summer mission trip to Israel. The deli made 120 donations, giving 12 dozen brownies each time. What was the total number of brownies the students received from the deli?

5. In the area surrounding New Orleans, land is being cleared to build new housing. The county will allow only 250 trees to be cut per square mile. If there are 105 square miles to be developed, what is the maximum number of trees that could be cut?

6. Many tourists in New Orleans take the "Swamp Tour" to view alligators living in their natural habitat. During one week in May, each of the five daily trips was filled to capacity with 45 people. How many people toured the swamp that week?

More Practice with Three-Digit Factors

Read the following. Tell what information is not needed to solve the problem. Then find the answer.

7. The average dairy cow in California gives 2,305 gallons of milk per year. A Holstein cow weighs between 1,000 and 1,500 pounds. How many gallons of milk would a herd of 215 cows in California produce in one year?

8. It takes 10 gallons of milk to make one pound of cheese, and 15.6 gallons of milk to obtain one gallon of cream. How many gallons of milk are used to make 125 pounds of cheese?

Use multiplication to find some interesting statistics.

9. In the United States, girls between the ages of 12 and 19 drink an average of two cans of soda a day. How many cans of soda does that "average" girl drink in 1 year?

10. Americans consume between one and three teaspoons of salt daily. This is about twice as much as is recommended. If you consume three teaspoons of salt per day, how many teaspoons will you eat in one year? Use a calculator to divide your answer by 48 to find how many cups of salt you would consume per year at this rate.

Baskets of salt produced in Africa

11. A taco salad from a fast food restaurant has 1,620 mg of sodium from salt. If you had a taco salad every day for a week, how many milligrams of sodium would that be?

12. The daily recommended intake of salt is 1,100 to 3,300 mg. What is the maximum amount, in milligrams, of safe salt intake for a week? How does the sodium total from a week of taco salads compare with that figure?

Lesson 37

Construct Meaning

Some problems require the use of more than one operation to solve. Carefully analyze the information given. Plan how to solve the problem one step at a time. Choose the numbers and the operation you will use for the first step: addition, subtraction, multiplication, or division. Then decide which operation to use next to solve the problem.

Mrs. Cox shops for Christmas gifts early so that in December she will be able to be with her family and focus on the birth of Christ. During the October sale at Son Valley Christian Bookstore, she bought the following items: Six compact discs at $12 each, seven devotional books at $22 each, and two Bibles at $39 each. If she had $325 to spend, what will she have left to return to her Christmas gift fund?

Understand the question. Analyze the data. Plan the strategy. Solve the problem. Evaluate the result.

Step 1 Estimate using mental math. Use a calculator to determine what was spent.

ON/C 6 × 1 2 M+ 7 × 2 2 M+ 2 × 3 9 M+ MRC = **$304** spent

To clear the memory, press MRC MRC ON/C .

Step 2 To compute the amount of money remaining,

press 3 2 5 − 3 0 4 = **$21** left

Check Understanding

When we purchase items in a store, we pay the <u>retail</u> price. Store owners buy the items from a supplier for a lesser amount, called the <u>wholesale</u> price. The chart below shows the wholesale prices for the items Mrs. Cox bought. Use the chart and your calculator to figure how much <u>profit</u> Mr. Samuels, the store owner, made on the items sold to Mrs. Cox.

| Wholesale Prices | CD's $6 each | Devotional books $12 each | Bibles $15 each |

a. Figure the total amount that Mr. Samuels paid for the items Mrs. Cox bought.

Press ON/C 6 × 6 M+ 7 × 1 2 M+ 2 × 1 5 M+ MRC .

Clear the calculator. MRC MRC ON/C

b. Calculate the profit Mr. Samuels made from this sale by finding the difference between what Mrs. Cox paid and the amount the store owner paid.

Use a calculator.

1. Rebecca and Brian earn $9 per hour at the Son Valley Christian Bookstore. Last week Rebecca worked for 24 hours and Brian clocked 16 hours. What was the total amount Mr. Samuels paid to Rebecca and Brian last week?

2. Chad is an avid fan of Christian music. He purchased a CD for $16 and a tape that had originally been marked $11.97, but a sticker on the tape said, "Take $2.49 off." What did Chad pay for the CD and tape?

3. Michelle has worked at Mr. Samuels' store for five years and now earns $12 an hour. This week, she and Brian each worked 32 hours. How much more did Michelle earn than Brian?

Choose a problem-solving strategy that best helps you to solve each of the following problems.

Possible Strategies
- Use a calculator.
- Draw a picture.
- Make a chart.
- Write an equation.

4. Rebecca was responsible for setting up a display near the entrance of the bookstore. She used Bibles, calendars, Christian novels, and family albums. She placed Bibles on one end. The novels were between the albums and the calendars. If the calendars are not next to the Bibles, what is?

5. During December, the bookstore sells many Scripture calendars for the coming year. They sold a total of 580 calendars during the first two weeks of December. If they sold 179 calendars the first week, how many were sold during the second week?

6. Mr. Samuels usually buys best-selling Christian books for $180 per box. The publisher is now offering a reduced price of $112 per box. Since he is going to order 45 boxes of books, how much money will he save?

7. The Son Valley Christian Bookstore is closed on Sunday. Mr. Samuels is planning to close on one additional day, either Monday or Tuesday. He compared the total sales on Mondays during October with the total sales on Tuesdays for that month. He will close the store on the day with the lower total sales. Based on the following information, which day will he choose?

October Sales				
Monday	$2,884	$1,223	$2,506	$1,989
Tuesday	$2,949	$2,361	$1,428	$2,029

Lesson 38

Construct Meaning

Astronomers often work with very large numbers in their study of objects in the universe. In astronomy, as well as other fields of science, large numbers may be expressed in shorter form using exponents.

Another way to express 100,000 is 10 × 10 × 10 × 10 × 10. It can also be written as 10^5 and read as "10 to the fifth power." 10 is the base number, and 5 is the exponent.

base number 10^5 exponent

Read the following base numbers and exponents. The **exponent** tells the number of times the **base number** is used as a factor.

$$2^5 \qquad 5^8 \qquad 10^7 \qquad 3^9 \qquad 4^6$$

Powers of 10
$10 = 10 \times 1 = 10^1$
$100 = 10 \times 10 = 10^2$
$1,000 = 10 \times 10 \times 10 = 10^3$
$10,000 = 10 \times 10 \times 10 \times 10 = 10^4$

In each row, note the relationship between the exponent and the number of zeros in the first number.

People from around the world bring their balloons to participate in the Balloon Fiesta held in Albuquerque, New Mexico. Over one million spectators enjoy this event each fall. Write this number as a power of ten.

$$1,000,000 = 10^6$$

The diameter of Earth is 12,756 kilometers (km). An astronomer would change that figure for scientific purposes.

12,756 km could be rounded to 13,000 km.
$$13,000 = 13 \times 1,000 = 13 \times 10^3 \text{ km}$$

Check Understanding

Round to the highest place value and express using exponents.

a. 4,030   b. 65,892   c. 41,738   d. 125,640

e. 38,618   f. 7,955   g. 89,750   h. 192,214

i. The distance from the earth to its moon is 238,613 miles. Round that figure to the highest place value and express using exponents of 10.

Mathematics Grade 5

The chart shows the diameter of each planet in our solar system, ordering the planets from smallest to largest. Round the diameter of each planet to the nearest thousand and express using powers of 10. Use your answers to compare the relative sizes of the planets.

Planets in Our Solar System

Planet	Diameter (in Km)	Rounded figure	Expressed with Exponents
Pluto	2,284	1.	
Mercury	4,878	2.	
Mars	6,786	3.	
Venus	12,104	4.	
Earth	12,756	5.	
Neptune	48,600	6.	
Uranus	52,142	7.	
Saturn	120,000	8.	
Jupiter	142,800	9.	

 Review

Write the letter of the correct estimated product.

1. 536×120
   a. 6,000
   b. 60,000
   c. 600,000

2. 420×277
   a. 120,000
   b. 12,000
   c. 1,200

3. 312×702
   a. 2,100,000
   b. 2,100
   c. 210,000

4. 675×435
   a. 280,000
   b. 28,000
   c. 2,800

Use the Distributive Property to find the product.

5. 5×532
6. 7×924
7. 8×860
8. 9×235

Name the property of multiplication shown by each equation and then solve.

9. $495 \times 0 = 0$
10. $895 \times 42 = 42 \times 895$
11. $8 \times (9 \times 7) = (8 \times 9) \times 7$

Find the product.

12. $\begin{array}{r} 498 \\ \times\ \ \ 5 \\ \hline \end{array}$

13. $\begin{array}{r} 863 \\ \times\ \ 19 \\ \hline \end{array}$

14. $\begin{array}{r} 4,500 \\ \times\ \ \ \ \ 22 \\ \hline \end{array}$

15. $\begin{array}{r} 22,607 \\ \times\ \ \ \ \ \ \ 84 \\ \hline \end{array}$

16. $\begin{array}{r} 5,289 \\ \times\ \ \ 363 \\ \hline \end{array}$

17. $\begin{array}{r} 937 \\ \times\ 684 \\ \hline \end{array}$

18. $\begin{array}{r} 2,934 \\ \times\ \ \ \ \ 25 \\ \hline \end{array}$

19. $\begin{array}{r} 12,630 \\ \times\ \ \ \ \ \ 767 \\ \hline \end{array}$

20. $\begin{array}{r} 4,152 \\ \times\ \ \ \ 984 \\ \hline \end{array}$

21. $\begin{array}{r} 898 \\ \times\ 257 \\ \hline \end{array}$

 Construct Meaning

A lattice is made from wooden or metal strips placed in a diagonal pattern with open spaces between the strips. Often a lattice supports ivy or roses as they grow. In **lattice multiplication**, a framework resembling a lattice supports us as we multiply using factors with two digits or more.

Use lattice multiplication to find the product of 52 × 43. Follow the steps.

1 **Write** the digits of one factor across the top edge of the lattice and the digits of the other factor down the right edge.

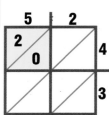

2 Beginning with the box in the **upper left corner, multiply** the digit at the top of the column by the digit at the right of the row. **Record** the product.

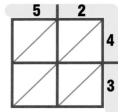

3 Do the same for each box in the lattice.

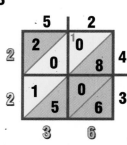

4 Beginning in the **lower right corner**, **add** the digits in each diagonal. Write each sum below its colored diagonal. Regroup to the next diagonal if necessary.

5 The product is read from top to bottom, left to right on the lattice edge.

52 × 43 = 2,236

 Check Understanding

Find the product of 756 × 819 using lattice multiplication.

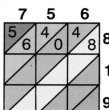

a. Copy and complete the lattice multiplication. Multiply for each box in the lattice. (Start at upper left.)

b. Add diagonally. (Start at lower right.)

c. Write the product. (Read from top left to bottom right.)

Practice

Use lattice multiplication to find the product.

1. 33 × 16
2. 42 × 27
3. 128 × 356
4. 345 × 62

5. 272 × 54
6. 545 × 236
7. 87 × 44
8. 72 × 99

9. 120 × 619
10. 651 × 477
11. 19 × 66
12. 58 × 236

CUMULATIVE REVIEW: Chapters 1–3

1. Choose the statement that is true.

   a. 0.03 > 0.30
   b. 0.20 > 0.40
   c. 0.40 > 0.04
   d. 0.40 < 0.04

2. 3,483,610 rounded to the nearest thousand is:

   a. 3,500,000
   b. 3,000,000
   c. 3,483,000
   d. 3,484,000

3. Choose the number that has 5 in the tenths place.

   a. 45.0
   b. 41.5
   c. 51.4
   d. 5.0

4. Which decimal shows the part of a dollar represented by a quarter?

   a. 0.25
   b. 2.5
   c. 25.0
   d. 0.025

5. What is the difference between 0.70 and 0.75?

   a. 0.5
   b. 5
   c. 0.05
   d. 5.0

6. What number is next in the pattern of 1, 2, 4, 8, 16?

   a. 24
   b. 32
   c. 30
   d. 18

7. What is the sum of 12.05 + 0.55?

   a. 12.60
   b. 12.65
   c. 12.055
   d. 13.0

8. Which number rounds to 32?

   a. 32.5
   b. 32.61
   c. 33.1
   d. 32.3

9. Which statement is true?

   a. 0.30 = 0.3
   b. 0.03 = 0.3
   c. 0.03 = 0.003
   d. 3.0 = 3.03

10. Bermuda, a group of islands in the Atlantic, is a popular tourist location. Use the graph to determine the months that receive about 4.5 inches of rain.

    a. January, February, March
    b. February, March, November
    c. June, July, August
    d. June and August

Bermuda's Rainfall

Multiply Like the Stars

Find the product.

1. 75 × 8	2. 49 × 63	3. 55 × 98	4. 687 × 26	5. 354 × 79	6. 262 × 45

7. 891 × 765	8. 4,328 × 33	9. 539 × 644	10. 7,870 × 141	11. 476 × 295	12. 5,820 × 36

Use mental math to find the product.

13. 800 × 4,000   14. 900 × 12,000   15. 5,000 × 110   16. 80 × 30,000

"... the LORD had said He would multiply Israel like the stars of the heavens." I Chronicles 27:23

Write the letter of the correct answer for problems 17–20.

Find an equivalent equation.

17. 42 × (18 + 69) =
    a. (42 + 18) × 69
    b. (42 × 18) + (42 × 69)
    c. (42 × 18) × (42 × 69)

18. 15 × (850 × 5) =
    a. (15 × 850) × 5
    b. (15 + 850) × 5
    c. 15 + 850 + 5

19. Marsha was using a calculator. She had written 27, 36, 45, 54, 63 on her paper. She was looking for

    a. factors of 9   **b.** multiples of 9   **c.** multiples of 7

20. Aaron was using a calculator to do a multiple-step problem. He found the first product he would need and pressed M+. Then he found the next product and pressed M+. What should he do in order to add the products?

    a. Press M+ again.   **b.** Press + .   **c.** Press MRC .

Find the Least Common Multiple for each pair of numbers.

21. 4 and 3   22. 5 and 8   23. 6 and 9   24. 7 and 12

25. Susan's brother is working to help pay his college tuition. He makes $8 an hour and works 15 hours per week. He also receives $175 a month for helping coach track at the high school. What are his total earnings for one month?

Estimate the product using front-end digits.

26. 46
×57

27. 92
×39

28. 55
×40

29. 81
×61

30. 33
×28

Estimate the product by rounding both factors to the greatest place value.

31. 482
× 56

32. 5,621
×   29

33. 843
× 81

34. 2,650
×   39

35. 999
× 71

36. Evan decided to read his entire Bible in one year. He thought he could read about 3 pages a day. His Bible has 1,045 pages. Can he complete reading the Bible in one year? Could he take off one day a week and finish within one year? Explain your answer.

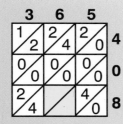

37. What are the missing numbers on the lattice? Use the lattice to find the product of 365 × 408.

38. Catherine is making a tile mosaic for an art project at school. It will be 12 inches by 18 inches. The tiles are available in the following sizes: 2-inch, 3-inch, 4-inch and 5-inch. The project requires that all the tiles in the mosaic be the same size. Which sizes of tile will work on her mosaic? What is the largest tile she could use?

"Brethren, join in following my example,
and note those who so walk,
as you have us for a pattern."
Philippians 3:17

Grade Five

4

Chapter

Lessons 41 – 60

Those who are wise shall shine
Like the brightness of the firmament,
And those who turn many to righteousness
Like the stars forever and ever.

Daniel 12:3

Construct Meaning

Mr. Borden hosted a space camp for the fifth grade students. He decided to divide the students into groups of five. On the first day, 65 students attended the camp. How many groups could Mr. Borden form?

How many groups of five are in 65?

Use base ten blocks to find the answer.

$5\overline{)65}$

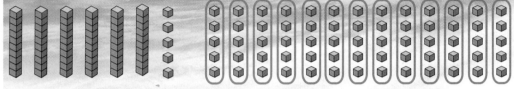

There are 13 groups of five in 65.

Check by multiplying $13 \times 5 = 65$.

A number is **divisible** by another number if it can be divided by that number with no remainder.

You can use the rules of divisibility to find out if a number is divisible by another number.

Is 65 divisible by 5?

A number is divisible by 5 if the digit in the ones place is 0 or 5.

Look at the number in the ones place.

tens | ones

$5\overline{)6\,5}$

The digit in the ones place is 5.

There is no remainder, so 65 is divisible by 5.

$5\overline{)65}^{\,13}$

RULES OF DIVISIBILITY

If a number is divisible by:

2 The digit in the ones place will be an even number. (0, 2, 4, 6, 8)

3 The sum of the digits will be divisible by 3. (15, 30, 45, 57)

5 The digit in the ones place will be 5 or 0. (15, 20, 25, 30)

6 It will be divisible by 2 and by 3. (12, 18, 24, 36)

9 The sum of the digits will be divisible by 9. (18, 27, 45, 72)

10 The digit in the ones place will be 0. (20, 30, 50, 60)

Check Understanding

Write the number of the model that shows the correct answer.

a. $6\overline{)36}$

b. $4\overline{)32}$

c. $6\overline{)24}$

d. $8\overline{)80}$

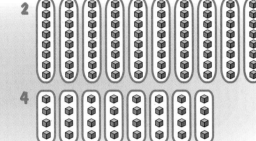
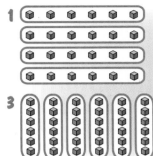

Practice

Write *yes* if the black number is divisible by the orange number. Write *no* if it is not. Use the rules of divisibility to help you.

1. 36 9	2. 24 10	3. 18 3	4. 142 2	5. 54 5
6. 49 6	7. 90 5	8. 700 10	9. 20 3	10. 81 9

Solve the problem. Check by multiplying.

11. $10\overline{)80}$ 12. $9\overline{)45}$ 13. $5\overline{)60}$ 14. $6\overline{)42}$ 15. $3\overline{)54}$

16. $2\overline{)96}$ 17. $6\overline{)24}$ 18. $9\overline{)81}$ 19. $10\overline{)110}$ 20. $5\overline{)75}$

21. $3\overline{)36}$ 22. $2\overline{)48}$ 23. $9\overline{)36}$ 24. $6\overline{)54}$ 25. $2\overline{)44}$

Challenge

By which numbers (2, 3, 5, 6, 9, or 10) is the given number divisible?

26. 72   27. 50   28. 78   29. 140   30. 228   31. 45

3-ounce
334
12-ounce
1,20

Review

Write the least common multiple of each pair.

1. 2 and 6   2. 3 and 4   3. 3 and 5

4. 4 and 8   5. 3 and 9   6. 5 and 10

 **Construct Meaning**

To purchase tickets to the baseball game, Steph, Randy, and Jenna had to save a total of $36. How much did each ticket cost?

Find $3)\overline{\$36}$. Think: ▦ × 3 = 36

12 × 3 = 36, so 36 ÷ 3 = 12

The price of each ticket was $12.

You can write four related multiplication and division sentences using 3, 12, and 36.

12 × 3 = 36   36 ÷ 12 = 3
3 × 12 = 36   36 ÷ 3 = 12

There are three different ways to show division. Each part of a division problem has a name: **dividend**, **divisor**, and **quotient**.

$$\overset{\text{12 quotient}}{\text{divisor } 3)\overline{36 \text{ dividend}}}$$

$$\underset{\text{dividend divisor quotient}}{36 \div 3 = 12}$$

$$\frac{\text{dividend } 36}{\text{divisor } 3} = 12 \text{ quotient}$$

Every division symbol is read as "divided by."

To read $3)\overline{36}$, begin with the number inside the box: "thirty-six divided by three."

To read 36 ÷ 3, work from left to right: "thirty-six divided by three."

To read $\frac{36}{3}$, work from top to bottom: "thirty-six divided by three."

At the game, Randy said to his friends, "I can find the quotient for 4,675,892 divided by 1 in one second." Randy knew his division rules. Can you find the rule that makes it possible for Randy to find the quotient in one second?

DIVISION RULES TO REMEMBER

1 When any number other than 0 is divided by itself, the quotient will be 1. 9 ÷ 9 = 1

2 When a number is divided by 1, the quotient will be that number. 9 ÷ 1 = 9

3 When zero is divided by any number, the quotient will be 0. 0 ÷ 9 = 0

4 It is impossible to divide by zero! How would you divide $100 among zero people?

Rule 2 makes it possible for Randy to divide quickly. 4,675,892 ÷ 1 = 4,675,892

  Check Understanding

Copy and solve each problem. Label the parts of the problem.

a. $4)\overline{36}$ b. 40 ÷ 5   c. $\frac{12}{2}$ d. $6)\overline{48}$

**ractice**

Solve if possible. Write the number of the division rule you used.

1. 237 ÷ 0
2. 360 ÷ 360
3. 400 ÷ 1
4. 0 ÷ 50

Divide.

5. 2)‾22‾
6. 5)‾15‾
7. 6)‾42‾
8. 7)‾21‾
9. 4)‾16‾

10. 3)‾33‾
11. 7)‾42‾
12. 9)‾27‾
13. 8)‾24‾
14. 2)‾24‾

15. 1)‾748‾
16. 4)‾44‾
17. 10)‾50‾
18. 6)‾18‾
19. 5)‾35‾

20. 36 ÷ 9
21. 12 ÷ 3
22. 35 ÷ 7
23. 70 ÷ 7
24. 540 ÷ 6

25. 55 ÷ 5
26. 90 ÷ 1
27. 24 ÷ 4
28. 120 ÷ 10
29. 35 ÷ 5

30. 30 ÷ 3
31. 32 ÷ 8
32. 990 ÷ 11
33. 72 ÷ 12
34. 0 ÷ 81

35. $\frac{45}{5}$
36. $\frac{18}{3}$
37. $\frac{81}{9}$
38. $\frac{72}{8}$
39. $\frac{40}{8}$

Write the related facts for each set of numbers.

40. 6, 9, 54
41. 56, 7, 8
42. 8, 8, 64
43. 9, 63, 7

pply

44. Kyra and her dad found 50 golf balls which she gave away. If she gives an equal amount of golf balls to 10 of her friends, how many will each friend receive?

45. Pedro has 48 marbles. He wants to share them with his three best friends. If Pedro and his friends divide the marbles among themselves, how many will each boy receive?

Review

Multiply.

1. 204
   × 3

2. 82
   × 6

3. 69
   × 4

4. 42
   × 8

5. 121
   × 2

Write >, < or = for each ⬚.

6. 0.08 ⬚ 0.008
7. 32.8 ⬚ 0.328
8. 0.12 ⬚ 1.2

Construct Meaning

The fifth grade students at Mt. Elim Bible Camp are going for a ride on the lake. Before departing, each boat must have three people aboard. If 14 people want to take a ride, how many boats will be needed? Find $14 \div 3$.

• Find the greatest number of threes in 14.

$3 \times 3 = 9$ too low $3 \times 4 = 12$ close $3 \times 5 = 15$ too high

The greatest number of threes in 14 is 4.

```
        4 R2  quotient
divisor 3)14  dividend
       -12
         2   remainder
```

Check by multiplying.

```
    4  ← quotient
  × 3  ← divisor
   12
 +  2  ← remainder
   14  ← dividend
```

Four boats will carry three students each. The remainder tells you that a fifth boat will be needed.

Large rafts carry nine passengers. How many rafts will be needed for 183 people? Find $183 \div 9$.

Step 1	Step 2	Step 3
Will the first digit of the quotient be in the hundreds place?	Divide the tens.	Divide the ones.

Step 1

```
9)183
```
No, there are not enough hundreds.
$9 > 1$

Step 2

Divide the tens.
```
     2
 9)183
  -18    Multiply
    0    Subtract
         Compare, 0 < 9
```

Step 3

Divide the ones.
```
    20 R3
 9)183
  -18↓
    03    Bring down
  -  0    Multiply
     3    Write the remainder
```

Step 4

Check by multiplying.
```
    20
  ×  9
   180
  +  3
   183
```

There are 20 groups of 9. The remainder is 3.

Twenty rafts will carry nine passengers each. One additional raft will be used for the remaining three passengers. Twenty-one rafts will be needed.

 **Check Understanding**

Copy and complete.

a.
```
      4 R▦
8) 34
  - 32
```

b.
```
      ▦ R▦
6) 28
  - 24
```

c.
```
      2 R▦
7) 141
  - 14
```

d.
```
      3 R▦
5) 161
  - 15
```

 Practice

Divide. Check by multiplying.

1. 6) 44   2. 5) 69   3. 3) 110   4. 2) 175   5. 4) 281

6. 5) 164   7. 9) 211   8. 7) 492   9. 8) 324   10. 3) 124

Divide.

11. 162 ÷ 4   12. 89 ÷ 9   13. 76 ÷ 3   14. 122 ÷ 6

15. 380 ÷ 7   16. 430 ÷ 6   17. 131 ÷ 2   18. 332 ÷ 5

19. 510 ÷ 9   20. 321 ÷ 8   21. 132 ÷ 5   22. 289 ÷ 9

Find the quotient.

23. $\frac{37}{5}$ 24. $\frac{61}{9}$ 25. $\frac{43}{7}$ 26. $\frac{440}{9}$ 27. $\frac{520}{6}$

 **Apply**

28. Scott, Todd, and Greg went to a weekend retreat for fathers and sons. A total of 123 people attended the retreat. How many groups of eight can be formed to stay in the cabins? How many will make a smaller group?

 **Review**

Write the numbers that are evenly divisible by 8.

1.   36   64   56   16   21   74   32

Write the numbers that are evenly divisible by 7.

2.   50   21   63   15   70   49   44

Lesson 44

Construct Meaning

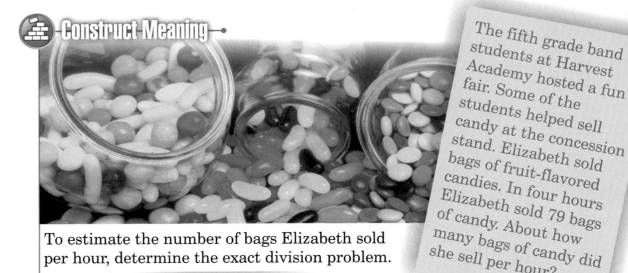

The fifth grade band students at Harvest Academy hosted a fun fair. Some of the students helped sell candy at the concession stand. Elizabeth sold bags of fruit-flavored candies. In four hours Elizabeth sold 79 bags of candy. About how many bags of candy did she sell per hour?

To estimate the number of bags Elizabeth sold per hour, determine the exact division problem.

$$79 \div 4$$

Compatible numbers are numbers that can be computed mentally and are near the given numbers. Find compatible numbers to help you determine the estimated quotient. Find a multiple of 4 that is close to 79.

$4 \times 10 = 40$ too low $4 \times 20 = 80$ close $4 \times 30 = 120$ too high

80 is close to 79, so 80 and 4 are the compatible numbers.

$$\begin{array}{r} 20 \\ 4\overline{)80} \end{array}$$

The estimated quotient is 20.
The exact quotient will be less than 20 because 80 > 79.
20 is an <u>overestimate</u>.

• Elizabeth sold about 20 bags of candy per hour.

Ben sold 131 lollipops in 4 hours.
About how many lollipops did Ben sell per hour? $131 \div 4$

Choose a multiple of 4 that is close to 131.
$4 \times 30 = 120$ $4 \times 40 = 160$
Use $120 \div 4$ as the compatible numbers. The estimated quotient is 30.

$$\begin{array}{r} 30 \\ 4\overline{)120} \end{array}$$
The exact quotient will be greater than 30 because 120 < 131.
30 is an <u>underestimate</u>.

Ben sold about 30 lollipops per hour.

Check Understanding

Choose the best estimate. Write *under* or *over* for each estimate.

a. $5\overline{)31}$ b. $3\overline{)149}$ c. $8\overline{)162}$ d. $7\overline{)419}$

50   20   6   60

Mathematics Grade 5

Practice

Write the letter of the best estimate for each quotient.

1. 4)250   **a.** 70   **b.** 50   **c.** 40   **d.** 60

2. 3)272   **a.** 90   **b.** 70   **c.** 60   **d.** 80

3. 6)423   **a.** 80   **b.** 40   **c.** 70   **d.** 60

4. 7)200   **a.** 20   **b.** 30   **c.** 40   **d.** 70

5. 5)618   **a.** 120   **b.** 130   **c.** 100   **d.** 110

6. 8)730   **a.** 40   **b.** 60   **c.** 70   **d.** 90

7. 9)350   **a.** 30   **b.** 40   **c.** 100   **d.** 70

Estimate. Write *under* or *over* for each estimated quotient.

8. 2)130   9. 3)220   10. 5)390   11. 6)359   12. 8)270

13. 4)430   14. 5)456   15. 9)185   16. 8)170   17. 2)157

Apply

Estimate the answer.

18. Sara sold 206 pieces of candy in three hours. About how many pieces did she sell per hour?

19. Luke sold 359 licorice sticks in six hours. About how many licorice sticks did Luke sell per hour?

**Review**

Solve.

1. 63 ÷ 7   2. 72 ÷ 9   3. 64 ÷ 8   4. 48 ÷ 6

5. Write the numbers which are evenly divisible by 3.

    33   22   27   37   9   19

Lesson 45

 Construct Meaning

The Vitt family reunion is next weekend. The 42 people attending the reunion will stay in seven cabins. If each cabin holds an equal number, how many people will stay in each cabin?

Draw a picture to show 42 ÷ 7.

Solve the problem by dividing.

$$\begin{array}{r} 6 \\ 7{\overline{\smash{\big)}\,42}} \\ -42 \quad \text{Multiply} \\ \hline 0 \quad \text{Subtract} \\ \text{Compare, } 0 < 7 \end{array}$$

6 people will stay in each cabin.

The cost of each cabin is $396. If six people pay an equal amount for one cabin, how much will each person pay? Divide $396 by six people.

Will the first digit of the quotient be in the hundreds place?

$$6{\overline{\smash{\big)}\,\$396}}$$
$\$$

No, there are not enough hundreds. 6 > 3

Divide the tens.

$$\begin{array}{r} \$\ 6 \\ 6{\overline{\smash{\big)}\,\$396}} \\ -36 \quad \text{Multiply} \\ \hline 3 \quad \text{Subtract} \\ \text{Compare, } 3 < 6 \end{array}$$

Divide the ones.

$$\begin{array}{r} \$\ 66 \\ 6{\overline{\smash{\big)}\,\$396}} \\ -36\downarrow \\ \hline 36 \quad \text{Bring down} \\ -36 \quad \text{Multiply} \\ \hline 0 \quad \text{Subtract} \\ \text{Compare, } 0 < 6 \end{array}$$

Multiply to check.

$$\begin{array}{r} \$66 \quad \leftarrow \text{quotient} \\ \times\quad 6 \quad \leftarrow \text{divisor} \\ \hline \$396 \quad \leftarrow \text{dividend} \end{array}$$

Each person paid $66.

 Check Understanding

Copy and complete each problem.

a. $\begin{array}{r} 1 \\ 5{\overline{\smash{\big)}\,75}} \\ -5 \\ \hline 2 \end{array}$ b. $2{\overline{\smash{\big)}\,96}}$ c. $\begin{array}{r} 8 \\ 4{\overline{\smash{\big)}\,324}} \\ -32 \end{array}$ d. $7{\overline{\smash{\big)}\,637}}$ e. $9{\overline{\smash{\big)}\,594}}$

Dividing Two- and Three-Digit Numbers

Divide. Check by multiplying.

1. 2)94   2. 4)88   3. 3)57   4. 5)80   5. 6)78

6. 9)459   7. 6)264   8. 2)796   9. 3)369   10. 8)968

Divide.

11. 72 ÷ 6   12. 56 ÷ 2   13. 81 ÷ 3   14. 88 ÷ 4

15. 125 ÷ 5   16. 176 ÷ 8   17. 252 ÷ 7   18. 138 ÷ 6

Divide. Circle the number of the problem if the quotient has a remainder.

19. 5)31   20. 7)46   21. 8)99   22. 7)56

23. 6)156   24. 9)563   25. 2)468   26. 3)478

27. 4)589   28. 5)697   29. 8)963   30. 6)546

31. 9)872   32. 3)952   33. 8)789   34. 9)567

35. Ashleigh and Skyler raise lilies in their pond. They sold nine plants for a total of $36. If each plant cost an equal amount, what was the price of one plant?

36. They sold a total of 312 plants in six days. If they sold an equal number each day, how many plants did they sell per day?

Review

Subtract.

1. 34,628
   − 22,819

2. 3,892
   − 904

3. 5,768
   − 3,979

4. 56,934
   − 9,845

5. 167,284
   − 38,395

6. 67,146 − 66,835   7. 7,031 − 5,008   8. 42,322 − 41,001   9. 300,002 − 175,934

Construct Meaning

Have you ever seen a "falling star"? Falling stars are meteors, bright streaks of light produced when a small meteoroid enters the earth's atmosphere. Most meteoroids disintegrate before reaching the earth's surface.

Ron and Diane counted the falling stars they saw in one month. During the first week they saw 27 meteors. The second week they saw 21, the third week, 30, and the fourth week, 38. What was the average number of meteors, or falling stars, they counted each week?

The **average**, also called the **mean**, can be found by adding the number of falling stars seen each week, and then dividing the sum by the number of addends.

Add the numbers.

Week 1	27
Week 2	21
Week 3	30
Week 4 +	38
	116

Divide the sum by the number of addends.

$$\begin{array}{r} 29 \\ 4\overline{)116} \\ \underline{-8} \\ 36 \\ \underline{-36} \\ 0 \end{array}$$

Ron and Diane saw an average of 29 falling stars per week.

The difference between the greatest number and the least number in a set of numerical data is the **range**.

The numbers in the chart are the data. The greatest number is 38; the least number is 21. The difference, 17, is the range of this set of numbers.

Check Understanding

Write the correct average, or mean.

a. 30	46	54	65	10				173	41	20	31
b. 72	89	272	193	32	44	152		122	160	55	110
c. 223	66	123	56	25	200	35	40	88	177	100	96

Practice

Find the average, or mean, of each set of numbers.

1. 126   254   331

2. 260   177   422   105

3. 47   208   144   230   36   325

4. 327   103   255   220   90

5. 75   77   28   56   106   10   75

Find the average of each set of numbers.

6. 105   153   144   110   104   112   120   128

7. 248   177   251   124   150

8. 125   143   102   189   140   147

9. 352   280   367

10. 123   140   204   113   107   118   112

Use a calculator to find the average and the range of each set of numbers.

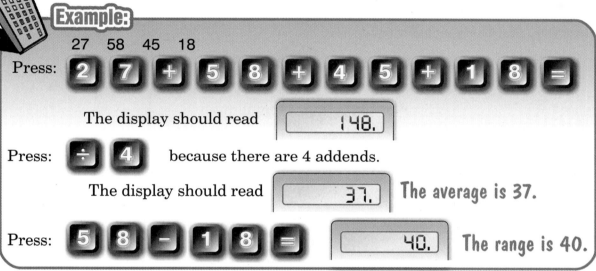

Example:

27   58   45   18

Press: 2 7 + 5 8 + 4 5 + 1 8 =

The display should read | 148. |

Press: ÷ 4   because there are 4 addends.

The display should read | 37. | The average is 37.

Press: 5 8 − 1 8 = | 40. | The range is 40.

11. 36   65   48   97   54

12. 150   132   122   168   100   60

13. 268   153   212

14. 126   178   132   107   113   140   198

Apply

Use pencil and paper or a calculator to find the average. Write the method you used.

15. Eric and Lori spent the afternoon hiking a nature trail. They spotted 56 birds the first hour, 45 birds the second, and 22 the third hour. What was the average number of birds they saw in an hour?

16. Brian, Susan, and Mari drove to their grandparents' home in Virginia. They traveled 388 miles the first day and 600 miles the second day. What was the average number of miles they drove per day?

Lesson 47

Construct Meaning

Did you know that bits of the solar system fall to Earth every day? Chunks of metallic or stony matter that survive a fiery fall through the earth's atmosphere and reach the earth's surface are called meteorites.

If 436 meteorites hit the earth in 4 years, what would be the average number in one year?

Estimate the quotient to help find the answer.
$4 \times 100 = 400$. The quotient should be close to 100.
Divide to find the exact quotient.

$$436 \div 4$$
$$\downarrow \qquad \downarrow$$
$$400 \div 4$$

| Divide the hundreds. $\quad 4 \div 4 = 1$ | $\begin{array}{r} 1 \\ 4\overline{)436} \\ -4\downarrow \\ \hline 03 \end{array}$ Multiply
Subtract
Compare, $0 < 4$
Bring down the tens | Divide the tens. There are not enough tens. Write a 0 in the quotient. | $\begin{array}{r} 10 \\ 4\overline{)436} \\ -4 \\ \hline 03 \\ -0\downarrow \\ \hline 36 \end{array}$ Bring down the ones |

| Divide the ones. $\quad 36 \div 4 = 9$ | $\begin{array}{r} 109 \\ 4\overline{)436} \\ -4 \\ \hline 03 \\ -0 \\ \hline 36 \\ -36 \\ \hline 0 \end{array}$ Multiply
Subtract | **An average of 109 meteorites would hit the earth in one year.** |

Check Understanding

Copy and complete each problem.

a. $5\overline{)525}$ = 10☐

b. $3\overline{)329}$ = 10☐ R☐

c. $6\overline{)642}$ = 1☐☐

d. $8\overline{)852}$ = 1☐☐ R☐

Practice

Write the letter of the correct quotient.

1. $7\overline{)743}$ a. 107 R2   b. 106 R1   c. 104   d. 102

2. $9\overline{)986}$ a. 108 R2   b. 108   c. 109 R5   d. 107

3. $4\overline{)422}$ a. 105 R2   b. 104 R1   c. 106 R2   d. 107 R3

4. $6\overline{)654}$ a. 110   b. 109   c. 103   d. 140

Find the quotient.

5. $7\overline{)707}$ 6. $4\overline{)429}$ 7. $3\overline{)319}$ 8. $2\overline{)212}$

9. $6\overline{)652}$ 10. $9\overline{)987}$ 11. $8\overline{)864}$ 12. $5\overline{)510}$

13. $4\overline{)416}$ 14. $7\overline{)714}$ 15. $3\overline{)301}$ 16. $6\overline{)647}$

17. $876 \div 8$ 18. $924 \div 9$ 19. $535 \div 5$

20. $411 \div 4$ 21. $754 \div 7$ 22. $327 \div 3$

Divide. Check by multiplying.

23. $540 \div 5$ 24. $206 \div 2$ 25. $831 \div 8$

26. $946 \div 9$ 27. $402 \div 4$ 28. $318 \div 3$

pply

29. The fifth grade students at Lake Hills Christian School raised money for a mission trip to Mexico by selling tickets to a school play. Three classes were given a total of 312 tickets to sell. If each class received the same amount of tickets, how many did one class receive?

30. The fifth grade students earned $468 from ticket sales. If the play was performed four times, how much money was earned from each performance?

Review

Use mental math to solve. Remember to first solve inside the parentheses.

1. $45 \div 9$ 2. $50 \div 5$ 3. $66 \div 6$

4. $(56 \div 8) \times 4$ 5. $(49 \div 7) \times 6$ 6. $5 \times (35 \div 5)$

7. $8 \times (81 \div 9)$ 8. $(12 \div 2) \times 9$ 9. $(36 \div 4) \times 3$

Lesson 48

Construct Meaning

When a large meteorite strikes the earth, a huge crater is formed. Meteor Crater near Winslow, Arizona, is 570 feet deep and over 4,000 feet across. Scientists believe an iron-nickel meteorite 150 feet in diameter, hurtling toward Earth at 40,000 miles per hour, left this crater.

If you ride your bike 7 miles per hour, how many times faster was the meteorite traveling?

$$40{,}000 \text{ miles per hour} \div 7 \text{ miles per hour}$$

Estimate the quotient of 40,000 miles per hour ÷ 7 miles per hour.
Use a basic fact close to these numbers: 42,000 ÷ 7 = 6,000.
The meteorite traveled about 6,000 times faster.
Because 42,000 > 40,000, 6,000 is an <u>overestimate</u>.

Find the exact quotient. Will the first digit in the quotient be in the ten thousands place? 7)40,000 No, 4 < 7.	Divide the thousands. Think: 7 × 5 is close to 40, without going over. 5 7)40,000 − 35 5 Multiply Subtract Compare, 5 < 7
Divide the hundreds. Think: 7 × 7 is close to 50, without going over. 5 7 7)40,000 − 35 ↓ 5 0 − 4 9 1 Bring down the hundreds Multiply Subtract Compare, 1 < 7	Divide the tens. Think: 7 × 1 is close to 10, without going over. 5 71 7)40,000 − 35 5 0 − 4 9 ↓ 10 − 7 3 Bring down the tens Multiply Subtract Compare, 3 < 7

Divide the ones.
Think: 7 × 4 is close to 30, without going over.

```
      5 714 R2
  7) 40,000
    − 35
      5 0
    − 4 9
        10
      −  7
        30
      − 28
         2
```

The meteorite was going about 5,714 times faster.

Check by multiplying.

```
        5,714  ←— quotient
     ×      7  ←— divisor
       39,998
    +       2  ←— remainder
       40,000  ←— dividend
```

 **Check Understanding**

Copy the problem. Write only the first digit of the quotient in the correct place.

Example:
$$\frac{6}{6)\overline{37,318}}$$

a. $8)\overline{1,624}$ b. $5)\overline{45,555}$ c. $9)\overline{18,290}$ d. $3)\overline{21,500}$

Practice

Divide. Multiply to check.

1. $4)\overline{1,200}$ 2. $2)\overline{2,600}$ 3. $7)\overline{2,800}$ 4. $4)\overline{3,456}$

5. $9)\overline{6,934}$ 6. $6)\overline{5,246}$ 7. $4)\overline{1,425}$ 8. $2)\overline{7,834}$

9. $8)\overline{48,254}$ 10. $7)\overline{64,318}$ 11. $3)\overline{27,988}$ 12. $5)\overline{25,789}$

Find the quotient.

13. $67,428 \div 2$ 14. $78,565 \div 5$ 15. $38,422 \div 4$

16. $45,727 \div 3$ 17. $97,516 \div 8$ 18. $56,488 \div 7$

19. $23,152 \div 6$ 20. $17,369 \div 4$ 21. $82,360 \div 9$

Did You Know?

A crater formed by the collapse of a volcano is called a *caldera*. This is a picture of Crater Lake, a caldera formed by the eruption and collapse of Mount Mazama. Crater Lake is 1,932 feet deep, making it the deepest lake in the United States and the fifth deepest lake in the world.

Crater Lake National Park, Oregon

Review

Find the product.

1. 62×73 2. 471×653 3. $3,245 \times 14$

Find the sum.

4. $647 + 745 + 893$ 5. $1,256 + 3,578 + 701$ 6. $4,208 + 3,551 + 2,001$

Find the quotient.

7. $834 \div 9$ 8. $643 \div 3$ 9. $520 \div 5$

Lesson 49

Construct Meaning

Jill's family has an apple orchard. Each year Jill and her friends help harvest the apples by placing them into produce crates. On Saturday, they picked 173 apples. Jill's dad asked them to distribute an equal number of apples into 8 crates. How many apples were placed in each crate?

173 apples ÷ 8 crates

```
      21 R5
  8) 173
    -16↓
      13
    - 8
       5
```

Jill and her friends placed 21 apples into each crate.

What should happen to the remainder?

When solving a word problem with a remainder, you may need to . . .

- round the quotient to the next higher number, or
- drop the remainder, or
- use the remainder as your answer.

Since there were not enough apples for each box to get another apple, the remainder was dropped.

Check Understanding

Solve the problem. Decide if you should round the quotient to the next higher number, drop the remainder, or use the remainder as the answer. Write the correct answer.

a. Nate's family is making gift baskets for the fifth grade teachers. They have 150 stickers to divide equally into four baskets. How many stickers will be placed in each basket?

40 stickers
37 stickers
38 stickers

b. Tatum's class is having a pool party. The students will ride in cars to the pool. There are 28 students in her class. If each car carries no more than five, how many cars will be needed?

6 cars
5 cars
7 cars

Write the quotient. Explain how you used the remainder.

1. Micah's class cut 230 sunflowers to give to nine nursing homes. Each home will receive the same number of flowers. Micah and his classmates will be able to keep the extra flowers for their room. How many sunflowers will they keep?

2. Claudia's fifth grade class is helping the kindergarten students sharpen and organize their pencils. Each pencil basket may contain no more than nine pencils. If there are 58 pencils, how many baskets will be needed?

Solve.

3. Morgan and Jamal work at a balloon shop. They fill helium balloons for birthday parties. On Monday they filled 122 balloons. Tuesday, they filled 153 and on Wednesday they filled 121. What was the average number of balloons filled per day?

4. At the balloon shop, Morgan and Jamal need to separate 1,899 balloons into 9 groups. How many balloons will be in each group?

5. 147 balloons were inflated for seven parties. If the balloons are divided equally among the parties, how many will be at each party?

6. Carrie's older sister, Jenna, is going away to college. She has $350 to spend on dorm room essentials. Jenna's roommate is willing to share the cost of items they can both use.

Work with your partner to decide what Jenna should purchase. Remember that although the cost of some items can be divided, Jenna cannot spend more than a total of $350. You may use calculators. Write your names on the final list you make.

Room Accessories		Bedding		Cooking		Personal	
desk lamp	$11	pillow	$10	"cube" refrigerator	$108	hair dryer	$16
bulletin board	$12	sheet set	$28	dishes	$12	shower basket	$4
calculator	$12	blanket	$19	can opener	$9	laundry bag	$8
clock radio telephone	$50	comforter	$40	microwave oven	$92	backpack	$49
alarm clock	$9	lap desk	$9	"hot pot"	$10		
phone with answering system	$45	under-bed storage box	$10				
CD rack	$22						

 Construct Meaning

Travis and his friends planned a lunch for the World Impact Mission Conference. The pizzas were cut into a total of 240 slices. Each person was given a plate with an equal number of slices. If 80 people were fed, how many slices of pizza did each one receive?

240 ÷ 80

1. Think of the basic multiplication facts. Observe the pattern.

$8 \times 3 = 24$
$80 \times 3 = 240$
$800 \times 3 = 2,400$

2. Remember that division is the inverse operation. Use basic division facts to find larger quotients.

$24 \div 8 = 3$ Each person received
$240 \div 80 = 3$ 3 slices of pizza.
$2,400 \div 80 = 30$

Here are some examples of division patterns.

$54 \div 9 = 6$	$49 \div 7 = 7$	$400 \div 50 = 8$	$240 \div 60 = 4$
$540 \div 90 = 6$	$490 \div 70 = 7$	$4,000 \div 50 = 80$	$2,400 \div 60 = 40$
$5,400 \div 90 = 60$	$4,900 \div 70 = 70$	$40,000 \div 50 = 800$	$24,000 \div 60 = 400$

 **Check Understanding**

Copy and complete each division pattern.

a. $16 \div 4 = 4$
  $160 \div 40 = \blacksquare$
  $1,600 \div 40 = \blacksquare$

b. $32 \div 8 = \blacksquare$
  $320 \div 80 = \blacksquare$
  $3,200 \div \blacksquare = 40$

c. $360 \div 60 = \blacksquare$
  $\blacksquare \div 60 = 60$
  $36,000 \div \blacksquare = 600$

Use mental math to find the quotient.

d. $450 \div 50$ e. $8,100 \div 90$ f. $3,500 \div 70$ g. $18,000 \div 60$

Practice

Copy the chart. Write the missing numbers to complete the division pattern.

Example: $420 \div 70 = 42$ tens $\div 7$ tens = ⟶

1. $4,200 \div 70 = 42$ hundreds $\div 7$ tens = ⟶

2. $42,000 \div 70 = 42$ thousands $\div 7$ tens = ⟶

3. $420,000 \div 70 = 42$ ten thousands $\div 7$ tens = ⟶

thousands	hundreds	tens	ones
			6

Find the quotient.

Example:
$$20\overline{)600}$$ = 30

4. $40\overline{)800}$ 5. $30\overline{)900}$ 6. $70\overline{)140}$ 7. $20\overline{)160}$

8. $50\overline{)200}$ 9. $90\overline{)360}$ 10. $60\overline{)420}$ 11. $80\overline{)560}$

Example:
$$30\overline{)1,200}$$ = 40

12. $40\overline{)2,400}$ 13. $60\overline{)3,000}$ 14. $90\overline{)5,400}$ 15. $70\overline{)2,800}$

16. $50\overline{)4,500}$ 17. $80\overline{)3,200}$ 18. $30\overline{)2,100}$ 19. $20\overline{)4,000}$

Example:
$$50\overline{)40,000}$$ = 800

20. $30\overline{)15,000}$ 21. $70\overline{)35,000}$ 22. $60\overline{)12,000}$

23. $40\overline{)32,000}$ 24. $50\overline{)20,000}$ 25. $80\overline{)48,000}$

26. $90\overline{)27,000}$ 27. $30\overline{)24,000}$ 28. $70\overline{)49,000}$

29. $63,000 \div 70$ 30. $40,000 \div 80$ 31. $45,000 \div 90$

32. $24,000 \div 60$ 33. $21,000 \div 70$ 34. $30,000 \div 50$

Apply

35. Over a 30-day period 60,000 people attended the fair. If an equal number of people attended the fair each day, how many would have attended in one day?

36. 14,000 cups of lemonade were sold in 70 days during the fair. What was the average number of cups sold each day?

Review

Multiply.

1. $\begin{array}{r} 27 \\ \times\ 3 \\ \hline \end{array}$
2. $\begin{array}{r} 482 \\ \times\ 24 \\ \hline \end{array}$
3. $\begin{array}{r} 971 \\ \times\ 87 \\ \hline \end{array}$
4. $\begin{array}{r} 5,603 \\ \times\ \ \ 2 \\ \hline \end{array}$
5. $\begin{array}{r} 4,050 \\ \times\ \ \ 9 \\ \hline \end{array}$

Solve.

6. $\begin{array}{r} 8.6 \\ +9.4 \\ \hline \end{array}$
7. $\begin{array}{r} 5.33 \\ -4.63 \\ \hline \end{array}$
8. $\begin{array}{r} 84.12 \\ +\ 9.39 \\ \hline \end{array}$
9. $\begin{array}{r} 90.14 \\ +10.23 \\ \hline \end{array}$
10. $\begin{array}{r} 3.6 \\ -2.72 \\ \hline \end{array}$

Lesson 51

Construct Meaning

Did you know that the most popular fruit in America is the banana? Maybe that is because bananas are available year-round.

Last year the fifth grade classes conducted a survey to find out how many pounds of bananas were eaten by friends and family members. If 1,980 pounds of bananas were eaten by 60 people, about how many pounds were eaten by one person?

1,980 pounds ÷ 60 people

To find the approximate number of pounds of bananas eaten by one person, estimate the quotient.

Find compatible numbers.	Think of the multiplication pattern to help find the quotient.
1,980 ÷ 60 ↓ ↓ 1,800 ÷ 60	$60 \times 3 = 180$ $60 \times 30 = 1,800$ $60 \times 300 = 18,000$

Divide.	Check.	
$$\begin{array}{r} 30 \\ 60\overline{)1,800} \\ -1\ 80\downarrow \\ \hline 00 \\ -\ 0 \\ \hline 0 \end{array}$$	$$\begin{array}{r} 60 \\ \times 30 \\ \hline 1,800 \end{array}$$	*One person ate about 30 pounds of bananas.*

Estimate 3,490 ÷ 48 by finding compatible numbers.

Use the front-end digit of the divisor.

3,490 ÷ 48
↓ ↓
3,600 ÷ 40 = 90

OR

Round the divisor.

3,490 ÷ 48
↓ ↓
3,500 ÷ 50 = 70

Which estimate is closer to the actual answer?

Check Understanding

Copy and complete each problem. Use compatible numbers to find the estimated quotient.

a. 2,377 ÷ 65
↓ ↓
2,400 ÷ ▦ = 40

b. 5,540 ÷ 92
↓ ↓
▦ ÷ 90 = 60

c. 1,023 ÷ 35
↓ ↓
1,200 ÷ 30 = ▦

d. 71,900 ÷ 94
↓ ↓
72,000 ÷ 90 = ▦

e. 62,566 ÷ 71
↓ ↓
▦ ÷ 70 = 900

f. 44,023 ÷ 53
↓ ↓
45,000 ÷ ▦ = 900

108

Estimating Quotients with Two-Digit Divisors

 **Practice**

Write the letter of the best estimate.

1. 1,650 ÷ 43
    a. 1,600 ÷ 40 = 40
    b. 2,000 ÷ 40 = 50
    c. 1,800 ÷ 30 = 60

2. 2,170 ÷ 33
    a. 2,000 ÷ 40 = 50
    b. 2,500 ÷ 50 = 50
    c. 2,100 ÷ 30 = 70

3. 55,000 ÷ 71
    a. 60,000 ÷ 60 = 1,000
    b. 56,000 ÷ 70 = 800
    c. 54,000 ÷ 90 = 600

Use compatible numbers to find the estimated quotient.

4. 41)‾2,750   **5.** 23)‾1,890   **6.** 72)‾2,300   **7.** 92)‾8,120

8. 50)‾3,600   **9.** 30)‾1,908   **10.** 62)‾3,100   **11.** 91)‾5,320

12. 74)‾1,502   **13.** 47)‾1,300   **14.** 92)‾89,200   **15.** 64)‾26,010

16. 38)‾14,500   **17.** 53)‾51,000   **18.** 31)‾17,900   **19.** 63)‾37,444

20. 6,401 ÷ 82   **21.** 2,319 ÷ 34   **22.** 1,260 ÷ 23   **23.** 56,201 ÷ 84

24. 23,050 ÷ 84   **25.** 66,488 ÷ 67   **26.** 15,080 ÷ 52   **27.** 4,490 ÷ 91

 Apply

28. Donna's Bakery baked 2,455 loaves of banana bread in 63 days. About how many loaves were baked each day?

29. Customers at the bakery ordered 1,390 muffins in 71 days. About how many muffins were ordered per day?

30. Donna sold 1,670 cups of hot chocolate in 45 days. About how many cups of hot chocolate were sold each day?

 **Review**

Write the product.

1. 40
× 5

2. 132
× 6

3. 29
×16

4. 430
× 30

5. 235
× 45

6. 4,281
× 65

7. 5,741
× 70

8. 2,400
× 40

9. 3,266
× 55

10. 4,100
× 10

 **Construct Meaning**

In the fall, Aimee's family helped plant bulbs in the front yard of their church. There were 288 bulbs to be planted by 32 people. If each person planted an equal number of bulbs, how many did one person plant?

288 bulbs ÷ 32 people

Use front-end digits and compatible numbers to estimate the quotient.

$30 \times 8 = 240$ (too low)

$30 \times 9 = 270$ (close)

$30 \times 10 = 300$ (too high)

Since 270 is close to 288, use **9** as the estimated quotient.

Divide.
$$\begin{array}{r} 9 \\ 32\overline{)288} \\ -288 \\ \hline 0 \end{array}$$

Check.
$$\begin{array}{r} 32 \\ \times\ 9 \\ \hline 288 \end{array}$$

Each person planted 9 bulbs.

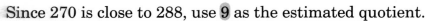

What if the 32 people had been given 224 bulbs to plant? If each person planted an equal number of bulbs, how many would one person have planted?

224 bulbs ÷ 32 people

Find the estimated quotient. $210 \div 30 = 7$ $240 \div 30 = 8$

Because $240 > 224$, 8 is an <u>overestimate</u>. Instead of using 8 as the quotient, try the next lower number, 7.

Divide.
$$\begin{array}{r} 7 \\ 32\overline{)224} \\ -224 \\ \hline 0 \end{array}$$

Check.
$$\begin{array}{r} 32 \\ \times\ 7 \\ \hline 224 \end{array}$$

Each person planted 7 bulbs.

 **Check Understanding**

Choose the correct quotient.

a. $18\overline{)144}$
9
8
7 R9

b. $62\overline{)558}$
7
8 R3
9

c. $38\overline{)345}$
9 R3
6 R2
5

d. $55\overline{)228}$
5 R6
6
4 R8

Practice

Estimate.

1. 24)68   2. 46)79   3. 21)82   4. 33)89

5. 44)92   6. 12)39   7. 55)308   8. 65)223

Write your estimate. Then find the quotient.

9. 78)457   10. 68)273   11. 32)81   12. 58)177

13. 559 ÷ 93   14. 255 ÷ 83   15. 394 ÷ 78   16. 199 ÷ 49

Divide. Multiply to check your answer.

17. 515 ÷ 73   18. 419 ÷ 65   19. 39)166   20. 18)169

21. 53)449   22. 47)326   23. 27)240   24. 91)811

25. 33)200   26. 64)498   27. 75)250   28. 83)125

29. 36)259   30. 34)170   31. 316 ÷ 41   32. 455 ÷ 53

Apply

33. Joshua brought 135 balloons for the school celebration. If 45 balloons were in each package, how many packages did he bring?

34. Lindsey folded brightly colored napkins for the celebration. If she folded 130 napkins in 26 minutes, how many napkins per minute did she fold?

35. Isaac and his friends baked 196 mini-cookies for the celebration. If 98 people each received the same number of cookies, how many would one person have?

Review

Write a multiplication sentence for the product given. Do <u>not</u> use 1 as a factor.

1. 88   2. 140   3. 99   4. 122   5. 153

6. 408   7. 576   8. 300   9. 378   10. 592

Construct Meaning

A comet is a small, celestial body of rock and ice. Most comets follow an oval-shaped path around the sun. When a comet nears the sun, some of the ice turns into gas. Solar wind blows the gas and dust away, forming a long, luminous tail.

The comet named for astronomer Edmund Halley is visible from the earth every 76 years. How many times would it be seen in 1,748 years?

Comet Halley

1,748 years ÷ 76 years

First, estimate the quotient.
Use compatible numbers.
Will the answer be more or less than the estimate?

$1,748 ÷ 76$
↓ ↓
$1,400 ÷ 70 = 20$

Decide where to place the first digit in the quotient. Since 76 > 17, but 76 < 174, place the **2** in the tens place.

$$
\begin{array}{r}
2 \\
76)\overline{1,748} \\
-1\,52 \\
\hline
22
\end{array}
$$
Divide
Multiply
Subtract
Compare, 22 < 76

Bring down. Estimate the ones place.
Use basic facts to help.

$228 ÷ 76$
↓ ↓
$210 ÷ 70 = 3$

Use **3** for the second digit in the quotient.

$$
\begin{array}{r}
23 \\
76)\overline{1,748} \\
-1\,52\downarrow \\
\hline
228 \\
-228 \\
\hline
0
\end{array}
$$
Divide
Multiply
Subtract
Compare, 0 < 76

Check. $76 × 23 = 1,748$

> Halley's Comet can be seen from Earth 23 times in 1,748 years.

Check Understanding

Write the correct answer.

a. $23)\overline{483}$ 21   21 R5   20

b. $46)\overline{1,381}$ 30   30 R1   33 R5

c. $67)\overline{4,157}$ 62 R3   60 R4   66

Copy and complete each problem.

1.
```
      8
31)2,759
  -2 48
    279
```

2.
```
      4
25)1,225
  -1 00
```

3.
```
      3
42)2,646
  -2 52
    126
```

4.
```
      8  R3
29)2,468
```

5.
```
      5  R
63)3,529
```

6.
```
      2 R
34)2,138
```

7.
```
      9
74)7,252
```

8.
```
        R
48)3,621
```

Find the quotient. Remember to estimate first.

9. 27)1,242

10. 17)515

11. 41)867

12. 63)3,278

13. 72)1,730

14. 58)3,659

15. 26)2,419

16. 63)1,476

17. 4,929 ÷ 53

18. 1,908 ÷ 36

19. 3,570 ÷ 42

20. 2,572 ÷ 82

21. 2,527 ÷ 72

22. 3,528 ÷ 86

23. 1,518 ÷ 52

24. 932 ÷ 61

25. Thom and Kate were stamping their wedding invitations. They bought 325 stamps. If the stamps came in packages of 25, how many packages did they buy?

26. Candles for the wedding were packaged 11 to a box. If Kate and Thom bought a total of 132 candles, how many boxes are there?

27. The flower arrangements were made with 17 flowers each. If they had a total of 391 flowers, how many arrangements were made?

Divide.

1. 3)218

2. 4)179

3. 6)378

4. 7)427

5. 9)136

6. 8)2,356

7. 5)4,505

8. 3)2,121

Construct Meaning

Asteroids are the largest of all the space rocks. All asteroids orbit the sun. Most are found in the "asteroid belt," a region between Mars and Jupiter. Asteroids are also called "minor planets" because they are too small to be classified as true planets.

The largest known asteroid, 1 Ceres, has a diameter of nearly 600 miles. If 1 Ceres rotates 46 times in 414 hours, how many hours does it take to complete one rotation on its axis?

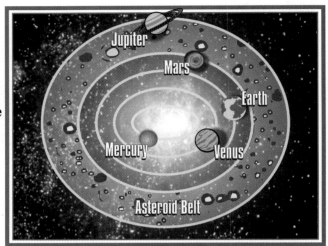

414 hours ÷ 46 rotations

If you round the divisor and use compatible numbers, 8 hours is the estimated quotient.

$$414 \div 46$$
$$\downarrow \qquad \downarrow$$
$$400 \div 50 = 8$$

Divide.
Try 8 as the quotient.

$$\begin{array}{r} 8 \\ 46 \overline{)414} \\ -368 \\ \hline 46 \end{array}$$

Multiply
Subtract
Compare,
46 = 46

Because the remainder 46 is equal to the divisor, raise the digit in the quotient to the next higher number, 9.

$$\begin{array}{r} 9 \\ 46 \overline{)414} \\ -414 \\ \hline 0 \end{array}$$

Multiply
Subtract
Compare,
0 < 46

1 Ceres completes one rotation in 9 hours.

If an asteroid rotates 54 times in 378 hours, how long does it take to complete one rotation?

Use compatible numbers to find the estimated quotient.

$$378 \div 54$$
$$\downarrow \qquad \downarrow$$
$$400 \div 50 = 8$$

Try 8 as the quotient.

$$\begin{array}{r} 8 \\ 54 \overline{)378} \\ -432 \end{array}$$

Multiply
Compare,
432 > 378

Because the estimate was too large, try the next lower number (7) for the quotient.

$$\begin{array}{r} 7 \\ 54 \overline{)378} \\ -378 \\ \hline 0 \end{array}$$

It takes seven hours for this asteroid to complete one rotation.

Check Understanding

If the estimated quotient is the same as the exact quotient, write *correct*. If the estimated quotient needs to be adjusted, write *adjust up* or *adjust down*.

a. $31\overline{)240}$ → 8

b. $51\overline{)458}$ → 9

c. $45\overline{)123}$ → 2

d. $47\overline{)332}$ → 6

e. $21\overline{)128}$ → 6

Practice

Find the quotient.

1. $19\overline{)855}$

2. $27\overline{)974}$

3. $38\overline{)646}$

4. $24\overline{)846}$

5. $56\overline{)674}$

6. $15\overline{)347}$

7. $42\overline{)672}$

8. $72\overline{)864}$

9. $28\overline{)759}$

10. $63\overline{)820}$

11. $32\overline{)576}$

12. $13\overline{)679}$

13. $416 \div 26$

14. $928 \div 58$

15. $798 \div 38$

16. $769 \div 24$

17. $585 \div 13$

18. $963 \div 72$

19. $394 \div 17$

20. $532 \div 19$

Divide. Check your answer.

21. $14\overline{)588}$

22. $41\overline{)422}$

23. $38\overline{)363}$

24. $25\overline{)226}$

25. $32\overline{)226}$

26. $63\overline{)514}$

27. $68\overline{)476}$

28. $42\overline{)128}$

Apply

29. 126 students met at the school football field to look at stars. They shared 14 telescopes. If an equal number of students shared each telescope, how many students would use one telescope?

30. Some students went home shortly after arriving. Only 84 students stayed to watch the stars. How many students share the telescopes now?

Construct Meaning

Asteroid 1998 KY26 is the fastest known spinning object in the solar system. 1998 KY26 spins so fast that it can complete a rotation in about 11 minutes. How many rotations will the asteroid make in 12 hours or 720 minutes?

$$11\overline{)720}$$

Decide where to place the first digit.
Since 11 > 7, but < 72, the first digit will be in the tens place.

$$\begin{array}{r} 6 \\ 11\overline{)720} \end{array}$$

Use compatible numbers.
Think: 6 × 11 = 66.

$$\begin{array}{r} 6 \\ 11\overline{)720} \\ -66 \\ \hline 6 \end{array}$$
Multiply
Subtract
Compare, 6 < 11

$$\begin{array}{r} 65 \text{ R5} \\ 11\overline{)720} \\ -66\downarrow \\ \hline 60 \\ -55 \\ \hline 5 \end{array}$$

Bring down.
Think: 5 × 11 = 55.
Repeat the steps.
Write the remainder.

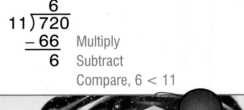

Asteroid 1998 KY26 makes over 65 rotations in a 12-hour period.

Check Understanding

Write whether the problem will have a *one-digit* or a *two-digit* quotient.

a. $62\overline{)758}$ b. $42\overline{)383}$ c. $84\overline{)506}$ d. $17\overline{)672}$

If the digit in the quotient is the right one, write *correct*. If it is not correct, write *adjust up* or *adjust down*.

e. $\begin{array}{r} 7 \\ 32\overline{)224} \end{array}$ f. $\begin{array}{r} 4 \\ 24\overline{)80} \end{array}$ g. $\begin{array}{r} 8 \\ 55\overline{)440} \end{array}$ h. $\begin{array}{r} 6 \\ 63\overline{)480} \end{array}$

Copy and complete.

i. $\begin{array}{r} \text{R} \\ 24\overline{)95} \\ -72 \\ \hline \end{array}$

j. $\begin{array}{r} 19\overline{)456} \\ -38 \\ \hline 7 \\ - \\ \hline 0 \end{array}$

k. $\begin{array}{r} 44\overline{)396} \\ -396 \\ \hline 0 \end{array}$

l. $\begin{array}{r} 1 \text{ R} \\ 35\overline{)484} \\ -35 \\ \hline 13 \\ - \\ \hline \end{array}$

More One- and Two-Digit Quotients

Divide. Check your answer with multiplication.

1. 37)83
2. 48)95
3. 17)93
4. 28)78
5. 54)166

6. 645 ÷ 18
7. 516 ÷ 24
8. 3,555 ÷ 79
9. 2,000 ÷ 34
10. 62)5,208

Divide.

11. 22)279
12. 41)1,460
13. 60)485
14. 82)1,073
15. 70)536

16. 92)564
17. 55)800
18. 38)494
19. 33)2,637
20. 29)1,851

Apply

21. Greenville Gymnastics has 144 students. There are 18 students in each class. How many classes are held at Greenville Gymnastics?

22. The students at Greenville Gymnastics have a meet on Saturday. 75 gymnasts will ride in vans that carry six passengers each. How many vans will be needed?

Review

Write >, < or =.

1. 57,630 ▦ 57,603
2. 69,992 ▦ 69,998
3. 14.79 ▦ 14.790
4. 360.028 ▦ 360.030
5. 23.25 ▦ 25.23
6. 0.710 ▦ 0.71
7. 48 × 13 ▦ 39 × 21
8. 128 ÷ 4 ▦ 168 ÷ 8

Lesson 56

Heidi organized a food drive at her school. Students from each grade were involved in donating food. Each class donated the same amount of food. If 2,214 pounds of food were donated by 18 classes, how many pounds did each class collect?

2,214 pounds ÷ 18 classes

First, estimate the quotient by using compatible numbers.

$$2{,}214 \div 18$$
$$\downarrow \qquad \downarrow$$
$$2{,}000 \div 20 = 100$$

Use 100 as the estimated quotient.

To find the exact quotient, divide 2,214 by 18.

Decide where to place the first digit of the quotient.	$18\overline{)2{,}214}$	There are not enough thousands. The first digit will be in the hundreds place because 22 can be divided by 18.

Try the first digit of the estimated quotient.
(1 × 18 = 18)

$$\begin{array}{r} 1 \\ 18\overline{)2{,}214} \\ -1\ 8 \\ \hline 4 \end{array}$$

Multiply. Subtract.
Compare, 4 < 18.

Bring down. Divide 41 by 18.
(2 × 18 = 36)

$$\begin{array}{r} 12 \\ 18\overline{)2{,}214} \\ -1\ 8\downarrow \\ \hline 41 \\ -36 \\ \hline 5 \end{array}$$

Multiply. Subtract.
Compare, 5 < 18.

Bring down. Divide 54 by 18.
(3 × 18 = 54)

$$\begin{array}{r} 123 \\ 18\overline{)2{,}214} \\ -1\ 8 \\ \hline 41 \\ -36\downarrow \\ \hline 54 \\ -54 \\ \hline 0 \end{array}$$

Multiply. Subtract.
Compare, 0 < 18.

Check.
$$\begin{array}{r} 123 \\ \times\ 18 \\ \hline 984 \\ 1\,230 \\ \hline 2{,}214 \end{array}$$

Each class donated 123 pounds of food.

Check Understanding

Choose the correct answer.

a. $23\overline{)5{,}428}$ 246   236   231

b. $45\overline{)6{,}615}$ 157   146   147

Copy and complete each problem.

1.
```
        14░
   26)3,770
    -26
     1 17
    -1 04
       130
```

2.
```
      2░
  32)8,256
   -6 4
    1 85
```

3.
```
      5░ R2
  13)7,399
```

4.
```
       ░░ R░
  41)5,826
   -4 1
```

5.
```
        37░
  53)19,822
   -15 9
     3 92
    -3 71
       212
```

6.
```
       2░
  47)12,173
    -9 4
     2 77
```

7.
```
       4░ R1
  39)16,459
    -15 6
```

8.
```
       ░░ R░
  27)17,146
```

Write the quotient.

9. 25)9,225

10. 47)5,875

11. 59)9,676

12. 28)9,129

13. 15)8,839

14. 21)14,658

15. 49)17,885

16. 34)29,755

17. 87)12,356

18. 46)21,988

19. 22)19,119

20. 17)14,369

21. 17,526 ÷ 69

22. 48,894 ÷ 87

23. 25,155 ÷ 39

24. 13,515 ÷ 85

25. 28,714 ÷ 49

26. 25,956 ÷ 63

27. 23,819 ÷ 52

28. 29,536 ÷ 33

29. If a total of 5,313 feet of cotton thread was needed to weave 21 panels of Guatemalan textiles, how many feet would be used for each piece?

30. Bible covers woven in Guatemala sell for $28 each. How many Bible covers would be in a shipment valued at $3,472?

Construct Meaning

Beautiful fireworks are often displayed during Fourth of July celebrations in America. One fireworks display launched 4,725 fireworks in 45 minutes. If an equal number was displayed each minute, how many fireworks were displayed in one minute?

4,725 fireworks ÷ 45 minutes

Estimate the quotient by finding compatible numbers.

$$4,725 \div 45$$
$$5,000 \div 50 = 100$$

The estimated quotient is 100 fireworks per minute.

Decide where to place the first digit. Divide the hundreds. Think: $45 \times 1 = 45$.

$$\begin{array}{r} 1 \\ 45\overline{)4,725} \\ -4\,5 \\ \hline 2 \end{array}$$

Multiply
Subtract
Compare, 2 < 45

Bring down.
Divide the tens.
There are not enough tens.
Think: $45 \times 0 = 0$.

$$\begin{array}{r} 10 \\ 45\overline{)4,725} \\ -4\,5\downarrow \\ \hline 22 \\ -\ 0 \\ \hline 22 \end{array}$$

45 > 22. Show that there are not enough tens by writing a zero in the tens place.

Bring down.
Divide the ones.
Think: $45 \times 5 = 225$.

$$\begin{array}{r} 105 \\ 45\overline{)4,725} \\ -4\,5 \\ \hline 22 \\ -\ 0\downarrow \\ \hline 225 \\ -225 \\ \hline 0 \end{array}$$

Multiply
Subtract
Compare, 0 < 45

Check.
$$\begin{array}{r} 105 \\ \times\ 45 \\ \hline 525 \\ +\ 4\,200 \\ \hline 4,725 \end{array}$$

105 fireworks were displayed each minute.

✓ Check Understanding

Choose the correct quotient from the answer box.

a. $23\overline{)7,061}$ b. $21\overline{)14,868}$ c. $36\overline{)18,036}$ d. $32\overline{)13,059}$

307	70	51	408 R3
37	780	501	480 R3
370	708	510	48 R3

Practice

Write the quotient. Check by multiplying.

1. $45\overline{)27,135}$ 2. $62\overline{)6,386}$ 3. $58\overline{)12,122}$ 4. $37\overline{)18,574}$

5. $22\overline{)13,288}$ 6. $41\overline{)12,548}$ 7. $85\overline{)8,673}$ 8. $72\overline{)21,748}$

9. $12\overline{)9,615}$ 10. $25\overline{)10,225}$ 11. $56\overline{)11,424}$ 12. $81\overline{)8,427}$

Divide.

13. $10,764 \div 52$ 14. $13,222 \div 22$ 15. $7,635 \div 15$

16. $4,983 \div 47$ 17. $19,572 \div 95$ 18. $11,594 \div 23$

19. $36\overline{)21,746}$ 20. $58\overline{)11,778}$ 21. $23\overline{)16,146}$

Use a calculator to find the quotient.

Example:

$99\overline{)89,892}$

Press: 8 9 8 9 2 ÷ 9 9 = .

The display should read: 908.

22. $86\overline{)43,516}$ 23. $55\overline{)44,495}$

24. $67\overline{)60,769}$ 25. $89\overline{)63,012}$

Review

Write how you would solve the problem: *divide, multiply, subtract,* or *add.*

1. Jane wanted to figure how many more cookies she baked than Anita.

2. Gary wanted to know the total number of tickets sold by his class.

3. John wanted to find out how many pencils were lost per day.

 Construct Meaning

A local paint supply store donated 1,522 paintbrushes to Ridgeview Christian School. If the paintbrushes are equally divided among 13 classes, how many will each class receive?

1,522 paintbrushes ÷ 13 classes

First, estimate the quotient by using compatible numbers.

$$1,522 \div 13$$
$$1,500 \div 15 = 100$$

The estimated quotient is 100 paintbrushes per class.

Divide to find the exact quotient.

Will the first digit of the quotient be in the thousands place?

$$13\overline{)1,522}$$ No, 13 > 1. There are not enough thousands.

Try the hundreds place. 15 can be divided by 13 one time. (13 × 1 = 13)

```
      1
13)1,522
  -1 3
      2
```

Bring down. Divide the tens. (13 × 1 = 13)

```
     11
13)1,522
  -1 3↓
      22
    -13
       9
```

Bring down.
Divide the ones.
(13 × 7 = 91)
Write the remainder.

```
        117 R1
13)1,522
  -1 3
      22
    -13↓
       92
     -91
        1
```

Check.

```
    117 ←quotient
  × 13 ←divisor
    351
  1 17
  1,521
+     1 ←remainder
  1,522 ←dividend
```

**Each class will receive 117 paintbrushes.
1 paintbrush will be left over.**

✔ Check Understanding

Copy and complete each problem.

a.
```
      12
21)2,583
  -2 1
     48
```

b.
```
        8 R1
36)9,289
  -7 2
    2 0
```

c.
```
      63
89)56,337
  -53 4
```

d.
```
      8   R
54)53,192
```

Write the letter of the correct quotient.

1. 42)9,030

   a. 205
   b. 215
   c. 21

2. 58)21,460

   a. 37
   b. 317
   c. 370

3. 64)23,619

   a. 369 R3
   b. 369
   c. 309 R6

4. 23)21,898

   a. 902 R2
   b. 952 R2
   c. 950 R2

Find the quotient.

5. 22)15,290

6. 67)21,517

7. 75)15,900

8. 99)36,535

9. 53)43,725

10. 69)29,532

11. 85)12,326

12. 44)16,196

13. 96)26,592

14. 29)10,121

15. 57)39,559

16. 35)16,177

17. 14,218 ÷ 74

18. 54,596 ÷ 61

19. 44,352 ÷ 84

20. 31,826 ÷ 78

21. 19,776 ÷ 24

22. 11,435 ÷ 45

23. 18,528 ÷ 96

24. 15,437 ÷ 63

25. 17,958 ÷ 34

26. Fifth grade students at Eastview Christian Academy volunteered to wash windows for elderly people in their community. They washed 1,113 windows in 21 days. If they washed the same number of windows each day, how many did they wash in one day?

27. The students used an average of 23 buckets of cleaning solution on each of the 21 days. How many buckets of solution did they use during their "Wash-a-thon?"

Lesson 59

Construct Meaning

The softball tournament was won by Bayberry Christian School. Coach Starcher credited the win to the time the players spent practicing their hitting. During the tournament, Bayberry had the highest batting average, or the most hits per time at bat. The team batting average is figured by adding each player's average and dividing by the number of players.

Help the Bayberry coach find the team average by using a calculator and the information in the chart.

Bayberry Christian School Softball Team

Name	Batting Average
Nia	0.312
Donovan	0.283
Andrew	0.189
Nicole	0.234
Jeff	0.251
Tiffany	0.308
Rolland	0.273
Anne	0.261
Dirk	0.273

The Problem-Solving Guide Can Help You

1. Understand the question. Write the problem in your own words.
   - Find the team batting average.

2. Analyze the data.
   - The batting averages and number of players are listed in the chart.

3. Plan the strategy.
   - Use a calculator to add the players' batting averages and divide by the number of players.

4. Solve the problem.

   - Look at the information. Add each average by using a calculator. Do not forget to press  when entering each average!

   Your sum should be   `2.284`

   - Divide the total of the averages by the number of players.

   `2.284`   players   `0.253777`

   - Find the three numbers that immediately follow the decimal point. Now look at the fourth number following the decimal point (**7**). If it is greater than 5, round the third number (**3**) to the next higher digit. Because 7 > 5, round 3 up to 4.

   `0.253777`

   The team average is 0.254.

5. Evaluate the result.

   Does the average 0.254 seem reasonable? Compared to the individual averages, 0.254 seems like a reasonable team average.

Use a calculator to find the average of each set of numbers. Round to the nearest thousandth.

1. 0.357   0.451   0.208   0.135   2. 0.561   0.123   0.340   0.308

3. 0.213   0.184   0.133   4. 0.223   0.302   0.138

5. 0.309   0.236   0.337   0.196   0.203   6. 0.202   0.348   0.400   0.168

CUMULATIVE REVIEW: Chapters 1–4

Write the letter of the correct answer.

1. Which number, when rounded, will be 6?   **a.** 5.43   **b.** 5.56   **c.** 7.78

2. Which number is greater than 2.36?   **a.** 2.33   **b.** 2.10   **c.** 2.40

3. Which number is less than 5.47?   **a.** 5.49   **b.** 5.45   **c.** 5.50

4. Stacy's new car costs $17,893. It is $9,322 more than her old car. How much did she pay for her old car?   **a.** $9,271   **b.** $7,930   **c.** $8,571

5. The attendance for last year's weekend retreat was 8,032 people. This year's attendance was 3,596 more than last year's. What was the attendance for this year?
   a. 10,528 people   **b.** 11,438 people   **c.** 11,628 people

6. Which set of numbers are all multiples of 8?   **a.** 48, 16, 23, 59, 60
   b. 24, 72, 40, 56, 64
   c. 27, 36, 48, 64, 80

7. Sam baked 36 muffins. Tammie baked 24. The baking pans they used held the number of muffins that is the greatest common factor of 36 and 24. How many muffins could be baked in each pan?   **a.** 2   **b.** 12   **c.** 3

8. Mitzi packed 9 pairs of socks for the camping trip. Dave packed 7. What is the least common multiple of 9 and 7?   **a.** 56   **b.** 72   **c.** 63

9. Parker counted the geese along the way to school. He counted a total of 105 geese in five days. If he counted an equal number of geese each day, how many did he count in one day?   **a.** 22   **b.** 21   **c.** 19

10. What is the estimated quotient for 490 ÷ 52?
    a. 10   **b.** 100   **c.** 5

The Quest for Quotients

1. Which group of numbers is evenly divisible by 5? Write the letter.

   a. 22, 26, 41, 53   **b.** 15, 20, 45, 30   **c.** 62, 74, 86, 98

2. List five numbers evenly divisible by 2.

Write the letter of the correct quotient.

3. 7)49
   a. 9
   b. 6
   c. 7

4. 3)27
   a. 8
   b. 9
   c. 7

5. 6)48
   a. 6
   b. 7
   c. 8

Estimate the quotient by using compatible numbers.

6. $359 \div 4$ 7. $640 \div 9$ 8. $244 \div 82$

9. $329 \div 33$ 10. $374 \div 12$ 11. $2{,}111 \div 30$

12. $5{,}603 \div 52$ 13. $31{,}210 \div 80$ 14. $15{,}489 \div 32$

Find the average for each set of numbers.

15. 21   36   12   44   32   16. 56   14   72   99   10   25

17. 110   235   150   484   121   18. 266   454   164   388

Copy and complete each problem.

19. 2⬚
   5)125
   −10
    25

20. ⬚⬚ R3
   4)359
   −32

21. ⬚⬚ R⬚
   40)1,624

22. ⬚⬚ R⬚
   17)10,340

Write the letter of the correct quotient.

23. 639 ÷ 7

24. 459 ÷ 5

25. 736 ÷ 61

26. 989 ÷ 43

27. 2,688 ÷ 28

28. 42,390 ÷ 54

29. 35,464 ÷ 36

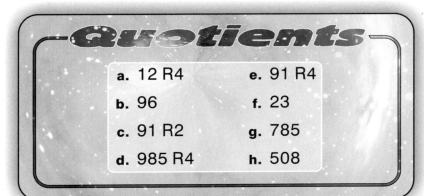

Quotients

a. 12 R4   e. 91 R4

b. 96   f. 23

c. 91 R2   g. 785

d. 985 R4   h. 508

Find the quotient. Check by multiplying.

30. 624 ÷ 48   31. 1,725 ÷ 69   32. 3,278 ÷ 52

33. 2,889 ÷ 74   34. 1,932 ÷ 84   35. 5,952 ÷ 62

36. 9,225 ÷ 25   37. 35,786 ÷ 42   38. 26,524 ÷ 38

39. Carrie's family visited relatives for a week. They drove 639 miles in two days. About how many miles did they drive each day?

40. Carrie's cousins had to drive 963 miles to visit. If they drove an equal number of miles in three days, how many miles did they drive in one day?

"We can't understand the universe in any clear way without the supernatural." Allan Sandage, astronomer

"O Lord, how manifold are Your works! In wisdom You have made them all." Psalm 104:24

Grade Five

5

Chapter

Lessons 61–70

You alone *are* the LORD; You have made heaven, the heaven of heavens, with all their host.

Nehemiah 9:6a

Construct Meaning

Tommy's science club spent 3.5 days at the planetarium. They spent 2.4 hours each full day focused on the planet Mercury. They learned that Mercury is the closest planet to the sun and that it travels around the sun faster than any other planet; hence, the Romans named it to honor the swift messenger of their gods.

The club members gathered information about Mercury's temperature. One of the facts they learned was that the average temperature of the side facing the sun is 810°F and the side away from the sun is –300°F.

About how much time did the club members spend focused on Mercury?

Estimate decimal products two ways.
- Round both factors to the greatest place value and multiply.

$$\begin{array}{r} 3.5 \longrightarrow 4 \\ \times 2.4 \longrightarrow \times 2 \\ \hline 8 \end{array}$$ **About 8 hours were spent focused on Mercury.**

- Round a factor to a multiple of five so that computing mentally is easy.

$$\begin{array}{r} 33.5 \longrightarrow 30 \\ \times4.6 \longrightarrow \times5 \\ \hline 150 \end{array} \text{ or } \begin{array}{r} 35 \\ \times5 \\ \hline 175 \end{array}$$

The exact answer of 154.10 is in the estimated range.

150 < 154.10 < 175

Decimal products and whole-number products can be estimated the same way.

Check Understanding

Estimate the product by rounding to the greatest place value.

a. 4.6
   ×1.3

b. 8.2
   ×4.7

c. 5.4
   ×7.3

d. 26.5
   × 8.1

e. 32.3
   × 6.4

f. 2.4 × 42   g. 3.5 × 11   h. 18 × 4.6   i. 27 × 3.4

Estimate. Write > or <.

j. 2.6 × 4.7 ▒ 8   k. 3.2 × 7.3 ▒ 25   l. 4.4 × 24.31 ▒ 76

m. 7.25 × 26.5 ▒ 175   n. 5.3 × $42.95 ▒ $270   o. 2.31 × 7.18 ▒ 25

p. 21.3 × 4.5 ▒ 80   q. 63.5 × 9.8 ▒ 660   r. 200.4 × 6.3 ▒ 1,100

Estimating Decimal Products

Estimate.

1. 7.2
   × 3.4

2. 28.3
   × 1.6

3. 4.3
   × 4.5

4. 37.1
   × 49.4

5. 7.8
   × 6.1

6. 42 × 1.6

7. 56 × 2.3

8. 8.7 × 19

9. 2.6 × 279

Choose the best estimate. Write *a*, *b*, or *c*.

10. 31.2 × 6.81 ≈ *y*   **a.** 210   **b.** 280   **c.** 310
11. 27.6 × 4.54 ≈ *y*   **a.** 100   **b.** 150   **c.** 200
12. 19.8 × 7.66 ≈ *y*   **a.** 160   **b.** 190   **c.** 260
13. 8.4 × 52.1 ≈ *y*   **a.** 300   **b.** 200   **c.** 400
14. 4.5 × 392.6 ≈ *y*   **a.** 1,000   **b.** 2,000   **c.** 3,000
15. 15 × 9.86 ≈ *y*   **a.** 150   **b.** 300   **c.** 250
16. 842 × 7.3 ≈ *y*   **a.** 5,000   **b.** 560   **c.** 5,600

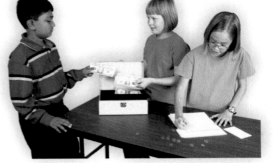

17. Club dues are $28.75 per person per year. There are ten members in the club. Using the two closest multiples of five to round the money amount, what is the range of the estimated amount paid in dues each year? Which estimate is closer to the exact amount of $287.50?

18. Ed rode his bike 6.5 miles to the planetarium. Tom rode his bike 2.4 times that distance. About how many miles did Tom ride his bike?

Review

Round each addend to the greatest place value and add.

1. 829 + 1,104 + 102   2. 83 + 204 + 12 + 46   3. 36,406 + 23,653 + 42,856

Multiply.

4. 24
   × 6

5. 314
   × 9

6. 5,782
   × 7

7. 46
   × 39

8. 287
   × 145

Solve the problem. Check by multiplying.

9. 2)68   10. 9)657   11. 16)704   12. 27)6,431   13. 9)568

Write *yes* if the black number is evenly divisible by the purple number. Write *no* if it is not.

14. 36   9   15. 44   7   16. 83   9   17. 56   8

Lesson 62

Construct Meaning

The science club researched the planet Venus prior to their planetarium visit. Here are some facts they found.

- Venus is the closest planet to Earth.
- Venus is the brightest planet.
- Its temperature, about 860°F, is higher than that of any other planet.
- The surface consists of flat ground, mountains, canyons, and valleys.
- The U.S. *Mariner 2* first observed Venus in 1962.
- In 1970 the Soviet spacecraft *Venera 7* landed on Venus.

> Encyclopedias, magazines, books, and the Internet were sources the club members used. Four websites each provided 0.15 of the data researched.

What part of the data came from the websites?
Use graph paper divided into hundredths to find $4 \times 0.15 = x$.

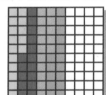

$$\begin{array}{r} 0.15 \\ \times \quad 4 \\ \hline \end{array}$$

Sixty-hundredths is the amount of data retrieved from the websites.

Was the <u>whole</u> project researched from the websites?

$$\begin{array}{r} \overset{2}{0.15} \\ \times \quad 4 \\ \hline 0.60 \end{array}$$

Multiply the hundredths. Regroup 20 as 2 tenths and 0 hundredths.
Multiply the tenths, then the ones.
Total the number of decimal places in both factors. **2**
Show the product with the same number of decimal places. **2**

More Examples

$$\begin{array}{r} \overset{4\ 2}{2.74} \\ \times \quad 6 \\ \hline 16.44 \end{array}$$
2 decimal places
$+\ 0$ decimal places
2 decimal places

$$\begin{array}{r} \overset{1}{4.132} \\ \times \quad 4 \\ \hline 16.528 \end{array}$$
3 decimal places
$+\ 0$ decimal places
3 decimal places

$$\begin{array}{r} \overset{1}{5.069} \\ \times \quad 12 \\ \hline 10138 \\ 50690 \\ \hline 60.828 \end{array}$$
3 decimal places
$+\ 0$ decimal places

3 decimal places

Check Understanding

Copy the equation that matches the graph model.

a.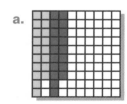

$2 \times 18 = 36$
$2 \times 0.18 = 0.36$

b.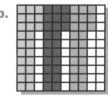

$3 \times 0.23 = 0.69$
$3 \times 23 = 69$

c.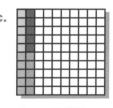

$4 \times 0.05 = 0.20$
$4 \times 5 = 20$

d.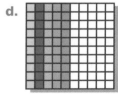

$5 \times 10 = 50$
$5 \times 0.10 = 0.50$

132

Multiplying a Decimal by a Whole Number

 **ractice**

Show each equation on graph paper to help you find the product.

1. $3 \times 0.12 = z$ 2. $2 \times 0.31 = z$ 3. $4 \times 0.10 = z$ 4. $6 \times 0.06 = z$

Write the number of decimal places counted for each product.

5. $9 \times 0.4 = n$ 6. $35 \times 0.86 = n$ 7. $6 \times 0.905 = n$ 8. $17 \times 1.84 = n$

Find the product.

9.	10.	11.	12.	13.
0.4	1.8	3.072	7.62	2.64
× 5	× 9	× 8	× 24	× 17

The gravitational pull of Venus is 0.91 times that of the earth.
Find how much the object would weigh on Venus.
If the product is a decimal, round it to the nearest whole number.

WEIGHT ON EARTH	× 0.91 =	WEIGHT ON VENUS
14. 100-pound boat		
15. 35-pound swordfish		
16. 300-pound football player		
17. 11-pound watermelon		

Multiply using pencil and paper. Compare your product with the one displayed if you multiply using a calculator. Do you see any similarities or differences? Explain.

18.
YOUR WORK
25
× 8

CALCULATOR DISPLAY
25
× 8

19.
YOUR WORK
0.25
× 8

CALCULATOR DISPLAY
0.25
× 8

 **eview**

Write the least common multiple of each pair.

1. 6 and 4   2. 2 and 8   3. 3 and 5   4. 5 and 4

Multiply.

5.	6.	7.	8.	9.
305	74	59	45	269
× 4	× 6	× 3	× 8	× 4

Divide.

10. $6\overline{)456}$ 11. $8\overline{)749}$ 12. $9\overline{)847}$ 13. $7\overline{)658}$ 14. $5\overline{)870}$

Construct Meaning

Tommy's science club probed into the night sky. They wanted to find the celestial poles—points on the celestial sphere above the north and south poles. They used paper, pencil, and a skymap to note the brightest stars. Two hours later they noted changes. Some stars had moved, and some appeared motionless. The areas where the stars seemed motionless are the locations of the celestial poles in the sky. In the northern hemisphere that area is between the Big Dipper and Cassiopeia; in the southern hemisphere it is between the Southern Cross and the Small Magellanic Cloud.

0.3 of an hour was spent looking at the sky. 0.7 of that time included taking notes. What part of the hour was spent on note taking?

Solve $0.7 \times 0.3 = x$.

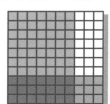

$$\begin{array}{r} \overset{2}{0.7} \\ \times\ 0.3 \\ \hline 0.21 \end{array}$$

Multiply the tenths. Regroup the 21.
Multiply the ones.
Count the decimal places in both factors. **2**
Show the product with 2 decimal places.

0.21 of the hour was spent taking notes.

Compare 0.7×0.3 with 7×3.

decimal model

whole-number model

Which model shows more than one whole?

Which model shows less than one whole?

In 0.7×0.3 the product 0.21 is less than 1.
In 7×3 the product 21 is more than 1.

More Examples

$$\begin{array}{r} 0.24 \\ \times\ \ 0.3 \\ \hline 0.072 \end{array}$$

2 decimal places
+1 decimal place
3 decimal places

$$\begin{array}{r} 34.781 \\ \times\ \ \ \ .03 \\ \hline 1.04343 \end{array}$$

3 decimal places
+2 decimal places
5 decimal places

$$\begin{array}{r} 1.62 \\ \times 3.24 \\ \hline 648 \\ 3240 \\ 48600 \\ \hline 5.2488 \end{array}$$

2 decimal places
+2 decimal places

4 decimal places

Check Understanding

Copy the equation that matches the model.

a.

b.

c. (grid model)

$0.6 \times 0.2 = 0.12$

$0.2 \times 0.4 = 0.08$

$0.3 \times 0.5 = 0.15$

Practice

Rewrite the product with the decimal in the correct place.

1. 7.1
   ×4.9
   ────
   3479

2. 25.8
   × 0.7
   ────
   1806

3. 18.32
   ×   0.7
   ─────
   12824

4. 126
   × 0.2
   ────
   252

5.   1.5
   ×0.306
   ─────
   04590

Multiply.

6. 0.8 × 0.3

7. 241 × 1.3

8. 4.3 × 0.6

9. 0.01 × 10

10. 9.7
   ×0.3
   ────

11.   24
   ×0.16
   ────

12. 3.562
   × 0.14
   ─────

13. 5.90
   ×0.02
   ────

14.   0.84
   ×0.135
   ─────

15. 10.6
   × 0.9
   ────

16. 82.37
   ×   0.5
   ─────

17. 0.46
   × 0.6
   ────

18. 1.2
   ×.09
   ────

19. 83.6
   ×   2
   ────

20. 0.6 × 0.5

21. 2.2 × 8.6

22. 8.52 × 0.9

23. 11.1 × 20.42

Apply

24. The gravitational pull of the sun is 27.8 times greater than that of Earth. If a man who weighed 116.5 pounds on Earth could stand on the sun, how much would he weigh? Round the product to the nearest whole number.

25. Land forms about 0.3 of the surface of planet Earth. The oceans cover 2.33 times more surface than land. How much of Earth is covered by oceans? Round the product to the nearest tenth.

Review

Add.

1. 6.5 + 3.6

2. 8.3 + 4.8

3. 13.936 + 6.881

4. 7.43 + 1.96

Subtract.

5. 5.7 − 4.05

6. 92.4 − 21.9

7. 16.82 − 12.096

8. 2.03 − 1.30

Estimate the product.

9. 4.8
   ×1.9

10. 6.3
   ×3.7

11. 5.3
   ×2.9

12. 5.67
   × 2.8

13. 8.55
   ×5.97

Lesson 64

Earth   Sun

The earth traveling through space around the sun is only a small part of the universe. People, plants, and animals can live on Earth because it is the right distance from the sun. When the northern hemisphere is tilting away from the sun and the days get shorter, the leaves of deciduous trees change colors and fall from the trees.

Ray's neighborhood is full of trees, and the neighbors are willing to pay him to rake and bag the leaves. Ray charges $0.75 per bag. How much would Ray make if he raked 10 bags of leaves? How much would Ray make if he raked 100 bags of leaves?

1 bag × $0.75 each = $0.75
10 bags × $0.75 each = $7.50
100 bags × $0.75 each = $75.00

Ray would make $7.50 for raking 10 bags of leaves and $75.00 for 100 bags of leaves.

The number of zeros in 10, 100, and 1,000 tells you how many places to move the decimal to the right.

10 ⟶
100 ⟶
1,000 ⟶

Use mental math. Observe how the number becomes larger as the decimal point moves to the right.

1 × 1.75 = 1.75
10 × 1.75 = 17.5
100 × 1.75 = 175
1,000 × 1.75 = 1,750 ← Write a zero so there are 3 places to move the decimal.

1 × 14.03 = 14.03
10 × 14.03 = 140.3
100 × 14.03 = 1,403
1,000 × 14.03 = 14,030

Multiply. Write extra zeros in the product if needed.

Find 0.03 × 0.069.

  0.069   3 decimal places
× 0.03   + 2 decimal places
0.00207   5 decimal places

Because there are only 4 places, write an extra zero and place the decimal.

Find $4.25 × 0.50.

  $4.25
× 0.50
$2.1250   rounded to the nearest cent is $2.13.

Multiply. Observe the pattern.

a.   1 × $0.79
    10 × $0.79
  100 × $0.79

b.   1 × 2.04
      10 × 2.04
    100 × 2.04
  1,000 × 2.04

c.   1 × 52.98
      10 × 52.98
    100 × 52.98
  1,000 × 52.98

Find the product. Write extra zeros if needed.

d. 10 × 0.9

e. 1,000 × 0.069

f. 100 × 0.32

g. 0.04 × 0.03

h. 1.6 × 0.007

i. 0.09 × 0.007

136

Practice

Use mental math to multiply. Observe the pattern.

1. 1 × 1.37
   10 × 1.37
   100 × 1.37
   1,000 × 1.37

2. 1 × 20.68
   10 × 20.68
   100 × 20.68
   1,000 × 20.68

3. 1 × $4.59
   10 × $4.59
   100 × $4.59
   1,000 × $4.59

Multiply. Write extra zeros if needed.

4. 0.03 × 0.6
5. 0.13 × 0.5
6. 0.081 × 0.09
7. 0.01 × 0.05

8. 36 × 0.005
9. 1.7 × 0.62
10. 37.01 × 0.003
11. 44 × 0.2

12. 84 × 0.07
13. 0.008 × 65
14. 0.4 × 0.4
15. 100 × 63.2

Multiply the number by 10, 100, and 1,000.

16. 84.013
17. 34.9
18. 1.6
19. 2.82
20. 0.798

Apply

21. Ray bought four packages of plastic lawn and garden bags that cost a total of $10.98. The cashier added $0.07 tax for each dollar of the price. How much tax did he pay? Round your answer to the nearest cent.

22. Ten bags of leaves weighed 113.5 pounds. How much did 100 bags weigh?

23. The waste management department picked up the bags on 10 different occasions. The cost of each trip was $0.75. How much did the department charge Ray to pick up the bags?

24. Use the chart to find how much Ray made after he had bagged 30, 50, and 80 bags of leaves.

×	30	50	80
$0.75			

Challenge

25. If you multiply 100,000 × 35.8, how many zeros will you need to add to the product?

Review

Write the decimal for each word form.

1. two and thirty-four hundredths
2. thirteen and five-tenths
3. three hundred sixty-three and eight thousandths
4. one and one-thousandth

Find the product.

5. 153
   × 416

6. 531
   × 382

7. 718
   × 395

8. 274
   × 947

9. 8,343
   × 535

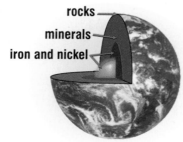

rocks
minerals
iron and nickel

Our planet Earth is the third planet in order from the sun. The earth's interior is iron and nickel surrounded by a mantle of minerals with a rocky crust. Tommy's dad, a geologist, gave him a valuable rock collection. Having the collection prompted Tommy to collect rocks wherever he goes until his pockets are bulging.

Data — information, facts, figures, statistics — are used to solve equations. Check the following paragraph to determine if the information is . . .

sufficient — just enough
insufficient — not enough
extra — unnecessary

Southgate Christian School ordered a <u>rock collection that cost $24.99 for each of the 4 fifth grade classrooms.</u> <u>Each collection contained 18 samples of igneous, sedimentary, and metamorphic rocks.</u> How much money did the school invest in the rock collections?

Understand the question.

How much money did the school spend on the four rock collections?

Analyze the data.

Each rock collection cost $24.99. The school bought four. All other data are extra and can be ignored.

Plan the strategy.

Since the problem asks how much, we will need to multiply the price of one rock collection by four. Round $24.99 to $25 to estimate the answer. $4 \times \$25 = \$100$

Solve the problem.

$4 \times \$24.99 = \$99.96$ spent on the rock collections

Evaluate the result.

Yes, it is reasonable that the school spent $99.96 on four rock collections, since the predicted amount was $100.

Problem Solving: Multiplication of Decimals

Solve. Label each problem as having *sufficient*, *insufficient*, or *extra* information. If the problem contains insufficient information, tell what is needed. Write the first and last words of any sentence containing extra information.

1. Tommy priced a geologist hammer at $7.59 and a hand lens for $6.89. He bought two of each of the tools. He found a nearby quarry that provided an opportunity to use the tools to break off rock specimens for $10 an hour. How much did Tommy spend on the tools?

2. Cullen's father, a gemologist, cut and polished five emeralds for a jewelry show. He charged $75.00 per emerald. How much money did he make?

3. A high school ring may contain a gemstone. The company that sells high school rings displayed various rings at an assembly. Five students bought the same style ring with a blue sapphire stone. What is the amount of money the company received from the sale of those five rings?

4. For Valentine's Day, Mr. Hall bought a 3-piece ruby set of jewelry for his wife. Each piece cost $52.50. For Christmas he bought a 4-piece pearl set. Each piece cost $27.50. Which set of jewelry cost more? How much more?

Japanese pearl sorter

5. The weight of Ashley's tanzanite ring is 1.5 carats. A tanzanite carat is worth $300.00. How much is her ring worth?

6. A gemcutter repaired some jewelry for Mrs. Miles. He charged $8.75 per piece. How much did Mrs. Miles pay for the repairs?

7. Mrs. Walter paid $0.06 sales tax on every dollar when she purchased a topaz necklace that cost $113.00. The matching earrings were on sale for $49.00. What was the final amount she paid for the necklace?

Find the price of each gemstone. Round the final cost to the nearest dollar.

	Gemstone	Number of carats	Price per carat	Final cost
8.	Specimen A	37.87	$0.66	
9.	Specimen B	141.50	$0.53	
10.	Specimen C	94.33	$5.30	
11.	Specimen D	164.55	$3.95	

12. In the parable of the pearl of great price, Jesus relates the kingdom of heaven to a merchant seeking beautiful pearls. Read Matthew 13:45 and 46 to find out what the merchant did when he found a pearl of great price. What is the lesson for us?

Construct Meaning

Did you know that space shuttle astronauts have taken radar images of much of Earth's surface to make a three-dimensional map of our planet? The map will help experts deal with issues such as climate changes, military missions, cell phone towers, and beach erosion.

When a hurricane hits an area, beach erosion and major property destruction occur. Ron spent a total of 4.38 hours on two different days taking safety measures prior to the forecasted hurricane. How many hours did he average per day?

Solve 4.38 ÷ 2 = *x*.

Use flats, rods, and units to show dividing decimals by a whole number.

4 flats   3 rods   8 units
(4 ones) (3 tenths) (8 hundredths)

Divide the 4 ones (flats) into 2 equal groups.

Share the 3 tenths (rods) between each group.

left over

Regroup the 1 tenth (rod) left over as 10 hundredths (units). Share the 18 hundredths between each group.

2 flats in each group
1 rod in each group
9 units in each group

$$\begin{array}{r} 2.19 \\ 2\overline{)4.38} \\ \underline{-4}\downarrow \\ 0\,3 \\ \underline{-2}\downarrow \\ 18 \\ \underline{-18} \\ 0 \end{array}$$

Place the decimal in the quotient.
Divide the whole number. 4 ÷ 2.
Divide the tenths. 3 ÷ 2
Divide the hundredths. 18 ÷ 2

Ron spent 2 and 19 hundredths hours each day taking safety measures.

Dividing Decimals by Whole Numbers

 Remember to place the decimal first. Divide as with whole numbers.

$$\begin{array}{r} 0.3 \\ 6\overline{)1.8} \\ \underline{-} \\ 0 \end{array}$$

$$\begin{array}{r} 2.4 \\ 2\overline{)4.8} \\ \underline{-4}\downarrow \\ 0\,8 \\ \underline{-8} \end{array}$$

$$\begin{array}{r} 6.3 \\ 4\overline{)25.2} \\ \underline{-}\downarrow \\ 1\,2 \\ \underline{-1\,2} \\ 0 \end{array}$$

$$\begin{array}{r} 5.67 \\ 7\overline{)39.69} \\ \underline{-35}\downarrow \\ 4\,6 \\ \underline{-}\downarrow \\ 49 \\ \underline{-49} \\ 0 \end{array}$$

$$\begin{array}{r} 0.132 \\ 12\overline{)1.584} \\ \underline{-1\,2}\downarrow \\ 36 \\ \underline{-36}\downarrow \\ 24 \\ \underline{-} \\ 0 \end{array}$$

Check Understanding

Write a decimal division problem shown by the model.

a.

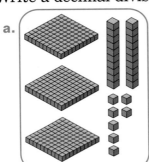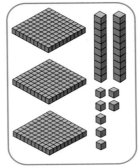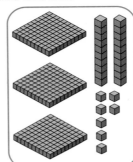

Practice

Divide.

1. $2\overline{)6.54}$

2. $6\overline{)3.6}$

3. $4\overline{)2.8}$

4. $3\overline{)9.33}$

5. $5\overline{)4.5}$

6. $8\overline{)67.12}$

7. $5\overline{)25.75}$

8. $9\overline{)85.5}$

9. $7\overline{)14.994}$

10. $3\overline{)14.853}$

11. $17\overline{)3.978}$

12. $42\overline{)8.82}$

13. $26\overline{)54.6}$

14. $35\overline{)423.5}$

15. $18\overline{)2.16}$

Apply

16. Diana and her two roommates share a phone. If they equally divide the January bill of $59.55, what is the amount each one must pay?

17. After the hurricane 235.4 miles of beachfront property contained debris. It took 11 days to clean up the entire area. What was the average number of miles cleaned each day?

18. The Johnson family drove 8 hours and covered 412.8 miles while the sun was shining. The weather changed to snow, so they stopped to spend the night. Had they averaged more or less than 50 miles per hour?

Review

Find the product.

1. 0.15×0.2 2. 0.04×1.3

Find the quotient.

3. $912 \div 24$ 4. $2,652 \div 17$

 Construct Meaning

Do you know how long it takes a jet airplane to fly around the earth?

Do you know how long it takes an astronaut to circle the earth in space?

0°

The equator, an imaginary circle on the earth, is found at 0° latitude on a globe or map. Other circles, spaced specific distances apart, help to locate places in relation to the equator and the prime meridian, which is located at 0° longitude. On a globe or map, zero has significance.

0°

Zero also has significance in dividing decimals.

⦿ A zero holds place value in the quotient of a decimal problem just as it does in the quotient of a whole-number problem.

```
      4.01       Place the decimal.
 3) 12.03        Divide 12 by 3.
  − 12           Divide the tenths.
    0 03         Write 0.
   −   3         Divide the hundredths.
       0
```

```
       401       Divide 12 by 3.
 3) 1,203        Divide the tens.
   − 1 2         Write 0.
     003         Divide the ones.
   −   3
       0
```

More Examples of Zero in the Quotient

```
    0.003     There are 0 ones,
 3) 0.009     tenths, and
  −     9     hundredths.
        0     Place a 0 in those
              places in the
              quotient. Continue
              to divide.
```

```
    0.513     2 cannot be
 4) 2.052     divided by 4, so
  − 2 0       place a 0 in the
      05      ones place in the
   −   4      quotient. Continue
       12     to divide.
     − 12
        0
```

```
     50.8     4 cannot be
 6) 304.8     divided by 6,
  − 30        so place a 0 in
    04 8      the quotient.
  − 4 8       Continue to
      0       divide.
```

⦿ A zero placed at the end of the dividend can sometimes help to complete a decimal problem so there is no remainder.

```
      3.47
 25) 86.85
   − 75
     11 8
   −10 0
     1 85
   −1 75
       10 ← Continue to divide to eliminate any remainder.
```

```
      3.474
 25) 86.850
   − 75
     11 8
   −10 0
     1 85
   −1 75
      100
     −100
        0
```

Check by using the inverse operation.

```
     3.474
 ×      25
    17370
  +69480
   86.850 ✓
```

 **Check Understanding**

Place the decimal and divide.

a. $2\overline{)0.008}$ b. $7\overline{)49.70}$ c. $8\overline{)209.6}$ d. $15\overline{)65.19}$

 **Practice**

Find the quotient.

1. $3\overline{)1.08}$ 2. $6\overline{)0.024}$ 3. $7\overline{)205.1}$ 4. $35\overline{)40.6}$ 5. $24\overline{)5.40}$

6. $9\overline{)0.234}$ 7. $14\overline{)19.04}$ 8. $4\overline{)0.06}$ 9. $11\overline{)0.242}$ 10. $25\overline{)4.075}$

Divide and check.

11. $5\overline{)1.705}$ 12. $8\overline{)83.04}$ 13. $18\overline{)38.052}$ 14. $2\overline{)4.9}$ 15. $7\overline{)0.014}$

 Apply

16. The five-member Welch family spent $2,046.50 on their summer vacation in 2000. One of their daughters got married and did not go on the family vacation in 2001 when the family spent $1,804.00 on their vacation. Which year did the Welch family spend more per person?

Erin and Chelsee went shopping for the Sunday school department. Packages of items were bought and divided among several classes. Help the girls find the price per item.

Item	Number Per Package	Price Per Package	Price Per Item
Pencils	8	$2.08	17.
Pens	10	$2.00	18.
Erasers	15	$0.75	19.
Glue Sticks	2	$2.40	20.
Colored pencils	12	$2.28	21.
Stickers	2	$2.80	22.
Glitter	6	$4.26	23.

 **Review**

Solve.

1. 401
   × 18

2. 2,456
   ×   8

3. 1,608
   ×   23

4. 53.46
   × 1.9

5. 25.62
   ×   32

6. $7\overline{)846}$ 7. $46\overline{)1,450}$ 8. $23\overline{)7,694}$ 9. $10\overline{)1,480}$ 10. $5\overline{)49,723}$

**Construct Meaning**

Mars is the fourth planet in order from the sun. Known as the Red Planet, it seems fiery red in the sky at night. Phobos and Deimos are its two moons. The core is believed to be iron with some nickel. Olympus Mons, located on Mars, is the largest volcano in the solar system; it is two times as high as Earth's Mt. Everest. Robotic rovers have explored Mars' surface and given us exciting information about the planet.

If a rover analyzed 10 rock samples that weighed a total of 86.5 pounds, what would the average sample weigh?

Find 86.5 ÷ 10.

USE MENTAL MATH OR LONG DIVISION.

When you divide by 10, all the digits change to a lower place value. 86.5 becomes 8.65 when the decimal point moves one place to the left.

```
       8.65
10) 86.50
   -80
     6 5
    -6 0
       50
      -50
        0
```

The average sample weight would be 8.65 pounds.

- Dividing decimals by 10, 100, and 1,000 can be done mentally.
  The number of zeros tells how many places to move the decimal point to the left.

$$10 \longrightarrow \qquad 86.5 \div 10 = 8.65$$
$$100 \longrightarrow \qquad 86.5 \div 100 = 0.865$$
$$1{,}000 \longrightarrow \qquad 86.5 \div 1{,}000 = 0.0865$$

Write a zero so there are 3 places to move the decimal.

Look for a pattern. Observe how the number becomes smaller as the decimal point moves to the left.

$$17.6 \div 10 = 1.76 \qquad 239.74 \div 10 = 23.974$$
$$17.6 \div 100 = 0.176 \qquad 239.74 \div 100 = 2.3974$$
$$17.6 \div 1{,}000 = 0.0176 \qquad 239.74 \div 1{,}000 = 0.23974$$

- Divide decimals by 10, 100, and 1,000 using long division.

```
       1.76            0.176              0.0176
10) 17.60      100) 17.600      1,000) 17.6000
   -10            -10 0                -10 00
     7 6            7 60                  7 600
    -7 0           -7 00                 -7 000
      60             600                   6000
     -60            -600                  -6000
       0               0                      0
```

Dividing decimals by 10, 100, and 1,000 is easier using mental math than long division.

Dividing Decimals by 10, 100, and 1,000

 **Check Understanding**

Use mental math to divide.

a. 25.9 ÷ 10
25.9 ÷ 100
25.9 ÷ 1,000

b. 4.76 ÷ 10
4.76 ÷ 100
4.76 ÷ 1,000

c. 591.7 ÷ 1,000
d. 873.9 ÷ 100
e. 7.4 ÷ 10

 Practice

Use mental math to divide. Observe the pattern.

1. 16.2 ÷ 10
16.2 ÷ 100
16.2 ÷ 1,000

2. 25.38 ÷ 10
25.38 ÷ 100
25.38 ÷ 1,000

3. 748.9 ÷ 10
748.9 ÷ 100
748.9 ÷ 1,000

Use mental math to divide.

4. 4.3 ÷ 100
5. 39.1 ÷ 10
6. 46.23 ÷ 1,000
7. 843.7 ÷ 100
8. 0.05 ÷ 10
9. 0.18 ÷ 1,000
10. 5.7 ÷ 100
11. 91.23 ÷ 10
12. 487.32 ÷ 100
13. 116.4 ÷ 1,000
14. 1.1 ÷ 10
15. 61.1 ÷ 100

Compare the quotient with the dividend.
Count how many places each digit moved.
Write whether the divisor is *10, 100,* or *1,000.*

16. 39.4 ÷ x = 0.394
17. 125.6 ÷ x = 12.56
18. 8.9 ÷ x = 0.0089
19. 2.1 ÷ x = 0.021

20. Copy and complete the chart.

÷	10	100	1,000
6.2			
18.5			
243.7			

 **Apply**

21. If Anna worked on a Martian project for 10 weeks and earned $1,250, how much did she earn each week?

22. The corporation paid student scientists $9,750 for 1,000 hours of research on the project. Was the hourly rate more or less than $10 per hour?

MARTIAN SUNDIAL

Review

Solve.

1. 0.08
× 13.7

2. 12.8
× 0.06

3. 8.9
× 4.7

4. 0.09 × 14
5. 35.5 × 0.24

6. 14)73.92
7. 26)598.78
8. 56.304 ÷ 9
9. 16.64 ÷ 8
10. 10.010 ÷ 10

© Copyright 2001

145

Lesson 69

✓ Check Understanding

The fifth grade students at Pinecreek Christian School are making plans to raise money for Teacher Appreciation Day. They would like to give their teacher a classroom gift and a gift certificate to spend at the mall. They plan to raise money by setting up booths that contain fun things to do. They will invite other classes and parents to participate.

Complete the chart to find out the amount each person raised.

Activity	Number of Students Working	Amount Raised	Amount Raised Per Student
Dart Game	4	$40.56	a.
Put on a Skit	4	$52.72	b.
Cupcake Decorating	4	$23.72	c.
String Shell Necklace	4	$68.96	d.
Volleyball Game	4	$47.52	e.
Video Game	4	$66.52	f.

g. The total amount of $300 is to be evenly divided between a classroom gift and a personal gift. How much money will go toward each gift?

h. The dart and volleyball games together profited $88.08. If all 8 students worked in a combined effort, what would be the amount raised per student?

i. Three shell necklaces are made from one package of shells. One package of shells cost $4.95. What is the cost of one necklace?

j. 100 people participated in the cupcake decorating activity. How much profit did each cupcake provide? Round to the nearest cent.

k. $66.52 was raised by playing five different videos at equal intervals of time. How much did each video profit the class? Round to the nearest dollar.

l. A $150 mobile of the sun, Mercury, Venus, Earth, and Mars was presented as the classroom gift. What is the amount each student raised for the mobile?

"But the fruit of the Spirit is love, joy, peace, longsuffering, kindness, goodness, faithfulness, gentleness, self-control. Against such there is no law." Galatians 5:22, 23

Problem Solving: Division of Decimals

Practice

Solve.

1. Did you ever wonder how much you would weigh on Mars? The gravitational pull on Mars is 0.38 times that of Earth. To find out how much you would weigh on Mars, multiply your weight times 0.38.

2. The town of Creekview had a record 33.6 inches of rain over an 8-month period. What was the average rainfall per month?

3. Mr. Kline's car gets 18 miles to a gallon of gasoline. Realizing his gasoline tank was almost empty, he stopped and put in 8.765 gallons of gasoline. He reset the odometer and figured he should be able to drive a certain number of miles. How many miles did Mr. Kline figure he would be able to drive on 8.765 gallons of gasoline?

4. The fishermen caught 167.5 pounds of seafood. If a bushel basket holds 25 pounds of seafood, how many bushels of seafood do the fishermen have?

5. Cal drove an average of 58 miles per hour on his trip from Florida to South Carolina. He started driving at night and drove for 12.5 hours. How many miles did he travel?

6. Mother made a refreshing pitcher of iced tea. She used one large tea bag with eight cups of water. How many cups of water would she use with three large tea bags?

7. Four mail trucks ran their regular deliveries. The total mileage report for those four trucks on Monday was 678.8 miles. What was the average number of miles each truck traveled?

8. Grandmother's prescription cost $12.57 per month. How much does she pay for a yearly prescription?

9. Tonya bought 2.5 dozen of doughnuts to be shared among her 15-member Sunday school class. How many doughnuts could each member receive?

10. Jack and three friends folded letters for a local business. The job paid a total of $250. How much did each person get paid for the job?

11. Michelle's father invited his fellow employees over for a cookout. He bought nine pounds of steak at $3.29 per pound. What was the cost of the meat?

Lesson 70

Where Is the Point?

Estimate the product by rounding to the greatest place value.

1. 5.2	2. 8.1	3. 3.8	4. $22.50	5. 317.2
×1.6	×5.7	×2.5	× 5.1	× 45.6

Estimate. Write > or <.

6. 24.6 × 3.4 ▦ 55   7. 5.64 × 8.17 ▦ 58   8. $14.98 × 7.2 ▦ $68

Write the equation that matches the model.

9.

3 × 12   = 36
3 × 0.12 = 0.36
0.3 × 0.12 = 0.36

10.

0.4 × 0.8 = 0.32
4 × 8   = 32
0.4 × 8   = 3.2

11.
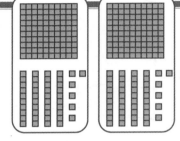

2.92 ÷ 2 = 1.46
1.46 ÷ 2 = 0.73

Find the product.

12. 0.5	13. 2.7	14. 4.093	15. 6.74	16. 4.72
× 6	× 8	× 7	× 32	× 16

17. 8.4	18. 28	19. 4.732	20. 76.3	21. 64.37
×0.6	×0.19	× 0.13	× 2	× 0.8

22. 0.7 × 0.4   23. 351 × 1.4   24. 6.2 × 0.4   25. 12.3 × 30.41

26. 0.04 × 0.7   27. 24.01× 0.003   28. 45 × 0.3   29. 0.006 × 44

● Complete the pattern.

1 × 2.56 = 2.56
30.   10 × 2.56 = ▦
31. 100 × 2.56 = ▦
1,000 × 2.56 = 2,560

1 × 38.4 = 38.4
32.   10 × 38.4 = ▦
100 × 38.4 = 3,840
33. 1,000 × 38.4 = ▦

1 × $0.25 = $0.25
10 × $0.25 = $2.50
34. 100 × $0.25 = ▦
35. 1,000 × $0.25 = ▦

Divide.

36. $3\overline{)9.78}$ **37.** $6\overline{)12.882}$ **38.** $24\overline{)55.2}$ **39.** $12\overline{)4.788}$ **40.** $8\overline{)\$65.84}$

41. $4\overline{)0.008}$ **42.** $5\overline{)3.065}$ **43.** $25\overline{)81.65}$ **44.** $18\overline{)24.84}$ **45.** $3\overline{)9.021}$

46. $6.8 \div 100$ **47.** $286.2 \div 1{,}000$ **48.** $13.8 \div 10$ **49.** $0.18 \div 100$

Write the equation that is a match for the given answer.

50. Answer: *0.143*

$14.3 \div 10 = n$
$14.3 \div 100 = n$
$14.3 \div 1{,}000 = n$

51. Answer: *2.435*

$24.35 \div 10 = n$
$24.35 \div 100 = n$
$24.35 \div 1{,}000 = n$

52. Answer: *0.5638*

$563.8 \div 10 = n$
$563.8 \div 100 = n$
$563.8 \div 1{,}000 = n$

Solve.

53. Mr. Richardson, his wife, and two children attended a baseball series that lasted five days. They drove 64.8 miles round trip each day. How many miles did traveling to this event add to the odometer on their car?

54. The Richardson family spent $127.95 on refreshments and memorabilia while at the games. What was the average amount spent per day?

Complete the chart to find the weight on various surfaces.

×	Gravitational Factor	Mercury 0.28	Venus 0.91	Earth's Moon 0.17	Mars 0.38
Weight on Earth — 75 pounds		55.	56.	57.	58.
Weight on Earth — 98 tons		59.	60.	61.	62.

Bonus questions are related to the information you supplied on the chart above.

63. On which planet would a 75-pound person weigh the most?

64. On which two planets would a 75-pound person weigh close to the same amount?

65. On which location would a 98-kilogram object weigh the least?

Grade Five

6

Chapter

Lessons 71–85

Therefore, since we are the offspring of God, we ought not to think that the Divine Nature is like gold or silver or stone, something shaped by art and man's devising.

Acts 17:29

Construct Meaning

The term geometry comes from two Greek words that mean earth (geo) and to measure (metry). It is important to know geometric terms in order to study the many lines, shapes, and figures that are part of God's creation.

Geometric Terms

Point	A fixed location in space. It is named with a capital letter.	A •	Point A
Line	A straight path that continues without end in both directions.	B C ←——→	Line BC or Line CB $\overleftrightarrow{BC}$ or $\overleftrightarrow{CB}$
Line segment	Part of a line between two endpoints.	D E •——•	Segment DE or Segment ED $\overline{DE}$ or $\overline{ED}$
Ray	Part of a line that has one endpoint and goes on without end in one direction.	F G •——→	Ray FG or $\overrightarrow{FG}$
Intersecting lines	Lines which cross each other, meeting at a common point.	J H L K I	$\overleftrightarrow{HI}$ intersects $\overleftrightarrow{JK}$
Perpendicular lines	Intersecting lines which form right angles.	L N M O	$\overleftrightarrow{LM}$ is perpendicular to $\overleftrightarrow{NO}$ $\overleftrightarrow{ML} \perp \overleftrightarrow{ON}$
Parallel lines	Lines in the same plane which do not intersect.	P Q R S	$\overleftrightarrow{PQ}$ is parallel to $\overleftrightarrow{RS}$ $\overleftrightarrow{QP} \parallel \overleftrightarrow{SR}$
Plane	A flat surface that extends without end in all directions. It is named by a letter.	t	Plane t

Check Understanding

Name the figure.

a. V   W   *point* b. Z   c. X   Y   d. R   S   e.

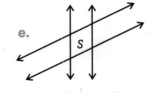

line segment   *line*   *Ray*   *plane*

Describe the line relationships.

f. A   B   C   D

Parallel lines

g.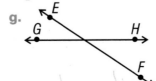

E   G   H   F

intersection line

h.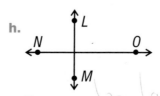

L   N   O   M

perpendicular lines

Draw each figure.

1. point *G*

2. line segment *AB*

3. line *RS*

4. ray *XY*

5. line *FG* parallel to line *HI*

6. lines *JK*, and *LM* intersecting at point *P*

7. line *CD* perpendicular to line *EF*

8. point *Y* on line *PQ*

9. plane *x*

Use the artist's simulation of *Pioneer 11*, an early unmanned space probe, to choose the best word(s) to complete each sentence.

10. The red line segment showing the electric cable appears to ____ the yellow line segment above it.

   a. intersect   **b.** be parallel to   **c.** be perpendicular to

11. The green rays near the Geiger counter are ____ .

   a. perpendicular
   b. parallel line segments
   c. neither choice applies

12. The purple rays that meet near the RTGs ____ .

   a. are parallel
   b. intersect
   c. are perpendicular

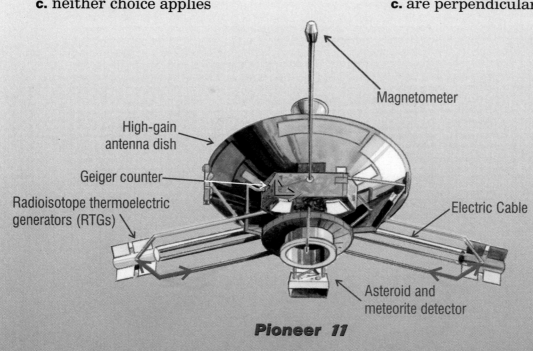

Pioneer 11

Lesson 72

Construct Meaning

An **angle** is formed by two rays with the same endpoint. The endpoint at which the rays intersect is called the **vertex**. Notice the angles formed at the corners of the level, by the scissor blades, and by the hands of the clock.

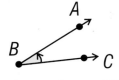

In this drawing of an angle, point B is the vertex of the angle. The letter of the vertex may name the angle, or the angle may be named with three letters, having the letter of the vertex in the middle. This is angle B, or angle ABC, or angle CBA. The unit used to measure an angle is the **degree**, shown by the symbol °.

∠B or ∠ABC or ∠CBA

Types of Angles

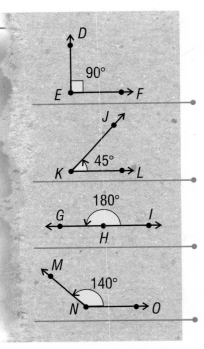

When two rays meet to form an angle of 90°, a **right angle** is formed.
$$\angle DEF = 90°$$

An angle measuring less than 90° is an **acute angle**.
$$\angle JKL = 45°$$

An angle of 180° is a **straight angle**.
$$\angle GHI = 180°$$

An angle greater than 90° but less than 180° is an **obtuse angle**.
$$\angle MNO = 140°$$

Reexamine the three photographs at the top of the page. Identify angles that appear to be right angles, acute angles, obtuse angles, and straight angles.

Check Understanding

a. Name the rays shown in the drawing.
b. Name the obtuse angles.
c. Name the acute angles.
d. Name the right angles.
e. Name the straight angle.

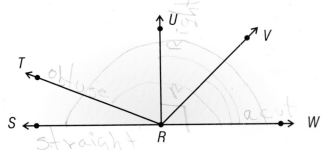

154

Mathematics Grade 5

ractice

Name the type of angle shown.

1. *acute* X
Y Z

2. *acute* I
G H

3. Right R
S T

4. *obtuse* L
M N

5. *obtuse* B C
D

6. straight A B C

7. *obtuse* D
E F

8. Right Q
R
S

Draw the hands on a clock to show each time. Identify the type of angle the hands display.

9. 9:10   10. 11:00   11. 9:00   12. 8:00   13. 6:00   14. 3:00

Apply

15. What is the name of the plane in this drawing?

16. Name a line segment that is parallel to $\overline{NO}$.

17. Name a line that is perpendicular to $\overleftrightarrow{VX}$.

18. Point W is within which angles?

19. Which angle has fewer degrees, ∠OST or ∠QSO?

20. Which is a right angle, ∠STN or ∠SVT?

21. Name the angle closest to point M.

22. Name two angles that have $\overline{TS}$ as a side.

23. Name all the points on $\overleftrightarrow{KQ}$.

24. What is the vertex of ∠LTV?

25. Name the point where $\overleftrightarrow{QK}$ and $\overleftrightarrow{VX}$ intersect.

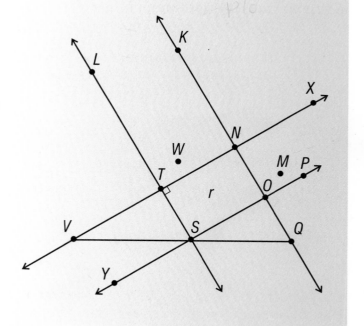

Review

1. 42.81
    ×   66

2. 0.733
    × 0.25

3. 589
    × 0.75

4. 321
    × 0.07

5. 0.92
    × 0.33

Construct Meaning

Many words begin with a prefix that gives you numerical information. In sports, the names biathlon, triathlon, and pentathlon tell how many events are involved. The Pentagon in Washington, D.C., is famous for its unique design with five sides. It follows that a **pentomino** is made using five parts, which are squares of equal dimensions.

MAKE A SET OF PENTOMINOES.

You will need:
  scissors
  three sheets of one-inch grid paper
  crayons or colored pencils

Cut five one-inch squares from one piece of the grid paper, being careful to cut on the lines exactly. You are ready to begin moving the squares into varied arrangements to design twelve different pentominoes.

The rule for making pentominoes is:
  At least one whole side of each square must touch a whole side of another square.

This is a pentomino.   This is not.

This is the pentomino shown above, but it has been flipped.

This is the same pentomino, but it has been rotated.

The challenge is to find twelve designs, following the rule.

Each time you find a new way to make a pentomino, check that only whole sides of squares touch. Then check using rules of motion in geometry.

MOTION IN GEOMETRY

Rotations or turns do not change the shape. Turn the piece on a point. Make a series of turns, including 90° (a quarter turn) and 180° (a half turn).

Reflections or flips change only the appearance of the shape. Flip each piece over to make a visual check to avoid repeating your designs.

Slides of pieces help when doing puzzles with pentominoes.

Practice

1. As you design a new pentomino, copy the arrangement by coloring five squares on another piece of one-inch grid paper and cutting around the outside edge. Continue working with your five separate squares to find each correct arrangement, color it on the grid sheet, and cut around its edge.

2. When you have a complete set of twelve pentominoes, you are ready to try some puzzles. Use the framework for the Wolf Puzzle and try the Stair Step Puzzle provided by your teacher.

Use one-inch grid paper or patterns from your teacher to make the framework for each puzzle listed below. Solve each puzzle using the correct number of pentominoes.

Puzzle Size	Number of Pentominoes
3. 3-inch × 5-inch rectangle	3
4. 4-inch × 5-inch rectangle	4
5. 5-inch × 5-inch rectangle	5
6. 3-inch × 10-inch rectangle	6
7. 6-inch × 10-inch rectangle	12

Lesson 74

⊞ Construct Meaning

When a kite is made from paper or fabric, its designer must measure the angles carefully. An instrument that is used for constructing and measuring angles is called a **protractor**.

A protractor is used to measure the angles of two-dimensional objects. It has two scales, marked from 0° to 180°, that allow you to measure from right to left or from left to right. A point at the center near the bottom of the protractor should be placed on the vertex of the angle you are measuring. The zero line across the bottom of the protractor is placed on one of the rays of the angle.

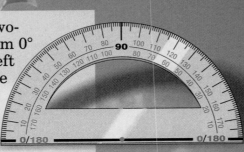

To measure ∠CDE, the protractor is placed as shown below.

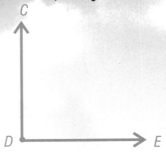 

Read the number of degrees where $\overrightarrow{CD}$ crosses the protractor.
∠CDE = 90°, a right angle.

∠FGH is an acute angle.
It measures 50°.

∠JKL is an obtuse angle.
It measures 130°.

 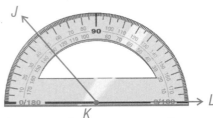

Why are there two opposite scales of numbers on the protractor?

To construct ∠RST, a 70° angle, use your protractor.

1. Make point S, the vertex.
2. Draw $\overrightarrow{ST}$.
3. Place the point of the protractor on point S, lining up $\overrightarrow{ST}$ with the zero line.
4. Make a mark below the line where you see 70° on the protractor.
5. Draw $\overrightarrow{SR}$ from point S to the mark you made.

158

Check Understanding

a. Use a protractor to measure ∠LMN, using these steps.

Step 1. Place the appropriate point on the protractor over the vertex of the rays.

Step 2. Line up the zero line of the protractor with $\overrightarrow{MN}$.

Step 3. Read the degrees from the zero line up to the point where $\overrightarrow{ML}$ crosses.

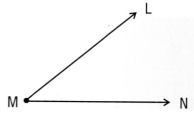

∠LMN = 40°

If your answer is different, reposition your protractor, using the steps above to guide you.

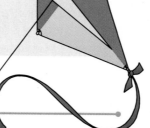

b. Why is the measure of ∠LMN equal to 40° rather than 140°?

Practice

Measure each angle.

1.

2.

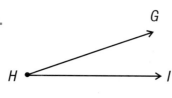

3.

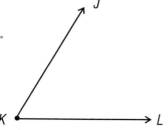

4.

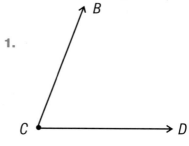

5.

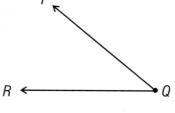

Use a protractor to draw each angle.

6. ∠KLM, a right angle

7. ∠RST, a straight angle

8. ∠EFG = 45°

9. ∠HIJ = 30°

10. ∠UVW = 150°

Apply

11. Could the sum of the degrees in two acute angles be greater than 180°? Explain your answer.

12. What type of angle do the hands on the clock show when your school day begins? What angle do you see when the final bell rings?

Construct Meaning

The Great Pyramid, which still stands near Cairo, Egypt, is the only survivor of the original Seven Wonders of the Ancient World. It was built approximately two thousand, six hundred years before the birth of Christ, and is an amazing architectural feat. It has a square base, and each visible face is a triangle that measures two hundred thirty meters at the base.

A **triangle** is a plane figure with three sides, three vertices, and three angles. A triangle is classified by the relative length of its sides or by the three angles it contains.

Triangles Classified by Relative Length of the Sides

	equilateral triangle	3 sides of equal length
	isosceles triangle	at least 2 sides of equal length
	scalene triangle	3 sides of unequal length

Triangles Classified by Angles

	right triangle	1 right (90°) angle
	acute triangle	3 acute (less than 90°) angles
	obtuse triangle	1 obtuse (greater than 90°) angle

What is the sum of the angles in a triangle?

Trace and cut out the triangle shown. Tear off each corner. Place on a straight angle to see the sum of the degrees of the three angles. Draw another triangle and try again.

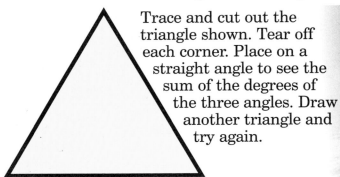

One of God's many architectural feats, the "final pyramid" of Mount Everest.

Classifying Triangles

✔ Check Understanding

Classify each triangle according to its sides.

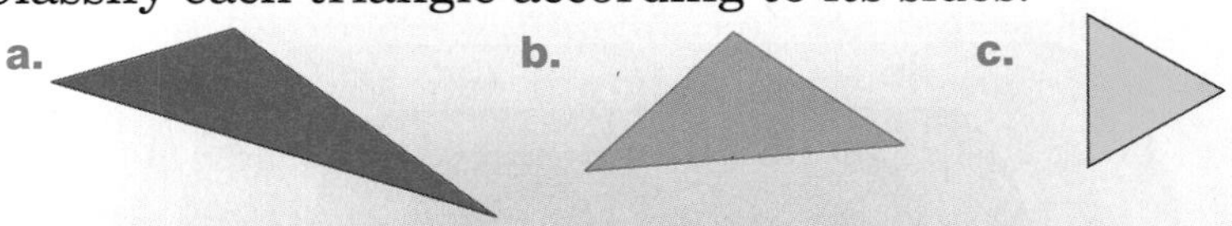

a.  b. c.

Classify each triangle according to its angles.

d.  e. f.

g. If △ABC has two 60° angles, how many degrees does the third angle contain?

Practice

Label each triangle as equilateral, isosceles, or scalene.

1. isosceles

2. equilateral

3. Isa lene

4. isosceles

5. obtuse

6. acute

160

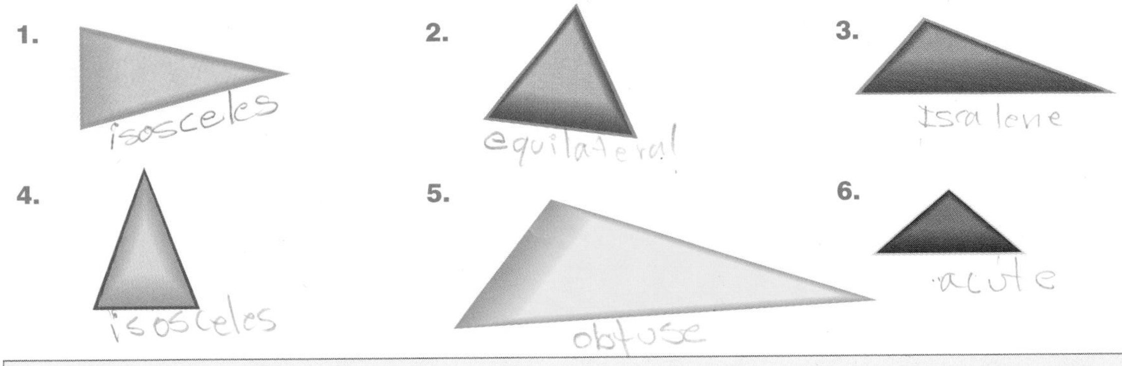

Label each triangle as *right*, *acute*, or *obtuse*. Tell the number of degrees in the third angle for each triangle.

360
180

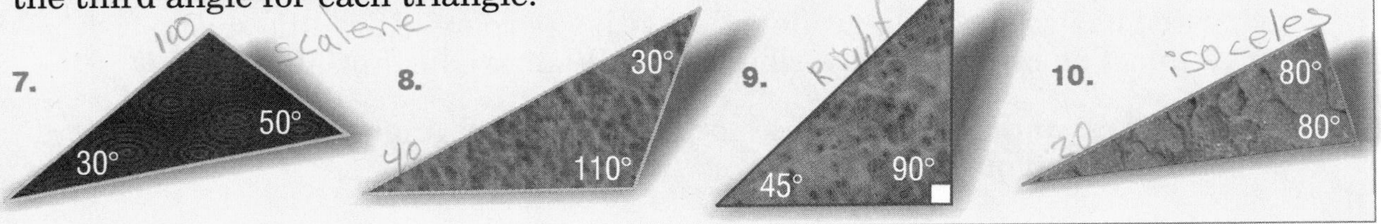

7. 100 scalene 50° 30°

8. scalene 40 30° 110°

9. Right 45° 90°

10. isosceles 20 80° 80°

Apply

11. Use a ruler and a protractor to construct a right triangle. Label each vertex and name the triangle. Use the protractor to measure each angle and write the number of degrees in it. Use the ruler to measure each side and write the length of each side in inches. Is your triangle an equilateral, isosceles, or scalene triangle?

12. Draw a two-inch square. Use one diagonal line to divide the square into triangles. What type of triangles result? Try the same with three-, four-, and five-inch squares. Is the result the same?

© Copyright 2001

161

Lesson 76

 **Construct Meaning**

 The students in Mr. Warner's class discovered that many letters of the alphabet display interesting geometric concepts. They devised a guessing game called *Geometry Letters*. When it was Maria's turn to give clues, she said, "I am thinking of three uppercase letters that form a word that is something we all like to do." Here are the clues she gave.

One of the letters looks like a triangle at the top and has no parallel or perpendicular lines.

One letter is formed by two perpendicular lines and has two right angles at the top.

Another letter begins with a straight angle that has three shorter lines perpendicular to it.

Can you write and unscramble the letters to form a word?

Making designs and diagrams are problem-solving strategies that are helpful when you work with geometry. These strategies help you make visual representations to solve problems, just as an architect or engineer would design and use a blueprint to construct a building or bridge.

Practice

Use visual representations to help you solve the following. You will need a pencil and a ruler.

1. Diana asked her classmates to guess her cousin's initials. His first initial is constructed of two vertical parallel lines with a perpendicular line segment at their center. The last initial is a right angle. What are his initials?

2. Draw your first and last initials as block letters. What angles do you see? What types of line segments?

3. Your class is making a quilt. You need to cover a 4-inch by 4-inch square with colored rectangles that measure 1" × 2". How many rectangles will you need to cover your square?

Moments with Careers

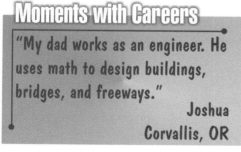

"My dad works as an engineer. He uses math to design buildings, bridges, and freeways."

Joshua
Corvallis, OR

4. Shelly's family is visiting a wilderness area that is newly opened. Although there are hiking trails, no trail maps are available for hikers yet. Mr. and Mrs. Riggs, Shelly's neighbors, have already hiked in the area and gave her family the directions below. Draw the trail map Shelly and her parents will make as they follow the directions. When you are finished, tell what polygon you see on your map.

Begin at the wooden sign at the trailhead. The path goes north, running parallel to the creek for about two miles. You will come to a trail that runs perpendicular to this one, and you will turn right. This trail is parallel to a large meadow of wildflowers that you will see on your left. After about two miles, you will see two trails on your right, one that makes a 90° turn to the south, and a second trail that makes a 45° angle with your present trail. Choose the second trail, and you will return to the point where you started.

5. C.J. lives by a park that is shaped like a square. A path that goes around the perimeter of the park is eight miles long. A diagonal path goes across the park, dividing it into two triangles that are the same size. C.J.'s brother, Zach, says the diagonal path is also 2 miles long. C.J. disagrees. Who is correct? Why?

6. Janna wanted to draw an obtuse triangle. After drawing it, she measured and found one angle was 40° and the next angle was 60°. Does she need to measure the third angle? Has she made an obtuse triangle?

7. Mrs. Milligan told her students to follow these directions to make a design of triangles.
   a. Draw an equilateral triangle with four-inch sides and a horizontal base.
   b. Measure the bottom side and make point S halfway across this side.
   c. Draw a line from point S to the vertex at the top.
   d. Place a ruler on the vertical centerline with 0 at point S.
   e. Mark point T on the vertical line one inch above point S. Draw a horizontal line crossing the triangle and intersecting the vertical line at point T.

How many triangles can be seen in the final design?

Lesson 77

Habitat for Humanity is an organization dedicated to building housing for people who are unable to purchase a home. In a short period of time, Habitat's many volunteers will do all of the necessary work to make a home for a family in need.

As you observe the silhouette of a house shown above, notice the many polygons that can be seen. A **polygon** is a closed plane figure with three or more sides. How many polygons do you count in the house silhouette?

Polygon	Sides	Vertices	Angles
Triangle	3	3	3
Quadrilateral	4	4	4
Pentagon	5	5	5
Hexagon	6	6	6
Octagon	8	8	8
Decagon	10	10	10

A **regular polygon** has sides that are equal in length and angles that are equal in size. These are called congruent sides and angles. An equilateral triangle is a regular polygon with congruent sides and angles. Scalene and isosceles triangles are not regular polygons. Identify the regular polygons in the drawing of the house.

Compare the pentagons shown. Identify the regular pentagon with congruent sides and angles.

Discuss why each statement is *true* or *false*.
- a. A scalene triangle is a regular polygon. F
- b. An equilateral triangle and a square are regular polygons. T
- c. Cubes are sometimes polygons. T
- d. Pentagons, hexagons, and octagons are often, but not always, regular polygons. F
- e. A right triangle may be a regular polygon. F

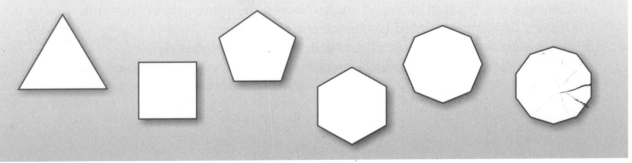

164

Name each polygon. Decide if it is a regular polygon as shown. Write *yes* or *no*.

1.

2. regular polygono

3. 0

4. regular polygano

5.

6.

7. regular poligano

8.

9. regular Poligono

10. regular poligono

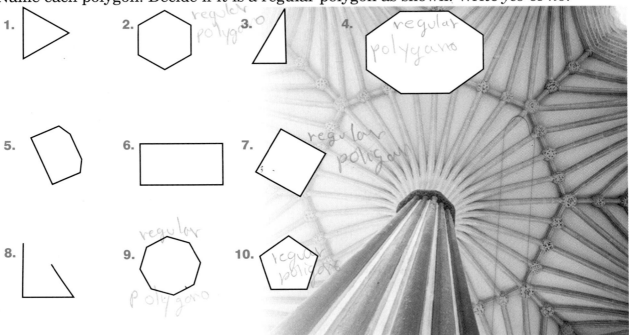

Complete each analogy.
11. Triangle is to quadrilateral as pentagon is to ░░░░.
12. Scalene triangle is to polygon as equilateral triangle is to ░░░░ ░░░░.
13. Quadrilateral is to octagon as hexagon is to ░░░░.

14. Mrs. Keenan wants her students to consider the attributes of various polygons. As she describes a specific polygon, the students need to identify and draw it. For each description below, tell which polygon the students should draw.

   a. A polygon that has three angles. The angles are 90°, 45°, and 45°.
   b. A polygon with two pairs of parallel line segments that are the same length. It has four right angles.
   c. This regular polygon has three pairs of parallel line segments and six angles.
   d. It is a polygon with two pairs of parallel line segments; one pair is greater in length than the other pair. There are four right angles.
   e. A regular polygon with four pairs of parallel line segments and eight angles.

15. Select an object in the classroom that is a polygon. Write a complete description of the polygon, including the number of sides and vertices, the types of angles, and properties of the line segments. Is it a regular polygon? Why or why not?

Lesson 78

Construct Meaning

The students planning the school fair developed a layout for ten booths. They wanted to use a quadrilateral shape for each booth. The plan the students drew is shown here. Is every booth a quadrilateral?

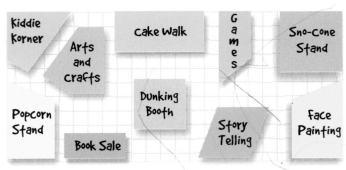

A **quadrilateral** is a polygon with four sides. The most common quadrilaterals in geometry are the parallelogram, rectangle, rhombus, square, and trapezoid.

parallelogram

A quadrilateral having opposite sides that are parallel. The opposite sides are congruent, or same length.

rectangle

A parallelogram with four right angles. Pairs of sides are congruent.

rhombus

A parallelogram having all sides congruent.

square

A rectangle having four congruent sides.

trapezoid

A quadrilateral with only two opposite sides parallel. The parallel sides are called **bases**.

Check Understanding

a. Which quadrilateral named above is not a parallelogram?

b. Name the quadrilaterals defined above that are apparent in the drawing of the layout of booths.

c. What is the total number of degrees in a rectangle? Will the total be the same for the square? Explain.

d. Which of the quadrilaterals are regular polygons?

166

Practice

Identify the figure that does not belong.

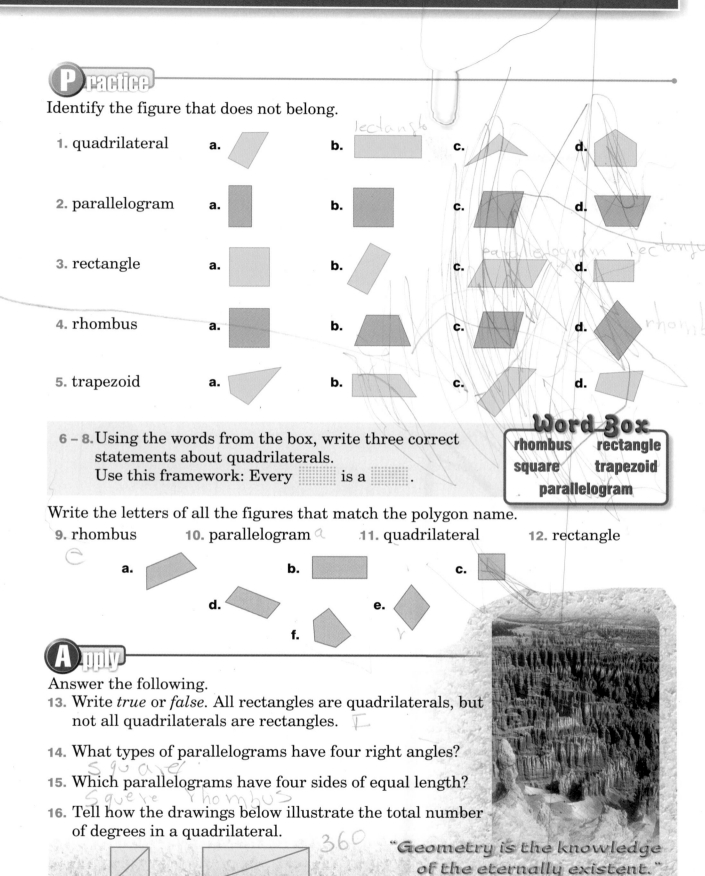

1. quadrilateral   a.   b.   c.   d.

2. parallelogram   a.   b.   c.   d.

3. rectangle   a.   b.   c.   d.

4. rhombus   a.   b.   c.   d.

5. trapezoid   a.   b.   c.   d.

6 – 8. Using the words from the box, write three correct statements about quadrilaterals.
Use this framework: Every ▦ is a ▦ .

Word Box

rhombus	rectangle
square	trapezoid
parallelogram	

Write the letters of all the figures that match the polygon name.

9. rhombus   10. parallelogram   11. quadrilateral   12. rectangle

a.   b.   c.

d.   e.

f.

Apply

Answer the following.

13. Write *true* or *false*. All rectangles are quadrilaterals, but not all quadrilaterals are rectangles.

14. What types of parallelograms have four right angles?

15. Which parallelograms have four sides of equal length?

16. Tell how the drawings below illustrate the total number of degrees in a quadrilateral.

"Geometry is the knowledge of the eternally existent."

Plato

Construct Meaning

When Mrs. Dale asked her fifth graders to compare a plane figure with a solid, Tyler drew a rectangle and compared his drawing to his math book. He said, "The rectangle I drew is a plane figure, but the book is a solid."

A solid has length, width, and height.

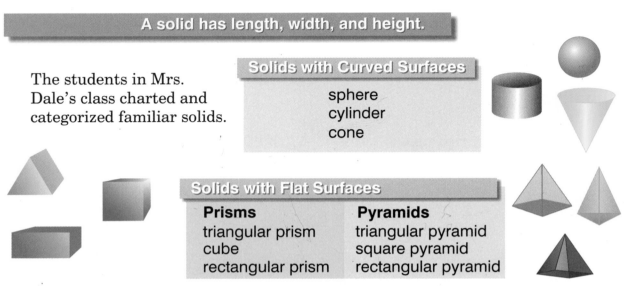

The students in Mrs. Dale's class charted and categorized familiar solids.

Solids with Curved Surfaces

sphere
cylinder
cone

Solids with Flat Surfaces

Prisms	Pyramids
triangular prism	triangular pyramid
cube	square pyramid
rectangular prism	rectangular pyramid

Any solid having only flat surfaces is called a **polyhedron**. Polyhedrons have faces, vertices, and edges.

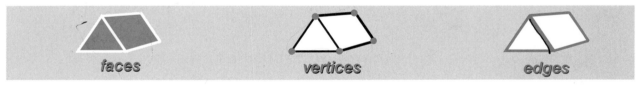

faces   vertices   edges

A **prism** is a polyhedron with two congruent bases and rectangular sides. Count the faces, vertices, and edges on the triangular prisms shown.

Each student in Mrs. Dale's class constructed a **pyramid**, which is a polyhedron named for its base with all other faces being triangles. The table shows the polygons needed to construct each type of pyramid.

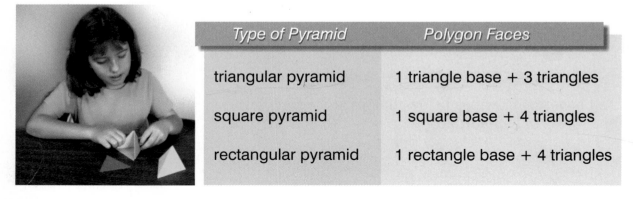

Type of Pyramid	Polygon Faces
triangular pyramid	1 triangle base + 3 triangles
square pyramid	1 square base + 4 triangles
rectangular pyramid	1 rectangle base + 4 triangles

✓ **Check Understanding**

a. How many faces, edges, and vertices do you count on the triangular pyramid?
4 faces   5 vertices

b. Are cones and cylinders polyhedrons? Explain your answer.

Complete the following chart.

Type of Prism	Polygon Faces
cube	c. 6 faces
triangular prism	d. 4 faces
rectangular prism	e. 5 faces

P ractice

1. Write the letter of each figure that is a polyhedron.

a.   b.   c.    d.

e.    f.   g.   h.

2. Construct at least three of the polyhedrons from the paper models supplied by your teacher. Make a table that shows each polyhedron you made and the number of faces, edges, and vertices it has.

Use a dictionary to find the geometric meaning of each of the following terms. Write each term with the appropriate definition.

3. face   4. edge   5. vertex   6. polyhedron   7. polygon

R eview

1. If two angles of a triangle are 30° and 40°, what is the third angle?

Write *acute, right,* or *obtuse* to describe the angle.

2. 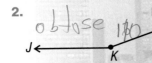 obtuse 180

3. 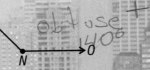 obtuse +90 140

4. 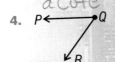 acute —90

5. Square is to rhombus as rectangle is to _____.

© Copyright 2001

169

Lesson 80

Construct Meaning

It is important to know many problem-solving strategies in mathematics. We use these strategies alone or in combination with each other to solve problems every day.

| WRITE AN EQUATION | USE A KNOWN EQUATION |
| USE DATA FROM A TABLE | USE LOGICAL REASONING |

Only part of Polygon A is showing. Visualize what may be hidden by the box using logical reasoning. Name each polygon.

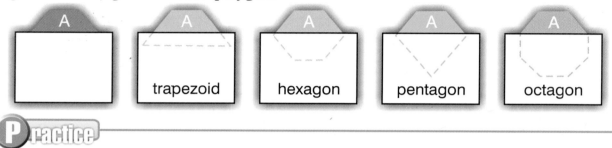

Practice

Use Table 1 to solve the following.

1. The angles in a parallelogram are 60°, 120°, and 60°. What is the measure of the fourth angle?

2. If a stop sign is a regular octagon, what is the measure of each of its angles?

3. A triangle has angles that measure 20° and 85°. What is the measure of the third angle?

4. The length of each of the five outer walls of the Pentagon building in Washington, D.C., is 921 feet. What is the angle where two walls of the Pentagon meet?

5. What is the measure of each angle in a regular hexagon?

6. Can a triangle have two right angles? Why or why not?

Polygon	Degrees
Triangle	180°
Quadrilateral	360°
Pentagon	540°
Hexagon	720°
Octagon	1,080°

Table 1

Write the names of some of the polygons which may be hidden by each box.

7. 8. 9.

In 1752, a mathematician names Leonhard Euler made a discovery that is true for solid figures. He wrote his findings in an equation:

$$Faces + Vertices - Edges = 2$$

Use the information about a cube to try Euler's equation. Then solve the following problems using the information from Table 2. Write an equation to show your work.

Table 2 Solid	Faces	Vertices	Edges
cube	6	8	12
triangular pyramid	4	4	
square pyramid	5	1	8
triangular prism	5	5	9
rectangular prism	6	8	12

10. How many edges are on a triangular pyramid?

11. What is the total number of vertices on a triangular prism?

12. How many vertices are found on a square pyramid?

13. The number of edges on a rectangular prism is ▦ .

14. Paul and his parents are planning to construct a frame for a flowerbed using large blocks of wood. The frame will be a 6-foot by 4-foot rectangle. The blocks of wood may be purchased as 1-foot squares for $3 each or 1-foot by 2-foot rectangles for $5 each. Paul drew a picture to determine the cost of using the square blocks. What will be the cost of the frame using the square blocks? the rectangular blocks?

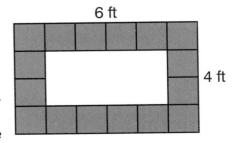

6 ft

4 ft

15. Megan said, "I can draw a parallelogram, a rhombus, a rectangle, a square, and a trapezoid by drawing only two polygons." Is that possible? If so, use a ruler to draw the two polygons.

Moments with Careers

My dad is a carpenter. He uses math in his work to estimate lumber and concrete and to figure roof pitches and proper stair layout.

Ryan
Colorado Springs, CO

Construct Meaning

A **circle** is a closed plane figure with all points an equal distance from the center. It is a part of many beautiful designs, including the Rose Window of the Great Cathedral of Chartres, France.

When you construct a circle, you discover its characteristics. A **compass** is a tool used to draw a circle with precision.

Use a compass and a ruler to draw a circle.

 1 Open the compass, set the point firmly on your paper, and move the pencil in a complete curve.

 **2** Mark a point at the center and label it with a letter. The letter is the name of your circle.

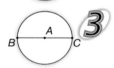 **3** Cut out the circle and fold it in half, making a **semicircle**. Open it and trace across the fold line. This is the **diameter**, a line segment crossing the center of a circle. Name the endpoints of the diameter.

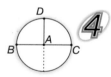 **4** Fold the semicircle in half. Open it and trace the vertical fold line from point A to the top of the circle. This line segment shows a **radius** of the circle, which is any line segment from the center to a point on the circle.

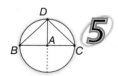 **5** Join the endpoint of this radius with each endpoint of the diameter. These are **chords**, line segments with both endpoints on the circle.

 6 The diameter of the circle divides it into two straight angles, each having 180°. The total measure of a circle is 360°.

Check Understanding

Set your compass to make a circle with a two-inch diameter. Be careful. If you open the compass 2 inches, what diameter results?

a. Draw the circle and name it.

b. Draw a diameter, name each endpoint, and measure with a ruler.

c. Make three radii and name all the endpoints. How long is the radius?

d. Use a protractor to measure the angles made by the diameter and each radii.

e. Draw three chords and name the endpoints.

**ractice**

1. What is the name of the circle?

2. Name the diameter.

3. Name the radius.

4. Name the chords which are not diameters.

5. Measure ∠*LIK* and ∠*JIL*, recording each measure. What is the sum of the two angles?

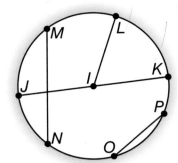

**pply**

6. A circle has 360°. If it is divided into four equal parts, what is the measure of each angle? Draw a model.

7. If the radius of circle *S* is 4.5 inches, what is the diameter?

8. How many degrees are in a semicircle?

9. If you want to make an octagon within a circle, would you draw chords or radii for the edges of the octagon? How many?

Write *true* or *false*.

10. Every point on a circle is an equal distance from the center.

11. A chord has the center of the circle as one endpoint.

12. A circle may have more than one diameter.

13. A circle may have more than one radius.

14. A circle divided into eight equal parts has 40° in each part.

15. The diameter of a circle may be three times as long as the radius.

Review

1. $3 \times 12 = \boxed{} \times 4$

2. $15 \times 4 = 3 \times \boxed{}$

3. $\boxed{} \times 2.5 = 5 \times 3$

4. $8.5 \times \boxed{} = 5 \times 17$

5. $9 \times 12 = 6 \times \boxed{}$

6. $\boxed{} \times 11 = 6 \times 22$

7. $5 \times 8 = 2 \times \boxed{}$

8. $12 \times 2 = \boxed{} \times 4$

9. $35 \times 2 = \boxed{} \times 5$

10. $16 \times 3 = 6 \times \boxed{}$

11. $\boxed{} \times 21 = 28 \times 3$

12. $7 \times 8 = \boxed{} \times 3.5$

Construct Meaning

Line symmetry exists when at least one line of symmetry can be drawn in a figure. A line of symmetry makes the two parts appear as mirror images. There are many examples of symmetry in the things created by God as well as in objects built by men.

These research aircraft from NASA's Dryden Flight Research Center in California show examples of both symmetry and **asymmetry**, where no lines of symmetry exist. Discuss your observations of the X-36 tailless fighter and the Gossamer Albatross.

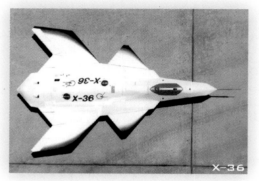

Imagine folding a figure on the line of symmetry. If the parts are an exact fit, it is symmetrical.

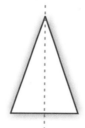
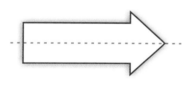
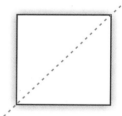

Do these figures have other lines of symmetry?

Look closely to determine how many lines of symmetry exist in each of the following designs.

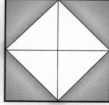
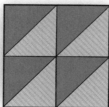
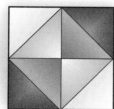

Check Understanding

Copy each figure. Draw the line(s) of symmetry on each figure.

a.

b.

c.

d.

e.

Practice

Copy each figure. Draw all the lines of symmetry. Write *none* if there are none.

1.
2.
3.
4.
5.

6.
7.
8.

Copy and complete each figure, using the red dotted line as the line of symmetry.

9.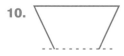
10.
11.
12.
13.

Apply

Observe each border pattern. Write how many lines of symmetry you find for each picture.

14.
15.
16.

17. How many possible lines of symmetry are in a circle?

18. On May 15, 1961, the first manned space flight of the U.S. Space Program took place. Astronaut Alan Shepard, Jr., flew a sub-orbital mission in a space capsule called *Freedom 7*. Write the name of the space capsule in uppercase letters. Which letters show horizontal symmetry? vertical symmetry?

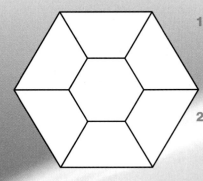

19. Consider the two hexagon designs. How many lines of symmetry can you count in the design at the left?

20. If you consider the colors shown on the right, how many lines of symmetry are there? (Pretend you are folding and yellow must touch yellow, blue must touch blue).

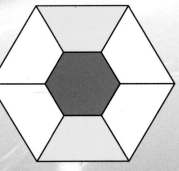

Lesson 83

 **Construct Meaning**

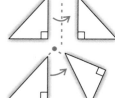

Transformations
Translations
Reflections
Rotations

Motion in geometry is often accomplished by making one of the transformations in this list of terms. Geometric **transformations** change the location or position of the figure, but not its size or shape.

A **translation**, or **slide**, requires moving the figure in a straight line. The figure changes its location, but not its position.

A **reflection**, or **flip**, is a move that turns the figure over on a line of symmetry.

A **rotation**, or **turn**, moves the figure around a fixed point.

Use a ruler to construct a scalene triangle with sides of 1 inch, $1\frac{1}{2}$ inches, and 2 inches. Cut it out carefully and follow the directions below. Make a chart.

1. Title your chart "Transformations."

2. List the name of each type of transformation in the left column of the chart.

3. Next to each term, trace your triangle, then use it to perform the transformation, tracing it in the new location or position to show your work.

Transformations		
Type	Figure 1	Figure 2
Translation		
Reflection		
Rotation		

Check Understanding

A pattern of right triangles may be made by using transformations. For example,

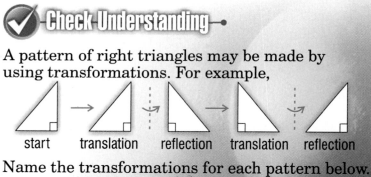

start   translation   reflection   translation   reflection

Name the transformations for each pattern below.

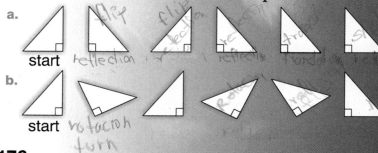

a.

start   reflection

b.

start   rotation
        turn

176

Practice

Identify each transformation using the terms *translation*, *reflection*, or *rotation*.

1. reflection

2. rotacion

3. rotacion

4. translation

5. translation

6. reflection

7. rotacion

8. reflection

Tell the possible series of transformations that were used.

9. translation

10. reflection

11. rotacion

Apply

12. Below are the first three steps for making an origami paper cup. Which step shows a reflection on a line of symmetry?

13. After step 2 is completed, what type of transformation is needed to reposition the paper to perform step 3?

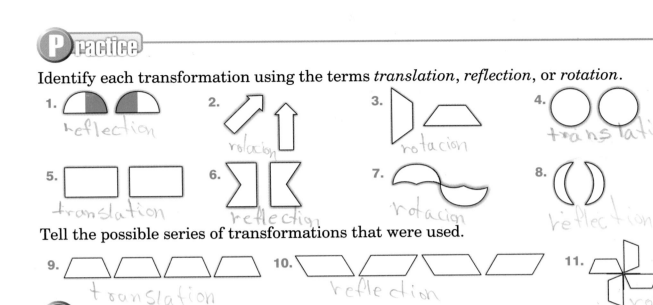

Step 1
Fold top corner to opposite corner.

Step 2
Fold top layer only, dividing the upper angle in half. Return to the position shown above.

Step 3
Hold it like this.

14. Use a square piece of dot paper and follow steps 1–6 to make an origami cup.

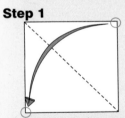

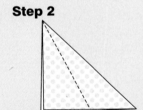

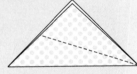

Step 4 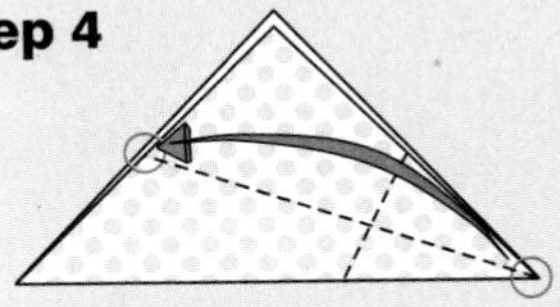
Fold the lower corner to the opposite edge.

Step 5 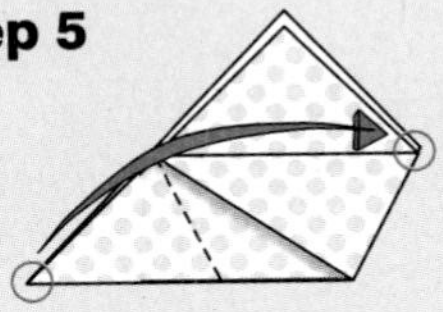
Fold the opposite side in a similar manner.

Step 6 
Separate top flaps and bring down to finish.

15. Look at the shape of your cup. Is it symmetrical? Does the drawing in step 6 show a symmetrical figure?

Construct Meaning

Samantha copied a picture of the *Skylab* to use on the cover of her report on space exploration. She needed to show more details of the satellite, so she copied the photograph again and enlarged it.

The photographs on the left show **congruent figures** that are the same shape and the same size.

If you compare *Skylab* in the enlarged photograph with the one in the original picture, you see figures that are the same shape but may not have the same size. These are called **similar figures**.

Rules of Congruence

A   B   M   N

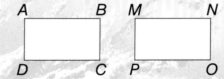

D   C   P   O

ABCD is congruent to *MNOP*.

$ABCD \cong MNOP$

The corresponding parts of congruent figures are congruent.

$\overline{AB} \cong \overline{MN}$ $\angle BAD \cong \angle NMP$

Name the other congruent line segments and angles.

The triangles below are congruent. They remain congruent when transformations are applied.

Congruent solids are the same shape and size. They have the same number of faces, edges, and vertices.

Rules of Similarity

Similar polygons must have the same shape. *diferen size*

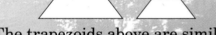

The trapezoids above are similar. The trapezoids below are not.

 *ds difen*

Rectangles and squares are not similar. Why?

These are similar triangles.

Equilateral

Isosceles

Scalene

Solids are similar if they are the same shape.

Congruence and Similarity

✓ Check Understanding

a. *MNOPQ* and *RSTUV* are both pentagons.
Name the congruent line segments and angles.

 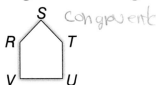 *Congruent*

b. Are the two pentagons shown below congruent or similar? Why?

  similar

Practice

Use a ruler to draw a congruent figure for each of the following. Each figure should face a different direction.

1.  **2.**  **3.**  *traslacion* **4.**

Draw a similar figure for each of the following.

5.  **6.**   **7.**  *rotacion* **8.**

Apply

9. Jeff built a model that was an exact replica of the *Vanguard 1* Satellite launched by the United States in 1958. After he built it, did Jeff have a congruent or a similar solid?

10. Juan and Katie had two identical sets of pattern blocks. Katie blocked Juan's view of her workspace. She asked him to listen and try to duplicate her design as he heard her explain which blocks she used and where she placed them. When finished, they discovered his design was a mirror image of hers. Were the designs similar or congruent? Why?

Review

Write the letter of the correct match for each term.

1. obtuse angles
2. line segments
3. lines of symmetry
4. parallel lines
5. perpendicular lines
6. acute angles
7. triangles
8. quadrilaterals
9. chords
10. rays

a. do not intersect
b. connect two points on a circle
c. sum of the angles is 360°
d. greater than 90°, less than 180°
e. intersect at right angles
f. line segments with one endpoint
g. divide figures into mirror images
h. sum of the angles is 180°
i. have two endpoints
j. less than 90°

Reflecting Your Geometry Knowledge

Identify each term.

1. An exact location in space.
2. An angle greater than 90°, but less than 180°.
3. A polygon having all sides equal in length and all angles equal in measure.
4. A polygon with four sides.
5. An infinite set of points going in both directions.
6. The endpoint where two rays intersect.
7. A closed, plane figure with three or more sides.
8. A tool used in the construction of angles.
9. A solid figure with flat faces.
10. A closed, plane figure having all points an equal distance from the center.

Identify each triangle as acute, obtuse, or right. Give the measure of the third angle.

11.
90
150

12.
90

13.
120
60

Write the letter of the best answer.

14. A quadrilateral having two sets of parallel lines, all the same length.
    a. parallelogram
    b. square
    c. rhombus
    d. both square and rhombus

15. A triangle with three sides of unequal length.
    a. isosceles triangle
    b. right triangle
    c. scalene triangle
    d. obtuse triangle

16. A polygon with eight congruent angles and eight congruent sides.
    a. pyramid
    b. hexagon
    c. octagon
    d. regular octagon

17. A polygon with only one set of perpendicular lines.
    a. regular hexagon
    b. right triangle
    c. parallelogram
    d. rhombus

18. A term describing many types of motion in geometry.
    a. transformation
    b. translation
    c. rotation
    d. reflection

19. A polyhedron with only triangular faces.
    a. prism
    b. pyramid
    c. triangular pyramid
    d. cylinder

Use the circle to answer the following.

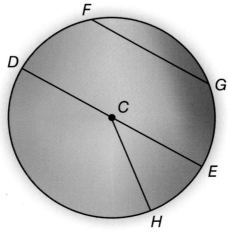

20. Name the circle.

21. Name the diameter shown.

22. $\overline{FG}$ is a ▒▒▒▒.

23. $\overline{CD}$ and $\overline{CE}$ are ▒▒▒.

24. ▒▒▒ is another radius of the circle.

25. $\angle HCE$ is a(n) ▒▒▒ angle.

26. $\angle DCH$ is a(n) ▒▒▒ angle.

27. $\angle ECD$ is a(n) ▒▒▒ angle.

Write *true* or *false*.

28. All intersecting lines are perpendicular.

29. An isosceles triangle and a scalene triangle could be similar.

30. When a symmetrical design is folded on a line of symmetry, the parts will match exactly.

31. A baseball and a soccer ball are congruent solids.

32. Draw a heart showing all lines of symmetry.

$\triangle LMN \cong \triangle POQ$

33. Name the congruent angles.

34. Name the congruent sides.

Name the transformation illustrated by each pair of figures.

35. rotation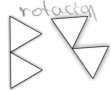

36. reflection

37. translation

38. reflection

39. Molly wants to use paper polygons to make polyhedrons. Name three polyhedrons she can make if she has seven squares and eight triangles.

40. Design a border that shows symmetry. Identify the line(s) of symmetry.

"Therefore thus says the Lord GOD: 'Behold, I lay in Zion a stone for a foundation. A tried stone, a precious cornerstone, a sure foundation; Whoever believes will not act hastily.'" Isaiah 28:16

Grade Five

7 Chapter

Lessons 86–96

Praise the LORD!
Praise the LORD from the heavens;
Praise Him in the heights!
Praise Him, all His angels;
Praise Him, all His hosts!

Psalm 148:1–2

Construct Meaning

Solar panels generate electrical power to energize satellites in space. Specialized equipment such as this Russian satellite helps with communication systems on earth.

• **Fractions can be used to describe the parts of a whole.**

A whole:

3 of the 4 sections are shaded.

number of parts shaded → $\underline{3}$ numerator
total number of equal parts → 4 denominator

Write $\frac{3}{4}$. Say "three-fourths."

• **Fractions can be used to describe the parts of a set.**

A set:

2 of the 5 satellites are colored.

number of parts shaded → $\underline{2}$ numerator
total number of equal parts → 5 denominator

Write $\frac{2}{5}$. Say "two-fifths."

• **Fractions can be counted on a number line.**

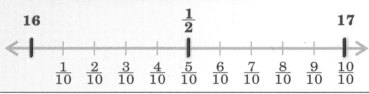

16     $\frac{1}{2}$ 17

$\frac{1}{10}$ $\frac{2}{10}$ $\frac{3}{10}$ $\frac{4}{10}$ $\frac{5}{10}$ $\frac{6}{10}$ $\frac{7}{10}$ $\frac{8}{10}$ $\frac{9}{10}$ $\frac{10}{10}$

Each section is $\frac{1}{10}$.

$\frac{10}{10}$ are one whole.

A **fraction** names part of a whole or part of a group.
A **numerator** represents the number of equal parts being considered.
A **denominator** represents the total number of equal parts of a whole.

Check Understanding

Write the fraction for the shaded part.

a.  $\frac{5}{25}$

b. $\frac{1}{3}$

c.  $\frac{2}{6}$

d. 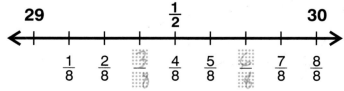 $\frac{2}{5}$

e. Write the missing eighths as you count from 29 to 30.

29     $\frac{1}{2}$ 30

$\frac{1}{8}$ $\frac{2}{8}$ $\frac{3}{8}$ $\frac{4}{8}$ $\frac{5}{8}$ $\frac{6}{8}$ $\frac{7}{8}$ $\frac{8}{8}$

Reviewing the Meaning of Fractions

P ractice

Write if the picture is a *whole* or a *set*. Write a fraction for the shaded part. Label the *numerator* and the *denominator*.

1.  $\frac{4}{7}$

2. 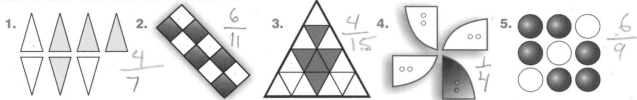 $\frac{6}{11}$

3. $\frac{4}{15}$

4. $\frac{1}{4}$

5. $\frac{6}{9}$

Draw a picture of a whole and another of a set to show each fraction.

6. $\frac{3}{8}$

7. $\frac{2}{9}$

8. $\frac{3}{4}$

9. $\frac{4}{5}$

10. $\frac{5}{6}$

Write each fraction.

11. five-eighths   12. two-thirds   13. seven-twelfths   14. one-fifth

15. What fraction of the week are Tuesday and Wednesday? $\frac{2}{7}$

16. What part of a dozen are three eggs?

17. What fraction of the year is January through June? $\frac{6}{12}$

18. What part of the year is the week of Christmas?

A pply

19. The Defense Support Program had nine satellites performing their function of detection. Two of the satellites had their solar paddles spread out. What fraction of the satellites had their solar paddles spread out?

20. One solar panel has 22 sections, but 15 are damaged. What part of this solar panel needs repair?

R eview

Write the letter of the figure that does not belong.

1. quadrilateral   a.   b.   c.   d.

2. parallelogram   a.   b.   c.   d.

Solve.

3. $\begin{array}{r} 42 \\ \times\ 7 \\ \hline \end{array}$

4. $\begin{array}{r} 56.2 \\ \times 0.19 \\ \hline \end{array}$

5. $\begin{array}{r} 53 \\ \times 23 \\ \hline \end{array}$

6. $61\overline{)38{,}552}$

7. $8\overline{)6.904}$

Construct Meaning

Christians around the world observe the birth of Christ in the month of December. Many families celebrate by preparing a birthday cake for Jesus.

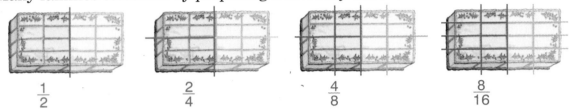

$\frac{1}{2}$ $\qquad$ $\frac{2}{4}$ $\qquad$ $\frac{4}{8}$ $\qquad$ $\frac{8}{16}$

Equivalent fractions name the same amount or number. One-half, two-fourths, four-eighths, and eight-sixteenths are equivalent fractions.

- To find equivalent fractions, multiply the numerator and the denominator by the same number.

$$\frac{1 \times 2}{3 \times 2} = \frac{2}{6}$$

$\frac{1}{3}$ $\qquad$ $\frac{2}{6}$ One-third and two-sixths are equivalent fractions.

- To find equivalent fractions, divide the numerator and the denominator by the same number.

$$\frac{4 \div 4}{12 \div 4} = \frac{1}{3}$$

$\frac{4}{12}$ $\qquad$ $\frac{1}{3}$ Four-twelfths and one-third are equivalent fractions.

To find a missing numerator of an equivalent fraction, find the number by which the denominator has been multiplied or divided. Perform the same operation on the numerator.	Use the same strategy to find a missing denominator.

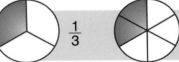

$\frac{3}{4} = \frac{6}{8}$ Think: $4 \times 2 = 8$ $3 \times 2 = 6$ $\frac{2}{3} = \frac{8}{12}$ Think: $2 \times 4 = 8$ $3 \times 4 = 12$

Use a number line to list equivalent fractions.

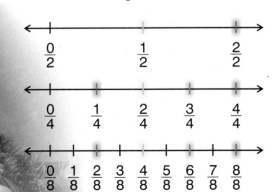

$\frac{1}{4} = \frac{2}{8}$ $\frac{1}{2} = \frac{2}{4} = \frac{4}{8}$

$\frac{3}{4} = \frac{6}{8}$ $\frac{2}{2} = \frac{4}{4} = \frac{8}{8}$

Mathematics Grade 5

Check Understanding

Draw two pictures to show equivalent fractions.

Example:

$\dfrac{3 \times 2}{5 \times 2} = \dfrac{6}{10}$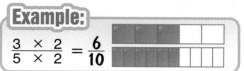

a. $\dfrac{2 \div 2}{12 \div 2} =$ b. $\dfrac{3}{8}$ c. $\dfrac{4}{16}$

Practice

Write equivalent fractions for the models.

1.  $\dfrac{6}{8}$ $\dfrac{2}{4}$

 $\dfrac{3}{4}$

2.  $\dfrac{4}{8}$

Write an equivalent fraction.

3. $\dfrac{3}{8} =$ ——   4. $\dfrac{2}{3}$ 5. $\dfrac{4}{6}$ 6. $\dfrac{5}{25}$ 7. $\dfrac{8}{32}$

Use the models to find the missing number.

8.    9.   10.

$\dfrac{1}{5} = \dfrac{2}{10}$ $\dfrac{3}{4} = \dfrac{6}{8}$ $\dfrac{2}{3} = \dfrac{8}{12}$

Write the missing number.

11. $\dfrac{2}{4} = \dfrac{8}{16}$ 12. $\dfrac{4}{5} = \dfrac{16}{20}$ 13. $\dfrac{1}{7} = \dfrac{4}{28}$ 14. $\dfrac{5}{9} = \dfrac{15}{27}$

$7 \times 4 = 28$ $5 \times 3 = 15$

$9 \times 3 =$

15. $\dfrac{10}{50} = \dfrac{20}{100}$ 16. $\dfrac{9}{10} = \dfrac{27}{30}$ 17. $\dfrac{7}{8} = \dfrac{35}{40}$ 18. $\dfrac{2}{7} = \dfrac{12}{42}$

$2 \times 6 = 12$

7×6

Write the next three equivalent fractions.

19. $\dfrac{1}{3}, \dfrac{2}{6}, \dfrac{3}{9}, \dfrac{4}{12}$ 20. $\dfrac{2}{7}, \dfrac{4}{14}, \dfrac{6}{21}, \dfrac{8}{28}$ 21. $\dfrac{4}{5}, \dfrac{8}{10}, \dfrac{12}{15}, \dfrac{16}{20}$

Apply

22. The Christmas tree was beautifully decorated. Two-fourths of the glass ornaments were red and four eighths were green. Was the number of red ornaments more, less, or equal to the amount of green ornaments?

23. Judy's sugar cookie recipe calls for one fourth dozen of eggs. Sue's recipe calls for four eggs. Whose recipe calls for fewer eggs?

 Construct Meaning

Jupiter has a rocky core and a diameter about eleven times that of Earth. The dark bands around Jupiter are called belts and the light bands are called zones. The distinctive feature of Jupiter is the Great Red Spot, a storm system. The color comes from chemicals in Jupiter's clouds. Nine-tenths of Jupiter is composed of hydrogen.

- Fractions and decimals can name numbers less than 1.

word form: nine-tenths

fraction: $\frac{9}{10}$

decimal: 0.9

ones	.	tenths	hundredths	thousandths
0	.	9	0	0

$\frac{1}{4}$ of Jupiter's moons are significantly larger than the others.

- Change $\frac{1}{4}$ to a decimal by multiplying the numerator and the denominator by the same number to make a fraction with a denominator of 10, 100, or 1,000. Then write a decimal.

$$\frac{1}{4} \overset{\times 25}{\underset{\times 25}{=}} \frac{25}{100} = 0.25$$

or - Change $\frac{1}{4}$ to a decimal by dividing the numerator by the denominator. Use long division.

```
     0.25
4)1.00
  - 8
    20
  - 20
     0
```

Use a calculator to check your division.

Press: 0.25

word form: twenty-five hundredths

fraction: $\frac{25}{100}$

decimal: 0.25

ones	.	tenths	hundredths	thousandths
0	.	2	5	0

- Fractions and decimals can name numbers greater than 1.

two and thirty-one hundredths

$2\frac{31}{100}$

2.31

ones	.	tenths	hundredths	thousandths
2	.	3	1	0

 Check Understanding

Write the selection from the shaded area on the right that matches the picture.

a.   b.   c.

ones	.	tenths	hundredths	thousandths
0	.	5	3	0

$\frac{1}{10}$

0.01

fifty-three hundredths

0.44

d. Use the denominator of 1,000 to rename the fraction. Then write it as a decimal on the place value chart.

$$\frac{31}{200} = \frac{}{}$$

ones	tenths	hundredths	thousandths

e. Divide the numerator by the denominator to find the decimal equivalent of $\frac{5}{8}$.

 31

Practice

Write the word form, a fraction, and a decimal for each model.

1. 2. 3.

Write an equivalent fraction using the given denominator.
Then write it as a decimal.

4. $\frac{1}{2} = \frac{}{10}$

5. $\frac{2}{5} = \frac{}{10}$

6. $\frac{7}{20} = \frac{}{100}$

7. $\frac{8}{25} = \frac{}{100}$

8. $\frac{32}{125} = \frac{}{1,000}$

9. $\frac{11}{250} = \frac{}{1,000}$

$$\frac{1}{5} = \frac{20}{100} = 0.20$$

Divide the numerator by the denominator to find the decimal equivalent.

10. $\frac{3}{4}$ 0.75

11. $\frac{4}{5}$ 0.80

12. $\frac{1}{8}$ 0.125

13. $\frac{5}{10}$ 0.50

14. $\frac{3}{20}$ 0.15

Write each decimal as a fraction.

15. 0.29 $\frac{29}{10}$

16. 0.2 $\frac{2}{10}$

17. 0.32 $\frac{32}{10}$

18. 0.07 $\frac{7}{10}$

19. 0.327 $\frac{327}{1000}$

Apply

20. The moon named Io orbits Jupiter in one and seventy-seven hundredths days. Write the orbital period as a decimal.

21. Two other moons complete their orbits faster than Io. Adrastea orbits Jupiter in 0.3 of a day. Thebe's orbital period is 0.68 of a day. Which moon orbits in less time than Amalthea, with an orbit time of 0.5 of a day? Which moon has a longer orbit than Amalthea?

Review

1. 4.07
   + 3.294

2. 89.5
   − 76.784

3. 0.54
   × 0.7

4. $18\overline{)96.912}$

5. 60.04
   − 13.15

Lesson 89

Jim's fifth grade class painted two large Christmas cards on 4' by 8' sheets of plywood to be displayed in the schoolyard during the holiday season. The first was a picture of an angel appearing to Mary; the second was Mary and Joseph going to Bethlehem. The class discussed arranging the cards horizontally or vertically.

> When a number has exactly two factors, one and itself, it is called a **prime number**. 2 is a prime number.

1 × 2

2 × 1

The class wanted the project to be an outreach to the city, so they showed the Christmas story using six cards. Showing the possible ways to arrange the cards helped to find the factors of the number 6.

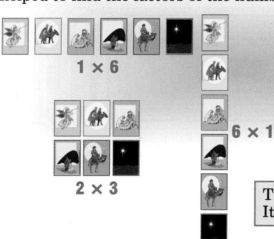

1 × 6

2 × 3

6 × 1

3 × 2

> The different factors used to make these arrangements are 1, 2, 3, and 6. When a number has more than two factors, it is called a **composite number**. 6 is a composite number.

> The number 1 has only one factor: itself. It is neither prime nor composite.

A **factor tree** is another way to find how many factors are in a number. Factoring a number until all the numbers are prime is called **prime factorization**.

> Think of two factors whose product is 24.
> List them.
>
> 3 is a prime number.
>
> Find two factors whose product is 8.
> List them.
>
> Find two factors of 4.
> List them.

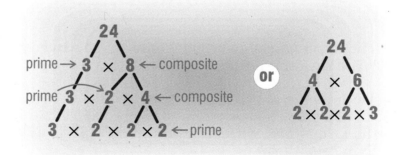

Since 24 has more than two factors (1, 2, 3, 4, 6, 8, 12, and 24), it is a composite number. The prime factors of 24 at the bottom of each tree are 3 × 2 × 2 × 2. The order of the factors on the second tree does not affect the product. Can you think of a third way to factor 24?

190

Mathematics Grade 5

Handwritten notes at top: 9×4=36. and XØ 11 12 13 14 and 18

Copy and complete each factor tree.

a.
```
      12
     /  \
    3  × 4
   /    / \
  3  × 2 × 2
```

b.
```
       32
      /  \
     4  × 8
    / \   / \
   2×2×2×4
  / | | | \
 2×2×2×1×4
```

c.
```
        48
       /  \
      8  × 6
     /|\   |\
    2×2×2×6
   /|  | | |\
  2×2×2×1×6
```

Handwritten: 30 ×10 / 60 / 800 / 00

List all the factors of each number. Write *prime*, *composite*, or *neither*.

1. 6   2. 30   3. 43   4. 10   5. 9   6. 5   7. 1

Copy and complete each factor tree.

8.
```
    4
   / \
  1 × 4
```

9.
```
     15
    /  \
 P 3 × 5 C
```

10.
```
     16
    /  \
   4  × 4
  / \  / \
 2×2×1×4
```

11.
```
        40
       /  \
      2  × 20
     /   / \
    2 × 5 × 4
   /   |   |\
  2 × 5 × 3 ×
```

List the prime factors.

12. 4   13. 15   14. 16   15. 40

Draw a factor tree for each number.

16. 24   17. 72   18. 6   19. 125   20. 248   21. 390

Use your calculator to multiply the prime numbers to check the accuracy of the factorization. Write *yes* or *no*. If no, correct the mistake.

22.
```
       418
      /  \
     2 × 209
    /   / \
   2 × 19 × 11
```

23.
```
          168
         /  \
        4 × 42
       / \  / \
      2×2×6×7
     / | | | \
    2×2×2×2×7
```

24.
```
         210
        /  \
       6 × 35
      / \  / \
     2×3×5×7
```

25. What are the two prime numbers whose product is 141?

1. Two angles of a triangle are 40° and 50°. What is the third angle?

2. Which angle is obtuse?

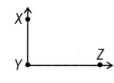
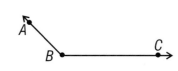

Construct Meaning

During the open house at Covenant Christian Academy, there were exhibits displayed that students had designed. One of the exhibits consisted of an impressive drawing of the planet Saturn with its rings. Saturn is the sixth planet from the sun, and its rings form from dust and ice orbiting the planet.

John's interactive exhibit included models of the planet Saturn which students could complete using attachable rings. John challenged his friends to make identical models using all of the black and yellow rings. What is the greatest number of identical models that can be made?

List the multiplication facts for each number.

12

1 × 12
OOOOOOOOOOOO

2 × 6
OOOOOO
OOOOOO

3 × 4
OOOO
OOOO
OOOO

18

1 × 18
OOOOOOOOOOOOOOOOOO

2 × 9
OOOOOOOOO
OOOOOOOOO

3 × 6
OOOOOO
OOOOOO
OOOOOO

List the factors of each number in numerical order.

12: 1, 2, 3, 4, 6, 12

18: 1, 2, 3, 6, 9, 18

> *Factors of a number divide a number evenly with <u>no</u> remainder.*

Compare the factors of 12 and 18.

The factors that appear for both products are 1, 2, 3, and 6. These factors are called **common factors** since they are factors of both products. The largest common factor is known as the **greatest common factor** (**GCF**). The GCF of 12 and 18 is 6.

There are 6 models of Saturn with each using 2 black and 3 yellow rings.

Check Understanding

List the factors of each number.

a. 30   b. 12   c. 9   d. 1   e. 21

List the common factors of each number. Identify the GCF by circling it.

f. 4 and 8   g. 6 and 15   h. 14 and 36   i. 9 and 24   j. 6, 18, and 27

k. List all the products that have a factor of 12.

24   36   40   48   60   69   72   81   84

List the factors of each number.

1. 12   **2.** 20   **3.** 11   **4.** 32   **5.** 45

List the common factors for each set of numbers. Circle the GCF.

6. 14 and 28   **7.** 24 and 32   **8.** 25 and 35   **9.** 55 and 66   **10.** 14, 21, 35, and 42

11. 18 and 27   **12.** 3 and 5   **13.** 18 and 81   **14.** 18 and 36   **15.** 10, 15, and 30

Write the letter of the pair of numbers that has the given GCF.

16. 4
  a. 8 and 12
  b. 9 and 12
  c. 6 and 12

17. 6
  a. 8 and 10
  b. 12 and 18
  c. 6 and 9

18. 9
  a. 14 and 16
  b. 36 and 54
  c. 27 and 45

19. 10
  a. 65 and 75
  b. 70 and 80
  c. 35 and 40

20. Kimberly's class sold school supplies at the open house. Pens and pencils were packaged separately, but the packages contained the same number of items. If there were 18 pencils and 14 pens, what was the greatest number of items in one package?

21. Gift baskets were presented to the winners of the exhibits. 30 lollipops, 42 pens, 48 stickers, and 18 notecards were divided evenly to make up the gift baskets.

  a. What is the greatest number of identical gift baskets you can make using all of the items?

  b. How many of each item will be in each basket?

  c. If you make three identical gift baskets using stickers and notecards, what is the maximum number of each that you could use?

Add.

1. 36,795
  +67,038

2. 2,456
    891
  +3,657

3. 1,356
  4,768
  2,347
  +6,902

4. 376
  894
   25
  +762

5. 2,576
  343
  555
  +4,809

Subtract.

6. 84,762
  −56,184

7. 6,000
  −2,597

8. 501
  −105

9. $98.79
  −96.97

10. 8.7
  −3.802

Solve.

11. 7,324
  ×   16

12. 0.724
  × 0.03

13. $7\overline{)0.049}$

14. $23\overline{)9,223}$

15. $14\overline{)786}$

 Construct Meaning

For a class field trip, Rhonda's teacher permitted the students to choose from the options of going to the zoo, the war memorial, or the space museum. 24 of the 32 students decided to go to the space museum where they could learn more about the planet Uranus that lies on its side instead of standing straight up.

The class vote of 24 out of 32 can be expressed as a fraction.

$\dfrac{24}{32}$ numerator / denominator

24 out of 32

A fraction is in **simplest form**, or lowest terms, when the greatest common factor of the numerator and denominator is 1. Write $\frac{24}{32}$ in simplest form.

- List the factors of 24 and 32 to find the greatest common factor (GCF).
  24: 1, 2, 3, 4, 6, 8, 12, 24
  32: 1, 2, 4, 8, 16, 32   The GCF of 24 and 32 is 8.

  The GCF is the largest number that will divide evenly into the numerator and the denominator.

- Divide the numerator and denominator by the GCF, 8.

  $\dfrac{24 \div 8}{32 \div 8} = \dfrac{3}{4}$ $\frac{24}{32}$ in the simplest form is $\frac{3}{4}$.

Write $\frac{24}{32}$ in simplest form using another method.

- Divide the numerator and denominator by any common factor until the GCF is 1.

  $\dfrac{24 \div 4}{32 \div 4} = \dfrac{6}{8} \longrightarrow \dfrac{6 \div 2}{8 \div 2} = \dfrac{3}{4}$ 3 and 4 have no common factor greater than 1.
  $\frac{3}{4}$ is in simplest form.

Look at the fraction drawing above. Can you see how $\frac{24}{32} = \frac{3}{4}$? Explain.

 Check Understanding

List the factors of the numerator and denominator of $\frac{6}{18}$ to find the GCF.

a. 6: ▦, ▦, ▦, ▦   b. 18: ▦, ▦, ▦, ▦, ▦, ▦   c. The GCF of 6 and 18 is 6.

Divide the numerator and denominator by the GCF to find the simplest form.

d. 6 ÷ 2 = 3   e. 18 ÷ 6 = 9   f. $\dfrac{6}{18} = \dfrac{3}{9}$ in simplest form.

g. $\dfrac{6 \div 2}{18 \div 2} = \dfrac{3}{9} \longrightarrow \dfrac{3 \div 3}{9 \div 3} = \dfrac{1}{3}$ The numerator and denominator were divided by ▦, and then ▦ until the GCF was 1.

List the factors of the numerator and the denominator. Use the GCF to divide. Write the fraction in simplest form.

1. $\frac{16}{24}$ 2. $\frac{15}{35}$ 3. $\frac{9}{12}$ 4. $\frac{3}{15}$ 5. $\frac{8}{24}$

Write each fraction in simplest form.

6. $\frac{8}{20}$ 7. $\frac{10}{15}$ 8. $\frac{28}{42}$ 9. $\frac{9}{15}$ 10. $\frac{4}{28}$

11. $\frac{3}{27}$ 12. $\frac{5}{25}$ 13. $\frac{16}{48}$ 14. $\frac{22}{44}$ 15. $\frac{5}{100}$

16. $\frac{63}{75}$ 17. $\frac{168}{224}$ 18. $\frac{200}{400}$ 19. $\frac{170}{198}$ 20. $\frac{102}{408}$

Is the fraction in simplest form? Write *yes* or *no*. If your answer is no, divide and write the simplest form of the fraction.

21. $\frac{6}{13}$ 22. $\frac{7}{11}$ 23. $\frac{6}{8}$ 24. $\frac{9}{18}$ 25. $\frac{3}{5}$

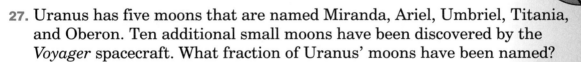

Write the fractions in simplest form (or lowest terms).

26. Nine out of the eleven rings of Uranus are less than six miles wide. What fraction of the rings are more than six miles wide?

27. Uranus has five moons that are named Miranda, Ariel, Umbriel, Titania, and Oberon. Ten additional small moons have been discovered by the *Voyager* spacecraft. What fraction of Uranus' moons have been named?

The atmosphere of Uranus consists of 85 parts hydrogen, 12 parts helium, and 3 parts methane. What fraction of the atmosphere is:

28. hydrogen?

a. $\frac{12}{100} = \frac{3}{25}$

b. $\frac{85}{100} = \frac{17}{20}$

c. $\frac{3}{100}$

29. helium?

a. $\frac{12}{100} = \frac{3}{25}$

b. $\frac{3}{100}$

c. $\frac{22}{25}$

30. hydrogen and methane?

a. $\frac{88}{100} = \frac{22}{25}$

b. $\frac{85}{100} = \frac{17}{20}$

c. $\frac{12}{100} = \frac{3}{25}$

31. helium and methane?

a. $\frac{85}{100} = \frac{17}{20}$

b. $\frac{3}{100}$

c. $\frac{15}{100} = \frac{3}{20}$

Write four equivalent fractions.

1. $\frac{1}{3}$ 2. $\frac{1}{4}$ 3. $\frac{1}{2}$ 4. $\frac{1}{5}$ 5. $\frac{1}{6}$

 **Construct Meaning**

Mrs. Shay invited the class to put up an interactive bulletin board. The class chose a space theme. There were planets, stars, moons, rings, pictures of astronauts, spacecraft, and interstellar material. Stars came in packages of 4 and moons came in packages of 6. If an equal number of stars and moons were used, what was the least number of stars and moons used?

The multiples of a number are found by multiplying that number by 1, 2, 3, etc.

List the multiples of 4 and 6.

| **4:** | 4, 8, 12, 16, 20, 24, 28, 32, 36, 40 |
| **6:** | 6, 12, 18, 24, 30, 36, 42, 48, 54, 60 |

The multiples that are the same for two or more numbers are called **common multiples**. The common multiples of 4 and 6 are 12, 24, and 36.

The smallest multiple that is common to two or more numbers is the **least common multiple (LCM)**. The LCM of 4 and 6 is 12.

12 moons and 12 stars were used.

Find the least common multiple of 2, 3, and 4.

2:	2, 4, 6, 8, 10, 12, 14, 16, 18, 20
3:	3, 6, 9, 12, 15, 18, 21, 24, 27, 30
4:	4, 8, 12, 16, 20, 24, 28, 32, 36, 40

The LCM of 2, 3, and 4 is 12.

The least common multiple can be used to find the **least common denominator (LCD)** for fractions.

The LCD of $\frac{1}{2}$ and $\frac{1}{3}$ is 6.

 **Check Understanding**

List six multiples of each number.

a. 5   b. 7   c. 8   d. 9   e. 10

List at least five multiples of each number.

f. 3 and 6   g. 5 and 3   h. 8 and 10   i. 4 and 5   j. 4 and 12

Find the least common multiple for each set of numbers.

k. 5 and 6   l. 2 and 5   m. 9 and 12   n. 3 and 8   o. 2, 4, and 6

p. What is the least common denominator for $\frac{1}{4}$ and $\frac{1}{5}$?

$\frac{1}{4}$: $\frac{1}{4}$, $\frac{2}{8}$, $\frac{3}{12}$, $\frac{4}{16}$, $\frac{5}{20}$

$\frac{1}{5}$: $\frac{1}{5}$, $\frac{2}{10}$, $\frac{3}{15}$, $\frac{4}{20}$, $\frac{5}{25}$

List four multiples of each number.

1. 6 2. 4 3. 12 4. 3 5. 11

List at least six multiples of each number.

6. 4 and 8 7. 5 and 10 8. 6 and 12 9. 4 and 6 10. 9 and 11

Find the least common multiple for each set of numbers.

11. 6 and 9 12. 3 and 7 13. 2 and 4 14. 7 and 9 15. 3, 6, and 9

16. Mrs. Shay divided her class into two groups. Group 1 was given permission to do the bulletin board activities three times a week. Due to scheduling, Group 2 received permission to use the board four times a week. Monday was the first day they all began to use it. When both groups had used the bulletin board the same number of times, how many weeks had passed for Group 1? How many weeks had passed for Group 2? How many times had permission been given to each group?

Group 1 | Week 1 | Week 2 | Week 3 | Week 4 | ⬚ times

Group 2 | Week 1 | Week 2 | Week 3 | ⬚ times

17. One group went for 15-minute sessions. Another group went for 20-minute sessions. How many minutes had each group spent when all the students had spent an equal amount of time?

18. Use your calculator to find the multiples of larger numbers. Find the LCM of 36 and 42.

Press [ON/AC] [+] [3] [6] [=] [=] [=] [=] [=] [=] [=] [=]

Press [ON/AC] [+] [4] [2] [=] [=] [=]

 What is the LCM of 36 and 42?

Continue pressing [=] until a common multiple appears.

Copy the set of fractions if they are equivalent. If they are not, write *not equivalent*.

1. $\frac{1}{2} = \frac{13}{26}$ 2. $\frac{3}{7} = \frac{22}{49}$ 3. $\frac{2}{5} = \frac{12}{30}$ 4. $\frac{4}{6} = \frac{12}{24}$ 5. $\frac{2}{3} = \frac{14}{21}$

Name each figure.

6. A———B 7. F· 8. J———K 9. O———P 10.

"Now the multitude of those who believed were of one heart and one soul; neither did anyone say that any of the things he possessed was his own, but they had all things in common." Acts 4:32

Lesson 93

 Construct Meaning

Two fifth grade classes were surveyed as to whether they would prefer an astronaut or an astronomer to share personal experiences at the conclusion of the study on planets. In Mrs. Marsh's room $\frac{1}{2}$ of the students voted to have an astronaut visit the classroom; in Mr. Alexander's room $\frac{3}{8}$ of the students voted for the astronaut. Compare the two fractions to find which classroom was more supportive of the astronaut coming to visit the classroom.

• Use fraction bars to compare fractions.

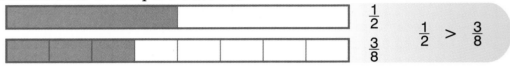

$\frac{1}{2}$

$\frac{3}{8}$

$\frac{1}{2} > \frac{3}{8}$

• Use a number line to compare fractions.

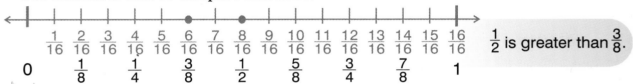

$\frac{1}{16}$ $\frac{2}{16}$ $\frac{3}{16}$ $\frac{4}{16}$ $\frac{5}{16}$ $\frac{6}{16}$ $\frac{7}{16}$ $\frac{8}{16}$ $\frac{9}{16}$ $\frac{10}{16}$ $\frac{11}{16}$ $\frac{12}{16}$ $\frac{13}{16}$ $\frac{14}{16}$ $\frac{15}{16}$ $\frac{16}{16}$

0   $\frac{1}{8}$ $\frac{1}{4}$ $\frac{3}{8}$ $\frac{1}{2}$ $\frac{5}{8}$ $\frac{3}{4}$ $\frac{7}{8}$ 1

$\frac{1}{2}$ is greater than $\frac{3}{8}$.

• Use equivalent fractions that have a common denominator.

Check the denominators of $\frac{1}{2}$ and $\frac{3}{8}$.

Since they are different, find a common denominator to write equivalent fractions.

The least common multiple of 2 and 8 is 8. Use the LCM as the denominator to rewrite the fractions.

$\frac{1}{2} = \frac{4}{8}$ $\frac{3}{8} = \frac{3}{8}$

Compare the numerators. Since $\frac{4}{8} > \frac{3}{8}$, then $\frac{1}{2} > \frac{3}{8}$.

REMEMBER:
If the denominators are the same, just compare the numerators.

$\frac{2}{5} < \frac{4}{5}$

> Mrs. Marsh's class was more supportive of the astronaut's visit.

Check Understanding

Follow the steps to compare $\frac{2}{3}$, $\frac{3}{4}$, and $\frac{1}{6}$. Write the missing multiple for each denominator.

a. 3: 3, 6, 9, ▦, 15

b. 4: 4, 8, ▦, 16

c. 6: 6, ▦, 18

d. The LCM is ▦.

Write an equivalent fraction using the LCM as the LCD.

e. $\frac{2}{3} = \frac{▦}{▦}$ f. $\frac{3}{4} = \frac{▦}{▦}$ g. $\frac{1}{6} = \frac{▦}{▦}$

h. Compare the numerators to order the fractions above from greatest to least.

Comparing and Ordering Fractions

ractice

Compare. Write >, < or = .

1. $\frac{1}{3}$ ⬚ $\frac{1}{4}$ 2. $\frac{1}{5}$ ⬚ $\frac{1}{2}$ 3. $\frac{3}{6}$ ⬚ $\frac{5}{6}$ 4. $\frac{2}{3}$ ⬚ $\frac{1}{2}$ 5. $\frac{6}{8}$ ⬚ $\frac{3}{4}$

6. $\frac{7}{9}$ ⬚ $\frac{5}{9}$ 7. $\frac{5}{8}$ ⬚ $\frac{9}{10}$ 8. $\frac{5}{20}$ ⬚ $\frac{1}{4}$ 9. $\frac{5}{12}$ ⬚ $\frac{1}{4}$ 10. $\frac{5}{7}$ ⬚ $\frac{6}{7}$

Write a fraction sentence which contains the symbol shown.

11. >   12. <   13. =

Draw and shade the models. Compare by writing >, < or = .

14.   15. ◯◯   16.   17. ◯◯

$\frac{2}{8}$ ⬚ $\frac{1}{4}$ $\frac{1}{6}$ ⬚ $\frac{1}{3}$ $\frac{4}{5}$ ⬚ $\frac{3}{5}$ $\frac{6}{10}$ ⬚ $\frac{3}{5}$

Write in order from the least to the greatest.

18. $\frac{1}{2}, \frac{1}{3}, \frac{1}{4}$ 19. $\frac{2}{5}, \frac{3}{4}, \frac{1}{10}$ 20. $\frac{3}{6}, \frac{1}{6}, \frac{3}{9}$ 21. $\frac{4}{6}, \frac{1}{3}, \frac{3}{8}$

pply

22. The astronaut brought some delicious freeze-dried snacks for a group of 20 students to sample. $\frac{1}{2}$ of the students chose the Berry Blast, $\frac{1}{5}$ chose the Double Chocolate Saucer, and $\frac{3}{10}$ chose the Ice-Cream Sandwich.

a. Which dessert was sampled by the most students?
b. Order the desserts from the most popular to the least popular.
c. Which would you have sampled?

Review

Find the GCF.

1. 24 and 32   2. 28, 42, and 35

Find the LCM.

3. 3 and 7   4. 3, 6, and 9

Solve.

5. 472×0.8 6. $94,763 + 8,507$ 7. $17\overline{)39.695}$ 8. $572.9 - 48.376$ 9. $1,207 \times 36$

Construct Meaning

The guest astronaut displayed two air tanks and discussed their features. He invited students to lift the tanks. Paul announced that one was heavier than the other. The gauge on one tank showed one whole tank. The other tank was $\frac{3}{4}$ full.

The amount of air contained in both tanks is $\frac{7}{4}$ or $1\frac{3}{4}$ of the tanks.

$\frac{7}{4}$ is an improper fraction. An **improper fraction** has a numerator greater than or equal to the denominator. An improper fraction is greater than or equal to one. A **proper fraction** is less than one.

$1\frac{3}{4}$ is a mixed number. A **mixed number** has a whole number and a fraction.

Rename the improper fraction $\frac{8}{5}$ as a mixed number.

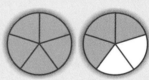

$$5\overline{)8} \quad \begin{array}{c} 1\frac{3}{5} \\ -5 \\ \hline 3 \end{array}$$

Divide the denominator into the numerator.

Write the remainder over the divisor in fractional form in the quotient.

$\frac{8}{5} = 1\frac{3}{5}$ mixed number

Rename the mixed number $2\frac{2}{3}$ as an improper fraction.

$3 \times 2 = 6$ Multiply the denominator by the whole number.

$6 + 2$ Add the numerator.

$\frac{8}{3}$ Write the sum over the denominator.

$2\frac{2}{3} = \frac{8}{3}$ improper fraction

Sometimes an improper fraction can be renamed as a whole number. $\frac{6}{3} \longrightarrow 3\overline{)6}^{\,2}$

A whole number can be renamed as an improper fraction. $9 \longrightarrow \frac{9}{1}$

 Check Understanding

Write a fraction and a mixed number for each picture.

a.   b.   c.

Identify each type of number.

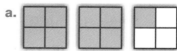

d. $\frac{9}{5} = 1\frac{4}{5}$ e. $\frac{4}{7} =$ f. $1\frac{2}{3} = \frac{5}{3}$ g. 8

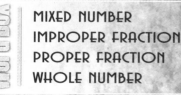

MIXED NUMBER
IMPROPER FRACTION
PROPER FRACTION
WHOLE NUMBER

200

Draw and shade models for each number.

1. $1\frac{1}{3}$ 2. $2\frac{3}{4}$ 3. $\frac{4}{2}$ 4. $3\frac{1}{5}$ 5. 4

Rename as a mixed number or a whole number. Write in simplest form.

6. $\frac{7}{4} = 1\frac{3}{4}$ 7. $\frac{6}{5} = 1\frac{1}{5}$ 8. $\frac{14}{2} = 7\frac{1}{2}$ 9. $\frac{9}{7} = 1\frac{2}{7}$ 10. $\frac{12}{9} = 1\frac{3}{9}$

11. $\frac{8}{3} = 2\frac{2}{3}$ 12. $\frac{10}{5} = 2$ 13. $\frac{11}{5} = 2\frac{1}{5}$ 14. $\frac{24}{7} = 3\frac{3}{7}$ 15. $\frac{50}{6} = 8\frac{2}{6}$

Rename as an improper fraction.

16. $4\frac{2}{3} = \frac{4}{5}$ 17. $1\frac{1}{2} = \frac{3}{2}$ 18. $6 = \frac{72}{12}$ 19. $7\frac{5}{8}$ 20. $9\frac{1}{4} = \frac{37}{4}$

21. $2\frac{1}{6} = \frac{13}{6}$ 22. $3\frac{4}{9} = \frac{31}{9}$ 23. $5\frac{3}{7} = \frac{38}{7}$ 24. $8\frac{2}{5} = \frac{42}{5}$ 25. $2 = \frac{8}{4}$

26. The class enjoyed the visiting astronaut. Their behavior was exceptional and they asked interesting questions. The teacher was pleased and asked a parent to provide a treat for the class. For snack time the next day each student was given one slice of pizza. The pizzas were cut into eight slices each. There were 23 students in the class. Write an improper fraction then rename it as a mixed number to show how much pizza was eaten.

27. If the parent brought in three whole pizzas, was there a slice left for the teacher?

28. The parent also brought strawberry string licorice. Each student was given a piece $\frac{1}{2}$ foot long. Write an improper fraction then rename it as a mixed number to show how many feet of licorice were given to the students.

29. Pluto is 1,430 miles in diameter, and its moon Charon is 745 miles in diameter. How many miles larger in diameter is Pluto than Charon?

Review

Write in order from the least to the greatest.

1. $\frac{1}{2}, \frac{1}{8}, \frac{1}{4}, \frac{3}{8}$ 2. $\frac{3}{4}, \frac{5}{8}, \frac{1}{2}, \frac{1}{3}$ 3. $\frac{2}{5}, \frac{6}{10}, \frac{4}{5}, \frac{5}{10}$

Solve.

4. $4\overline{)90.72}$ 5. 596×34 6. $87,002 - 30,863$ 7. $17\overline{)16,779}$ 8. $0.247 + 1.8$

 **Check Understanding**

The class wanted to show their appreciation to the visiting astronaut by making some cookies. Miss Randall assigned different ingredients to be measured by the students. Who measured the larger amount of each ingredient?

a. Tim measured $\frac{3}{4}$ cup of flour and John measured $\frac{2}{3}$ cup.
b. Michelle measured $\frac{1}{4}$ cup of shortening and Tina measured $\frac{1}{3}$ cup.
c. Erin measured $\frac{1}{8}$ teaspoon of salt and Jill measured $\frac{1}{4}$ teaspoon.
d. Bruce measured $\frac{1}{2}$ cup of sugar and Josie measured $\frac{1}{3}$ cup.

 **Practice**

Write the fraction in its simplest form.

1. Mother uses a recipe that calls for nine ingredients. She has five of the ingredients. What fraction of the ingredients does Mother need to purchase?

2. Jane made a birthday cake for her husband. If it took 0.4 of an hour to bake, what fraction of an hour did it take?

3. A salad requires two-fourths of a cup of green peppers. The recipe book records that amount in fractional form. How would it appear in the recipe book?

The banquet was a success! Many students received awards. Out of 100 students, 35 received athletic awards, 42 received academic awards, and 23 received musical awards. Write the letter of the fraction of the awards for each category.

4. athletic
   a. $\frac{42}{100} = \frac{21}{50}$
   b. $\frac{35}{100} = \frac{7}{20}$
   c. $\frac{23}{100}$

5. academic
   a. $\frac{35}{100} = \frac{7}{20}$
   b. $\frac{58}{100} = \frac{29}{50}$
   c. $\frac{42}{100} = \frac{21}{50}$

6. musical
   a. $\frac{23}{100}$
   b. $\frac{35}{100} = \frac{7}{20}$
   c. $\frac{42}{100} = \frac{21}{50}$

7. athletic and musical
   a. $\frac{42}{100} = \frac{2}{50}$
   b. $\frac{23}{100}$
   c. $\frac{58}{100} = \frac{29}{50}$

Use the chart to tell which piece(s) of fabric each person should buy.

Precut for Craft Activities

COLOR	LENGTH
red	$\frac{3}{6}$ yard
blue	$\frac{2}{3}$ yard
green	$\frac{3}{4}$ yard
yellow	$\frac{1}{4}$ yard
pink	$\frac{4}{8}$ yard

8. Susie calculates she can use $\frac{6}{9}$ yard of this color to make a head scarf.

9. Tonya needs a little more than $\frac{2}{3}$ yard to decorate a table.

10. Paula needs $\frac{1}{2}$ yard of two different colors.

11. Tasha needs $\frac{3}{8}$ yard to make a rag doll. Is there enough yellow fabric?

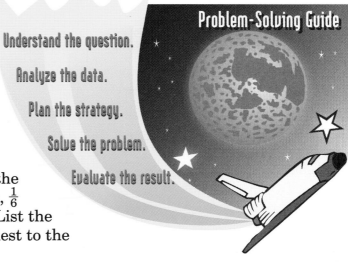

Problem-Solving Guide

Understand the question.

Analyze the data.

Plan the strategy.

Solve the problem.

Evaluate the result.

12. Walter's grandfather planted a small garden last spring. He planted 20 rows of vegetables. Three of the rows were corn. What fraction of the garden was planted in corn?

13. For a Super Bowl party, Barton's mother made a nut bowl mix. $\frac{1}{5}$ of the bowl was Brazil nuts, $\frac{1}{2}$ was pecans, $\frac{1}{6}$ was almonds, and $\frac{2}{15}$ was walnuts. List the nuts that were used from the smallest to the greatest quantity.

14. During a typical February, the United States celebrates the birthdays of two of its presidents—George Washington and Abraham Lincoln—honored as great leaders. What fraction of the month do these two days represent?

15. Dole drank $2\frac{1}{3}$ glasses of milk while enjoying some of his mother's fresh chocolate chip cookies. The glasses show thirds. Copy the drawing and shade sections to show how much milk Dole drank. Write that amount as an improper fraction.

16. Melissa has three brothers. Their ages are 24, 32, and 18. What is the greatest common factor of the ages of the brothers?

17. After the retreat, Jason spent $1\frac{3}{4}$ hours driving home. Charles spent $1\frac{5}{6}$ hours driving to his home. Who spent more time driving?

18. Dad used a board $16\frac{1}{2}$ feet long to replace a rotten board in the fence. The other boards in the fence were $\frac{33}{2}$ feet long. Was the replacement board too long, too short, or just the right length?

19. If 90 out of 100 people asked said that they watched some part of the Olympics 2000, which decimal represents this group?

    a. 0.9   **b.** 0.09   **c.** 0.009

20. The mechanic needs to make each fraction equivalent to $\frac{1}{2}$.

    a. $\frac{}{12}$ **b.** $\frac{}{16}$ **c.** $\frac{}{56}$

21. Make each fraction equivalent to $\frac{1}{3}$.

    a. $\frac{}{9}$ **b.** $\frac{}{24}$ **c.** $\frac{}{30}$

22. What is the greatest number of identical Valentine bags that could be made if 20 stickers, 40 heart candies, and 30 Valentine cards were divided equally?

In the 1980s Pluto was closer to the sun than Neptune. NASA reports that the last time Pluto was this close to the sun, George Washington was a boy!

23. Leon has completed through Lesson 95 of this book. What part of the book has he completed?

Focusing on Fractional Forms

Write the letter of the definition that matches the term.

_____ 1. equivalent fractions
_____ 2. composite number
_____ 3. LCM
_____ 4. fractions and decimals
_____ 5. improper fraction
_____ 6. prime number
_____ 7. mixed number
_____ 8. GCF

a. a number with exactly two factors
b. largest common factor of two or more products
c. numerator is greater than or equal to the denominator
d. a number with more than two factors
e. name the same amount or number
f. a whole number and a fraction
g. smallest multiple that is common to two or more numbers
h. name part of a whole

Write a fraction for the shaded part.

9.

10.

11.

12.

Write the fraction.

13. three-sevenths   14. four-eighths   15. nine-seventeenths

Write the word form, the fraction, and the decimal for each picture.

16.

ones	tenths	hundredths	thousandths
1	4	5	0

17.

18.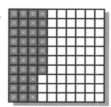

Rename the fraction by using the given denominator.

19. $\frac{2}{5} = \frac{}{10}$ 20. $\frac{1}{2} = \frac{}{100}$ 21. $\frac{13}{250} = \frac{}{1,000}$

Write the decimal.

22. four and thirty-six hundredths   23. one-tenth   24. two and thirteen-thousandths

Find the missing number of the equivalent fraction.

25. $\frac{2}{3} = \frac{}{12}$ 26. $\frac{4}{7} = \frac{}{35}$ 27. $\frac{3}{25} = \frac{6}{}$

List all the factors of each number. Write *prime* or *composite*.

28. 20   **29.** 17   **30.** 36

Draw a factor tree for each number.

31. 72   **32.** 25   **33.** 164

List the common factors. Circle the GCF.

34. 9 and 12   **35.** 4 and 16   **36.** 6, 18, 24

Write each fraction in simplest form.

37. $\frac{18}{21}$ **38.** $\frac{10}{45}$ **39.** $\frac{12}{24}$ **40.** $\frac{10}{60}$

Find the least common multiple for each set of numbers.

41. 3 and 4   **42.** 7 and 9   **43.** 6, 9, and 12

Compare. Write >, < or = .

44. $\frac{2}{3}$ ⬚ $\frac{6}{9}$ **45.** $\frac{3}{6}$ ⬚ $\frac{4}{6}$ **46.** $\frac{5}{6}$ ⬚ $\frac{3}{4}$ **47.** $\frac{1}{8}$ ⬚ $\frac{1}{4}$

Write in order from the least to the greatest.

48. $\frac{1}{2}, \frac{1}{3}, \frac{1}{4}$ **49.** $\frac{3}{4}, \frac{2}{3}, \frac{4}{5}$ **50.** $\frac{3}{8}, \frac{4}{6}, \frac{1}{3}$

Rename as a mixed number.

51. $\frac{8}{3}$ **52.** $\frac{35}{6}$ **53.** $\frac{78}{7}$

Rename as a fraction.

54. $3\frac{2}{5}$ **55.** $6\frac{1}{8}$ **56.** $4\frac{5}{7}$

57. Marci brought candy bars to share with her classmates for her birthday. She gave each one a third. There are 22 students in her class. Write an improper fraction, then rename it as a mixed number to show how many candy bars were eaten.

Grade Five

8
Chapter
Lessons 97–110

Lift up your eyes to the heavens,
And look on the earth beneath.

Isaiah 51:6a

Construct Meaning

Cyndi and her mother made trail mix for a family camping trip. They put $\frac{2}{3}$ cup of sunflower seeds into the mixture. Cyndi's friend Molly brought $\frac{1}{3}$ cup of sunflower seeds for the trail mix when she came to help with the food preparation. What was the total amount of sunflower seeds?

$$\frac{2}{3} \text{ cup} + \frac{1}{3} \text{ cup} = \frac{3}{3} \text{ cup} = 1 \text{ cup}$$

At the campground, Cyndi and Molly found a one-mile fitness course marked with signs showing tenths of a mile. Molly completed $\frac{9}{10}$ of the course, and Cyndi finished at the sign that said $\frac{6}{10}$ mile. What is the difference between the distances the girls covered?

$$\frac{9}{10} \text{ mile} - \frac{6}{10} \text{ mile} = \frac{3}{10} \text{ mile}$$

> When fractions have like denominators, add or subtract the numerators. The denominator stays the same.

Molly asked Cyndi's mother to tell her the proportions, or parts, of the trail mix. The proportions may be stated as fractions.

$\frac{1}{6}$ nuts $\qquad$ $\frac{2}{6}$ sunflower seeds $\qquad$ The rest of the trail mix was raisins.

What proportion of the trail mix was raisins?

Add $\frac{1}{6} + \frac{2}{6} =$ ▦ Subtract $\frac{6}{6} -$ ▦ $=$ ▦

Express the proportion of raisins in the simplest form.

Make a model to show the fractional parts of the trail mix. Use your circle divided into six equal parts. To show the proportions of the trail mix, label the appropriate fractional parts as *nuts*, *sunflower seeds*, or *raisins*.

Check Understanding

Write the correct answer in simplest form.

a. $\frac{8}{12} + \frac{3}{12}$
b. $\frac{3}{8} + \frac{1}{8}$
c. $1 - \frac{5}{10}$
d. $\frac{7}{8} -$ ▦ $= \frac{3}{8}$

Add and Subtract Like Fractions

ractice

Find the sum. Write your answer in simplest form.

1. $\frac{2}{4} + \frac{1}{4}$ 2. $\frac{3}{8} + \frac{3}{8}$ 3. $\frac{5}{7} + \frac{1}{7}$ 4. $\frac{2}{6} + \frac{3}{6}$ 5. $\frac{2}{5} + \frac{2}{5}$

Find the missing addend.

6. $\frac{1}{2} + \boxed{} = 1$ 7. $\frac{1}{3} + \boxed{} = \frac{2}{3}$ 8. $\frac{6}{11} + \boxed{} = \frac{10}{11}$ 9. $\boxed{} + \frac{3}{8} = \frac{7}{8}$ 10. $\frac{2}{9} + \boxed{} = 1$

Subtract. Write your answer in simplest form.

11. $\frac{11}{12} - \frac{9}{12}$ 12. $\frac{5}{6} - \frac{3}{6}$ 13. $\frac{8}{11} - \frac{2}{11}$ 14. $\frac{5}{9} - \frac{3}{9}$ 15. $\frac{9}{17} - \frac{4}{17}$

Complete each equation.

16. $\frac{11}{15} - \boxed{} = \frac{8}{15}$ 17. $\frac{3}{4} - \boxed{} = \frac{1}{4}$ 18. $\frac{5}{8} - \boxed{} = \frac{3}{8}$ 19. $\frac{7}{9} - \boxed{} = \frac{5}{9}$ 20. $\frac{5}{12} - \boxed{} = \frac{1}{12}$

Use the drawing to write the equation.

21.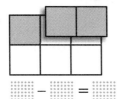

$\boxed{} - \boxed{} = \boxed{}$

22.

$\boxed{} - \boxed{} = \boxed{}$

23. $\boxed{} + \boxed{}$

$\boxed{} + \boxed{} = \boxed{}$

 pply

24. A recipe for salt dough is one part flour and three parts salt. Express the amount of salt in the recipe as a fraction. If you double the recipe to make the dough for crafts, using two cups of flour, how much salt will you need?

25. Jean had a chocolate bar that was divided into eight equal segments. She gave three friends two segments each. Express as a fraction the amount each friend received. How much does Jean have left?

26. Mr. Murray drives twenty miles to work each weekday. He fills the tank of his car with gasoline on Monday morning and calculates that he uses $\frac{1}{6}$ of a tank each day. Use a fraction to tell how much gasoline is in the tank on Thursday morning.

R eview

Find the least common multiple.

1. 3, 4, 2   2. 2, 5, 6   3. 3, 6, 12   4. 6, 9, 12   5. 2, 5, 8

Lesson 98

Construct Meaning

Captain Dominic L. Gorie, United States Navy, became an astronaut in 1995. He was the pilot of the *Discovery* Space Shuttle for a mission that orbited and docked with the Russian space station *Mir*. On his second trip into space, Captain Gorie and his crew were part of the Shuttle Radar Topography Mission that mapped more than forty-seven million square miles of the earth's land surface.

Astronauts use prepackaged food. If two packages of drink mix weighing $1\frac{1}{4}$ ounces each are combined, what is the total weight?

To add mixed numbers

$1\frac{1}{4}$ **ounces**	Add the fractions.
$+\ 1\frac{1}{4}$ **ounces**	Add the whole numbers.
$2\frac{2}{4} = 2\frac{1}{2}$ ounces	Write the answer in simplest form.

A large container of juice contained $48\frac{6}{10}$ ounces. If $16\frac{1}{10}$ ounces are poured into a pitcher, how many ounces are left in the jar?

To subtract mixed numbers

$48\frac{6}{10}$ **ounces**	Subtract the fractions.
$-\ 16\frac{1}{10}$ **ounces**	Subtract the whole numbers.
$32\frac{5}{10} = 32\frac{1}{2}$ ounces	Write the answer in simplest form.

Check Understanding

a. Write the steps needed to add or subtract mixed numbers. Explain why it is important to work in this order.

b. A student worked on homework for $1\frac{1}{4}$ hours, $\frac{3}{4}$ hour, 1 hour, and $1\frac{3}{4}$ hours. Was the total time period greater than or less than five hours? Express the difference between five hours and the total time spent doing homework as a fraction and as minutes.

210

Mathematics Grade 5

ractice

Add or subtract the mixed numbers. Write the answer in simplest form.

1. $21\frac{1}{2}$
$+ 19\frac{1}{2}$

2. $15\frac{2}{8}$
$+ 2\frac{3}{8}$

3. $18\frac{4}{5}$
$- 7\frac{2}{5}$

4. $6\frac{7}{10}$
$+ 5\frac{1}{10}$

5. $33\frac{6}{8}$
$- 29\frac{1}{8}$

6. $9\frac{2}{3}$
$- 8\frac{1}{3}$

7. $14\frac{11}{12}$
$- 9$

8. $50\frac{1}{4}$
$- 25\frac{1}{4}$

9. $15\frac{1}{3}$
$+ 15\frac{1}{3}$

10. $37\frac{8}{9}$
$- 4\frac{5}{9}$

11. $19\frac{5}{16}$
$- 6\frac{1}{16}$

12. $31\frac{5}{12}$
$- 2\frac{3}{12}$

13. $8\frac{1}{10} + 18\frac{6}{10} + 13$

14. $2\frac{5}{12} + 23\frac{1}{12} + 16\frac{4}{12}$

15. $17 + 9\frac{2}{9} + 6\frac{5}{9}$

pply

16. A ten-kilometer race is $6\frac{2}{10}$ miles in length and a five-kilometer race is $3\frac{1}{10}$ miles long. What is the mileage a runner covers in a fifteen-kilometer race?

17. An astronaut involved in a medical study recorded his liquid intake. On Monday, he drank $40\frac{5}{8}$ ounces of orange drink. On Tuesday, he drank $38\frac{5}{8}$ ounces of orange drink and $8\frac{2}{8}$ ounces of milk. What was his total liquid intake on Tuesday? What was the difference between his liquid intake on Monday and Tuesday?

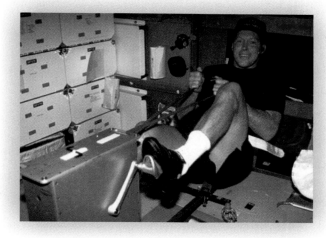

18. Astronauts are required to exercise daily while orbiting the earth in the Space Shuttle. If an astronaut exercised $\frac{3}{4}$ of an hour on Monday, Wednesday, and Friday, and $\frac{1}{4}$ hour on Tuesday and Thursday, what is the total exercise time for the five days?

eview

Write >, < or = for each pair of fractions.

1. $\frac{5}{6}$ ⬚ $\frac{2}{3}$

2. $\frac{3}{8}$ ⬚ $\frac{3}{4}$

3. $\frac{8}{16}$ ⬚ $\frac{12}{24}$

4. $\frac{4}{5}$ ⬚ $\frac{7}{10}$

5. $\frac{7}{21}$ ⬚ $\frac{1}{3}$

6. $\frac{2}{3}$ ⬚ $\frac{3}{4}$

7. $\frac{7}{8}$ ⬚ $\frac{1}{2}$

8. $\frac{1}{3}$ ⬚ $\frac{4}{12}$

9. $\frac{5}{8}$ ⬚ $\frac{3}{4}$

10. $\frac{1}{4}$ ⬚ $\frac{1}{12}$

 **Construct Meaning**

The fifth grade classes at King's Kids' Academy received pizza for their help with a community project. After school, the pizza remaining from three classes was served at the Bible Club meeting. Determine the amount of pizza given to the Bible Club.

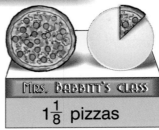

MRS. BABBITT'S CLASS
$1\frac{1}{8}$ pizzas

MR. GORDON'S CLASS
$1\frac{5}{8}$ pizzas

MRS. BURDICK'S CLASS
$1\frac{6}{8}$ pizzas

Add the mixed numbers.

$$
\begin{array}{r}
1\frac{1}{8} \\
1\frac{5}{8} \\
+\,1\frac{6}{8} \\
\hline
3\frac{12}{8}
\end{array}
$$

Add the fractions

Add the whole numbers.

Rename the sum.

$3\frac{12}{8} = 3 + 1\frac{4}{8}$ Change the improper fraction to a mixed number.

$= 4\frac{4}{8}$ Add.

$= 4\frac{1}{2}$ Write the answer in simplest form.

The Bible Club was given $4\frac{1}{2}$ pizzas.

Use mental math when possible.

Suppose the remaining pizza had been $1\frac{1}{8}$, $1\frac{5}{8}$, and $1\frac{7}{8}$. $1\frac{1}{8} + 1\frac{5}{8} + 1\frac{7}{8}$

Find the mixed numbers with fractions having a sum of 1.

$1\frac{1}{8} + 1\frac{7}{8} = 2\frac{8}{8} = 2 + 1 = 3$

Add the whole number to the remaining mixed number. $3 + 1\frac{5}{8} = 4\frac{5}{8}$

 **Check Understanding**

Choose the correct sum.

a. $2\frac{4}{5} + 3\frac{2}{5}$ b. $6\frac{3}{10} + 7\frac{9}{10}$ c. $15\frac{7}{8} + 12\frac{7}{8}$ d. $1\frac{2}{7} + 2\frac{5}{7} + 4\frac{2}{7}$

$5\frac{1}{5}$ $6\frac{1}{5}$ $5\frac{4}{5}$ $14\frac{3}{10}$ $13\frac{9}{10}$ $14\frac{1}{5}$ $27\frac{6}{8}$ $28\frac{3}{4}$ $28\frac{5}{8}$ $8\frac{3}{7}$ $7\frac{2}{7}$ $8\frac{2}{7}$

e. Use mental math to find the sum of $21\frac{3}{4} + 10 + 5\frac{1}{4}$.

Add the mixed numbers, renaming the sum. Write the answer in simplest form.

1. $5\frac{6}{10}$
   $+ 3\frac{5}{10}$

2. $2\frac{5}{6}$
   $+ 4\frac{5}{6}$

3. $6\frac{2}{5}$
   $+ 7\frac{4}{5}$

4. $3\frac{1}{7}$
   $+ 7\frac{6}{7}$

5. $2\frac{7}{8}$
   $+ 3\frac{3}{8}$

6. $17\frac{2}{5}$
   $+ 3\frac{3}{5}$

7. $4\frac{3}{8}$
   $+ 3\frac{6}{8}$

8. $9\frac{5}{9}$
   $+ 5\frac{6}{9}$

9. $8\frac{3}{4}$
   $+ 2\frac{3}{4}$

10. $10\frac{4}{6}$
    $+ 11\frac{3}{6}$

11. $13\frac{9}{8}$
    $+ \quad\frac{9}{8}$

12. $8\frac{2}{3}$
    $+ 4\frac{2}{3}$

13. $5\frac{3}{10} + 11\frac{8}{10}$

14. $20\frac{5}{9} + 32\frac{4}{9}$

15. $15\frac{5}{12} + 14\frac{7}{12}$

16. $1\frac{6}{8} + 4\frac{3}{8} + 7\frac{7}{8}$

17. $8 + 32\frac{2}{3} + 24\frac{2}{3}$

18. $7\frac{4}{5} + 9\frac{2}{5} + 8\frac{3}{5}$

Use mental math to find and rename the sum.

19. $2\frac{1}{7} + 10 + 3\frac{6}{7}$

20. $3\frac{2}{3} + 5\frac{1}{3} + 6\frac{1}{3}$

21. $3\frac{3}{4} + 4 + 6\frac{1}{4}$

22. $5\frac{6}{8} + 2\frac{2}{8} + 9$

Space Shuttle Crew Floating

Apply

23. Astronauts spend three hundred hours in the Shuttle Mission Simulator (SMS) to complete training in all aspects of operating the Space Shuttle. If an astronaut trains for $7\frac{2}{4}$ hours on Monday, $6\frac{3}{4}$ hours on Tuesday, and $7\frac{3}{4}$ hours on Wednesday, what is the total training time?

24. On a space mission, an astronaut tells time according to how long it has been since liftoff. Suppose an astronaut ate a meal $5\frac{1}{4}$ hours after liftoff and slept $8\frac{3}{4}$ hours after starting the meal. At the time she went to sleep, how many hours had passed since liftoff?

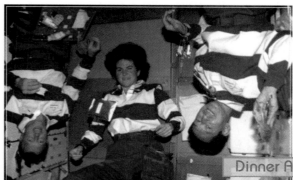

25. Compute the total mileage of an exercise program for female astronauts if they ran the following distances during one week: $3\frac{1}{10}$ miles, $4\frac{5}{10}$ miles, $5\frac{6}{10}$ miles, $6\frac{2}{10}$ miles.

Dinner Aboard the Space Shuttle

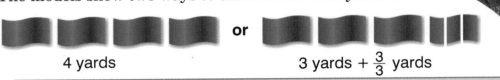 **Construct Meaning**

A student at New Life Christian Academy donated four yards of fabric to his teacher. The class used two-thirds of a yard for an art project. How much fabric was left after the project was completed?

The models show two ways to think of the four yards of fabric.

4 yards   **or**   3 yards + $\frac{3}{3}$ yards

To subtract a fraction from a whole number, rename the whole number using fractional parts that match the number being subtracted.

$$\begin{array}{r} 4 \\ -\ \frac{2}{3} \\ \hline \end{array}$$ Rename the whole number to match the fraction. $\longrightarrow$ $\begin{array}{r} 3\frac{3}{3} \\ -\ \frac{2}{3} \\ \hline 3\frac{1}{3} \end{array}$ Subtract the fractions.
Subtract the whole numbers.
yards remaining

Suppose the class had used $2\frac{1}{4}$ yards of fabric for the art project.

$$\begin{array}{r} 4 \\ -\ 2\frac{1}{4} \\ \hline \end{array}$$ Rename the whole number. $\longrightarrow$ $\begin{array}{r} 3\frac{4}{4} \\ -\ 2\frac{1}{4} \\ \hline 1\frac{3}{4} \end{array}$ Subtract the fractions.
Subtract the whole numbers.
yards remaining

Julia bought one yard of fabric. If she used $\frac{3}{8}$ yard to make book covers, how much fabric does she have left?

$$1 \text{ yard} - \frac{3}{8} \text{ yard} = \boxed{}$$

A fraction may be subtracted from the number one by changing it to a fraction with the same denominator.

$$1 - \frac{3}{8} = \frac{8}{8} - \frac{3}{8} = \frac{5}{8} \text{ yard}$$

 **Check Understanding**

Rename and subtract.

a. $5 - 2\frac{3}{5}$ b. $1 - \frac{7}{16}$ c. $6 - \frac{3}{10}$

d. A student wrote the following during math practice.

$$4 - 2\frac{3}{8} = 2\frac{5}{8} \qquad 12 - 9\frac{1}{6} = 3\frac{5}{6}$$

What error was made when the student renamed the whole numbers?

ractice

Write the missing number to rename each whole number.

1. $2 = 1\dfrac{}{10}$ 2. $12 = 11\dfrac{}{3}$ 3. $1 = \dfrac{}{20}$ 4. $7 = 6\dfrac{}{5}$ 5. $14 = 13\dfrac{}{6}$

Subtract. Write the answer in simplest form.

6. $\begin{array}{r} 9 \\ -3\frac{1}{3} \\ \hline \end{array}$
7. $\begin{array}{r} 1 \\ -\frac{5}{6} \\ \hline \end{array}$
8. $\begin{array}{r} 15 \\ -5\frac{1}{2} \\ \hline \end{array}$
9. $\begin{array}{r} 6 \\ -3\frac{3}{8} \\ \hline \end{array}$
10. $\begin{array}{r} 4 \\ -\frac{1}{4} \\ \hline \end{array}$

11. $\begin{array}{r} 7 \\ -3\frac{2}{6} \\ \hline \end{array}$
12. $\begin{array}{r} 10 \\ -\frac{6}{10} \\ \hline \end{array}$
13. $\begin{array}{r} 7 \\ -3\frac{3}{5} \\ \hline \end{array}$
14. $\begin{array}{r} 8 \\ -\frac{3}{8} \\ \hline \end{array}$
15. $\begin{array}{r} 20 \\ -\frac{2}{5} \\ \hline \end{array}$

16. $\begin{array}{r} 43 \\ -12\frac{5}{9} \\ \hline \end{array}$
17. $\begin{array}{r} 14 \\ -13\frac{2}{3} \\ \hline \end{array}$
18. $\begin{array}{r} 62 \\ -40\frac{5}{8} \\ \hline \end{array}$
19. $\begin{array}{r} 38 \\ -17\frac{1}{7} \\ \hline \end{array}$
20. $\begin{array}{r} 50 \\ -10\frac{3}{12} \\ \hline \end{array}$

pply

21. Tom practiced playing the guitar for three-fourths of an hour on Monday and played the same amount of time on Tuesday. If his goal was to practice for three hours before his lesson on Wednesday, how much more time will he need to practice before the lesson?

22. Mrs. Ledger filled the eighteen-gallon gasoline tank of her car. She used three gallons of gasoline on her weekend trip. What fraction of the gasoline was left in the tank?

eview

Solve. Write the answer in simplest form.

1. $\begin{array}{r} \frac{9}{10} \\ -\frac{5}{10} \\ \hline \end{array}$
2. $\begin{array}{r} \frac{3}{4} \\ +\frac{2}{4} \\ \hline \end{array}$
3. $\begin{array}{r} 1\frac{2}{3} \\ +\frac{2}{3} \\ \hline \end{array}$
4. $\begin{array}{r} 3\frac{5}{6} \\ +2\frac{3}{6} \\ \hline \end{array}$
5. $\begin{array}{r} 5\frac{3}{5} \\ -1\frac{2}{5} \\ \hline \end{array}$
6. $\begin{array}{r} \frac{7}{8} \\ -\frac{3}{8} \\ \hline \end{array}$

7. $\begin{array}{r} 20\frac{1}{2} \\ +14\frac{1}{2} \\ \hline \end{array}$
8. $\begin{array}{r} 18\frac{4}{5} \\ -11\frac{2}{5} \\ \hline \end{array}$
9. $\begin{array}{r} 10\frac{6}{7} \\ -\frac{2}{7} \\ \hline \end{array}$
10. $\begin{array}{r} 4\frac{2}{10} \\ +7\frac{9}{10} \\ \hline \end{array}$
11. $\begin{array}{r} \frac{8}{15} \\ +\frac{7}{15} \\ \hline \end{array}$
12. $\begin{array}{r} 6\frac{5}{9} \\ +\frac{7}{9} \\ \hline \end{array}$

 Construct Meaning

Juan and his sister Marta need $2\frac{1}{3}$ cups of flour for a birthday cake they are making for their mother. They found $\frac{2}{3}$ cup of flour in the pantry. How much more flour do they need for the cake?

Subtract to find the difference between $2\frac{1}{3}$ and $\frac{2}{3}$.
Rename the mixed number to increase the numerator of its fraction.

Rename $2\frac{1}{3}$ in order to subtract $\frac{2}{3}$.

$$2\frac{1}{3}$$
$$-\ \ \frac{2}{3}$$

$$2\frac{1}{3} = 2 + \frac{1}{3}$$
$$= 1 + 1 + \frac{1}{3}$$
$$= 1 + \frac{3}{3} + \frac{1}{3}$$
$$= 1 + \frac{4}{3}$$
$$= 1\frac{4}{3}$$

Use the renamed number.

$1\frac{4}{3}$ Subtract the fractions.

$-\ \ \frac{2}{3}$ Subtract the whole numbers.

$1\frac{2}{3}$ cups of flour needed

Solve $8\frac{3}{8} - 2\frac{7}{8}$. Rename $8\frac{3}{8}$ and use the renamed number to subtract.

$$8\frac{3}{8} = 7 + 1 + \frac{3}{8}$$
$$= 7 + \frac{8}{8} + \frac{3}{8}$$
$$= 7 + \frac{11}{8}$$
$$= 7\frac{11}{8}$$

$7\frac{11}{8}$ Subtract the fractions.

$-\ 2\frac{7}{8}$ Subtract the whole numbers.

$5\frac{4}{8} = 5\frac{1}{2}$ Write in simplest form.

 Check Understanding

Rename each mixed number as a whole number with an improper fraction.

a. $7\frac{3}{8}$ b. $12\frac{1}{10}$ c. $3\frac{1}{4}$

d. Select the problem that requires renaming the first number. Explain your reasoning. Solve.

$3\frac{5}{8} - 2\frac{3}{8}$ $11\frac{5}{7} - 9\frac{6}{7}$ $20\frac{7}{9} - 15\frac{5}{9}$

Practice

Rename and subtract. Write the answer in simplest form.

1. $9\frac{1}{4}$
   $-4\frac{3}{4}$

2. $3\frac{2}{5}$
   $-2\frac{3}{5}$

3. $6\frac{5}{8}$
   $-3\frac{6}{8}$

4. $10\frac{3}{5}$
   $-3\frac{4}{5}$

5. $12\frac{2}{6}$
   $-6\frac{5}{6}$

6. $15\frac{2}{9}$
   $-9\frac{7}{9}$

7. $16\frac{3}{11}$
   $-4\frac{9}{11}$

8. $24\frac{2}{7}$
   $-12\frac{6}{7}$

9. $20\frac{5}{13}$
   $-18\frac{9}{13}$

10. $5\frac{1}{3}$
    $-2\frac{2}{3}$

Subtract, renaming when necessary. Write the answer in simplest form.

11. $10\frac{4}{5} - 7\frac{2}{5}$

12. $4\frac{1}{4} - \frac{3}{4}$

13. $13 - 3\frac{5}{9}$

14. $21\frac{6}{8} - 4\frac{3}{8}$

15. $9\frac{1}{7} - \frac{5}{7}$

16. $7\frac{1}{7} - 3$

Apply

17. Mrs. Lirley measured her classroom bulletin board before asking her students to make border designs. The height of the bulletin board is $3\frac{7}{8}$ feet and the width is $5\frac{5}{8}$ feet. What is the difference between the height and the width of the bulletin board?

18. The border the students made for the longer side of the bulletin board extended to $6\frac{1}{8}$ feet. How much of the border must be trimmed to make it fit the bulletin board?

Review

Write each improper fraction as a mixed number. Write the answer in simplest form.

1. $\frac{12}{10}$

2. $\frac{15}{2}$

3. $\frac{26}{3}$

4. $\frac{30}{7}$

5. $\frac{21}{4}$

Subtract. Write the answer in simplest form.

6. $7 - \frac{2}{3}$

7. $16 - \frac{3}{8}$

8. $9 - 1\frac{3}{4}$

9. $12 - \frac{7}{8}$

10. $15 - 3\frac{3}{10}$

Construct Meaning

The owner of Sew Fine Fabrics donated partial bolts of fabric and ribbon to a group of students planning a mission trip to an orphanage in Ukraine. The students sorted the ribbon by the length written on each bolt. In one box, they placed the ribbon that had $\frac{1}{2}$ yard or less remaining. In the second box, the bolts with more than $\frac{1}{2}$ yard of ribbon were saved for sewing projects at the orphanage. The students used the guidelines below as they read the fraction on each bolt and sorted the ribbon.

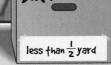

Box 1 — less than $\frac{1}{2}$ yard

$y < \frac{1}{2}$

The numerator is 1 and the denominator is greater than 2.

$$\frac{1}{3} < \frac{1}{2} \qquad \frac{1}{4} < \frac{1}{2}$$

The numerator is less than half of the denominator.

$$\frac{5}{12} < \frac{1}{2} \qquad \frac{4}{16} < \frac{1}{2}$$

You can find an equivalent fraction that is less than $\frac{1}{2}$.

$$\frac{3}{7} = \frac{6}{14} \qquad \boxed{\frac{7}{14} = \frac{1}{2}} \qquad \frac{3}{7} < \frac{1}{2}$$

THINK

Box 2 — greater than or equal to $\frac{1}{2}$

$y = \frac{1}{2}$

The fraction may be written in simplest form as $\frac{1}{2}$.

$$\frac{4}{8} = \frac{1}{2} \qquad \frac{8}{16} = \frac{1}{2}$$

$y > \frac{1}{2}$

The numerator is almost equal to the denominator.

$$\frac{7}{8} > \frac{1}{2} \qquad \frac{6}{7} > \frac{1}{2}$$

You can find an equivalent fraction that is greater than $\frac{1}{2}$.

$$\frac{5}{9} = \frac{10}{18} \qquad \boxed{\frac{9}{18} = \frac{1}{2}} \qquad \frac{5}{9} > \frac{1}{2}$$

THINK

The students had boxes weighing $3\frac{1}{4}$ pounds, $1\frac{3}{8}$ pounds, $2\frac{7}{8}$ pounds, and $5\frac{1}{2}$ pounds to mail in one package. Estimate the total weight.

To estimate a sum (or difference), round each fraction to the nearest whole number.

Round down (whole number stays the same) if the fraction is less than $\frac{1}{2}$. Round up if the fraction is equal to or greater than $\frac{1}{2}$. Then add (or subtract).

$$3\frac{1}{4} + 1\frac{3}{8} + 2\frac{7}{8} + 5\frac{1}{2}$$
$$\downarrow \qquad \downarrow \qquad \downarrow \qquad \downarrow$$
$$3 + 1 + 3 + 6 = 13 \text{ pounds}$$

Or

For a more precise estimate, round to the nearest half.

Round to the nearest half. Add (or subtract) the whole numbers and the fractions.

$$3\frac{1}{4} + 1\frac{3}{8} + 2\frac{7}{8} + 5\frac{1}{2}$$
$$\downarrow \qquad \downarrow \qquad \downarrow \qquad \downarrow$$
$$3\frac{1}{2} + 1\frac{1}{2} + 3 + 5\frac{1}{2} = 12\frac{3}{2} = 13\frac{1}{2} \text{ pounds}$$

 **Check Understanding**

Identify the correct box for each bolt of ribbon. Write *Box 1* or *Box 2*.

a. $\frac{4}{5}$ yard

b. $\frac{3}{8}$ yard

c. $\frac{5}{10}$ yard

d. Estimate the difference between $8\frac{9}{10}$ and $4\frac{1}{2}$. Use both methods.

 **Practice**

Write each fraction. Use <, > or = to compare it with $\frac{1}{2}$.

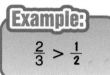 **Example:**

$\frac{2}{3} > \frac{1}{2}$

1. $\frac{3}{4}$

2. $\frac{3}{8}$

3. $\frac{7}{8}$

4. $\frac{1}{3}$

5. $\frac{4}{5}$

6. $\frac{4}{16}$

7. $\frac{5}{6}$

8. $\frac{2}{7}$

9. $\frac{4}{9}$

10. $\frac{7}{12}$

11. $\frac{6}{10}$

Estimate the sum or difference by rounding to whole numbers.

12. $7\frac{5}{9}$
$\;\;-3\frac{2}{18}$

13. $10\frac{3}{10}$
$\;\;+12\frac{4}{5}$

14. $3\frac{3}{4}$
$\;\;+2\frac{2}{3}$

15. $8\frac{1}{8}$
$\;\;+5\frac{3}{5}$

16. $12\frac{6}{9}$
$\;\;-6\frac{5}{10}$

Estimate the sum or difference by rounding to the nearest half.

17. $5\frac{1}{4} + 6\frac{7}{8} + 9\frac{1}{2}$

18. $22 + 3\frac{4}{8} + 10\frac{6}{7}$

19. $33\frac{1}{3} - 8\frac{5}{6}$

 Apply

20. Rosie eats $2\frac{1}{2}$ cups of dog food in the morning and $1\frac{3}{4}$ cups at night. Estimate how many cups she eats daily by:
   a. rounding to the nearest half.
   b. rounding to whole numbers.

21. What is the difference between each estimate and the actual amount needed? Which estimate would be better to use for planning the amount of dog food to take on a one-week vacation if space is limited? Explain your reasoning.

Rosie

 **Review**

Subtract, renaming when necessary. Write the answer in simplest form.

1. $3\frac{1}{4} - 2\frac{3}{4}$

2. $8 - \frac{7}{8}$

3. $12\frac{5}{6} - 3\frac{1}{6}$

4. $50 - 25\frac{1}{4}$

5. $31\frac{9}{10} - 27\frac{3}{10}$

6. $7 - 3\frac{2}{3}$

7. $4\frac{1}{8} - 2\frac{3}{8}$

8. $3\frac{3}{5} - 2$

Lesson 103

While shopping at the fruit and vegetable stand, Carolyn and her mother found that pineapples cost $1 each. Carolyn selected one pineapple that weighed $\frac{3}{4}$ pound and another that was $\frac{5}{8}$ pound. She thought the pineapple weighing $\frac{3}{4}$ pound was a better buy. Was she correct?

Fractions with unlike denominators may require renaming only one fraction. Is $\frac{3}{4}$ >, < or = $\frac{5}{8}$? Find the **least common denominator** (**LCD**).

Find the least common multiple (LCM) of the denominators.	The LCM of 4 and 8 is the least common denominator (LCD) for fourths and eighths.	Rename $\frac{3}{4}$ using the least common denominator.	Compare the fractions using the LCD.
4: 4, 8, 12, 16 8: 8, 12, 16, 24		$\frac{3 \times 2}{4 \times 2} = \frac{6}{8}$	$\frac{6}{8} > \frac{5}{8}$, so $\frac{3}{4} > \frac{5}{8}$

The pineapple weighing $\frac{3}{4}$ pound is the better buy. Why was only one fraction renamed to compare $\frac{3}{4}$ and $\frac{5}{8}$?

When you are working with fractions with unlike denominators, more than one fraction may require renaming. Compare $\frac{2}{3}$ and $\frac{3}{5}$. Find the least common denominator.

Multiples of 3: 3, 6, 9, 12, <u>15</u>   The LCM of 3 and 5 = 15.
Multiples of 5: 5, 10, <u>15</u>   15 is the least common denominator.

Rename both fractions, using 15 as the LCD.

$\frac{2}{3} = \frac{}{15}$ $\frac{2 \times 5}{3 \times 5} = \frac{10}{15}$

$\frac{3}{5} = \frac{}{15}$ $\frac{3 \times 3}{5 \times 3} = \frac{9}{15}$

Compare the renamed fractions.
$\frac{10}{15} > \frac{9}{15}$, so $\frac{2}{3} > \frac{3}{5}$

Is it necessary to rename both fractions with the LCD? Write *yes* or *no*.

a. $\frac{1}{2}$ and $\frac{3}{4}$ b. $\frac{1}{3}$ and $\frac{3}{7}$ c. $\frac{1}{2}$ and $\frac{1}{9}$ d. $\frac{1}{3}$ and $\frac{5}{6}$

e. Rename $1\frac{3}{4}$ and $2\frac{5}{12}$ with the least common denominator.

Rename the fractions with the least common denominator.

1. $\frac{1}{2}$ and $\frac{1}{3}$

2. $\frac{2}{5}$ and $\frac{3}{10}$

3. $\frac{2}{3}$ and $\frac{3}{4}$

4. $\frac{3}{5}$ and $\frac{5}{8}$

5. $\frac{1}{2}$ and $\frac{1}{9}$

6. $\frac{2}{3}$ and $\frac{1}{8}$

7. $\frac{1}{4}$ and $\frac{3}{5}$

8. $\frac{1}{6}$ and $\frac{5}{9}$

Rename the mixed numbers using the least common denominator.

9. $4\frac{1}{2}$, $1\frac{2}{3}$

10. $10\frac{3}{4}$, $5\frac{5}{8}$

11. $2\frac{2}{3}$, $6\frac{5}{6}$

12. $1\frac{2}{5}$, $2\frac{1}{6}$

Write the fraction pair that requires renaming both fractions with the least common denominator.

13. $\frac{1}{4}$ and $\frac{1}{12}$ or $\frac{1}{4}$ and $\frac{1}{9}$

14. $\frac{1}{16}$ and $\frac{1}{3}$ or $\frac{1}{5}$ and $\frac{1}{15}$

15. Betsy lives $\frac{5}{6}$ mile from school, and Ben's house is $\frac{7}{8}$ mile from the school. Who lives closer to school? How much closer?

16. Ben's father wanted to purchase a backpack for a long, difficult hiking trip. He saw a pack that weighed $5\frac{3}{5}$ pounds and another that weighed $5\frac{7}{10}$ pounds. If he purchased the lighter backpack, which one did he buy?

17. On the backpack trip, the hikers needed $2\frac{3}{4}$ cups of water to cook the rice for dinner. One of the men put 2 cups of water in the pot and another gave $\frac{5}{8}$ cup from the last of his water supply. Did they have enough water to prepare the rice? Compare the amount of water they had for the rice with the amount needed.

18. Do $\frac{3}{4}$ and $\frac{2}{3}$ have more than one common denominator? Why is it important to use the <u>least</u> common denominator with fractions?

**Construct Meaning**

Mark was making snack mix to take to school. He put $\frac{3}{4}$ cup of pretzels in the bowl of mix before going to answer the telephone. His sister entered the room and dumped an additional $\frac{3}{8}$ cup of pretzels into the bowl. What is the total amount of pretzels in the bowl of snack mix?

To add fractions with unlike denominators, find the least common denominator.

$\frac{3}{4}$ cup   What is the LCD of $\frac{3}{4}$ and $\frac{3}{8}$?

$+\ \frac{3}{8}$ cup   8 is a multiple of 4. The LCD is 8.

Only the fraction $\frac{3}{4}$ needs to be renamed. $\frac{3}{4} = \frac{}{8}$ $\frac{3 \times 2}{4 \times 2} = \frac{6}{8}$

Add, using fractions with the LCD.

$\frac{6}{8}$ cup

$+\ \frac{3}{8}$ cup

$\frac{9}{8}$ cup $= 1\frac{1}{8}$ cups of pretzels

Remember: If one denominator is a multiple of the other denominator, only one fraction must be renamed.

To subtract fractions with unlike denominators, find the least common denominator.

$\frac{8}{10}$
$\frac{3}{5}$

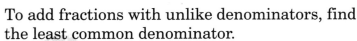

Compare the fraction bars to determine the LCD of $\frac{8}{10}$ and $\frac{3}{5}$. How many fractions must be renamed? Why?

Rename $\frac{3}{5}$ with the LCD.

$\frac{3}{5} = \frac{}{10}$ $\frac{3 \times 2}{5 \times 2} = \frac{6}{10}$

Subtract the fractions with the LCD.

$\frac{8}{10} - \frac{6}{10} = \frac{2}{10} = \frac{1}{5}$

**Check Understanding**

Write the least common denominator for each pair of numbers.

a. $\frac{1}{4}, \frac{3}{8}$

b. $\frac{5}{24}, \frac{3}{8}$

c. $\frac{5}{6}, \frac{5}{12}$

Rename the fractions using the LCD and solve. Write the answer in simplest form.

d. $\frac{11}{12} - \frac{3}{4}$

e. $\frac{1}{6} + \frac{11}{18}$

f. $\frac{8}{9} - \frac{2}{3}$

Rename the fractions using the LCD. Add or subtract, writing the answer in simplest form.

1. $\frac{3}{5} - \frac{1}{10}$
2. $\frac{1}{2} + \frac{1}{6}$
3. $\frac{1}{6} + \frac{3}{12}$
4. $\frac{5}{8} - \frac{1}{4}$

5. $\frac{4}{9} + \frac{1}{18}$
6. $\frac{5}{6} - \frac{2}{3}$
7. $\frac{14}{15} - \frac{1}{5}$
8. $\frac{3}{7} + \frac{2}{21}$

9. $\frac{3}{4} - \frac{5}{12}$
10. $\frac{9}{20} - \frac{2}{5}$
11. $\frac{5}{8} + \frac{3}{24}$
12. $\frac{5}{16} - \frac{1}{8}$

13. $\frac{2}{3} + \frac{1}{12}$
14. $\frac{7}{10} - \frac{1}{5}$
15. $\frac{8}{18} + \frac{5}{6}$
16. $\frac{2}{3} + \frac{5}{9}$

Diane's favorite brand   **Ann's favorite brand**

Diane and Ann each brought a package of their favorite brand of mixed nuts to an "Educated Shopper" class. Both packages were the same price and each held one cup of nuts, but they found that the brands differed in the amount of each type of nut in the package. Answer the questions based on their findings.

17. What is the total amount of cashews and peanuts in Diane's brand?

18. Add the amount of cashews to the amount of peanuts in Ann's brand. Is that figure greater than, less than, or equal to the amount in Diane's brand?

19. Find the difference between the amounts of walnuts in the two brands.

20. If cashews and walnuts are the most expensive types of nut, whose brand is the better buy?

21. If your personal favorites are cashews and almonds, whose brand should you buy?

Solve. Write each answer in simplest form.

1. $6\frac{7}{8} - 4\frac{5}{8}$
2. $15\frac{9}{10} - 2\frac{3}{10}$
3. $3 - 3\frac{1}{3}$
4. $25 - 10\frac{1}{4}$

5. $20\frac{1}{4} + 35\frac{2}{4}$
6. $19\frac{5}{12} + 10\frac{7}{12}$
7. $7\frac{3}{4} - 5$
8. $15\frac{5}{8} + 4\frac{3}{8}$

Construct Meaning

Sean and his family visited Space Adventure Camp for students who enjoy studying space. They toured the camp for a day to determine if Sean's attendance there would help him pursue his goal of becoming an astronaut.

Sean's family walked from the entrance to the Information Center. They walked on to the Lecture Hall, where they heard a short talk by a retired astronaut. How far had they walked from the entrance?

To add $\frac{1}{4}$ mile and $\frac{2}{3}$ mile, find the least common denominator.

| Multiples of 4: 4, 8, (12), 16 | The LCD is 12. |
| Multiples of 3: 3, 6, 9, (12) | Rename both fractions to add. |

$$\frac{1}{4} = \frac{}{12} \qquad \frac{1 \times 3}{4 \times 3} = \frac{3}{12} \qquad\qquad \frac{2}{3} = \frac{}{12} \qquad \frac{2 \times 4}{3 \times 4} = \frac{8}{12}$$

Add the renamed fractions. $\frac{3}{12} + \frac{8}{12} = \frac{11}{12}$ mile

Check Understanding

a. Sean and his parents left the Lecture Hall to go to lunch at the Dining Hall. Then they walked to Student Housing. What is the distance they traveled from the Lecture Hall?

b. List the necessary steps for adding fractions with unlike denominators when neither denominator is a multiple of the other.

Add the fractions using the least common denominator. Write the answers in simplest form.

1. $\frac{1}{6} + \frac{3}{5}$

2. $\frac{2}{4} + \frac{7}{8}$

3. $\frac{2}{3} + \frac{2}{5}$

4. $\frac{1}{2} + \frac{1}{3}$

5. $\frac{1}{4} + \frac{3}{5}$

6. $\frac{2}{3} + \frac{1}{8}$

7. $\frac{5}{6} + \frac{1}{5}$

8. $\frac{2}{9} + \frac{1}{6}$

9. $\frac{1}{3} + \frac{4}{9}$

10. $\frac{3}{7} + \frac{2}{3}$

11. $\frac{1}{6} + \frac{3}{8}$

12. $\frac{3}{10} + \frac{6}{15}$

13. $\frac{5}{8}$ $+ \frac{4}{5}$

14. $\frac{3}{4}$ $+ \frac{2}{9}$

15. $\frac{5}{6}$ $+ \frac{1}{4}$

16. $\frac{7}{20}$ $+ \frac{9}{10}$

Use the map of Space Adventure Camp to answer the questions.

17. If Sean took the Tourist Trolley from the station to the Launch Pad and went on to the Rocket Site, what distance would he travel?

18. Sean can easily jog a half mile in five minutes. Could he make it from the Rocket Site to the Space Theater in five minutes?

19. A group of students got up early every morning and jogged from Student Housing to the Lecture Hall and back to change before breakfast. Another group jogged every evening, making a round trip from Student Housing to the Flight Simulator. Which group ran a longer distance each day?

20. How much greater is the distance between the Launch Pad and the Rocket Site than the distance between the Rocket Site and the Flight Simulator?

21. Think of equivalent fractions to determine if a trip from the Tourist Trolley Station to the Rocket Site is greater or less than half a mile. Explain your reasoning.

22. If a student at Space Adventure Camp made three daily round trips from Student Housing to the Dining Hall, how many miles would he or she walk in one day?

Lesson 106

Construct Meaning

When Mrs. Sommer was previewing books for her reading students, she found two books of adventure stories. One of the books contained $\frac{3}{4}$ non-fiction selections, while the other had $\frac{1}{3}$ non-fiction adventures. What is the difference in the amount of non-fiction the books contain?

To find the difference, rename and subtract the fractions with unlike denominators.

Find the LCD.

$\frac{3}{4}$ multiples of 4: 4, 8, **12**, 16

$-\frac{1}{3}$ multiples of 3: 3, 6, 9, **12**

Rename the fractions and subtract.

$$\frac{3}{4} = \frac{3 \times 3}{4 \times 3} = \frac{9}{12}$$

$$-\frac{1}{3} = \frac{1 \times 4}{3 \times 4} \quad \frac{4}{12}$$

$$\frac{5}{12}$$

The difference is $\frac{5}{12}$.

The fraction bars show renaming with the least common denominator and subtracting.

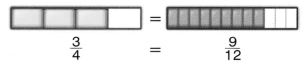

$$\frac{3}{4} = \frac{9}{12} \qquad \frac{1}{3} = \frac{4}{12}$$

$$\frac{9}{12} - \frac{4}{12} = \frac{5}{12}$$

Solve $\frac{5}{6} - \frac{7}{10}$.

Find the LCD.

$\frac{5}{6}$ multiples of 6: 6, 12, 18, 24, **30**

$-\frac{7}{10}$ multiples of 10: 10, 20, **30**

Rename and subtract.

$$\frac{5}{6} = \frac{}{30}$$

$$-\frac{7}{10} = \frac{}{30}$$

$$\frac{}{} = \frac{}{}$$

Check Understanding

a. Draw fraction models with circles to show renaming with the LCD and subtracting $\frac{1}{4}$ from $\frac{5}{8}$.

Rename with the LCD and subtract, writing the answers in simplest form.

b. $\frac{2}{3} - \frac{1}{6}$ c. $\frac{3}{5} - \frac{1}{3}$ d. $\frac{3}{4} - \frac{2}{5}$

226

Rename the fractions using the LCD. Subtract, writing the answers in simplest form.

1. $\frac{1}{2} - \frac{2}{5}$ 2. $\frac{7}{8} - \frac{2}{3}$ 3. $\frac{9}{10} - \frac{1}{5}$ 4. $\frac{3}{4} - \frac{1}{8}$ 5. $\frac{2}{3} - \frac{1}{4}$

6. $\frac{5}{6}$ 7. $\frac{4}{5}$ 8. $\frac{7}{8}$ 9. $\frac{5}{6}$ 10. $\frac{7}{10}$
$-\frac{1}{7}$ $-\frac{2}{3}$ $-\frac{3}{4}$ $-\frac{1}{4}$ $-\frac{1}{8}$

11. $\frac{11}{12}$ 12. $\frac{5}{9}$ 13. $\frac{1}{4}$ 14. $\frac{3}{5}$ 15. $\frac{1}{3}$
$-\frac{3}{5}$ $-\frac{1}{3}$ $-\frac{1}{5}$ $-\frac{4}{10}$ $-\frac{3}{12}$

16. A bag of flower bulbs contained $\frac{1}{5}$ daffodil bulbs and $\frac{1}{3}$ narcissus bulbs. The remainder of the bag contained iris bulbs. What portion of the bag was iris bulbs?

17. After planting the flower bulbs, Sharon and her mother walked $\frac{3}{5}$ mile from their home to a convenience store. Sharon suggested walking on to the park, but Mother said that would require walking about another half mile. It is $\frac{9}{10}$ mile from their home to the park. What is the exact distance from the convenience store to the park?

18. Sharon and her brother Doug each had a Nutty Chocolate Bar. Sharon divided her candy bar equally with one friend. Doug divided his candy equally among two friends and himself. How much more Nutty Chocolate Bar did Sharon and her friend each eat than Doug and his friends?

Write each fraction. Compare with $\frac{1}{2}$ by writing $> \frac{1}{2}$, $< \frac{1}{2}$ or $= \frac{1}{2}$.

1. $\frac{9}{10}$ 2. $\frac{3}{4}$ 3. $\frac{2}{3}$ 4. $\frac{5}{12}$ 5. $\frac{4}{7}$ 6. $\frac{8}{16}$ 7. $\frac{9}{20}$

Estimate the sum or difference by rounding to whole numbers.

8. $2\frac{3}{5}$ 9. $15\frac{3}{4}$ 10. $19\frac{7}{8}$ 11. $3\frac{1}{3}$ 12. $6\frac{2}{10}$
$+5\frac{1}{3}$ $-6\frac{1}{2}$ $-9\frac{7}{9}$ $+2\frac{1}{4}$ $+10\frac{1}{2}$

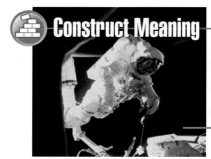

Construct Meaning

Changes in gravitational pull affect the body of an astronaut in space. An astronaut may "grow" $\frac{7}{8}$ inch to $1\frac{1}{4}$ inches in height because his or her spine lengthens after an extended time in a weightless environment.

Suppose a female astronaut is 5 feet $5\frac{1}{2}$ inches tall on earth. She gains $\frac{7}{8}$ inch in height while living aboard the Space Station. What is her total height while in space?

> To add mixed numbers and fractions with unlike denominators, find the least common denominator.

5 feet $5\frac{1}{2}$ inches

$+\qquad \frac{7}{8}$ inch

What is the LCD of $\frac{1}{2}$ and $\frac{1}{8}$?

8 is a multiple of 2. The LCD is 8.

Only the fraction $\frac{1}{2}$ is renamed. $\frac{1}{2} = \frac{}{8}$ $\frac{1 \times 4}{2 \times 4} = \frac{4}{8}$

Add the fractions with the LCD, then add the whole numbers.

5 feet $5\frac{4}{8}$ inches

$+\qquad \frac{7}{8}$ inch

5 feet $5\frac{11}{8}$ inches = 5 feet $6\frac{3}{8}$ inches

> Her height in space would be 5 feet $6\frac{1}{2}$ inches.

Solve $9\frac{2}{9} + 5\frac{1}{6}$. Rename the mixed numbers with the LCD.

$9\frac{2}{9} = 9\frac{}{18}$

THINK $\frac{2}{9} = \frac{2 \times 2}{9 \times 2} = \frac{}{18}$

$9\frac{2}{9} = 9\frac{}{18}$

$5\frac{1}{6} = 5\frac{}{18}$

THINK $\frac{1}{6} = \frac{1 \times 3}{6 \times 3} = \frac{}{18}$

$5\frac{1}{6} = 5\frac{}{18}$

Add the renamed mixed numbers, writing the answers in simplest form.

$9\frac{}{18}$ Add the fractions

$+5\frac{}{18}$ Add the whole numbers.

$14\frac{}{18}$

> **Man's Footprint on the Moon**

Check Understanding

Add the mixed numbers, renaming when necessary.
Write the answer in simplest form.

a. $3\frac{2}{3} + 10\frac{1}{3}$ b. $18\frac{1}{4} + 22\frac{1}{5}$ c. $5\frac{3}{4} + \frac{1}{2}$ d. $2\frac{1}{4} + \frac{3}{8} + \frac{1}{2}$

Add, writing the sum in simplest form.

1. $9\frac{1}{8}$
$+7\frac{4}{5}$

2. $21\frac{6}{10}$
$+13\frac{2}{20}$

3. 52
$+\ 3\frac{7}{8}$

4. $65\frac{2}{3}$
$+30\frac{4}{9}$

5. $33\frac{1}{3}$
$+25\frac{1}{4}$

6. $1\frac{5}{6}$
$+43\frac{2}{10}$

7. $12\frac{1}{2}$
$+\ 5\frac{3}{7}$

8. $50\frac{1}{12}$
$+16\frac{2}{3}$

9. $71\frac{6}{15}$
$+\ \ \frac{1}{2}$

10. 85
$+10\frac{5}{9}$

11. $4\frac{1}{3} + 6\frac{1}{4} + 8\frac{1}{2}$

12. $10\frac{1}{10} + 9\frac{1}{5} + 4\frac{3}{5}$

Coach Schwartz requires the cross-country runners to do short sprints called intervals as part of their training. He set a goal of $1\frac{1}{2}$ miles of interval training over a period of three days. Adam recorded his interval training in his running log.

Adam's Running Log	
Day	**Distance**
MONDAY	$\frac{3}{8}$ MILE
TUESDAY	$\frac{3}{4}$ MILE
WEDNESDAY	$\frac{1}{2}$ MILE

13. What was the total distance of Adam's interval training for the three-day period?

14. How much greater or less than the coach's goal was Adam's total mileage for interval training?

15. In addition to the interval training, Adam ran a total of $9\frac{3}{4}$ miles on a cross-country course during the same three-day period. What was the total amount of interval training and cross-country running for the three days?

16. At the cross-country meet, Adam ran the first half of the course in $8\frac{1}{2}$ minutes and the second half in $9\frac{1}{4}$ minutes. What was his time for the race?

17. Adam's grandfather stays fit by jogging daily on a track. One trip around the track equals $\frac{1}{4}$ mile. He ran completely around the track twice on Thursday, three times on Friday, and five times on Saturday. What was his total mileage?

Lesson 108

 **Construct Meaning**

At Fairview Christian School, the fifth graders worked with kindergarten "buddies." They invited the younger children to an event they called "Tasting Fruits and Vegetables from A to Z." Each child chose a letter of the alphabet and brought a fruit or vegetable beginning with that letter.

Pam and her buddy brought $3\frac{2}{3}$ pounds of grapes. Only $2\frac{1}{2}$ pounds were eaten. How many pounds were left?

$$3\frac{2}{3} - 2\frac{1}{2} \text{ pounds} = \boxed{}$$

To subtract mixed numbers with unlike denominators, rename the fractions with the LCD.	Use the renamed mixed numbers to subtract.

$$3\frac{2}{3} = 3\frac{4}{6}$$
and
$$2\frac{1}{2} = 2\frac{3}{6}$$

$3\frac{4}{6}$ Subtract the fractions.
$-2\frac{3}{6}$ Subtract the whole numbers.
$1\frac{1}{6}$ pounds remaining

The total amount of fruits and vegetables for the tasting event was $68\frac{1}{4}$ pounds. If $33\frac{2}{3}$ pounds were vegetables, what was the amount of fruit?

Rename with the LCD.
$$68\frac{1}{4} = 68\frac{3}{12} \qquad 33\frac{2}{3} = 33\frac{8}{12}$$

Rename $68\frac{3}{12}$ to increase the numerator.
$$68\frac{3}{12} = 67 + 1 + \frac{3}{12} = 67 + \frac{12}{12} + \frac{3}{12} = 67\frac{15}{12}$$

$$68\frac{1}{4} = 68\frac{3}{12} = 67\frac{15}{12}$$
$$-33\frac{2}{3} = 33\frac{8}{12} = 33\frac{8}{12}$$
$$34\frac{7}{12}$$

There were $34\frac{7}{12}$ pounds of fruit.

Check Understanding

a. Write all the steps that may be required to subtract mixed numbers with unlike denominators.

Subtract. Write the answer in simplest form.

b. $7\frac{7}{9}$
$-5\frac{1}{3}$

c. $25\frac{1}{4}$
$-15\frac{7}{8}$

d. 30
$-4\frac{3}{4}$

230

Mathematics Grade 5

 ractice

Subtract, renaming as needed. Write the answers in simplest form.

1. $2\frac{5}{8}$
   $-1\frac{1}{2}$

2. $25\frac{2}{10}$
   $-\ 9\frac{3}{5}$

3. $8\frac{4}{9}$
   $-3\frac{2}{6}$

4. $3\frac{2}{3}$
   $-2\frac{1}{6}$

5. $16\frac{4}{5}$
   $-\ 5\frac{3}{4}$

6. $7\frac{1}{4}$
   $-5\frac{3}{8}$

7. $12\frac{5}{6}$
   $-10\frac{2}{3}$

8. $18\frac{1}{3}$
   $-\ 4\frac{1}{2}$

9. $6\frac{2}{9}$
   $-1\frac{2}{3}$

10. $16\frac{4}{5}$
    $-\ 8\frac{5}{6}$

11. $9\frac{6}{16}$
    $-5\frac{1}{4}$

12. $5\frac{7}{10}$
    $-3\frac{3}{20}$

Identify the value of y in each equation.

13. $3\frac{1}{3} - 2\frac{y}{6} = 1\frac{1}{6}$

14. $10\frac{3}{4} - 5\frac{y}{3} = 5\frac{1}{12}$

15. $16\frac{1}{10} - 8\frac{y}{5} = 7\frac{1}{2}$

Write the next two numbers in the subtraction pattern.

16. $12, 10\frac{1}{2}, 9, 7\frac{1}{2}$

17. $18\frac{1}{2}, 16\frac{1}{4}, 14, 11\frac{3}{4}$

18. $20, 18\frac{2}{3}, 17\frac{1}{3}, 16$

 pply

19. David contributed $3\frac{7}{10}$ pounds of zucchini to the tasting event. He sliced $1\frac{1}{2}$ pounds and set it out for the students. When that was eaten, he sliced and served another $1\frac{1}{4}$ pounds. What amount of zucchini was left?

20. Helen brought $\frac{3}{4}$ pound of bananas, A.J. brought $1\frac{3}{8}$ pounds, and May brought $1\frac{1}{2}$ pounds of bananas. What was the total weight of the bananas?

21. There were plenty of fruits and vegetables for the letter "T" at the tasting event. $1\frac{3}{4}$ pounds of tomatoes were served and $\frac{5}{8}$ pound was eaten. Of the $2\frac{1}{4}$ pounds of tangerines, $\frac{3}{4}$ pound was eaten. Was there a greater amount of tomatoes or tangerines left? Compare the remaining amounts using >, < or = .

 eview

Write the fractions in order from least to greatest.

1. $\frac{1}{3}, \frac{1}{4}, \frac{1}{2}$

2. $\frac{2}{3}, \frac{3}{4}, \frac{1}{2}$

3. $\frac{5}{6}, \frac{7}{12}, \frac{3}{4}$

4. $\frac{2}{5}, \frac{3}{10}, \frac{5}{8}$

5. In Miss Roger's class, $\frac{5}{8}$ of the students said they eat citrus fruit. In Mr. Walter's class, $\frac{3}{5}$ of the students enjoy citrus fruit. Which class has the greater number of students that do <u>not</u> eat citrus fruit?

Construct Meaning

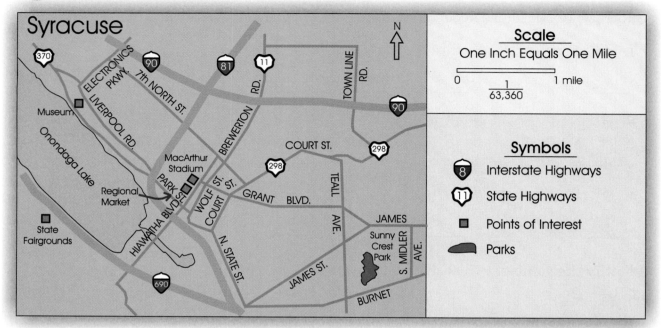

Laila and her family are planning a trip to Syracuse, New York. They looked at this Internet map showing part of the city. A map is an abstract representation of reality. The symbols on a map describe streets, locations, and other features. The **scale** shows the relationship between a unit of distance on the map and a unit of distance on the ground.

There are three types of map scales.

Verbal scale: The scale is expressed with words.

Visual scale: The unit of measurement is shown and labeled.

Representative fraction: $\dfrac{\text{map distance}}{\text{ground distance}}$

Check Understanding

a. Identify the three types of scales on the map of Syracuse.

b. Explain why the representative fraction for a scale of one inch equals one mile is $\frac{1}{63,360}$.

c. Use the map symbols to name the interstate highways, state highways, parks, and points of interest.

Use the map and a ruler to solve problems 1 through 5.

1. How many miles are traveled on I-90 from Town Line Road to Brewerton Road?

2. Suppose you are in front of MacArthur Stadium at Hiawatha Boulevard and Grant Boulevard. What is the shortest street route from there to the point where Seventh North Street intersects I-81? What is a reasonable whole number estimate of the distance?

3. To travel from the point where I-90 and Electronics Parkway meet to the Regional Market, you would travel $\frac{1}{4}$ mile on Electronics Parkway, $1\frac{9}{16}$ miles on Seventh North Street, and $\frac{1}{2}$ mile on Hiawatha Boulevard. What is the total distance?

4. What is the length of South Midler Avenue?

5. What is the length of James Street between North State Street and Teall Avenue to the nearest quarter mile?

6. If a map has a scale of one-half inch equals one mile, what is the ground distance between two points that are $3\frac{1}{2}$ inches apart on the map?

7. A state map has a representative fraction of $\frac{1}{500,000}$. About how many miles are represented by one inch on that map? (Remember: $\frac{1}{63,360}$ means one inch equals one mile.)

8. Use a ruler to draw the visual scale for a map with a representational fraction of $\frac{1}{316,800}$.

SYRACUSE UNIVERSITY

Pondering Parts and Proportions

Write the equation shown by the fraction models. Write the answer in simplest form.

1. ▭▭▭▭▭▭ + ▭▭▭▭▭

2.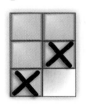

3.

Complete each equation.

4. $\frac{4}{15} + \boxed{} = \frac{7}{15}$

5. $\boxed{} - \frac{1}{4} = \frac{1}{2}$

6. $1\frac{2}{3} + \boxed{} = 2\frac{1}{3}$

7. $5 - \boxed{} = 3\frac{5}{8}$

Find the least common denominator for each pair of fractions. Write the equivalent fractions with the LCD.

8. $\frac{1}{10}$ and $\frac{3}{5}$

9. $\frac{3}{4}$ and $\frac{1}{12}$

10. $\frac{5}{8}$ and $\frac{3}{5}$

11. $\frac{2}{3}$ and $\frac{6}{7}$

12. $\frac{5}{6}$ and $\frac{2}{9}$

Write each fraction or mixed number in simplest form.

13. $\frac{3}{21}$

14. $\frac{7}{8}$

15. $12\frac{4}{12}$

16. $10\frac{2}{5}$

17. $\frac{15}{30}$

18. $\frac{12}{36}$

19. $\frac{25}{100}$

Add or subtract the fractions using the LCD. Write the answer in simplest form.

20. $\frac{3}{5}$
$+ \frac{1}{5}$

21. $\frac{13}{14}$
$- \frac{3}{7}$

22. $\frac{5}{6}$
$+ \frac{7}{12}$

23. $\frac{7}{8}$
$- \frac{1}{4}$

24. $\frac{1}{6}$
$+ \frac{4}{9}$

25. $\frac{3}{4}$
$- \frac{1}{3}$

26. $\frac{9}{10}$
$+ \frac{1}{3}$

27. $\frac{2}{7}$
$+ \frac{5}{8}$

28. $\frac{11}{12}$
$- \frac{1}{5}$

29. $\frac{2}{3}$
$- \frac{1}{5}$

Identify the value of y renaming each whole number.

30. $12 = 11\frac{y}{3}$

31. $7 = 6\frac{y}{5}$

32. $9 = y\frac{4}{4}$

33. $14 = 13\frac{15}{y}$

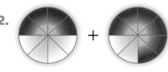

Moments with Careers

"My dad works as an artist. In his work, he uses math to mix certain amounts of colors to make the exact color he needs."

Katie
Trumbull, CT

Rename the mixed numbers using the LCD.

34. $19\frac{1}{3}$ and $3\frac{4}{5}$ **35.** $5\frac{7}{8}$ and $16\frac{1}{4}$ **36.** $9\frac{5}{6}$ and $3\frac{1}{3}$

Estimate the sum or difference by rounding to whole numbers.

37. $\begin{aligned}18\frac{5}{8}\\+\ \ 3\frac{1}{3}\end{aligned}$ **38.** $\begin{aligned}50\frac{1}{2}\\-13\frac{2}{3}\end{aligned}$ **39.** $\begin{aligned}7\frac{3}{4}\\+5\frac{1}{3}\end{aligned}$ **40.** $\begin{aligned}39\frac{2}{5}\\-21\frac{4}{5}\end{aligned}$ **41.** $\begin{aligned}45\frac{1}{3}\\-\ \ 9\frac{3}{5}\end{aligned}$

Estimate the sum or difference by rounding to the nearest half.

42. $10\frac{9}{10} + 3\frac{1}{2} + 16 + 8$ **43.** $9\frac{7}{8} - 6\frac{5}{10}$

Add or subtract, renaming as needed. Write the answer in simplest form.

44. $\begin{aligned}5\frac{9}{10}\\+\ 4\frac{2}{3}\end{aligned}$ **45.** $\begin{aligned}6\frac{1}{5}\\-\ 2\frac{1}{4}\end{aligned}$ **46.** $\begin{aligned}17\frac{1}{2}\\+19\frac{5}{6}\end{aligned}$ **47.** $\begin{aligned}9\frac{7}{12}\\-3\frac{3}{4}\end{aligned}$

48. $\begin{aligned}20\\-\ 5\frac{7}{8}\end{aligned}$ **49.** $\begin{aligned}7\frac{2}{3}\\+18\frac{2}{3}\end{aligned}$ **50.** $\begin{aligned}98\\-10\frac{3}{5}\end{aligned}$ **51.** $\begin{aligned}8\frac{1}{6}\\+9\frac{5}{9}\end{aligned}$

Use mental math to add.

52. $16 + 1\frac{6}{8} + 2\frac{2}{8}$ **53.** $9\frac{1}{5} + 14 + 10\frac{4}{5}$ **54.** $3\frac{1}{3} + 17\frac{2}{3} + 5 + 20$

---

55. Tim's parents budget their household income carefully. They give $\frac{1}{10}$ to the church, $\frac{2}{5}$ of the total is used for their house payment, and $\frac{1}{4}$ of the income is budgeted for groceries. What fraction of the total remains after they have paid their tithe, house payment, and grocery bill?

"And the Lord said, 'Who then is that faithful and wise steward, whom *his* master will make ruler over his household, to give *them their* portion of food in due season?'"

Luke 12:42

Grade Five

9

Chapter

Lessons 111–120

Your faith should not be
in the wisdom of men
but in the power of God.

I Corinthians 2:5

Astronaut repairing the Hubble

Construct Meaning

The National Aeronautics and Space Administration (NASA) is an agency consisting of explorers who are involved in air and space missions to further the development of technology. They research areas of industry and business to make our universe a better place in which to live.

To explore our universe, the Hubble Space Telescope, a satellite observatory, was placed into orbit in April, 1990. It is 43.3 feet (13 meters) long and 14 feet (4 meters) wide and weighs 25,500 pounds (11,000 kg). The telescope was named after Edwin Powell Hubble (1889–1953) who helped define galaxies. An amazing feature of the telescope is that it can point to a certain position in space for days at a time while traveling 17,000 mph orbiting our planet!

If $\frac{3}{4}$ of an image was visible with $\frac{1}{3}$ of the visible area being blurred, how much of the image was blurred?

A model can help you find $\frac{1}{3}$ of $\frac{3}{4}$.

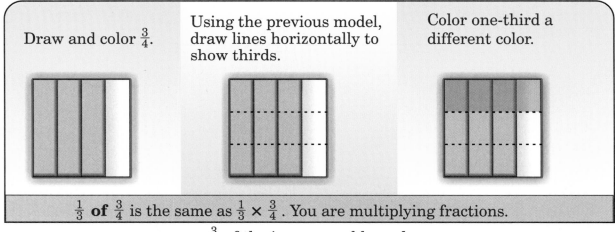

Draw and color $\frac{3}{4}$.

Using the previous model, draw lines horizontally to show thirds.

Color one-third a different color.

$\frac{1}{3}$ **of** $\frac{3}{4}$ is the same as $\frac{1}{3} \times \frac{3}{4}$. You are multiplying fractions.

$\frac{3}{12}$ of the image was blurred.

If you changed the order of the fractions, would you get the same product? Draw a model to explain your answer. Is the product greater or less than one?

Check Understanding

Use the model to tell which fractions to multiply. Use *of* and × to write each equation two ways. Solve.

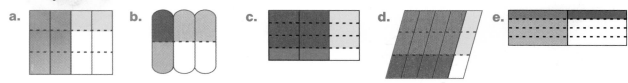

a.   b.   c.   d.   e.

Draw a model that shows the fractions being multiplied.

1. $\frac{1}{2} \times \frac{1}{4}$ 2. $\frac{1}{3} \times \frac{3}{4}$ 3. $\frac{1}{5} \times \frac{2}{4}$ 4. $\frac{1}{4} \times \frac{1}{3}$ 5. $\frac{2}{3} \times \frac{1}{6}$

Write a number sentence for each model.

6.   7. 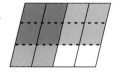 8. 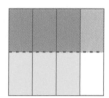 9.

10.  11. 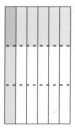 12.   13.

14. Julien spent $\frac{1}{4}$ of an hour drawing a picture of the Hubble Telescope in his math journal. He spent $\frac{1}{3}$ of that time adding color to his picture. What part of an hour did he spend coloring the telescope?

15. Mr. Morris read $\frac{1}{2}$ of a magazine article about the Hubble Space Telescope and saw that $\frac{2}{3}$ of each page was planet images. What fraction represents $\frac{2}{3}$ of $\frac{1}{2}$?

16. To prepare for the race on Saturday, Dennis needed to run five miles. On Monday he ran $1\frac{3}{4}$ miles; on Tuesday he ran $1\frac{1}{2}$ miles; and on Wednesday he ran $1\frac{1}{3}$ miles. Had he met the goal? Why or why not?

PHOTO TAKEN FROM THE TELESCOPE

Identify the greatest common factor.

1. 6 and 8 2. 24 and 36 3. 20 and 30 4. 15 and 45

5. 4 and 12 6. 7 and 21 7. 8 and 16 8. 18 and 24

Construct Meaning

What happens to the data collected by the Hubble Space Telescope? All the information gathered by the observatory as well as the commands to the telescope are manned by NASA's Goddard Space Flight Center in Greenbelt, Maryland. The center is named after Dr. Robert Hutchins Goddard (1882–1945) who built and tested the first rocket using liquid fuel. His feat impacted the exploration of space just as the Wright Brothers influenced aviation.

A scientist at Goddard was assigned a project on Monday and was to complete $\frac{1}{2}$ of it by Friday. Her goal was to finish $\frac{1}{5}$ of that fraction per day. What part of the project would she complete each day?

Because the scientist worked on the project some part <u>of</u> one-half of the project each day, we multiply to solve the problem. Draw a model to multiply fractions.

$\frac{1}{5}$ of $\frac{1}{2}$ is $\frac{1}{10}$.

Is the product greater than or less than the whole number 1?

How do you multiply fractions?

$\frac{1 \times 1}{5 \times 2} = \frac{1}{10}$ Multiply the numerators.
Multiply the denominators.
Write the product in simplest form.

The scientist would complete $\frac{1}{10}$ of the project each day.

When you multiply fractions, you can multiply either the numerators or the denominators first—the order does not change the product.

When you multiply fractions, the denominators can be different.

$$\frac{2}{4} \times \frac{1}{3} = \frac{2}{12} = \frac{1}{6} \qquad \frac{3}{4} \times \frac{5}{7} = \frac{15}{28} \qquad \frac{1}{2} \times \frac{9}{4} = \frac{9}{8} = 1\frac{1}{8}$$

✓ **Check Understanding**

Write a multiplication equation for each model.

  a. 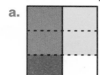   **b.**   **c.**    **d.** 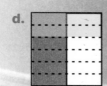   **e.**

Copy and complete.

  f. $\frac{3}{4} \times \frac{1}{2} = \frac{\quad \times \quad}{\quad \times \quad} = \quad$

  g. $\frac{2}{3} \times \frac{9}{10} = \frac{\quad \times \quad}{\quad \times \quad} = \frac{\quad}{\quad} = \frac{\quad}{\quad}$

**ractice**

Multiply. Write the product in simplest form.

1. $\frac{2}{5} \times \frac{2}{4}$

2. $\frac{8}{10} \times \frac{2}{3}$

3. $\frac{6}{7} \times \frac{1}{6}$

4. $\frac{10}{11} \times \frac{4}{5}$

5. $\frac{5}{8} \times \frac{3}{4}$

6. $\frac{1}{3} \times \frac{7}{8}$

7. $\frac{1}{2} \times \frac{2}{3}$

8. $\frac{8}{2} \times \frac{1}{3}$

9. $\frac{1}{2} \times \frac{15}{17}$

10. $\frac{5}{4} \times \frac{9}{2}$

11. $\frac{3}{10} \times \frac{4}{10} = \frac{12}{100}$

12. $\frac{1}{4} \times \frac{2}{3}$

Use > or < to complete the number sentence.

13. $\frac{1}{2} \times \frac{1}{3}$ ⬚ $\frac{2}{6}$

14. $\frac{2}{3} \times \frac{4}{5}$ ⬚ $\frac{6}{15}$

15. $\frac{3}{4} \times \frac{2}{7}$ ⬚ $\frac{3}{28}$

16. $\frac{3}{6} \times \frac{2}{4}$ ⬚ 1

pply

17. Liam's fifth grade is assigned to clean the schoolyard. His class is responsible for the playground area, which is $\frac{1}{3}$ of the schoolyard. Liam's group is designated to clean $\frac{1}{2}$ of the playground area. What part of the schoolyard did Liam's group clean?

18. Waste cans are placed in different locations. The can in the playground area was five-eighths full. The can in the parking area was one-fourth full. Tom emptied the can from the parking area into the can from the playground area. How full is the can from the playground area now?

19. The playground area is $\frac{3}{4}$ of an acre. The parking area is $\frac{2}{3}$ of an acre. Which area is larger? How much larger?

20. The scientist at Goddard finished $\frac{1}{2}$ of a project the first week. She finished $\frac{1}{3}$ of the project the second week. What part of the project was completed by the end of the second week?

**eview**

Solve. Write the answer in simplest form.

1. $25\frac{1}{3}$
$+ 17\frac{2}{3}$

2. $72\frac{2}{5}$
$- 65\frac{3}{10}$

3. $46\frac{1}{2}$
$- 18\frac{5}{8}$

4. $38\frac{3}{7}$
$+ 49\frac{9}{14}$

5. $50\frac{1}{8}$
$- 24\frac{1}{3}$

Construct Meaning

Satellites come in different shapes and sizes and are used in various ways. Some similar features of all kinds of satellites include a strong frame that holds the parts together in space, a source of power, a computer, a radio system with an antenna, and a control system that keeps the satellite pointed in the right direction.

Weather satellites help meteorologists be aware of current weather conditions and also predict the weather.

There are 15 meteorologists in the midwestern part of the United States predicting a snowy forecast. If $\frac{3}{5}$ of them predict blizzard-like conditions, how many are making that prediction?

- Find a fraction of a whole number by drawing a picture.

   $\frac{3}{5}$ of 15 or $\frac{3}{5} \times 15$ 3 out of 5 equal groups = 9

- Find a fraction of a whole number by multiplying.

   $\frac{3}{5} \times \frac{15}{1}$ Write a 1 under the whole number. The whole number may be listed first. $15 \times \frac{3}{5}$ is the same as $\frac{15}{1} \times \frac{3}{5}$.

   $\frac{3 \times 15}{5 \times 1} = \frac{45}{5}$ Multiply the numerators. Multiply the denominators.

   $5\overline{)45}$ (9)   Write the product in simplest form. Change the improper fraction to a whole or mixed number by dividing the denominator into the numerator.

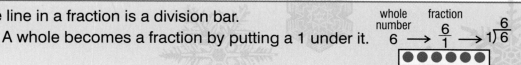

The line in a fraction is a division bar.
A whole becomes a fraction by putting a 1 under it.

whole number   fraction
$6 \longrightarrow \frac{6}{1} \longrightarrow 1\overline{)6}$

Check Understanding

Write a multiplication sentence for each picture.

a.    b.   c.   d.   e.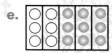

Multiply. Write the product in simplest form.

   f. $\frac{1}{2} \times 20$ g. $42 \times \frac{2}{3}$ h. $\frac{1}{6} \times 38$ i. $81 \times \frac{2}{9}$ j. $\frac{3}{7} \times 53$

Multiply. Write the product in simplest form.

1. $\frac{3}{5} \times 10$
2. $\frac{7}{8} \times 4$
3. $5 \times \frac{2}{7}$
4. $\frac{5}{6} \times 8$
5. $3 \times \frac{5}{9}$

6. $\frac{1}{4} \times 48$
7. $\frac{2}{3} \times 24$
8. $40 \times \frac{4}{5}$
9. $19 \times \frac{3}{6}$
10. $\frac{1}{2} \times 6$

11. $6 \times \frac{1}{7}$
12. $\frac{2}{12} \times 10$
13. $\frac{4}{8} \times 15$
14. $2 \times \frac{2}{9}$
15. $9 \times \frac{3}{10}$

16. $\frac{4}{11} \times 2$
17. $1 \times \frac{9}{10}$
18. $\frac{1}{2} \times 76$
19. $64 \times \frac{3}{4}$
20. $\frac{1}{13} \times 4$

21. Heat and humidity may affect people negatively. Dr. Willis Carrier designed the first modern air conditioning system. Out of 100 new homes built, only 80 of those installed an air conditioning system. $\frac{1}{4}$ of these homes with an air conditioning system had fewer windows. How many homes had fewer windows?

22. The classroom temperature is set for 78°F. There are 28 students in the classroom. $\frac{2}{7}$ of the students are comfortable. How many students are uncomfortable?

23. For three hours Ralph researched the effects of pollutants such as smoke and fumes on the quality of the air we breathe; Jason spent $1\frac{3}{4}$ hours; and Steven spent $\frac{2}{3}$ of an hour. How much time did the three boys spend?

24. As a result of a thunderstorm, $\frac{1}{2}$ of the 200 homes on the south side of town had no electricity. $\frac{1}{4}$ of the 100 homes on the north side of town had no electricity. $\frac{2}{5}$ of the 300 homes on the east side and $\frac{7}{10}$ of the 100 homes on the west side experienced the same power outage. Which side of town had the greatest number of homes affected by the storm?

25. If $\frac{2}{10}$ of an area with a population of 4,000 people felt the effects of a flood, how many people were affected?

Write > or <.

1. $\frac{5}{6}$ ⬚ $\frac{24}{30}$
2. $\frac{3}{4}$ ⬚ $\frac{8}{9}$
3. $\frac{10}{30}$ ⬚ $\frac{2}{5}$
4. $\frac{27}{42}$ ⬚ $\frac{4}{7}$
5. $\frac{2}{3}$ ⬚ $\frac{7}{21}$

Construct Meaning

Telstar and Intelsat are communication satellites that relay telephone conversations and data transmissions. To do this, a communication satellite has a special radio called a transponder that receives a conversation or transmission at one frequency and sends it back to earth at a different frequency.

Vernon was doing a research paper on communication satellites and needed more information on transponders. His friend Doug sent him a fax of photographs of satellites that filled $1\frac{1}{2}$ sheets of paper. Vernon later received a fax from Martin about the Telstar satellite. This fax was $3\frac{1}{3}$ times longer than the fax he received from Doug. How many sheets of paper did the fax from Martin require?

Multiply mixed numbers.

$3\frac{1}{3} \times 1\frac{1}{2} = n$ — Rename both mixed numbers as improper fractions.

$\frac{10}{3} \times \frac{3}{2} = \frac{30}{6}$ — Multiply the fractions.

$\frac{30}{6} = 5$ — Write the product in simplest form.

The fax from Martin took 5 sheets of paper.

Multiply a mixed number by a fraction.

$2\frac{1}{4} \times \frac{2}{5} = n$ — Rename the mixed number as an improper fraction.

$\frac{9}{4} \times \frac{2}{5} = \frac{18}{20}$ — Multiply the fractions.

$\frac{18}{20} = \frac{9}{10}$ — Write the product in simplest form.

Muliply a mixed number by a whole number.

$4\frac{1}{2} \times 5 = n$ — Rename the mixed number as an improper fraction. Rename the whole number as a fraction by putting 1 under it.

$\frac{9}{2} \times \frac{5}{1} = \frac{45}{2}$ — Multiply the fractions.

$\frac{45}{2} = 22\frac{1}{2}$ — Write the product in simplest form.

Check Understanding

Copy and complete.

a. $2\frac{1}{3} \times 4\frac{2}{4} = \frac{\square}{3} \times \frac{18}{\square} = \frac{\square}{\square} = \square = \square$

b. $6\frac{3}{5} \times \frac{4}{7} = \frac{33}{\square} \times \frac{4}{7} = \frac{\square}{\square} = \square$

c. $8\frac{1}{2} \times 4 = \frac{\square}{\square} \times \frac{\square}{\square} = \frac{\square}{\square} = \square$

Multiply. Write the letter of the answer in simplest form.

1. $1\frac{1}{3} \times 2\frac{1}{2}$ **a.** 4   **b.** $3\frac{1}{3}$ **c.** $5\frac{1}{2}$ **d.** 7

2. $3\frac{5}{6} \times \frac{6}{7}$ **a.** $3\frac{2}{7}$ **b.** $3\frac{1}{7}$ **c.** $2\frac{2}{7}$ **d.** $3\frac{3}{7}$

3. $4\frac{3}{4} \times 6$ **a.** $27\frac{1}{2}$ **b.** $28\frac{2}{3}$ **c.** $28\frac{1}{2}$ **d.** $29\frac{1}{2}$

4. $\frac{5}{8} \times 1\frac{1}{6}$ **a.** $\frac{36}{49}$ **b.** $1\frac{13}{48}$ **c.** $\frac{34}{49}$ **d.** $\frac{35}{48}$

Multiply. Write the product in simplest form.

5. $2\frac{1}{3} \times 5\frac{1}{3}$ 6. $4\frac{1}{8} \times 2\frac{2}{3}$ 7. $6\frac{2}{5} \times 5$ 8. $10\frac{2}{3} \times 4$ 9. $12\frac{1}{2} \times 6\frac{1}{2}$

10. $1\frac{1}{6} \times \frac{3}{8}$ 11. $2\frac{1}{5} \times 1\frac{3}{7}$ 12. $3\frac{1}{2} \times 9\frac{5}{6}$ 13. $3\frac{3}{5} \times 5$ 14. $1\frac{4}{5} \times 9\frac{1}{2}$

15. $8\frac{3}{4} \times 3\frac{1}{3}$ 16. $8\frac{5}{6} \times \frac{2}{7}$ 17. $\frac{1}{4} \times 12$ 18. $11\frac{1}{4} \times 7$ 19. $2\frac{4}{7} \times \frac{1}{2}$

20. Telstar helps to provide the current news. For a history assignment, Chris watched the news on television $1\frac{1}{2}$ hours each day for four days. How many hours did Chris spend on the assignment?

21. Chris invited eleven friends over to watch the basketball game and the reviews. If $\frac{3}{4}$ of the group, including Chris, agreed with the reviews, how many friends disagreed?

22. Chris' mother was in the kitchen making a dip recipe. It required $1\frac{1}{2}$ cups of sour cream. She made it $2\frac{1}{2}$ times. How many cups of sour cream did she use?

23. $\frac{2}{3}$ bag of corn chips, $\frac{3}{4}$ bag of barbecue chips, and $\frac{1}{2}$ bag of ruffled potato chips were served. How many bags of chips were served?

24. A bag contained $3\frac{1}{3}$ dozen cookies. The boys ate $2\frac{1}{2}$ dozen. How many dozen cookies were left over?

Write *prime* if the number is prime and *composite* if it is composite.

1. 15   2. 7   3. 24   4. 19   5. 99

Solve.

6. $\begin{array}{r} 479 \\ 58 \\ 102 \\ + \quad 7 \\ \hline \end{array}$ 7. $\begin{array}{r} 58{,}403 \\ -19{,}084 \\ \hline \end{array}$ 8. $\begin{array}{r} 43.7 \\ -\ 2.801 \\ \hline \end{array}$ 9. $13\overline{)5.278}$ 10. $\begin{array}{r} 3.7 \\ \times 0.65 \\ \hline \end{array}$

 Check Understanding

"It's a great project!" The fifth graders at Evangel Christian School sell homemade cookies to the middle schoolers during their lunch time. The profit from the sales goes toward the purchase of a series of videos on satellites, rockets, and robots. _____

Mrs. Jensen wrote the Sand Art Candy Cookie recipe on the board and told the students to triple the amount of each ingredient. To triple a recipe means to use exactly three times each of the listed ingredients.

Multiply by three to determine each amount.

Sand Art Candy Cookies

Ingredient	Triple Recipe
$\frac{3}{4}$ cup packed brown sugar	$\frac{3}{4} \times 3 = \frac{3}{4} \times \frac{3}{1} = \frac{9}{4} = 2\frac{1}{4}$ cups
$\frac{3}{4}$ cup white sugar	a. $\frac{3}{4} \times 3$
$1\frac{1}{2}$ cups all-purpose flour	b. $1\frac{1}{2} \times 3$
1 teaspoon baking soda	c. 1×3
1 teaspoon salt	d. 1×3
$1\frac{1}{2}$ cups rolled oats	e. $1\frac{1}{2} \times 3$
$1\frac{1}{3}$ cups candy-coated chocolates	f. $1\frac{1}{3} \times 3$
$\frac{2}{3}$ cups butterscotch chips	g. $\frac{2}{3} \times 3$
$1\frac{1}{4}$ cups chocolate chips	h. $1\frac{1}{4} \times 3$
1 cup shortening	i. 1×3
2 eggs	j. 2×3
1 teaspoon vanilla	k. 1×3

The cookies were a big success and the fifth graders were pleased to purchase the series of videos!

The dry ingredients in the sand art design can be used to make a beautiful gift. Layer and pack down each dry ingredient in a clear glass container in the order it is given. Attach a copy of the baking directions which you may obtain from your teacher.

Problem Solving: Multiply Fractions

1. Bryce surveyed 45 fifth graders. If $\frac{1}{5}$ said they preferred strawberry ice cream, how many preferred a different flavor?

2. Brynne's brother began the first grade with 20 teeth. During the year he lost $\frac{1}{4}$ of them. How many permanent teeth will replace the missing ones?

3. If $\frac{2}{3}$ of the 15 ice skaters in the race decreased their pace when it started to snow, how many were affected by the snow?

4. Alicia, Desiree, and Todd ordered a pizza with twelve slices. Alicia ate $\frac{1}{6}$ of the pizza, Desiree ate $\frac{1}{3}$, and Todd ate the remaining slices. What part of the pizza did Todd eat?

5. Ryan finished $\frac{3}{4}$ of a test which had 20 questions. How many questions were unfinished?

6. Mr. Hill owns $9\frac{1}{2}$ acres of farmland. If $\frac{1}{6}$ of the land is designated for dairy cows, and $\frac{2}{3}$ of the land is used for growing wheat and corn, how many acres remain for his home and yard?

7. Susie is 28 years old. Nory's age is $\frac{3}{4}$ the age of Susie. Kristy is $1\frac{1}{3}$ times as old as Nory. How old is Kristy?

8. If the ingredients of the Sand Art Candy Cookie recipe are multiplied by four, how many cups of flour are needed? How many cups of chocolate chips are needed?

9. A ball drops 50 feet from a window of a building. When it hits the ground, it bounces $\frac{2}{5}$ of the height it was dropped. Calculate the total distance the ball traveled after being dropped.

10. The fisherman caught $17\frac{1}{2}$ pounds of seafood. The next day he caught $3\frac{1}{5}$ times as much as the first day. How many pounds did he catch the second day?

11. To prepare for the basketball tournament, Eric shot baskets for $\frac{1}{3}$ hour. Mike shot baskets $1\frac{1}{2}$ times as long as Eric. Jack shot baskets $1\frac{1}{4}$ times as long as Mike. What is the total number of hours the boys shot baskets?

12. 486 tourists visited the U. S. Olympic Training Center in Colorado Springs, Colorado. If $\frac{2}{3}$ of the tourists visited the U. S. Olympic Spirit Store, how many were there?

Brandon Slay trained at the Olympic Training Center in Colorado Springs. He won a silver medal in wrestling in 2000. He is a devout Christian, and of the Olympic experience he said, "There's more to life than gold."

 **Construct Meaning**

The Global Positioning System is a satellite network that assists with navigation for both ships and airplanes. The GPS may also assist a farmer with tasks such as measurement of fields and record-keeping.

If about $\frac{1}{3}$ of 16 ships received the same route for sailing up the United States Atlantic coast, about how many received it?

Estimate products using fractions.

- Substitute a compatible number for the whole number.

  $\frac{1}{3} \times 16$ 16 is not evenly divisible by 3. 15 is evenly divisible by 3.
  $15 \div 3 = 5$. Substitute 15 in the place of 16.

  About 5 ships received the same sailing route.

  $\frac{1}{3}$ of 15 is 5, so $\frac{1}{3}$ of 16 is about 5.

  $\frac{1}{4} \times 21$ 21 is not evenly divisible by 4. 20 is evenly divisible by 4.
  $20 \div 4 = 5$. Substitute 20 in the place of 21. $\frac{1}{4}$ of 20 is 5, so $\frac{1}{4}$ of 21 is about 5.

- Round each number to the nearest whole number.

  $4\frac{3}{4} \times 3\frac{1}{3}$ Round, then multiply. $5 \times 3 = 15$.

  Solve. $4\frac{3}{4} \times 3\frac{1}{3} = \frac{19}{4} \times \frac{10}{3} = \frac{190}{12} = 15\frac{5}{6}$

  15 is a reasonable estimate for $4\frac{3}{4} \times 3\frac{1}{3}$.

- When you multiply a proper fraction by a proper fraction, the product will be less than 1. This is true because you begin with a number less than 1, and the other factor is also less than one.

  $\frac{2}{3} \times \frac{5}{6}$

  $\frac{2}{3} \times \frac{5}{6} = \frac{10}{18} = \frac{5}{9}$

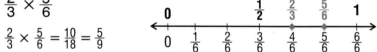

 **Check Understanding**

Use compatible numbers to complete the estimate.

a. $\frac{1}{7} \times 58 \longrightarrow 56 \div 7 = $ ▦ , so $\frac{1}{7}$ of 58 is about ▦ .

b. $\frac{1}{8} \times 39 \longrightarrow 40 \div 8 = $ ▦ , so $\frac{1}{8}$ of 39 is about ▦ .

Use rounding to the nearest whole number to estimate.

c. $12\frac{2}{3} \times 12\frac{1}{8} \longrightarrow 13 \times 12 = $ ▦ , so $12\frac{2}{3} \times 12\frac{1}{8}$ is about ▦ .

d. $5\frac{1}{3} \times 7\frac{1}{2} \longrightarrow $ ▦ $\times$ ▦ $= $ ▦ , so $5\frac{1}{3} \times 7\frac{1}{6}$ is about ▦ .

e. What do you know about the product of two proper fractions?

Substitute compatible numbers to complete the estimate.

1. $\frac{1}{4} \times 25$ 2. $\frac{1}{5} \times 36$ 3. $\frac{1}{3} \times 29$ 4. $\frac{1}{2} \times 55$ 5. $\frac{1}{5} \times 14$

6. $\frac{1}{3} \times 34$ 7. $\frac{1}{3} \times 41$ 8. $\frac{1}{4} \times 11$ 9. $\frac{1}{7} \times 65$ 10. $\frac{1}{10} \times 43$

11. $\frac{1}{25} \times 27$ 12. $\frac{1}{7} \times 15$ 13. $\frac{1}{9} \times 16$ 14. $\frac{1}{8} \times 21$ 15. $\frac{1}{2} \times 51$

Estimate by rounding each number to the nearest whole number.

16. $7\frac{1}{2} \times 9\frac{1}{3}$ 17. $14\frac{2}{3} \times 15\frac{1}{8}$ 18. $20\frac{2}{5} \times 6\frac{7}{9}$ 19. $4\frac{1}{2} \times 5\frac{3}{8}$ 20. $8\frac{2}{3} \times 1\frac{2}{3}$

21. There are 43 new yachts in the harbor. About how many of them take evening cruises if $\frac{1}{6}$ of them do?

22. The airplane flew $4\frac{3}{4}$ hours and signaled help for $1\frac{1}{3}$ hours of that time due to losing contact with the radar system. About how much time did the airplane fly with radar connection?

23. The farmer chose an area of land that was $\frac{1}{3}$ of a mile long and $\frac{5}{6}$ of a mile wide for the cattle to feed. Estimate the product to find the approximate number of square miles in this section of land.

24. The Global Positioning System was able to assist $\frac{1}{4}$ of 244 farmers, $\frac{1}{3}$ of 246 airplane pilots, and $\frac{1}{2}$ of 248 ship captains. Which group of people benefited the most by the network? What was the total number of occasions where assistance was given?

Moments with Careers

"My dad works as a farm manager. In his work he uses math to measure almonds for shipping and how much it costs to fertilize his farmland."

Stevinson
Modesto, CA

Write each fraction as a decimal.

1. $\frac{2}{10}$ 2. $\frac{25}{100}$ 3. $\frac{7}{10}$ 4. $\frac{250}{1,000}$ 5. $\frac{9}{100}$

Write each decimal as a fraction (in simplest form) or a mixed number.

6. 2.95   7. 0.01   8. 56.349   9. 1.17   10. 0.4

Construct Meaning

Space technology has led to the development of products that are being used on Earth. The insulation material used by the Space Shuttle to resist extreme temperatures is being used in thermal blanket kits and also in NASCAR drivers' cockpits to protect them from heat during a race. Freeze-dried foods used by manned space missions are also used for outdoor sports such as backpacking, fishing, and hunting.

Sam and Anneleis ate two packages of the freeze-dried ice cream they took on a hike. Each package was divided into four parts. How many fourths were in the two packages? A model can help you to divide a whole number by a fraction.

$$2 \div \frac{1}{4} = n \rightarrow \text{number of parts}$$

wholes   4 parts in each whole

There are eight fourths in two whole packages.

How many geoboards do you see?

What part of a whole board is each section?

$$3 \div \frac{1}{2} = n$$

There are six halves in three geoboards.

$$n = 6$$

How many cups do you see?

What part of a cup is each section?

$$4 \div \frac{1}{3} = n$$

There are twelve thirds in four cups.

$$n = 12$$

How many fraction bars do you see?

What part of a bar is each section?

$$5 \div \frac{1}{5} = n$$

There are twenty-five fifths in five bars.

$$n = 25$$

How many circles do you see?

What part of the circle is each section?

$$1 \div \frac{1}{3} = n$$

There are three thirds in the circle.

$$n = 3$$

Models can help you to divide a fraction by a fraction. A whole pie was divided into eighths. How many eighths are in $\frac{1}{2}$ of the pie?

$$\frac{1}{2} \div \frac{1}{8} = n \longrightarrow \text{number of eighths}$$

Consider one half of the whole.   8 parts in the whole

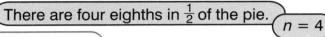
There are four eighths in $\frac{1}{2}$ of the pie. $n = 4$

 This box has been divided into fourths. How many fourths are in half of the box?
$\frac{1}{2} \div \frac{1}{4} = n$ There are two fourths in $\frac{1}{2}$. $n = 2$

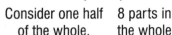

This egg carton has 12 sections. Each section is $\frac{1}{12}$. How many eggs are in $\frac{1}{3}$ of the carton?

$$\frac{1}{3} \div \frac{1}{12} = n$$

There are four eggs in $\frac{1}{3}$ of the carton. $n = 4$

This muffin pan has six sections. How many muffins are in $\frac{5}{6}$ of the pan?

$$\frac{5}{6} \div \frac{1}{6} = n$$

There are five muffins in $\frac{5}{6}$ of the pan. $n = 5$

✓ Check Understanding

Choose the number sentence that matches the model.

a. 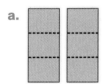   b.   c.   d.

$\frac{1}{2} \div \frac{1}{12} = 6$

$2 \div \frac{1}{3} = 6$

$\frac{3}{4} \div \frac{1}{8} = 6$

$3 \div \frac{1}{3} = 9$

Practice

Write the letter of the number sentence that matches the model.

1.    2.    3.    4.

1.
a. $3 \div \frac{1}{3} = 9$
b. $3 \div \frac{1}{4} = 12$
c. $3 \div \frac{1}{3} = 12$

2.
a. $2 \div \frac{1}{8} = 16$
b. $2 \div \frac{1}{7} = 14$
c. $2 \div \frac{1}{8} = 14$

3.
a. $6 \div \frac{1}{6} = 36$
b. $\frac{1}{2} \div \frac{1}{6} = 3$
c. $1 \div \frac{1}{6} = 6$

4.
a. $4 \div \frac{1}{5} = 20$
b. $2 \div \frac{1}{5} = 10$
c. $2 \div \frac{1}{4} = 8$

Draw a model for each number sentence. Copy and solve the equation.

5. $\frac{1}{3} \div \frac{1}{9} = n$ 6. $2 \div \frac{1}{5} = n$ 7. $1 \div \frac{1}{7} = n$ 8. $\frac{1}{4} \div \frac{1}{12} = n$

Construct Meaning

The Fisher Space Pen was designed with a special ink cartridge to be used on all manned space flights. It is guaranteed not to leak, to write smoothly, to write upside down, to write in extreme temperatures or in a gravity-free environment, and underwater.

Dan's father uses one of these pens in his outdoor work as a researcher in Northern Alaska. He carefully labels soil samples to send to two labs in Anchorage. One-half of each of three samples is sent to each lab for testing. How many halves (fraction) are in three (whole number) samples?

When dividing a fraction into a whole number, you are actually asking, "How many of this fraction are in this whole number?"

There are six halves in three samples.
This is the division equation that illustrates the picture.

$$3 \div \frac{1}{2} = 6$$

wholes   fraction   parts in 3 wholes

In Michael's lunch bag was a roll of chocolate candy. His mother had cut the roll into thirds. Michael cut each third in half so that he had 6 pieces. How many sixths are in $\frac{1}{3}$?

There are two sixths in $\frac{1}{3}$.

This is the division equation that illustrates the picture.

$$\frac{1}{3} \div \frac{1}{6} = 2$$

each of the   there are 6   parts in
3 parts of   total parts   each $\frac{1}{3}$
the whole

How many sixths are in $\frac{2}{3}$? Write a division equation.

Check Understanding

Decide if the model shows division of a whole number or division of a fraction. Write *whole number* or *fraction*.

a.    b.   c.    d.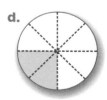

ractice

Use the model to write a division equation.

1.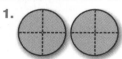

2.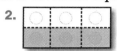

3.

4.

5.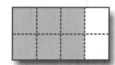

6.

7.

8.

Use models, if needed, to find the quotient.

9. $3 \div \frac{1}{3} = x$

THINK: How many thirds are in 3 whole models?

10. $5 \div \frac{1}{4} = x$

THINK: How many fourths are in 5 whole models?

11. $\frac{1}{2} \div \frac{1}{4} = x$

THINK: How many fourths are in $\frac{1}{2}$ of a model?

12. $\frac{1}{3} \div \frac{1}{9} = x$

THINK: How many ninths are in $\frac{1}{3}$ of a model?

pply

Write a division sentence to solve.

13. A piece of insulated fabric is $\frac{12}{18}$ of a yard long. Mrs. Marsh cuts the fabric into pieces that are $\frac{6}{18}$ of a yard long.

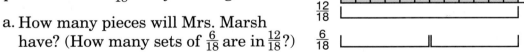

a. How many pieces will Mrs. Marsh have? (How many sets of $\frac{6}{18}$ are in $\frac{12}{18}$?)

b. If she cuts the fabric into pieces that are $\frac{4}{18}$ of a yard long, how many pieces will she have? (How many sets of $\frac{4}{18}$ are in $\frac{12}{18}$?)

c. If she cuts the fabric into pieces that are $\frac{3}{18}$ of a yard long, how many pieces will she have? (How many sets of $\frac{3}{18}$ are in $\frac{12}{18}$?)

14. Brent cut a round brownie into 11 slices. If each person eats $\frac{2}{11}$ of the brownie, how many people can be served? Will the whole brownie be eaten? Explain.

eview

Solve.

1. $1\frac{2}{3}$
   $+ 5\frac{2}{3}$

2. $9\frac{3}{4}$
   $- 6\frac{2}{5}$

3. 2.4
   $\times 7.9$

4. $8\overline{)26.064}$

5. 47.9
   $\times 0.62$

Construct Meaning

The Expedition One crew was launched on October 31, 2000 and arrived safely at the International Space Station. The first resident crew, United States Astronaut Bill Shepherd and Russian Cosmonauts Yuri Gidzenko and Sorgei Krikalev, were sent to activate systems, conduct experiments, do on-orbit construction, and welcome space shuttle missions.

Russian Space Station Mir was used as the International Space Station Phase 1

Conrad, Laurence, and Kenneth are on-line in the media center watching videos of life in space. They are getting facts for a creative writing class. The assignment is to write about a day at the ISS. Conrad got three facts per session, Laurence got two, and Kenneth got four. How many facts will Laurence and Kenneth have when Conrad has 15? Make a table to find a pattern.

Conrad	3	6	9	12	
Laurence	2	4	6	8	
Kenneth	4	8	12	16	

There is a pattern in the way each person's number of facts increases. Conrad's facts increase by three each session, so the next number is 15. Laurence's facts increase by two; the next number is 10. Kenneth's facts increase by four; the next number is 20.

When Conrad has 15 facts, Laurence will have 10 and Kenneth will have 20.

Mrs. Russell gave the students five sessions to brainstorm and write about a day at the ISS. The first session was for 15 minutes. The second session was five minutes longer than the first. The third was five minutes longer than the second session. If the pattern continues, how many minutes will the fifth session last?

Session	1	2	3	4	5
Minutes Per Session	15	20	25	30	

The pattern increases by five. The next number is 35.

The fifth session will last 35 minutes.

Check Understanding

Copy and complete the table. Solve by finding the pattern.

a. 32 fifth graders are anxiously waiting for their turn on a simulated space mission. If each ride takes eight minutes and four people ride each time, how long would it take 32 students to get a ride?

Time	8	16	24	32	40	48	56	
People	4	8	12	16	20	24	28	32

b. Betsy was saving her baby-sitting money for spring vacation. The first week she earned $15.00, but for each of the following weeks she earned $8.00. Using the pattern, how much money had she saved after the fifth week?

Week	1	2	3	4	5
Money Saved	$15	$23	$31	$39	

Practice

Solve by finding a pattern. Make a table if necessary.

1. If 720 people cast a vote every two minutes, how long will it take to cast 5,040 votes?

2. To help pay for the cost of the retreat, the students had a car wash. If four cars were washed hourly, how many cars were washed by the end of the sixth hour? If $3.00 profit was made per hour, how much money was raised?

3. Lorne delivers newspapers every morning. For every 30 papers he sells, he makes $2.50. How many newspapers will he need to sell to make $20?

4. Mrs. Brooks walks for 25 minutes every day and burns 125 calories. How many minutes will it take to burn off 1,000 calories? How many 25-minute sessions will it require?

5. Space technology has led to the use of cellular phones. During an eight-hour period, a company sold three phones during each of the first four hours and four phones during each of the last four hours. What was the total number of sales during the eight-hour period? If the number of sales increased at the same rate, how many phones would sell during each of the next four hours?

6. Dad enjoys putting a puzzle together. During his first sitting, he put 25 pieces together. The next time, he put 30 pieces together. The third time, he put 35 pieces together. If the pattern continues, how many sittings will it take Dad to put a 225-piece puzzle together?

7. The lawn mower cuts a width of $1\frac{1}{2}$ feet. How many widths will it take to mow a strip of grass that is $16\frac{1}{2}$ feet wide?

8. During the state volleyball tournament, six student tickets were sold for every two adult tickets. At this rate, how many adult tickets had been sold when 96 student tickets were sold?

9. The fifth graders at Community Christian School were committed to raise support for a fifth grade student to attend Alliance Academy in Quito, Ecuador. If they pledged to raise $25.00 per week, how many weeks will it take to raise $1,148.75?

10. Read Exodus 25:31–40 to find the pattern God gave His people for making a lampstand of pure gold. How many bowls were on the lampstand?

Featuring Fractions

Write *T* for true and *F* for false.

1. When you multiply fractions, you must multiply the numerators first.
2. When you multiply fractions, the denominators must be the same.
3. When you multiply $\frac{1}{3} \times \frac{3}{4}$, the product is less than the whole number 1.
4. The line in a fraction represents division.

Copy and complete the multiplication sentence for each model. Write the product in simplest form.

5. $\frac{1}{2} \times \frac{1}{4} =$ ░░░

6. $\frac{2}{3} \times$ ░░ $=$ ░░ $=$ ░░

7.  $\frac{1}{2} \times$ ░░ $=$ ░░

Multiply. Write the product in simplest form.

8. $\frac{2}{3} \times \frac{1}{4}$

9. $\frac{3}{4} \times \frac{4}{7}$

10. $\frac{5}{2} \times \frac{3}{9}$

11. $\frac{3}{5} \times \frac{7}{2}$

12. $\frac{1}{4} \times 24$

13. $45 \times \frac{3}{5}$

14. $\frac{2}{3} \times 18$

15. $63 \times \frac{2}{7}$

Use > or < to complete the number sentence.

16. $\frac{1}{4} \times \frac{2}{3}$ ░░ $\frac{2}{6}$

17. $\frac{4}{5} \times \frac{1}{2}$ ░░ $\frac{2}{10}$

18. $\frac{7}{14} \times \frac{5}{10}$ ░░ 1

19. $\frac{1}{3} \times \frac{3}{7}$ ░░ $\frac{1}{8}$

20. $\frac{1}{2} \times \frac{3}{7}$ ░░ $\frac{7}{14}$

21. $\frac{2}{5} \times \frac{5}{6}$ ░░ $\frac{1}{2}$

22. $\frac{6}{7} \times \frac{2}{4}$ ░░ $\frac{5}{14}$

23. $\frac{5}{9} \times \frac{7}{7}$ ░░ $\frac{1}{3}$

Multiply. Write the letter of the answer in simplest form.

24. $2\frac{1}{3} \times 3\frac{1}{2}$ a. $7\frac{1}{2}$ b. $8\frac{1}{6}$ c. $8\frac{2}{3}$ d. $8\frac{1}{5}$

25. $4\frac{5}{6} \times \frac{4}{5}$ a. $3\frac{14}{15}$ b. $3\frac{2}{3}$ c. $2\frac{13}{15}$ d. $3\frac{13}{15}$

26. $5\frac{3}{4} \times 7$ a. $40\frac{1}{2}$ b. $40\frac{1}{3}$ c. $39\frac{3}{4}$ d. $40\frac{1}{4}$

27. $\frac{6}{7} \times 1\frac{1}{4}$ a. $1\frac{1}{14}$ b. $1\frac{1}{4}$ c. $1\frac{1}{3}$ d. $1\frac{1}{2}$

28. $11\frac{1}{8} \times \frac{1}{2}$ a. $4\frac{9}{16}$ b. $6\frac{7}{16}$ c. $5\frac{9}{16}$ d. $5\frac{7}{16}$

Estimate the product by substituting a compatible number.

29. $\frac{1}{5} \times 29$

30. $\frac{1}{7} \times 58$

Round each number to the nearest whole number to estimate the product.

31. $15\frac{1}{6} \times 2\frac{7}{8}$

32. $6\frac{1}{2} \times 7\frac{3}{8}$

33. $10\frac{1}{2} \times 4\frac{1}{2}$

34. $8\frac{1}{3} \times 4\frac{3}{4}$

Captain Gorie reads God's Word in space.

Choose the letter of the number sentence that matches the model.

35.

a. $3 \div \frac{1}{3} = 9$

b. $3 \div \frac{1}{9} = 27$

c. $3 \div \frac{1}{6} = 18$

36.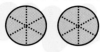

a. $\frac{1}{4} \div \frac{1}{8} = \frac{1}{32}$

b. $\frac{1}{4} \div \frac{1}{8} = 2$

c. $\frac{1}{5} \div \frac{1}{4} = \frac{1}{12}$

37.

a. $2 \div \frac{1}{5} = 10$

b. $2 \div \frac{1}{7} = 14$

c. $2 \div \frac{1}{6} = 12$

38.

a. $\frac{1}{2} \div \frac{1}{8} = 4$

b. $\frac{1}{2} \div \frac{1}{4} = \frac{1}{8}$

c. $\frac{1}{2} \div \frac{1}{8} = \frac{1}{16}$

Find the quotient.

39. $\frac{1}{3} \div \frac{1}{9}$

40. $\frac{1}{2} \div \frac{1}{10}$

41. $4 \div \frac{1}{4}$

42. $3 \div \frac{1}{5}$

The hand-held locator which contains the Global Positioning System helps people to navigate in the wilderness. If the high-tech locator sales progress accordingly, what is the projected number of sales for week seven? Solve by finding a pattern.

Week	1	2	3	4	5	6	7
Hikers	7	14	21	28	35	42	43.
Anglers	3	6	9	12	15	18	44.
Hunters	3	7	12	18	25	33	45.

46. The Penguin Water Corporation uses the filtration module that was designed for the International Space Station to have pure drinking water. If $\frac{1}{5}$ of the 60 local businesses use bottled water with this system, how many companies are benefitting from space technology?

47. Medical researchers have been able to give diabetics a better form of insulin due to experimenting with crystals in space where there is no weight. If each of four crystals were broken into thirds, how many pieces would there be?

48. Jackie shares 13 candy apples by cutting each one in half. How many people can be served if each person gets one half?

49. Clarke studied $1\frac{3}{4}$ hours on Monday and $2\frac{1}{3}$ hours on Tuesday for a math test. How many hours did he study for the perfect score he received on the test?

"For by Him all things were created that are in heaven and that are on earth, visible and invisible, whether thrones or dominions or principalities or powers. All things were created through Him and for Him. And He is before all things, and in Him all things consist."

Colossians 1:16–17

Grade Five

10
Chapter
Lessons 121–133

For the LORD God *is* a sun and shield;
The LORD will give grace and glory;
No good *thing* will He withhold
From those who walk uprightly.

Psalm 84:11

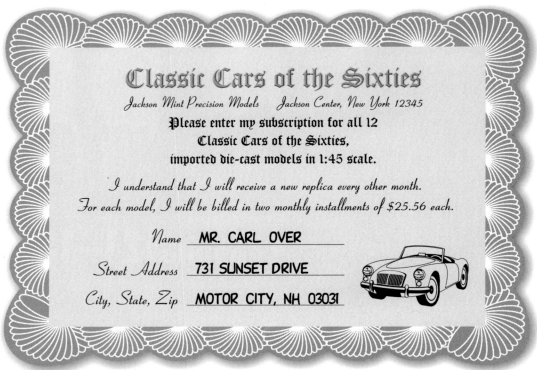

Classic Cars of the Sixties

Jackson Mint Precision Models   Jackson Center, New York 12345

Please enter my subscription for all 12
Classic Cars of the Sixties,
imported die-cast models in 1:45 scale.

I understand that I will receive a new replica every other month.
For each model, I will be billed in two monthly installments of $25.56 each.

Name   MR. CARL OVER

Street Address   731 SUNSET DRIVE

City, State, Zip   MOTOR CITY, NH 03031

The classic car models are made in a 1:45 scale. What does that mean? The notation 1:45 is a ratio. It means that the actual car was 45 times as large as the model. If the model of the 1967 Corvette is four inches long, the actual 1967 Corvette is 45 times four, or 180 inches long.

A **ratio** compares two quantities.

In this group of Canadian coins, the ratio of pennies to dimes is 3 to 4.

$$3 \quad \text{to} \quad 4$$
$$\downarrow \qquad\qquad \downarrow$$
Number of pennies   *Number of dimes*

A ratio can be written in three ways.   3 to 4   3:4 $\frac{3}{4}$

This ratio is being used to compare <u>one part to another part</u>, pennies to dimes.
The ratio for dimes to pennies would be 4 to 3, 4:3, or $\frac{4}{3}$.
The order in which you write a ratio is important.

$$\frac{\text{pennies}}{\text{dimes}} \quad \frac{3}{4} \quad \text{is different from} \quad \frac{\text{dimes}}{\text{pennies}} \quad \frac{4}{3}$$

You can also write a ratio to compare <u>one part to the whole</u>.

$$\frac{\text{pennies}}{\text{coins}} \quad \frac{3}{7} \quad \text{and} \quad \frac{\text{dimes}}{\text{coins}} \quad \frac{4}{7}$$

 **Check Understanding**

Write a ratio that shows each of the following.

a. minivans to motor homes

b. trolleys to trains

c. gas pumps to fuel gauges

 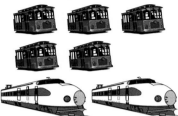 

 **Practice**

Use the table. Write each ratio in three ways.

VOTES FOR CLASS TRIP	
Brock Canyon	||||‖ ‖‖‖
Hamilton Park	‖‖‖
Latimer Zoo	‖‖‖ |||

1. Brock Canyon to Hamilton Park
2. Hamilton Park to Brock Canyon
3. Brock Canyon to total votes
4. Hamilton Park to Latimer Zoo
5. Latimer Zoo to Hamilton Park
6. Hamilton Park to total votes
7. Latimer Zoo to Brock Canyon
8. Latimer Zoo to total votes

9. Write the numbers of the problems that show part to part ratios.

10. Write the numbers of the problems that show part to whole ratios.

11. Using the table, what is being compared by the ratio of $\frac{10}{8}$?

 Apply

12. A survey found that out of 24 students, 11 listed chocolate chip ice cream as their favorite flavor. Write a ratio for the number of students who did <u>not</u> choose chocolate chip compared to the total number of students.

13. On a flight to Fairbanks, Alaska, there were two pilots, three flight attendants, and 72 passengers. What was the ratio of airline employees to passengers?

 **Review**

Solve each fraction problem. Watch the signs.

1. $2\frac{2}{3} + 3\frac{2}{3}$ 2. $\frac{1}{4} \times \frac{5}{9}$ 3. $11 - 6\frac{7}{8}$ 4. $\frac{3}{4} \times \frac{1}{2}$ 5. $\frac{3}{5} - \frac{1}{3}$

6. $\frac{6}{7} \times \frac{2}{3}$ 7. $5\frac{1}{12} + 7\frac{5}{6}$ 8. $\frac{9}{14} \times \frac{3}{5}$ 9. $20\frac{1}{8} - 16\frac{3}{4}$ 10. $12 + 4\frac{1}{8}$

 Construct Meaning

Chris loves to watch NASCAR racing. During a recent race, Chris's favorite driver averaged three miles per minute. At this rate, how long would it take the driver to travel 18 miles? Use equal ratios to find the number of minutes needed to travel 18 miles.

Two ratios are equal if they can be written as equivalent fractions. Finding an **equal ratio** is like finding an equivalent fraction.

$$\text{miles} \rightarrow \frac{3}{1} \quad \text{Find an equal ratio.} \quad \overset{\text{Think } \times 6}{\frac{3}{1} = \frac{18}{n}} \overset{\leftarrow \text{miles}}{\leftarrow \text{minutes}}$$
$$\times 6$$

The equal ratio would be $\frac{18}{6}$. Since $n = 6$, the car will travel 18 miles in 6 minutes.

A **ratio table** can show a series of equal ratios.

miles	3	6	9	12	15	18
minutes	1	2	3	4	5	6

The ratios 3:1, 6:2, 9:3, 12:4, 15:5, and 18:6 are equal ratios.

Pit crews are important to a driver's position on the track. When the driver pulls in for service, the fueling, tire changes, and minor adjustments need to be completed in seconds. If a driver pits four times in a race for a total of 76 seconds, what is the average number of seconds required for two pits?

$$\frac{\text{pits}}{\text{seconds}} \rightarrow \overset{\text{Think } \div 2}{\frac{4}{76} = \frac{2}{n}}$$
$$\div 2$$

The equal ratio would be $\frac{2}{38}$, so the average number

number of pits	1	2	3	4
number of seconds	19	38	57	76

The ratios $\frac{1}{19}$, $\frac{2}{38}$, $\frac{3}{57}$, and $\frac{4}{76}$ are equal ratios. They are named by equivalent fractions.

 **Check Understanding**

Copy and complete each ratio table.

a. To make two omelets, you need five eggs.

omelets	2	4	6	8
eggs	5			

b. To make one pie, you need six apples.

pies	1	2		4	
apples	6		18		30

ractice

Refer to the pictures. Tell what is being compared. Write each ratio as a fraction.

1. 5 to 3

2. 8 to 5

3. 3 to 8

4. 3 to 5

Write two ratios that are equal to the given ratio.

5. $\frac{3}{4}$

6. $\frac{2}{3}$

7. $\frac{3}{5}$

8. $\frac{6}{7}$

9. $\frac{4}{9}$

Find the missing number. Write your answer as $n =$ ▦ .

10. $\frac{3}{8} = \frac{15}{n}$

11. $\frac{4}{n} = \frac{16}{44}$

12. $\frac{9}{12} = \frac{n}{36}$

13. $\frac{n}{15} = \frac{8}{60}$

14. $\frac{16}{48} = \frac{n}{6}$

Write = or ≠ for each pair of ratios.

15. $\frac{3}{4}$ ▦ $\frac{9}{10}$

16. $\frac{9}{18}$ ▦ $\frac{27}{54}$

17. $\frac{18}{27}$ ▦ $\frac{6}{9}$

18. $\frac{8}{6}$ ▦ $\frac{32}{48}$

19. $\frac{12}{21}$ ▦ $\frac{4}{7}$

pply

Make a ratio table with the data given in the problem.

20. A pint of wild rice provides 11.5 milligrams of calcium. Show the number of milligrams of calcium in 1, 2, 3, 4, and 5 pints.

21. The ingredients for three submarine sandwiches cost $4.00. Show how many sandwiches can be made for $8.00, $12.00, and $16.00.

22. The ratio of NASCAR drivers to "over the wall" pit crew members is 1:7. Show the number of pit crew members required by 1, 2, 3, 4, and 5 drivers.

eview

Write the word or number that will complete each sentence.

1. A triangle with each side measuring a different length is called a ▦ triangle.

2. A ▦ is a line segment that connects the center with a point on the circle.

3. Lines that intersect at right angles are called ▦ lines.

4. The total measure of the three angles of a triangle is ▦ degrees.

 **Construct Meaning**

Are these two rugs proportional?

8 feet

6 feet

3 feet

4 feet

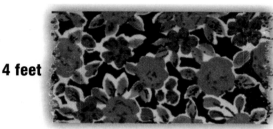

Each ratio compares the width of the rug to its length.

$$\frac{3 \text{ feet}}{6 \text{ feet}} \leftarrow \frac{\text{width}}{\text{length}} \rightarrow \frac{4 \text{ feet}}{8 \text{ feet}}$$

The numerator of each ratio represents width in feet. Both denominators show length in feet.

An equation that shows that the two ratios are equal is called a **proportion**. $\frac{3}{6} = \frac{4}{8}$

In a proportion the cross products are equal. To find **cross products** of two ratios, multiply each numerator by the denominator of the other ratio.

$\frac{3}{6} = \frac{4}{8}$ $3 \times 8 = 4 \times 6$
$24 = 24$

Because the cross products are equal, the rugs are proportional.

Evie and Marco are preparing bags of trail mix for the youth camping trip. If one recipe serves six, how many cups of mix will be needed for 24 students?

TRAIL MIX
Makes 8 cups. Serves 6.

4 cups cereal	1 cup banana chips
$\frac{1}{2}$ cup dried apricots	1 cup raisins
$\frac{1}{2}$ cup dried apples	1 cup yogurt-covered peanuts

To find the answer, write a proportion showing two equal ratios. Use cross products to solve for n.

$\dfrac{\text{number of servings}}{\text{cups of mix}} \longrightarrow \dfrac{6}{8} = \dfrac{24}{n}$

In the proportion $\frac{6}{8} = \frac{24}{n}$, n is the unknown term.

Find the cross products. $6 \times n = 24 \times 8$
$6 \times n = 192$
Divide to find n. $n = 192 \div 6$
$n = 32$

32 cups are needed for 24 students.

 Check Understanding

Write the cross products. Solve for the missing number.

a. $\frac{2}{7} = \frac{x}{28}$

b. $\frac{4}{5} = \frac{32}{n}$

c. $\frac{8}{3} = \frac{a}{21}$

d. $\frac{7}{3} = \frac{y}{9}$

 Practice

Write the cross products. Write = or ≠.

1. $\frac{3}{4} = \frac{6}{8}$

2. $\frac{4}{9} = \frac{6}{18}$

3. $\frac{6}{7} = \frac{2}{5}$

4. $\frac{17}{20} = \frac{34}{40}$

5. $\frac{9}{12} = \frac{7}{9}$

6. $\frac{6}{4} = \frac{18}{12}$

7. $\frac{12}{48} = \frac{3}{8}$

8. $\frac{6}{9} = \frac{2}{3}$

Find the value of the unknown term.

9. $\frac{x}{6} = \frac{2}{3}$

10. $\frac{8}{10} = \frac{4}{n}$

11. $\frac{20}{y} = \frac{4}{5}$

12. $\frac{6}{8} = \frac{n}{24}$

13. $\frac{32}{36} = \frac{8}{x}$

14. $\frac{4}{5} = \frac{x}{35}$

15. $\frac{n}{25} = \frac{6}{5}$

16. $\frac{2}{3} = \frac{x}{9}$

 Apply

Write a proportion. Solve for the unknown term.

17. An instant drink mix uses 3 tablespoons mix to 8 cups of water. How many tablespoons are needed for 32 cups of water?

18. A formula for paint takes 12 drops of yellow color to 1 gallon of green paint. How much yellow is needed for 3 gallons of green paint?

19. For every three drops of red color, Julia used four drops of yellow to make a certain shade of orange. If she used 21 drops of red, how many drops of yellow were needed?

 Review

Solve. Draw a model to help you if necessary.

1. $7 \div \frac{1}{3}$

2. $12 \div \frac{1}{2}$

3. $\frac{1}{2} \div \frac{1}{4}$

4. $\frac{1}{3} \div \frac{1}{9}$

Construct Meaning

For centuries, artists have worked with proportions. Greek sculptors used an 8 to 1 ratio for total body height to head height. Suppose you plan to make a clay sculpture of a human with a head that is 2 inches high. Using the Greek sculptor's 8 to 1 ratio, what would be the total height of the sculpture?

To find the height, you can write a proportion.

human body height	$\dfrac{8}{1} = \dfrac{x}{2}$	sculpture's body height
human head height		sculpture's head height

A proportion is an equation that states that two ratios are equal.

Remember:

There are two ways to find x.

1 You can use equal ratios. Multiply or divide both the numerator and the denominator of the fraction by the same number. _____

$$\overset{\times 2}{\overset{\frown}{\underset{\underset{\times 2}{\smile}}{\dfrac{8}{1} = \dfrac{x}{2}}}} \qquad \begin{array}{l} 8 \times 2 = 16 \\ x = 16 \end{array}$$

2 You can find the cross products of the two fractions. Multiply each numerator by the denominator of the other fraction. _____

$$\dfrac{8}{1} \times \dfrac{x}{2} \qquad \begin{array}{l} 8 \times 2 = x \times 1 \\ 16 = x \end{array}$$

To be proportional, the total height of the sculpture must be 16 inches.

Check Understanding

a. If an artist is using the 8 to 1 ratio to sculpt a statue of a human with a head height of 3 inches, what is the total body height?

b. If a life-size sculpture shows a man with a total height of 72 inches, what would you expect the head height to be?

c. If it takes an artist seven hours to cast three small copies of the sculpture shown, how many hours would it take to make 96 copies? Use cross products.

Use equivalent fractions or cross products to solve.

1. $\dfrac{4}{7} = \dfrac{n}{21}$

2. $\dfrac{5}{10} = \dfrac{50}{x}$

3. $\dfrac{4}{5} = \dfrac{48}{y}$

4. $\dfrac{n}{10} = \dfrac{12}{15}$

Copy and complete the ratio table to solve the problem.

5. You can walk 2 miles in 15 minutes. How far can you walk in 60 minutes?

MILES	2	4	6	
MINUTES	15			

6. The punch recipe uses two quarts of cranberry juice for each gallon of punch. How much cranberry juice is needed for seven gallons?

QUARTS OF CRANBERRY JUICE	2		8			
GALLONS OF PUNCH	1		3		6	

7. Randall, who is on a weight-loss program, has lost 3 pounds in five weeks. At the same rate, how long will it take him to lose 27 pounds?

8. A brick wall 24 feet in length contains 1,040 bricks. Using the same pattern, how many bricks will it take to build a wall 48 feet in length?

Great Wall of China seen through brick archway

9. Twenty-four jars can be packed in six identical boxes. How many jars can be packed in 15 boxes of that same size?

10. The dosage of a certain medication is 2 ounces for every 50 pounds of body weight. How many ounces are required for a 150-pound man?

11. Ron uses 2 pounds of fertilizer per 100 square feet of lawn. How much fertilizer is needed for a lawn that measures 2,500 square feet?

Order each set of fractions from greatest to least. Hint: Writing in simplest form may help you.

1. $\dfrac{7}{10}$ $\dfrac{3}{5}$ $\dfrac{4}{15}$ $\dfrac{15}{30}$

2. $\dfrac{2}{3}$ $\dfrac{4}{12}$ $\dfrac{3}{4}$ $\dfrac{14}{24}$

3. $\dfrac{1}{2}$ $\dfrac{6}{8}$ $\dfrac{4}{10}$ $\dfrac{8}{80}$

4. $\dfrac{7}{9}$ $\dfrac{18}{81}$ $\dfrac{2}{18}$ $\dfrac{27}{36}$

5. $\dfrac{3}{7}$ $\dfrac{2}{14}$ $\dfrac{25}{35}$ $\dfrac{16}{28}$

6. $\dfrac{1}{3}$ $\dfrac{2}{12}$ $\dfrac{21}{36}$ $\dfrac{5}{6}$

Construct Meaning

A **scale drawing** represents an area or an object as it is, but usually in a smaller or larger size. Maps, blueprints, landscaping plans, and diagrams are examples of scale drawings.

The scale of this map of Yosemite National Park tells you that 2 centimeters represent an actual distance of 5 kilometers. This can be expressed as the ratio 2 cm : 5 km. If the map distance of the road between Badger Pass and Glacier Point is 7 cm, what is the actual driving distance?

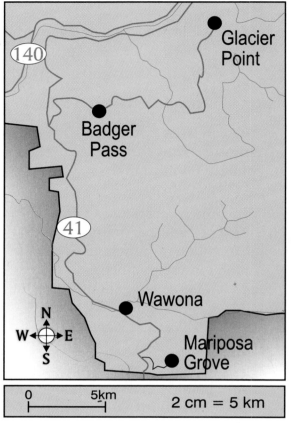

$$\frac{\text{map distance}}{\text{actual distance}} = \frac{2 \text{ cm}}{5 \text{ km}} = \frac{7 \text{ cm}}{x}$$

Use cross products.

$2 \text{ cm} \times x = 7 \text{ cm} \times 5 \text{km}$

$2 \times x = 35$

$x = 35 \div 2$

$x = 17.5$

The actual driving distance is 17.5 kilometers.

Check Understanding

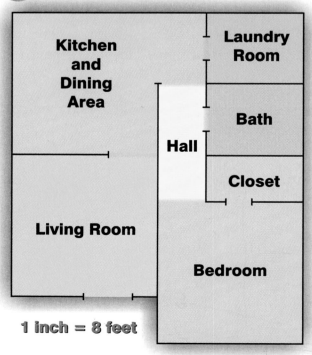

1 inch = 8 feet

Write and solve a proportion to answer each question. You will need a ruler.

a. What is the length of the apartment on its longest wall?

b. What is the length of the apartment from the front door to the back wall?

c. Will a rug that measures 12 feet by 10 feet fit into the living room?

d. What is the length of the wall that separates the dining area from the living room?

ractice

On a country map 2 centimeters represents 15 kilometers. Write an equation and solve to find the actual distance for each map measurement.

1. a wildlife preserve that is 4 centimeters long

2. a city located 8 centimeters from the wildlife preserve

3. a visitor center shown as 1 centimeter from the entrance

4. a lake along the eastern boundary of the preserve that is 3.2 cm long

5. the distance of 5 centimeters between the visitor center and the animal hospital

A scale drawing can be smaller than, larger than, or the same size as the object it represents. For each object, write if the scale is *reasonable* or *not reasonable*.

6.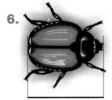

2 cm : 10 cm

7.

2 cm : 40 cm

8.

1 inch : 8 feet

9.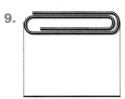

1 inch : 1 inch

Write an equation to solve each problem.

10. The length of the model car is 4 inches. The scale is 1 inch : 4 feet. What is the length of the actual car?

11. The scale model of the house is 12 inches long. The length of the actual house is 48 feet. Which scale was used: 1 inch = 4 feet or 1 inch = 8 feet?

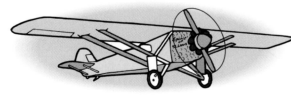

12. The *Spirit of St. Louis*, flown by Charles Lindbergh in 1927, had a wingspan of 14 feet. How long would the wingspan be in a scale drawing if the scale was 1 inch : 2 feet?

13. To fit on a Christmas card, an 8-inch by 10-inch photo must be reduced to 4 inches by 5 inches. Are the two sizes proportional?

14. A map scale is 1 inch equals 20 miles. How far apart are two towns if the map distance measures 3 inches?

Construct Meaning

Mrs. Bailey's fifth grade students conducted a poll of 100 fifth and sixth grade classmates. The students were asked to pick their favorite sport from a list of five choices. The chart shows the results.

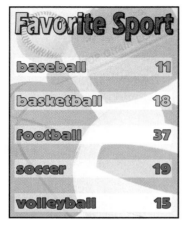

Favorite Sport

baseball	11
basketball	18
football	37
soccer	19
volleyball	15

Mrs. Bailey asked her students to show the results on a 10 by 10 grid, using five different colors. Then they wrote a ratio comparing the number of students who chose each sport to the total number of students polled. The students wrote: 11:100, 18:100, 37:100, 19:100, and 15:100.

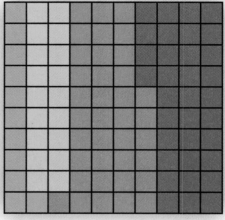

When you compare a number to 100, you are using a special ratio called a percent. **Percent** means "per one hundred." The symbol for percent is %.

What percent of the grid is colored?

The same number can be expressed in several ways.

Problem	Ratio	Fraction	Decimal	Percent
Show 89 out of 100.	89:100	$\frac{89}{100}$	0.89	89%
Show 43¢ out of $1.00.	43:100	$\frac{43}{100}$	0.43	43%

Check Understanding

Write a ratio, fraction, decimal, and percent to show what part is shaded.

a.    b.    c. 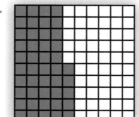   d.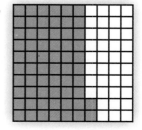

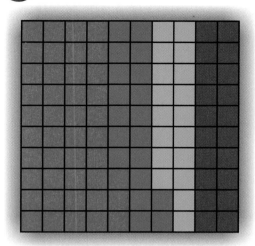

The grid shows the number of each type of book by color.

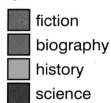

- fiction
- biography
- history
- science

1. Write the fraction and percent for each type of book.
2. What is the total percent of non-fiction books?
3. What percent of the books are art books?

Write each ratio as a percent.

4. $\frac{57}{100}$ 5. 1 to 100   6. 55:100   7. $\frac{79}{100}$ 8. 23 to 100

9. 10:100   10. 61 to 100   11. 75:100   12. $\frac{100}{100}$ 13. 5 to 100

Write as a fraction with a denominator of 100.

14. 16% $\frac{16}{100}$ 16%   15. 98% $\frac{98}{100}$ 16. 3% $\frac{3}{100}$ 17. 25% $\frac{25}{100}$ 18. 47% $\frac{47}{100}$

19. 9% $\frac{9}{100}$ 20. 50% $\frac{50}{100}$ 21. 88% $\frac{88}{100}$ 22. 33% $\frac{33}{100}$ 23. 65% $\frac{65}{100}$

24. Tom's mother has driven 33 of the 100 miles to their destination. What percent of the drive remains to be completed?

25. Out of the 100 problems on the test, Gary had 83 correct. What was the percentage of problems correct?

26. Six percent of 100 students chose the sun as the topic for their science project. What percent chose other topics?

Review

Solve. Write the answer in simplest form.

1. $9\frac{6}{8}$ $-6\frac{2}{3}$ 2. $10\frac{5}{6}$ $-4\frac{1}{2}$ 3. $16\frac{4}{9}$ $-3\frac{3}{4}$ 4. $13\frac{3}{6}$ -2 5. $21\frac{1}{2}$ $-5\frac{1}{3}$ 6. 31 $-11\frac{3}{22}$ 7. 7 $-5\frac{1}{2}$

 Construct Meaning

On a recent mission trip, Dr. Soduk examined the teeth of 50 children. He found that 17 of them had cavities.

What percent of the children had cavities?

Percent means per one hundred. If a ratio has a denominator of 100, it is easy to express it as a percent.

 Step 1 Write the ratio as a fraction.

$\dfrac{17}{50}$ ← number with cavities
← total children examined

 Step 2 Write a proportion in which one ratio has a denominator of 100.

$\dfrac{17}{50} = \dfrac{t}{100}$

 Step 3 Solve the proportion by using multiplication or cross products.

$\overset{\times 2}{\dfrac{17}{50}} = \underset{\times 2}{\dfrac{t}{100}} \quad t = 34$

 Step 4 Rewrite the fraction as a percent.

$\dfrac{34}{100} = 34\%$

34% of the children had cavities.

 Check Understanding

Copy and complete the chart.

	Ratio	Proportion	Solution		Percent
a.	$\dfrac{9}{25}$	$\dfrac{9}{25} = \dfrac{n}{100}$	$\dfrac{9}{25} =$	$\dfrac{\quad}{100}$	%
b.	$\dfrac{7}{20}$	$\dfrac{7}{20} = \dfrac{x}{100}$	$\dfrac{7}{20} =$	$\dfrac{\quad}{100}$	%
c.	$\dfrac{3}{5}$	$\dfrac{3}{5} = \dfrac{a}{\quad}$	$\dfrac{3}{5} =$	$\dfrac{\quad}{\quad}$	%

Write a percent to tell how much of each array is shaded.

1.

2.

Write each ratio as a percent.

3. 8 to 100   4. 6:10   5. $\frac{1}{5}$ 6. $\frac{3}{4}$ 7. $\frac{11}{25}$

8. 19:20   9. $\frac{55}{100}$ 10. $\frac{24}{25}$ 11. $\frac{7}{10}$ 12. $\frac{1}{4}$

Apply

13. When Dr. Soduk examined Solomon's teeth, he found twenty-five teeth were in place. Twelve of the teeth were incisors, the cutting teeth in front. What percent of Solomon's teeth were incisors?

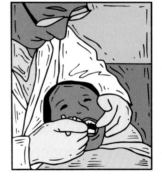

14. At 8:00 A.M. Dr. Soduk opened a package of disposable gloves. By noon, $\frac{2}{5}$ of the gloves had been used. What percent of the gloves were used?

15. The composition of dental fillings may include the metallic elements: silver, tin, copper, and zinc. If 69% of the mixture is silver, what percent is <u>not</u> silver?

Review

Write each fraction in simplest form.

1. $\frac{28}{35}$ 2. $\frac{18}{36}$ 3. $\frac{10}{25}$ 4. $\frac{49}{63}$ 5. $\frac{48}{54}$

6. $\frac{9}{60}$ 7. $\frac{24}{32}$ 8. $\frac{27}{81}$ 9. $\frac{40}{72}$ 10. $\frac{60}{100}$

Lesson 128

Carter's class recently voted for class president. Two-fourths of the class voted for Carter and two-fifths voted for his opponent. Which candidate received the larger percent of the votes?

You can write a fraction as a percent.

Percent means per one hundred. For each ratio, find an equal fraction with a denominator of 100.

$$\overset{\times 25}{\frac{2}{4}} = \frac{50}{100} = 50\%$$
×25

$$\overset{\times 20}{\frac{2}{5}} = \frac{40}{100} = 40\%$$
×20

50% > 40%
Carter received the larger percent of the vote.

You can also write a percent as a fraction with a denominator of 100. Then write the fraction in simplest form.

On a test of 20 spelling words, Pam received a 90% and Fred had 18 correct answers. Which student had the higher score?

Pam: $90\% = \frac{90}{100} = \frac{9}{10}$ Fred: $\frac{18}{20} = \frac{9}{10} = \frac{90}{100} = 90\%$

percent ⟶ fraction   fraction ⟶ percent

Both students had $\frac{9}{10}$ of the problems correct. Both had scores of 90%.

✔️ Check Understanding

Write a percent and a fraction in simplest form for each model.

a.  ____ % $\frac{35}{100} = \frac{}{20}$

b. ____ % $\frac{60}{100} = \frac{}{}$

c. ____ % $\frac{8}{100} = \frac{}{}$

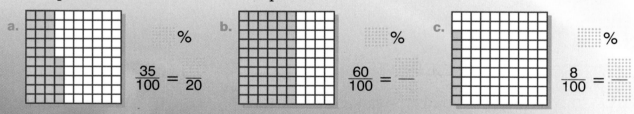

d. Write $\frac{2}{8}$ as a percent. Hint: Write the fraction in simplest form first.

e. Write 16% as a fraction in simplest form.

Practice

Write each fraction as a percent. It may be helpful to first write the fraction in simplest form.

1. $\frac{1}{4}$
2. $\frac{1}{2}$
3. $\frac{2}{5}$
4. $\frac{4}{4}$
5. $\frac{7}{10}$

6. $\frac{4}{5}$
7. $\frac{3}{4}$
8. $\frac{9}{100}$
9. $\frac{17}{20}$
10. $\frac{30}{50}$

11. $\frac{16}{25}$
12. $\frac{24}{30}$
13. $\frac{8}{25}$
14. $\frac{11}{50}$
15. $\frac{18}{90}$

Write each percent as a fraction in simplest form.

16. 40% $\frac{40}{100}$
17. 85%
18. 16%
19. 4%
20. 25%

21. 75%
22. 30%
23. 50%
24. 60%
25. 42%

26. 12%
27. 58%
28. 20%
29. 5%
30. 15%

Apply

31. A new fishing lure comes in six color combinations. If 20% of the order from Bob's Bait Shop was for the black and red fleck color, what part of the order was placed for the other color combinations? Show your answer as a fraction in simplest form.

32. In a test of the lure's effectiveness, a contest was held between the new "Worm in Constant Motion" and three other imitation lures. If nine of the 12 bass hooked were caught on the new lure, what percent of the fish were caught with the new lure?

33. Daryl completed $\frac{1}{3}$ of a project before dinner and $\frac{1}{4}$ after dinner. Is he closer to having the assignment half done or totally finished?

Review

Change each fraction to a mixed number. Then write in simplest form.

1. $\frac{160}{50}$
2. $\frac{24}{11}$
3. $\frac{14}{6}$
4. $\frac{62}{30}$
5. $\frac{175}{100}$

6. $\frac{80}{50}$
7. $\frac{65}{25}$
8. $\frac{58}{6}$
9. $\frac{14}{3}$
10. $\frac{22}{4}$

Lesson 129

Construct Meaning

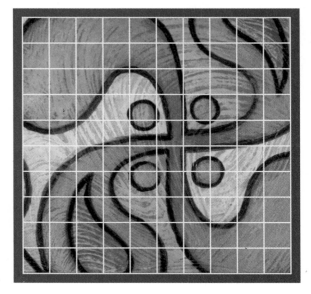

Look at the section of abstract art shown beneath the grid of 100 squares. What percent of the large square is colored blue? Count full squares and partial squares.

If you counted about six squares in blue, you can write this as a fraction, as a decimal, and as a percent.

6 out of 100 = $\frac{6}{100}$

Remember that a fraction bar represents division. Divide the numerator by the denominator to express a fraction as a decimal.

$$100\overline{)6.00} = 0.06$$
$$-6\ 00$$
$$\overline{0}$$

How do you write six-hundredths as a percent?

Use the model to read the decimal as a percent.

$\frac{6}{100} = 0.06 = 6\%$

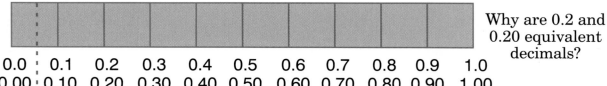

6%

| 0% | 10% | 20% | 30% | 40% | 50% | 60% | 70% | 80% | 90% | 100% |

0.0 0.1 0.2 0.3 0.4 0.5 0.6 0.7 0.8 0.9 1.0
0.00 0.10 0.20 0.30 0.40 0.50 0.60 0.70 0.80 0.90 1.00

0.06

Why are 0.2 and 0.20 equivalent decimals?

How would you show 120% on 10 by 10 grids? How would you write it as a decimal?

Check Understanding

Copy and complete each chart.

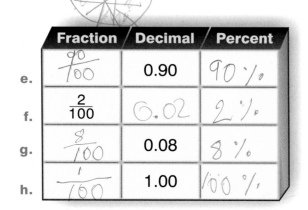

	Fraction	Decimal	Percent
a.	$\frac{15}{100}$	0.15	15%
b.	$\frac{7}{10}$	0.7	7%
c.	$\frac{34}{100}$	0.34	34%
d.	$\frac{3}{100}$	0.30	3%

	Fraction	Decimal	Percent
e.	$\frac{90}{100}$	0.90	90%
f.	$\frac{2}{100}$	0.02	2%
g.	$\frac{8}{100}$	0.08	8%
h.	$\frac{1}{100}$	1.00	100%

276

Mathematics Grade 5

Write the percent of one dollar (100 cents) represented by the coins.

1. 3 dimes, 4 nickels
2. 1 quarter, 1 dime
3. 3 nickels, 4 pennies
4. 3 quarters
5. 5 dimes, 3 nickels
6. 1 quarter, 2 pennies

Write each decimal as a percent.

7. 0.30 *30%*
8. 0.04 *4%*
9. 0.4 *4%*
10. 0.64 *64%*
11. 0.1 *10%*
12. 0.01 *1%*
13. 0.18 *18%*
14. 0.53 *53%*
15. 0.8 *8%*
16. 0.25 *25%*

Write each percent as a decimal.

17. 15% *0.15*
18. 76% *0.76*
19. 2% *0.02*
20. 93% *0.93*
21. 60% *0.60*
22. 26% *0.26*
23. 10% *0.10*
24. 88% *0.88*
25. 6% *0.06*
26. 33% *0.33*

Apply

Choose the most reasonable answer.

27. Cheryl has written ▦ of her research paper.

   30%   110% $\frac{4}{3}$

28. Martin's department store is having a sale. Everything is marked at ▦ off.

   100%   25%   1%

29. In the first three days of a two-week picking season, ▦ of the apple crop has been harvested.

   2%   20%   200%

Divide.

1. $7)\overline{2.457}$
2. $6)\overline{0.042}$
3. $5)\overline{1.505}$
4. $4)\overline{3.564}$

5. $3)\overline{2.79}$
6. $9)\overline{0.8172}$
7. $2)\overline{0.0466}$
8. $8)\overline{4.744}$

9. $0.036 \div 12$
10. $155.4 \div 37$
11. $324.16 \div 8$
12. $40.025 \div 25$

 Construct Meaning

Kip's father estimates that about 30% of his salary is withheld from his pay each month for taxes, retirement, and insurance. If Kip's father earns $4,245 per month, what is the approximate amount he takes home after deductions?

To estimate, round the dollars to the greatest place value.

Think $4,245 is about $4,000.

Remember that 10% can be written as $\frac{10}{100}$, which is $\frac{1}{10}$ when written in simplest form.

Think
$$10\% \text{ of } \$4,000 = \frac{1}{10} \times 4,000$$
$$= \frac{1}{10} \times \frac{4,000}{1}$$
$$= \frac{4,000}{10}$$
$$= \$400$$

Since 30% is three times 10%,

Think $3 \times \$400 = \$1,200$

Subtract.
$$\begin{array}{r} \$4,000 \\ -\ 1,200 \\ \hline \$2,800 \end{array}$$
Kip's father takes home about $2,800 per month.

Compare your answer to the model drawn below.

| 0% | 10% | 30% | | | | | | | 100% |

| 0 | $400 | $1,200 | | | | | | | $4,000 |

Does your answer make sense?

If you know 10% of a number, calculating a percent that is a multiple of ten can be done mentally.

Find 50% of 150.

$$10\% \text{ of } 150 = \frac{1}{10} \times \frac{150}{1} = \frac{150}{10} = 15$$
$$50\% \text{ of } 150 = 5 \times 15 = 75$$

Find 20% of 80.

$$10\% \text{ of } 80 = \frac{1}{10} \times \frac{80}{1} = \frac{80}{10} = \boxed{}$$
$$20\% \text{ of } 80 = 2 \times \boxed{} = \boxed{}$$

What is 100% of 5,600?   Remember that 100% is equal to one!

Using Mental Math to Estimate Percent

Use mental math to find each percent of 500.

a. 10% b. 50% c. 20% d. 70% e. 40%

 Practice

Use mental math to find each answer.

1. 10% of 40
2. 50% of 30
3. 20% of 350
4. 80% of 50

5. 10% of 1,000
6. 50% of 250
7. 40% of 700
8. 100% of 210

Estimate each answer by rounding to the highest place value.

9. 80% of 97
10. 30% of 61
11. 39% of 89
12. 51% of 203

Apply

13. About how much will Joel save if he wants to buy a $29.95 bicycle helmet when the store has a 30% off sale?

14. For Gabriella's birthday dinner, the total bill was $61.53. The restaurant suggested that the tip should be 20% of the bill. About how much should be given as a tip?

15. In Belle Valley, 10% of the days in September had some rain. Was this more or less than five days?

16. Mitchell has $60. The bicycle he wants to buy costs 70% of the original price of $90. Does he have enough money?

 Review

Subtract. Write the difference in simplest form.

1. $\frac{3}{5} - \frac{2}{10}$
2. $\frac{6}{8} - \frac{1}{3}$
3. $\frac{2}{5} - \frac{3}{15}$
4. $\frac{3}{4} - \frac{8}{16}$
5. $\frac{2}{3} - \frac{3}{9}$
6. $\frac{5}{6} - \frac{6}{24}$
7. $5\frac{2}{3} - 2\frac{2}{5}$
8. $16\frac{3}{4} - 7\frac{5}{9}$

Moments with Careers

"My dad works as a general manager. In his work he uses math for performing time trials and finding percentages."

Cale
Corvallis, OR

Construct Meaning

Caribbean Airlines decided to change its color scheme. If 15% of its 80 planes were repainted during the first year, what was the number of the Caribbean planes that were changed?

Find 15% × 80.

THREE METHODS

1. Change the percent to a fraction reduced to simplest form.

$15\% = \frac{15}{100} = \frac{3}{20}$

Multiply.

$\frac{3}{20} \times \frac{80}{1} = \frac{240}{20} = 12$ planes

2. Change the percent to a decimal.

$15\% = \frac{15}{100} = 0.15$

$$\begin{array}{r} 80 \\ \times\ 0.15 \\ \hline 400 \\ 800 \\ \hline 12.00 \end{array}$$

Multiply.

Remember to place the decimal.

12 planes

3. Use a calculator.

     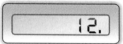 planes

By each method, the answer is 12 planes.

Find 25% of 540.

First, solve by using a fraction.　　$25\% = \frac{25}{100} = \frac{1}{4}$　　$\frac{1}{4} \times \frac{540}{1} = \frac{540}{4} = 135$

Next, solve by using a decimal. Check with a calculator.　　$25\% = \frac{25}{100} = 0.25$　　$0.25 \times 540 = 135$

When finding a percent of a number, it is sometimes easier to write the percent as a fraction. For example, 25% is $\frac{1}{4}$ and 75% is $\frac{3}{4}$. At other times, it is easier to convert the percent to a decimal. What operation do you use in either case?

Check Understanding

Choose the correct solution.

a. 60% of 1,200	72	720	7.2
b. 5% of 300	150	1.5	15
c. 25% of 900	225	2.25	22.5
d. 40% of 70	2.8	28	280
e. 50% of 3,500	175	17.5	1,750

 **ractice**

Find the percent of each number.

1. 1% of 100   2. 10% of 100   3. 40% of 340   4. 20% of 60

5. 30% of 210   6. 25% of 600   7. 50% of 62   8. 35% of 80

9. 100% of 19   10. 2% of 2,600   11. 30% of 40   12. 75% of 84

13. 60% of 365   14. 75% of 52   15. 19% of 500   16. 80% of 225

17. 75% of 12   18. 80% of 40   19. 34% of 700   20. 20% of 85

Compare. Write >, < or = .

21. 15% of 120 $\overset{18}{>}$ 5% of 300 ^15^   22. 12% of 400 $\overset{48}{<}$ 35% of 160 ^56^

23. 25% of 84 ☐ 30% of 80   24. 60% of 120 ☐ 40% of 180

 pply

Find the sale price for each of the following items.

25. camera: originally $75, on sale at 28% off the regular price

26. luggage: originally $80, being sold at 15% discount

27. computer: original price, $980, on sale at 20% off

28. basketball ticket: $25, sold at 80% of the original price to season ticket holders

29. bicycle: original price, $120, being sold at 35% discount

 **eview**

Estimate the product by rounding each factor to the greatest place value. Multiply.

1. 5.6 × 2.3   2. 4.67 × 4.4   3. 8.34 × 5.44   4. $5.77 × 6.5

5. $313.78 × 7.7   6. $456.77 × 4.2   7. $1,245.25 × 6.45   8. $13.99 × 3.45

Practice

Calculating <u>sales tax</u> is one use of percent.
Ben is helping his parents choose a birthday
present for his brother Matthew. They are
considering several options. Sales tax where
Ben lives is 6%. What will each item cost
after sales tax is added? Round each sales tax
amount to the nearest cent.

$29.99 $19.99

1. art set

2. trading card case

3. sport lamp

4. personal CD player

$34.99 $36.87

5. If the lamp is on sale at 20% off, what will be the total cost at the discounted price?

Another use of percent is a <u>tip</u> given for service. Find the total amount paid for the
service, including tip. Round to the nearest cent.

6. haircut: $14.95, 15% tip

7. soup, salad, drink: $7.30, 13% tip

8. pizza delivery: $11.95, 10% tip

9. hotel parking: $9.00, 15% tip

Salespersons often receive a <u>commission</u>, a percentage of the selling price. Find the
commission on each sale.

10. house: sold for $149,000
        7% commission

11. car: sold for $22,775
        4% commission

12. office building: sold for $565,000
        5% commission

13. truck: sold for $19,400
        3% commission

Interest is another common use of percent. When someone borrows money, he or she <u>pays</u> interest on the money owed. For example, Mr. Beauchamp borrowed $1,500 at 12% annual interest.

Money borrowed (principal) → $1,500
Rate of interest → 12% annually

$1,500 × 0.12 = $180 interest for 1 year
Total amount owed: $1,500 + $180 = $1,680

Find the <u>interest owed</u> for one year.

14. $1,000 at 13%

15. $2,500 at 9%

16. $4,000 at 18%

17. $7,500 at 15%

18. $875 at 12%

19. $10,000 at 8%

Interest is added to the amount of money to be repaid. For questions 20 through 25, add the interest to the principal in questions 14 through 19.

Find the <u>total amount owed</u> at the end of one year.

20. $1,000 at 13%

21. $2,500 at 9%

22. $4,000 at 18%

23. $7,500 at 15%

24. $875 at 12%

25. $10,000 at 8%

When someone saves money, he or she <u>earns</u> interest, which is added to the amount initially saved.

Find the <u>interest earned</u> for one year.

America's first bank, in Philadelphia

26. $750 at 4%

27. $1,200 at 5%

28. $10,000 at 19%

29. $5,550 at 7%

30. $925 at 6%

31. $3,000 at 8%

Find the <u>total amount saved</u> at the end of one year using the above amounts.

32. $750 at 4%

33. $1,200 at 5%

34. $10,000 at 19%

35. $5,550 at 7%

36. $925 at 6%

37. $3,000 at 8%

Complete the proportion.

1. $\frac{1}{3} = \frac{}{36}$

2. $\frac{5}{10} = \frac{}{100}$

3. $\frac{2}{8} = \frac{}{88}$

4. $\frac{2}{3} = \frac{}{60}$

5. $\frac{4}{6} = \frac{}{90}$

6. $\frac{1}{7} = \frac{}{21}$

7. $\frac{3}{5} = \frac{}{45}$

8. $\frac{4}{7} = \frac{}{56}$

9. $\frac{2}{4} = \frac{}{88}$

10. $\frac{4}{9} = \frac{}{72}$

Math for Every Day: Ratios, Proportion, Percent

Write each ratio in two different ways.

1. 3:4

2. 6 to 8

3. 13 out of 21

4. $\frac{5}{6}$

Write the next two equal ratios.

5. $\frac{9}{11}$

6. $\frac{3}{2}$

7. $\frac{4}{5}$

8. $\frac{8}{6}$

9. $\frac{4}{7}$

Is the ratio a proportion? Write = or ≠.

10. $\frac{2}{6}$ ▦ $\frac{6}{18}$

11. $\frac{4}{17}$ ▦ $\frac{8}{35}$

12. $\frac{8}{11}$ ▦ $\frac{14}{22}$

13. $\frac{16}{3}$ ▦ $\frac{48}{9}$

Find the missing number in each proportion.

14. $\frac{12}{45} = \frac{n}{15}$

15. $\frac{3}{8} = \frac{9}{n}$

16. $\frac{9}{n} = \frac{1}{3}$

17. $\frac{n}{6} = \frac{6}{12}$

18. $\frac{1}{3} = \frac{n}{30}$

19. $\frac{7}{n} = \frac{28}{16}$

20. $\frac{n}{5} = \frac{15}{25}$

21. $\frac{3}{4} = \frac{36}{n}$

Write each ratio as a percent.

22. 48:100

23. $\frac{24}{100}$

24. 35:100

25. $\frac{6}{100}$

26. 199:100

Write each percent as a decimal.

27. 88%

28. 54%

29. 7%

30. 1%

31. 40%

Write each percent as a fraction in simplest form.

32. 30%

33. 50%

34. 75%

35. 62%

36. 36%

Solve.

37. This standing mirror is $24.95. Sales tax is 6%. Round the sales tax to the nearest cent. What is the total cost?

38. The pocket watch with a chain is marked at 25% off. The original price was $149. What is the sale price?

39. 75% of the 40 sales clerks are working the 9 to 5 shift during the sale. How many sales clerks are working?

40. The sales manager reported that when the sale began, there were 250 pairs of shoes on the clearance racks. 30% have already been sold. How many pairs are left?

41. 700 new employees will be hired by the Topcomp Company. 25% will be in customer service. How many will be customer service employees?

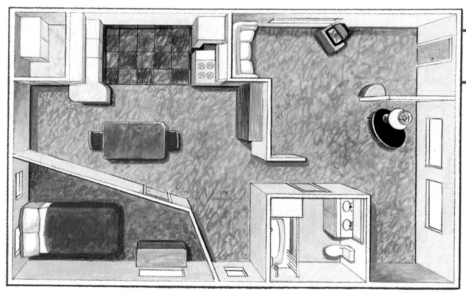

Scale

1 inch = 6 feet

42. Each inch in this floor plan represents six feet in the actual apartment. How long is the actual bed?

43. Write a proportion and solve to find the actual length of the apartment floor.

44. Will a rug that is five feet wide and eight feet long fit between the cabinets in the kitchen?

"For it is the God who commanded light to shine out of darkness, who has shone in our hearts to *give* the light of the knowledge of the glory of God in the face of Jesus Christ." 2 Corinthians 4:6

Grade Five

11

Chapter

Lessons 134–143

Who has measured the waters
  in the hollow of His hand,
Measured heaven with a span
And calculated the dust of the earth
  in a measure?
The everlasting God, the LORD,
The Creator of the ends of the earth.

Isaiah 40:12a, 28b

Construct Meaning

Ling's class took a trip to the Hoh Rain Forest in Olympic National Park, Washington. The guide explained that a meterologist (a scientist who studies weather) measures the rain that falls in the forest with a rain gauge. Each year Hoh Rain Forest receives about 150 inches of rain. Ling's teacher asked the students to determine how many feet of rain fall each year in Hoh Rain Forest.

When you know the number of inches, you can determine the number of feet. To change a smaller unit such as inches to a larger unit such as feet, consider the relationship between the two units.

Customary Units of Length

12 inches (in.) = 1 foot (ft)
3 feet = 1 yard (yd)
36 inches = 1 yard
5,280 feet = 1 mile (mi)
1,760 yards = 1 mile

12 inches = 1 foot
Divide the total number of inches by 12.

Divide.

```
      12 R6
12) 150
   -12
    30
   -24
     6  ← extra
          inches
```

Check.

```
    12
  × 12
   144
  +  6
   150
```

12 feet 6 inches of rain fall in Hoh Rain Forest each year.

Another rain forest receives 14 feet 3 inches of rain annually. How many inches of rain does it receive? Consider the relationship between the two units.

Step 1 Since one foot is equal to 12 inches, multiply the number of feet by 12.

```
  14  ← number of feet
× 12  ← number of inches
        in one foot
 168  ← number of inches
        in 14 feet
```

Step 2 Add the number of inches in 14 feet to the number of inches in the original measurement of rainfall.

```
 168  ← inches in 14 feet
+  3  ← inches from
        original measurement
 171  ← total inches in
        14 feet 3 inches
```

The rain forest receives 171 inches of rain annually.

**Check Understanding**

Multiply or divide to complete each equation.

a. 81 in. = ☐ ft ☐ in.   b. 46 in. = ☐ ft ☐ in.   c. 16 ft = ☐ in.

d. 13 ft 4 in. = ☐ in.   e. 7 ft 2 in. = ☐ in.   f. 144 in. = ☐ ft

**Practice**

Complete.

Example:

2 yd 1 ft = **7** ft

Multiply.   2 ← yards
　　　　　 ×3 ← feet in one yard
　　　　　 ———
　　　　　 6 ← feet in 2 yards

Add.   6 ← feet in 2 yards
　　　 +1 ← foot from the measurement
　　　 ———
　　　 7 ← feet total

1. 5 yd = ☐ ft
2. 7 yd 2 ft = ☐ ft
3. 4 yd = ☐ in.
4. 2 yd 1 ft = ☐ in.
5. 39 in. = ☐ yd ☐ in.
6. 5 ft = ☐ yd ☐ ft
7. 4 mi = ☐ yd
7. 3 mi = ☐ ft
9. 112 in. = ☐ ft ☐ in.
10. 8 ft = ☐ in.

This leaf is 6 inches long to the nearest inch. It is 6 inches to the nearest $\frac{1}{2}$ inch. It is $5\frac{3}{4}$ inches to the nearest $\frac{1}{4}$ inch. It is $5\frac{7}{8}$ inches to the nearest $\frac{1}{8}$ inch and $5\frac{13}{16}$ inches to the nearest $\frac{1}{16}$ inch.

Use your ruler to draw each line.

11. $1\frac{3}{4}$ in.   12. $4\frac{1}{16}$ in.   13. $\frac{1}{4}$ in.   14. $8\frac{1}{2}$ in.   15. $9\frac{1}{8}$ in.

Apply

16. Lily's curtain pattern calls for 6 yards 2 feet of fabric. She only has a twelve-inch ruler with which to measure. What is the total number of feet Lily should cut?

17. Robert measured two saplings in his yard. One stood $7\frac{1}{2}$ inches tall. The other was $7\frac{3}{8}$ inches. Which sapling was taller?

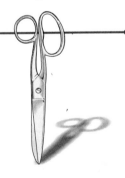

Construct Meaning

Did you know that seventy percent of the earth is covered by water? Most of that water is found in the oceans. Have you considered the amount of water in the atmosphere? Each day there are about 40 trillion gallons of water in the atmosphere above the United States in the form of clouds. About four trillion gallons of this water fall to the ground as rain, snow, or hail each day.

It takes about 20 gallons of water to fill a bath tub. Use the table of Customary Units of Capacity to find the number of quarts in 20 gallons.

To change larger units (gallons) to smaller units (quarts), multiply.

1 gallon = 4 quarts

Multiply the number of gallons by 4.

20 × 4 = 80 qt

Customary Units of Capacity
3 teaspoons (tsp) = 1 tablespoon (tbsp)
8 fluid ounces (fl oz) = 1 cup (c)
2 cups = 1 pint (pt)
2 pints = 1 quart (qt)
4 quarts = 1 gallon (gal)

There are 80 quarts in 20 gallons.

$$\begin{array}{r} 4 \\ + 4 \\ \hline 16 \end{array}$$

Kenton has 6 pints of juice. How many quart jars can he fill?

To change smaller units (pints) to larger units (quarts), divide.

Since 2 pints equal 1 quart, divide the number of pints by 2.

6 ÷ 2 = 3 qt   6 pints = 3 quarts

Kenton can fill 3 quart jars.

If you have 8 cups of juice and your friend has 3 pints, explain how to compare the amounts.

Check Understanding

Complete.

a. 16 fluid ounces = ⬚ cups

b. 10 tablespoons = ⬚ teaspoons

Write >, < or =.

c. 6 pints ⬚ 12 cups

d. 30 quarts ⬚ 8 gallons

Complete.

1. 48 fl oz = ▦ c

2. 6 qt = ▦ pt

3. 24 qt = ▦ gal

4. 15 tbsp = ▦ tsp

5. 4 gal = ▦ qt

6. 12 pt = ▦ c

7. 8 c = ▦ pt

8. 16 pt = ▦ qt

9. 3 c = ▦ fl oz

Sometimes changing the units takes more than one step.

Example: Change 16 pints to gallons.

- First, change 16 pints to quarts. $16 \div 2 = 8$ 16 pt = 8 qt
- Next, change 8 quarts to gallons. $8 \div 4 = 2$ 8 qt = 2 gal
- Write the equivalent measurement. 16 pints = 2 gallons

Example: Change 6 gallons to cups.

- First, change 6 gallons to quarts. $6 \times 4 = 24$ 6 gal = 24 qt
- Next, change 24 quarts to pints. $24 \times 2 = 48$ 24 qt = 48 pt
- Then, change 48 pints to cups. $48 \times 2 = 96$ 48 pt = 96 c
- Write the equivalent measurement. 16 gallons = 96 cups

Use the examples above and the table of Customary Units of Capacity to complete each equivalent measurement.

10. 24 pt = ▦ gal

11. 8 qt = ▦ c

12. 48 c = ▦ gal

13. 56 c = ▦ qt

14. 4 gal = ▦ pt

15. 8 gal = ▦ c

16. Ellery's math class was planning a celebration. He needed to bring enough juice for everyone in his class. Ellery determined he would need to bring two gallons of juice. How many cups of juice did Ellery bring?

17. Ellery's friend Allene brought 40 cups of snack mix for the celebration. How many quarts of snack mix did Allene bring?

Construct Meaning

One type of precipitation is hail. When rain falls from the clouds and is held in the atmosphere by wind, it freezes because of the cold temperatures in the sky. Very cold water freezes onto these tiny pieces of ice, and hail is formed. Hail can fall to the earth in various sizes. Sometimes a piece of hail is as large as a baseball.

Cammie's baseball team was given 16 new baseballs. Her coach asked her to carry the baseballs to the field. Each baseball weighed 5 ounces. What was the total weight of the baseballs in pounds?

Look at the Customary Units of Weight table.

First, multiply the number of baseballs by the weight of one baseball.

16 × 5 ounces = 80 ounces

Customary Units of Weight
16 ounces (oz) = 1 pound (lb)
2,000 pounds = 1 ton (T)

The total weight of 16 baseballs is 80 ounces.

Next, divide the total ounces by the number of ounces in one pound.

$$
\begin{array}{r}
5 \leftarrow \text{pounds in 80 ounces} \\
16\overline{)80} \leftarrow \text{total ounces} \\
-80 \\
\hline
0
\end{array}
$$

ounces in one pound →

16 baseballs weigh 5 pounds.

To change larger units (pounds) to smaller units (ounces), multiply.
To change smaller units (ounces) to larger units (pounds), divide.

 Check Understanding

Choose the equivalent amount from the answer box.

a. 4 lb

b. 144 oz

c. 3 T

d. 10,000 lb

e. 2 lb

f. 96 oz

9 lb	32 oz
5 T	6,000 lb
64 oz	6 lb

 **ractice**

Complete.

1. 112 oz = ▦ lb 　　　 2. 15 lb = ▦ oz 　　　 3. 6 T = ▦ lb

4. 32,000 lb = ▦ T 　　 5. 560 oz = ▦ lb 　　 6. 58 lb = ▦ oz

7. 1,072 lb = ▦ oz 　　 8. 1,568 oz = ▦ lb 　　 9. 14 T = ▦ lb

Complete.

> 6 lb 8 oz = **104** oz
> - Multiply to find the number of ounces in 6 pounds.
>   > 6 × 16 oz = 96 oz
> - Add the ounces in 6 pounds (96) to the ounces from the original measurement (8).
>   > 96 oz + 8 oz = 104 oz

10. 9 lb 10 oz = ▦ oz

11. 12 lb 4 oz = ▦ oz

12. 24 lb 6 oz = ▦ oz

13. 71 lb 11 oz = ▦ oz

14. 127 lb 3 oz = ▦ oz

15. 154 lb 9 oz = ▦ oz

Write each measurement in pounds.

16. 7 T 　　　　 17. 1,424 oz 　　　　 18. 11 T 　　　　 19. 400 oz

20. 832 oz 　　　 21. 688 oz 　　　　 22. 42 T 　　　　 23. 2,000 oz

 **pply**

24. Jace's baby sister weighs 17 lb 12 oz. How many ounces does she weigh?

25. Yeni is helping her grandfather make potato salad. The recipe calls for 48 ounces of potatoes. How many pounds of potatoes should they purchase?

C hallenge

26. Chuck weighs three times more than his sister. He weighs 84 pounds. How many pounds does Chuck's sister weigh?

27. Five more than six times Bonnie's weight is 317 pounds. What is Bonnie's weight?

 **Construct Meaning**

Michael arrived at school at 8:00 A.M. on a sunny morning. By the time he went to lunch at 12:20 P.M. it was snowing. How much time was Michael in school before lunch?

Find the elapsed time by counting forward from the beginning time.

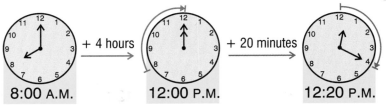

8:00 A.M.   + 4 hours   12:00 P.M.   + 20 minutes   12:20 P.M.

He was in school 4 hours 20 minutes.

Remember:
60 seconds (sec) = 1 minute (min)
60 minutes = 1 hour (hr)
A.M. begins at 12:00 midnight.
P.M. begins at 12:00 noon.

If it snowed for 1 hour 30 minutes before lunch, what time did it start to snow?

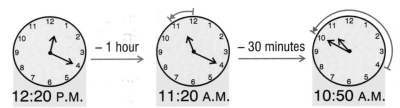

12:20 P.M.   − 1 hour   11:20 A.M.   − 30 minutes   10:50 A.M.

It started to snow at 10:50 A.M.

Orlando, Florida, had 10 hours 20 minutes between sunrise and sunset on December 19. On that same day in Anchorage, Alaska, there were only 5 hours 28 minutes of daylight. What was the difference in the amount of daylight residents in the two locations had that day?

$$\begin{array}{r} 10 \text{ hr } 20 \text{ min} \\ -\ 5 \text{ hr } 28 \text{ min} \end{array} \rightarrow \boxed{9 + 60 \text{ min} + 20 \text{ min}} \rightarrow \begin{array}{r} 9 \text{ hr } 80 \text{ min} \\ -\ 5 \text{ hr } 28 \text{ min} \\ \hline 4 \text{ hr } 52 \text{ min} \end{array}$$

Regroup

Orlando had 4 hours and 52 minutes more daylight than Anchorage.

It snowed in Ely, Minnesota, for 8 hours 20 minutes on one day, and 3 hours 45 minutes on the next day. What was the total time it snowed for both days?

$$\begin{array}{r} 8 \text{ hr } 20 \text{ min} \\ +\ 3 \text{ hr } 45 \text{ min} \\ \hline 11 \text{ hr } 65 \text{ min} \end{array} \rightarrow \boxed{11 \text{ hr} + 1 \text{ hr} + 5 \text{ min}} \rightarrow 12 \text{ hr } 5 \text{ min}$$

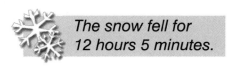

The snow fell for 12 hours 5 minutes.

 **Check Understanding**

Find the elapsed time.

a. 6:10 A.M. to 10:30 A.M   **b.** 4:55 P.M. to 7:35 P.M.   **c.** 11:45 A.M to 1:15 P.M.

Add or subtract.

d. 5 hr 20 min   **e.** 4 hr 51 min   **f.** 6 hr 25 min   **g.** 8 min 10 sec
    +2 hr 15 min   – 2 hr 40 min   +3 hr 35 min   – 3 min 40 sec

Practice

Write the elapsed time.

1. 2:35 P.M. to 8:10 P.M.   **2.** 9:50 A.M. to 3:14 P.M.   **3.** 6:42 P.M. to 1:45 A.M.

4. 10:23 A.M. to 5:55 P.M.   **5.** 11:36 A.M. to 4:19 P.M.   **6.** 1:12 P.M. to 12:00 A.M.

Solve.

Example:
```
        2 min  30 sec
      + 4 min  40 sec
Regroup → ¹6  min  7Q  sec
the seconds  7  min  10  sec
```

7. 10 min   5 sec   **8.** 12 min 34 sec
   + 1 min 58 sec   – 9 min 50 sec

9. 7 min 50 sec   **10.** 49 min 30 sec
   – 5 min 45 sec   +10 min 56 sec

11. 3 hr 45 min   **12.** 8 hr 56 min   **13.** 6 hr 13 min
   +6 hr 40 min   – 5 hr 13 min   – 4 hr 32 min

14. 7 hr 19 min   **15.** 9 hr 51 min   **16.** 5 hr
   +2 hr 24 min   +2 hr 32 min   – 3 hr 39 min

Apply

17. Mario's family drove to his grandparents' house for a weekend visit. If their trip began at 3:30 P.M. and ended at 7:48 P.M., how much time did it take to travel?

18. If Mario's family took a 30-minute break for dinner, how much time did they actually drive?

19. Sunrise was at 7:49 A.M. and sunset was at 5:09 P.M. in Columbus, Ohio, on December 19. How much time elapsed between sunrise and sunset?

Construct Meaning

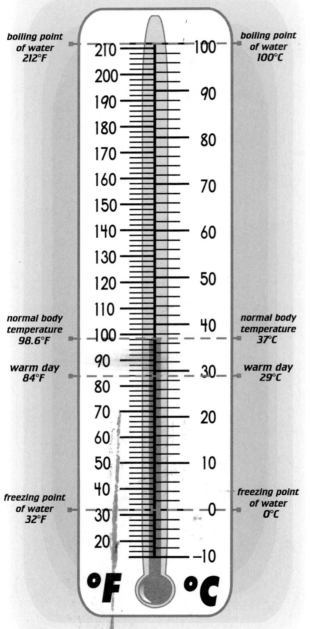

How is the weather today? Does it feel warm, hot, or cold? The way it feels to you is an indication of the temperature. A thermometer is used to measure temperature. The customary unit for temperature is degrees **Fahrenheit** (°F). The temperature can also be measured in metric units, degrees **Celsius** (°C). Identify each scale by locating the °F and °C at the bottom of the thermometer.

Locate the freezing point of water on the thermometer. What is the temperature when measured in degrees Fahrenheit? At what temperature does water freeze in degrees Celsius?

Thermometers may be marked in different ways. One may be marked by every degree, and another by every two degrees. How do you read a thermometer with every two degrees marked?

Check Understanding

Choose the temperature that is equivalent to the one given.

a. 32°F   b. 60°C   c. 190°F   d. 122°F   e. 70°C   f. 28°C

88°C   158°F   0°C   82°F   50°C   140°F

Fahrenheit and Celsius Temperatures

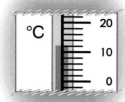 **ractice**

Write the temperature shown.

1.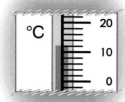

2.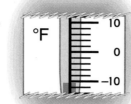

3.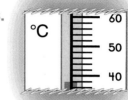

Choose the letter of the temperature closest to the one given.

4. 62°F   5. 24°F   6. 41°F   7. 180°F   8. 86°F

     a. −4°C   **b.** 30°C   **c.** 82°C   **d.** 17°C   **e.** 5°C

Solve.

9. On the Fahrenheit thermometer, how many degrees difference is there between the freezing point of water and normal body temperature?

10. Use the Celsius scale to determine the difference between normal body temperature and the boiling point of water.

 pply

11. This morning Kya read the temperature on her outdoor thermometer. It was 28°F. At noon, Granddad said it was 10°C. How many degrees Fahrenheit warmer was the temperature at noon?

12. Jonah's mom is a meteorologist. She predicted the high temperature for the week to be 68°F. The low temperature was predicted to be 35°F. How many degrees Fahrenheit above freezing are the high and low temperature predictions?

C **hallenge**

13. Find the difference between the freezing point and boiling point of water in degrees Celsius. Then find the difference in degrees Fahrenheit. Compare the two differences to determine about how many degrees on the Fahrenheit scale are equal to one degree on the Celsius scale.

Construct Meaning

The amount of new snowfall received at ski resorts is important to skiers. Each day, ski resorts report the amount of snow that has fallen within the last 24 hours. Sunlight Mountain Resort reported 22 centimeters of new snowfall. Change the number of centimeters to millimeters. Use the table of Metric Units of Length to convert the units.

Metric Units of Length
10 millimeters (mm) = 1 centimeter (cm)
10 centimeters = 1 decimeter (dm)
10 decimeters = 1 meter (m)
100 centimeters = 1 meter
1,000 meters = 1 kilometer (km)

Multiply to change larger units to smaller units.

Because there are 10 millimeters in one centimeter, multiply the number of centimeters by 10.

$22 \times 10 = 220$ mm

22 cm = 220 mm

220 mm of snow had fallen.

If Arapahoe Basin Ski Resort had 120 millimeters of new snow, how many centimeters of snowfall did Arapahoe Basin report?

Divide to change smaller units to larger units.

Because there are 10 millimeters in one centimeter, divide the number of millimeters by 10.

$120 \div 10 = 12$ cm

12 cm of snow were reported.

120 mm = 12 cm

Change 326 millimeters to centimeters. Since there are 10 millimeters in one centimeter, divide 326 millimeters by 10.

$$10\overline{)326.0} \quad 32.6 \text{ cm}$$

298

 **Check Understanding**

Complete the equation.

a. 13 cm = ⬚ mm

b. 145 mm = ⬚ cm

c. 380 mm = ⬚ cm

d. 63 cm 5 mm = ⬚ mm

e. 35.3 cm = ⬚ mm

f. 178 mm = ⬚ cm

 **Practice**

Complete the equation.

Example:

5.2 m = **52** dm

Multiply.   5.2 ← meters
         × 10 ← decimeters in 1 meter
         ‾‾‾‾
          0 0
          5 2
         ‾‾‾‾
         5 2.0 ← decimeters

1. 3 km = ⬚ m

2. 15 m = ⬚ dm

3. 24 cm = ⬚ mm

4. 6.5 cm = ⬚ mm

5. 6 m = ⬚ cm

6. 4,200 m = ⬚ km

7. 37 dm = ⬚ m   8. 450 cm = ⬚ dm   9. 3.4 m = ⬚ dm   10. 8.9 dm = ⬚ cm

Use a metric ruler to draw each line.

11. 20 mm   12. 5 cm   13. 5 mm   14. 38 mm

 Apply

15. A snowdrift in the mountains was 1.5 meters deep. State the equivalent amount of snow in centimeters.

16. A cross-country skier covered 100 meters in one minute. If he maintained that speed, how long would it take him to ski one kilometer?

 Review

1. $9)\overline{7.2}$ 2. $6)\overline{0.54}$ 3. $4)\overline{0.084}$ 4. $3)\overline{6.33}$

5. $8)\overline{3.20}$ 6. $7)\overline{0.0049}$ 7. $5)\overline{0.0095}$ 8. $5.87 \div 10$

9. $19.23 \div 10$ 10. $5.6 \div 10$ 11. $564.4 \div 100$ 12. $5.66 \div 100$

1 milliliter

1 Liter

2 Liters

Soda POP

Construct Meaning

When Karen's baby sister was sick, her mom gave her medicine with a medicine dropper. A medicine dropper holds about one milliliter of liquid. It would take 1,000 milliliters to fill a one-liter milk carton. How many milliliters would be needed to fill a two-liter bottle of soda?

Metric Units of Capacity
1,000 milliliters (mL) = 1 liter (L)

Since 1 liter equals 1,000 milliliters, multiply 2 by 1,000.

> $2 \times 1,000 = 2,000$ mL   *2,000 milliliters are needed to fill a 2-liter bottle.*

How many liters would be equal to 4,000 milliliters? Because there are 1,000 milliliters in 1 liter, divide 4,000 by 1,000.

> $4,000 \div 1,000 = 4$ L   *4 liters are the equivalent of 4,000 milliliters.*

Sometimes decimals are used when changing units. How would you write 9 milliliters as liters?

> $9 \div 1,000 = 0.009$ L   *9 milliliters would be the same as 0.009 L.*

 How many 500 mL bottles could you fill with a 2-liter bottle of sports drink? Explain your reasoning.

Check Understanding

Complete each equation.

a. 56 L = ▦ mL

b. 9,000 mL = ▦ L

c. 5 mL = ▦ L

Write >, < or =.

d. 120 mL ▦ 0.120 L

e. 20,000 mL ▦ 200 L

f. 5.7 L ▦ 57,000 mL

Choose the appropriate unit of measurement. Write *mL* or *L*.

1. a sink

2. a teaspoon

3. a pitcher of juice

4. a bottle of vanilla

5. an aquarium

6. a sample of shampoo

Complete.

7. 2 L = ____ mL

8. 5,678 mL = ____ L

9. 87 L = ____ mL

10. 700 mL = ____ L

11. 6 mL = ____ L

12. 0.14 L = ____ mL

13. 3.4 L = ____ mL

14. 134 mL = ____ L

15. 279 L = ____ mL

16. 3,456 mL = ____ L

17. 0.42 L = ____ mL

18. 0.076 L = ____ mL

19. 4.5 L = ____ mL

20. 67 mL = ____ L

21. 5.092 L = ____ mL

22. 3 mL = ____ L

23. 48,001 mL = ____ L

24. 45,000 mL = ____ L

25. Johanna bought a one-liter bottle of hand lotion for $17.50. Lara bought the same amount of lotion in 100-mL tubes which sold for $2.00 each. What was the better buy?

26. A one-cup measure holds about 250 milliliters of liquid. About how many cups of soda could Spencer pour if he had a two-liter bottle of soda?

27. Kay's recipe for one gallon of ice cream calls for 20 mL of vanilla. How many gallons of ice cream can be made using a half-liter bottle of vanilla?

Construct Meaning

The contents of a box of crackers have a mass of 255 grams (g). One serving of 16 crackers is 29 grams. Each cracker has a mass that is a little less than 2 grams.

When Lindy read the Nutrition Facts Label on the box, she was alarmed that one serving had 250 milligrams (mg) of sodium. However, she learned that 1,000 milligrams equal 1 gram and realized that 1 milligram has about the same mass as a grain of sand.

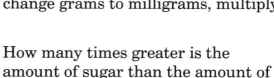

Metric Units of Mass

1,000 milligrams (mg) = 1 gram (g)

1,000 grams = 1 kilogram (kg)

There are 3 grams of sugar in one serving of crackers. To compare the amount of sugar with the amount of sodium in one serving, change 3 grams to milligrams. To change grams to milligrams, multiply the number of grams by 1,000.

$$3 \times 1,000 = 3,000 \text{ mg of sugar}$$

How many times greater is the amount of sugar than the amount of sodium in one serving?

If you need 1 kilogram of crackers for a party, how many boxes will you have to buy? One kilogram equals 1,000 grams. Divide this amount by the number of grams in one box.

$$
\begin{array}{r}
3 \text{ R}235 \\
255\overline{)1,000} \\
-765 \\
\hline
235
\end{array}
$$

Will you need three or four boxes?

Mass

A grain of sand is about 1 milligram (mg).

A large paper clip is about 1 gram (g).

A brick is about 1 kilogram (kg).

 **Check Understanding**

Complete.

a. 4 kg = ⬚ g   b. 5 g = ⬚ mg   c. 2,700 g = ⬚ kg   d. 450 mg = ⬚ g

Choose the more reasonable estimate of mass.

e. a balloon	f. a dime	g. an apple	h. a bicycle
1 mg or 1 kg	4 mg or 4 g	150 g or 150 kg	10 g or 10 kg

 **Practice**

Complete.

1. 23 g = ⬚ mg   2. 46 kg = ⬚ g   3. 290 mg = ⬚ g

4. 2 g = ⬚ mg   5. 3.2 kg = ⬚ g   6. 765 g = ⬚ kg

7. 2.3 kg = ⬚ g   8. 0.964 kg = ⬚ g   9. 2,300 g = ⬚ kg

10. 5.23 g = ⬚ mg   11. 5,600 mg = ⬚ g   12. 5 kg = ⬚ g

13. 9 g = ⬚ mg   14. 4.6 kg = ⬚ g   15. 0.034 g = ⬚ mg

Choose the appropriate unit of measurement. Write *mg*, *g*, or *kg*.

16. a snowflake   17. your math book   18. a car

19. a grain of rice   20. a safety pin   21. a pencil

Apply

22. Trina read the nutrition label on her box of cereal. She discovered one serving contained five grams of sugar. How many milligrams of sugar were in one serving?

23. There are 300 milligrams of sodium in one serving of the cereal. Would four servings contain more or less than one gram of sodium?

Lesson 142

Construct Meaning

The world is divided into 24 time zones, each differing by one hour. Six time zones divide the United States. The direction of the earth's rotation on its axis means that locations to the east will have daylight before your location. When the sun is rising in London, England, it is still dark in Toronto, Canada.

Use the Time-Zone Map to compare the time of various locations.

▶ If it is 7 A.M. eastern standard time in Boston, what is the time in Billings?

▶ A family in Honolulu is sleeping at 4 A.M. Hawaii standard time. Name several things their relatives in Omaha might be doing at that time.

▶ Emil's flight left Orlando at 11 A.M. eastern standard time and arrived in Los Angeles at 1:00 P.M. Pacific standard time. How long was his flight?

THINK: What time was it in Los Angeles when Emil's plane left Orlando?

How much time elapsed between the plane's departure from Orlando and its arrival in Los Angeles?

Time - Zone Map

304

Problem Solving: Using a Time-Zone Map

Check Understanding

Use the Time-Zone Map to answer each question.

a. If it is 3:00 P.M. in Cleveland, what is the time in Seattle?

b. It is 12:00 P.M. in Billings. What time is it in Philadelphia?

c. Name the time zone and a state within that time zone that is two hours ahead of Pacific standard time.

**ractice**

Use the Problem-Solving Guide and Time-Zone Map to help you find each answer.

1. Nyakim lives in Omaha, Nebraska. She called her grandparents who are located in Honolulu, Hawaii. If Nyakim called at 9:00 P.M. central standard time, what time was it in Honolulu?

2. Jonathon's flight from Denver, Colorado, to New Orleans, Louisiana, took two hours and 30 minutes. If Jonathon's flight departed at 10:00 A.M., what time did he arrive in New Orleans?

> **PROBLEM-SOLVING GUIDE**
>
> 1. UNDERSTAND THE QUESTION.
> 2. ANALYZE THE DATA.
> 3. PLAN THE STRATEGY.
> 4. SOLVE THE PROBLEM.
> 5. EVALUATE THE RESULT.

3. Reese is on an Alaskan cruise. She wants to call home to Orlando, Florida at 10:00 P.M. eastern standard time. At what time will Reese make the call?

4. Iveta, who lives in Dallas, has a watch that will show the time for two time zones. She set one face to show 12 P.M. (noon), which was the time in Anchorage where her grandparents live. She set the second clock face to show her own time zone. What time is displayed on the second clock face?

Challenge

5. The Janus family left their home at 11:30 A.M. to drive to a neighboring town to visit friends. When they arrived, the grandfather clock in their friends' home said 10:45 A.M. How could this occur?

Mastering Measuring

Use the Word Bank to complete each sentence.

Word Bank
yard
quart
Celsius
meter
milliliter
kilogram
centimeter
ounces
mass

1. The measurement of matter in an object is its _____.

2. The customary unit of length that measures 36 inches or 3 feet is the _____.

3. The metric unit of length that measures 10 decimeters is the _____.

4. The degree _____ is the metric unit of temperature.

5. The _____ is a small metric unit of capacity.

6. A metric unit of mass is the _____.

7. A _____ is equal to 4 cups or 2 pints.

8. Ten millimeters equal one _____.

9. Sixteen _____ equal one pound.

Choose the appropriate customary unit of capacity. Write *cup*, *pint*, *quart*, or *gallon*.

10.

11.

12.

13.

Complete each equation.

14. 72 fl oz = _____ c

15. 2 gal = _____ qt

16. 6 c = _____ pt

17. 16 qt = _____ pt

18. 20 pt = _____ qt

19. 12 pt = _____ c

20. 3 yd 2 ft = _____ ft

21. 42 in. = _____ yd _____ in.

22. 3 mi = _____ yd

23. 7 ft = _____ yd _____ ft

24. 4 mi = _____ ft

25. 8 ft 3 in. = _____ in.

San Diego, California

Write each measurement in pounds.

26. 5 T   27. 368 oz   28. 80 oz

Write each measurement in ounces.

29. 8 lb   30. 32 lb   31. 21 lb

Compare the measurements expressed in customary units. Write >, < or = .

32. 6 lb ⬚ 100 oz   33. 25 c ⬚ 1 gal   34. 3 mi ⬚ 705 yd

Write the elapsed time.

35. 7:10 A.M. to 11:30 A.M.

36. 11:37 A.M. to 2:25 P.M.

Find the time.

37.   9 hr 56 min   38.   6 min 49 sec
    − 2 hr 39 min   + 8 min 50 sec
    ‾‾‾‾‾‾‾‾‾‾‾‾‾   ‾‾‾‾‾‾‾‾‾‾‾‾‾

Use the thermometer to complete each equation.

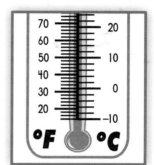

39. 64°F = ⬚ °C   40. 0°C = ⬚ °F

41. −10°C = ⬚ °F   42. 28°F = ⬚ °C

Complete each equation.

43. 2 dm = ⬚ cm   44. 300 cm = ⬚ m   45. 15 cm = ⬚ mm

46. 5 m = ⬚ cm   47. 47 dm = ⬚ m   48. 5,200 m = ⬚ km

49. 69 mL = ⬚ L   50. 0.52 L = ⬚ mL   51. 4,576 mL = ⬚ L

52. 6 g = ⬚ mg   53. 5.6 kg = ⬚ g   54. 450 mg = ⬚ g

Compare the measures expressed in metric units. Write >, < or = .

55. 5 kg ⬚ 5,000 g   56. 200 mL ⬚ 5 L   57. 420 cm ⬚ 3 m

58. Monica's best friend moved to San Diego, California. Monica still lives in Miami, Florida. She plans to call her friend at 9:00 P.M. Eastern Time. What time will it be in California?

59. The basketball tournament at Rohit's school begins at 9:45 A.M. Rohit's game begins at 1:25 P.M. How much time will Rohit have to wait until his game begins?

Miami, Florida

Grade Five

12 Chapter

Lessons 144–155

"Where were you when I laid the
foundations of the earth . . .
When the morning stars sang together,
And all the sons of God shouted for joy?"

Job 38:4a, 7

Construct Meaning

The **area** of a figure is the number of **square units** that cover the surface. In contrast, linear units measure only one dimension, length. Compare the linear unit with the corresponding square unit.

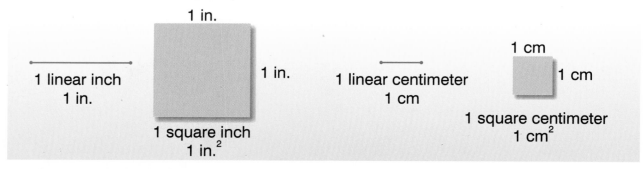

1 in.

1 linear inch
1 in.

1 in.

1 square inch
1 in.^{2}

1 cm

1 cm

1 linear centimeter
1 cm

1 square centimeter
1 cm^2

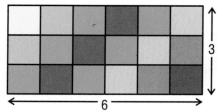

3

6

Isaac used a square-inch grid to plan a rectangular design of tiles each measuring one square inch. He figured the area of his design by counting the total square inches. What is the area of his design?

Later, Isaac painted a larger design on a piece of paper. To find the area of the new design, he used the formula for finding the area of a rectangle.

Area = length × width
$A = l \times w$

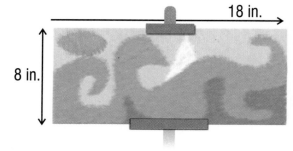

18 in.

8 in.

For the paper design, $A = 8 \times 18 = 144$ in.^{2}

Check Understanding

Identify the area for each figure. Label the answer using square units.

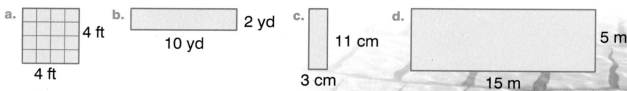

a.
4 ft
4 ft

b.
10 yd
2 yd

c.
3 cm
11 cm

d.
15 m
5 m

e. Write a formula for finding the area of a square.

f. Copy and complete the information in the table.

Rectangle	l	w	A
1	13 cm	6 cm	
2	2 m		24 m^2
3	5 yd		125 yd^2

Area of Rectangles

Practice

Use the formula to find the area.

1. Area of a room in square feet that measures 18 ft by 24 ft.

2. Area of a 12 mi by 6 mi ranch in square miles.

3. Area of a football field in square yards that measures 100 yd by 53.33 yd.

Identify the missing number.

4. $A = 49$ in.^{2}
   $l = 7$ in.
   $w = $

5. $A = 311$ yd^2
   $l = $
   $w = 62.2$ yd

6. $A = $
   $l = 59.8$ cm
   $w = 19.9$ cm

7. $A = 608$ mi^2
   $l = 19$ mi
   $w = $

Apply

8. A wooden chessboard made in Vermont is a square with 20-inch sides. A 2-inch border surrounds the actual grid for the game pieces. What is the area of the actual grid?

9. A garden has an area of 72 square feet. Corn is planted in all of the garden except $26\frac{1}{2}$ square feet. What amount of the garden is planted with corn?

10. Rachel drew a rectangle that measured 9 inches by 7 inches. After calculating the area, she decided to double the length of <u>one</u> side and draw a new rectangle. Compare the area of the second rectangle with the area of the first rectangle she drew.

11. When Rachel drew a third rectangle, she doubled the length of both sides of the original 9 inch by 7 inch rectangle. Compare the area of the third rectangle with the area of the 9 by 7 rectangle.

12. Mrs. James needs to carpet a room that is 15 feet by 18 feet. The carpet she wants is sold for $3.99 per <u>square yard</u>. What will it cost to carpet the room? Hint: 9 square feet = 1 square yard.

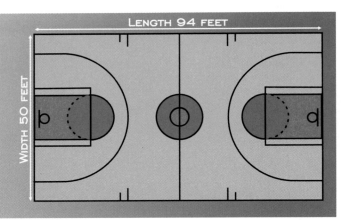

LENGTH 94 FEET
WIDTH 50 FEET

Construct Meaning

Perimeter is the distance around a figure. Professional basketball teams play on a rectangular court that has sides measuring 94 feet and 50 feet. The perimeter, or distance around the court, is the sum of its four sides.

To find the perimeter of a rectangle, use a formula.

Perimeter = (2 × length) + (2 × width)   **P = 2l + 2w**

Use the formula to find the perimeter of the basketball court.

P = 2l + 2w
P = (2 × 94) + (2 × 50) = 188 + 100 = 288
P = 288 feet

To find the perimeter of a square, use a formula.

If *s* means side, then P = s + s + s + s   **P = 4 × s**   **P = 4s**

If s = 6 cm, what is the perimeter?

P = 4s
P = 4 × 6
P = ▦ cm   6 cm

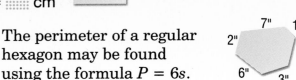

The perimeter of a regular hexagon may be found using the formula P = 6s.

P = 6 × 5 = ▦ inches

If the hexagon has sides of unequal length, add the length of each side to find the perimeter.

P = 1 + 5 + 3 + 6 + 2 + 7 = ▦ inches

Check Understanding

Find the perimeter of each figure.

a.

7"
3.5"

b.
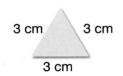
3 cm   3 cm
3 cm

c.

0.5 yd   1.2 yd   1 yd
1 yd   2.7 yd
3.3 yd

d. Explain why it is easier to find the perimeter of a regular polygon than to find the perimeter of a polygon having sides differing in measure.

 Practice

Find the perimeter for each figure. Label your answers.

1.
s = 5.1 yards

2.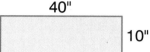
40"
10"

3.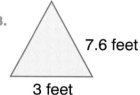
7.6 feet
3 feet

Identify the perimeter for each figure.

4. a regular pentagon, if $s = 215$ meters

5. a square, if $s = 16.5$ miles

6. a rectangle, if $l = 34$ inches, $w = 22$ inches

7. a scalene triangle, if the sides measure 18.8 yards, 29.9 yards, and 36 yards

8. a rhombus, if $s = 17$ centimeters

9. Write a formula for calculating the perimeter of each figure.
   a. an equilateral triangle
   b. a rhombus
   c. a regular octagon

 Apply

10. On a basketball court used for NBA games, the backboard must be a flat rectangle $3\frac{1}{2}$ feet on each vertical side. If the perimeter of the backboard is 19 feet, how wide is the backboard?

11. Tim, Kai, Abebi, and Lyn each drew a figure having only 6" sides. The figures drawn were a pentagon, a square, an octagon, and a hexagon. Rank the figures in order from the one with the largest perimeter to the one with the smallest perimeter.

12. Mr. Wright is planning to fence a rectangular play area that is 85 yards long and 48 feet wide. He will leave a four-foot opening for a gate that he will build later. How much fencing will he need?

13. The swimming pool used for the 2000 Olympics in Sydney, Australia, has a perimeter of 150 meters. The pool is twice as long as it is wide. Find the length and width of the pool.

Construct Meaning

The distance around a circle is called the **circumference**. Mr. Clark's students explored circumference using objects. They wrapped a piece of string around a flashlight and cut the string the length of the circumference. The students used the same piece of string to measure the diameter of the flashlight, cutting the string to see how many diameters would result. They were able to cut three diameter lengths with a small amount of string remaining. This resulted each time they measured the circumference of an object and cut the string the length of the diameter.

The students' findings confirm the ratio of the circumference of a circle to its diameter.

$$\frac{\text{circumference}}{\text{diameter}} = \text{approximately 3.14 or } pi \text{ (symbol } \pi \text{) or } \frac{C}{d} = \pi$$

To find the measure of the circumference of a circle, multiply the diameter by 3.14 (π).

$$\boxed{\text{Circumference} = \pi \times \text{diameter}} \qquad \boxed{C = \pi d}$$

Suppose you need to cut a piece of yarn to fit around the edge of a circular design you made. If the diameter of the design is eight inches, what is the approximate length of yarn needed? Use the formula for circumference.

$$C = \pi d$$
$$C \approx 3.14 \times 8$$
$$C \approx 25.12 \text{ inches}$$

If you cut a piece of yarn $25\frac{1}{4}$ inches long, will it be long enough?

Check Understanding

a. Perimeter is to polygon as ⬚ is to circle.

b. Use a whole number to estimate the circumference of a circle if the diameter measures 10 inches.

c. Use π (*pi*) to find the circumference if $d = 8.7$ centimeters.

d. How can you find C if you know the length of the radius?

Find the circumference. Round the answer to the nearest tenth.

1. 20 mm

2. 15 mm

3. 3.4 cm

4. 0.75 in.

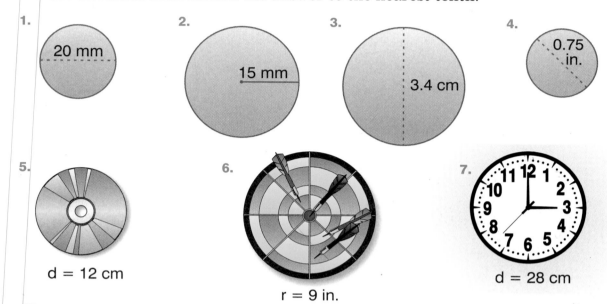

5. d = 12 cm

6. r = 9 in.

7. d = 28 cm

Apply

8. A city park has roses planted around its entire perimeter. Each end of the park is a half circle. Use the dimensions shown on the drawing to calculate the perimeter of the park. (Round your answer to the nearest tenth and label it.)

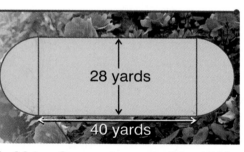

28 yards

40 yards

9. The first self-propelled bicycle was invented in 1839. The front wheel was about thirty inches in diameter and the diameter of the rear wheel was about ten inches greater. What was the approximate difference in the circumference of the two wheels?

10. Mrs. Martinez puts lace around the lids of pretty jars after filling them with homemade goodies. She has four feet of lace trim. How many lids with a two-and-a-half inch diameter can she trim?

11. A standard tennis ball has a diameter greater than $2\frac{1}{2}$ inches and less than $2\frac{5}{8}$ inches. If the diameter of a tennis ball is 2.55 inches, what is its circumference? (Round your answer to the nearest hundredth.)

Early Cyclists

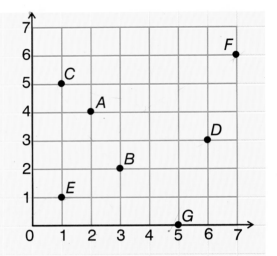

Construct Meaning

An archeologist used a **coordinate grid** similar to the one shown. The points were graphed on the grid to show the location of the objects that had been found.

Points on a grid are located using **ordered pairs** of numbers. The numbers are called the **coordinates** of the point, such as (2,4). The first number indicates how far to move to the <u>right</u> on the <u>horizontal</u> axis from 0. The second number indicates how far <u>up</u> to move. If you place your finger on (0,0) and trace two to the right and up four, you will see that (2,4) are the coordinates for point A.

Follow the steps to locate point B on the grid shown above.
 • Begin at (0,0).
 • Move three spaces to the right.
 • Move up two spaces.
What is the ordered pair for point B?

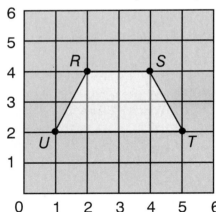

The points on this grid have been connected to form a trapezoid. The ordered pair for point R is (2,4). Name the ordered pair for each of the other vertices of the trapezoid.

Trip to Caesarea excavation
June 2000

Where is the line of symmetry for the trapezoid?

Check Understanding

a. Why are the coordinates of point T of the trapezoid called (5,2) instead of (2,5)?

b. Identify the only time when changing the order of the numbers in the pair will not change the location of the point.

c. Name the coordinates of points C through G on the grid at the top of the page.

d. Where is the vertical axis of a coordinate grid?

Practice

Name the point of the ordered pair.

1. (3,6)   2. (5,3)   3. (1,9)

Name the ordered pair for the point.

4. *G*   5. *E*   6. *A*   7. *B*

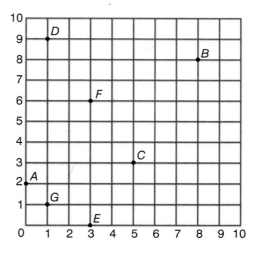

Identify the ordered pair for each vertex of the geometric figure. Name the polygon.

8.
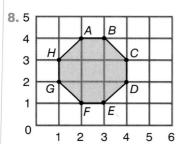

9.
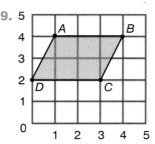

10. Predict what you will see on the grid if you graph and connect the points of the following ordered pairs: (0,0), (1,1), (2,2), (3,3), (4,4), and (5,5).

Apply

11. Use graph paper to draw and number a grid like the one at the top of this page. Draw a rectangle on the grid. Assign letter names to each of the vertices of the rectangle. Make a list of the ordered pairs that match each letter name.

12. Use your grid to graph the ordered pairs (2,1), (9,7), and (4,7). Connect the points, naming and classifying the polygon.

13. When Miss Michael's class played *Function Box,* she presented a series of ordered pairs. The students pretended the first number of the pair went into the "function box" and came out as the second number. They identified the rule, or function performed, that resulted in the second number. For example, the rule "multiply by two" makes the pairs (2,4), (4,8), and (8,16). State the function for the ordered pairs (3,6), (4,7), (5,8), (6,9), and (7,10). Graph the points on the grid. What do you discover when you connect the points?

14. Write an explanation of the correct process of locating and graphing the ordered pair (8,5).

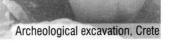

Archeological excavation, Crete

 Construct Meaning

Mrs. Bridges distributed square centimeter grid paper to her students and gave the following directions.

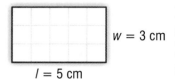
$w = 3$ cm
$l = 5$ cm

Draw a rectangle that measures 5 cm by 3 cm. Find the area of the rectangle.

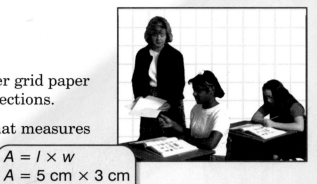
$A = l \times w$
$A = 5$ cm $\times$ 3 cm
$A = 15$ cm^2

Divide the rectangle with a diagonal line and cut on the line. What type of triangles result?
What fraction of the rectangle does each right triangle represent?
How does the area of each right triangle relate to the area of the rectangle?

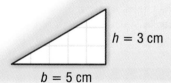
3 cm
5 cm

When you observe one of the triangles, you notice that the base and height of the right triangle are the same as the length and width of the rectangle. You know that the area of the right triangle is half that of the rectangle.

$h = 3$ cm
$b = 5$ cm

The formula for finding the area of a right triangle is: Area $= \frac{1}{2} \times$ base $\times$ height
$$A = \frac{1}{2} \times b \times h$$

Find the area of the triangle.

$$A = \frac{1}{2} \times b \times h$$
$$A = \frac{1}{2} \times 5 \text{ cm} \times 3 \text{ cm}$$
$$A = 7.5 \text{ cm}^2$$

Draw a rectangle on square centimeter grid paper and calculate the area. Divide your rectangle to form two congruent right triangles. Find the area of each triangle.

✓ Check Understanding

a. Find the area of a triangle with a height of 12 cm and a base of 29 cm.

b. A rectangular piece of stained glass measured 15 inches by 9 inches. It was divided into two congruent right triangles. What was the area of each triangle?

c. Name two characteristics of two triangles that form a rectangle when they are put together.

Practice

Identify the height, base, and area of each right triangle if □ = 1 square unit.

Example:

Example:
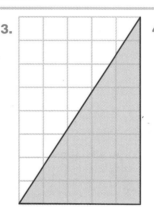
$b = 4, h = 2$
$A = 4$ square units

1.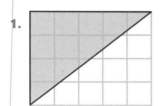

2.

3.

4.

Use the formula to find the area of each right triangle.

5.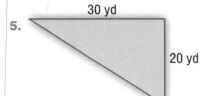
30 yd
20 yd

6. 13.4 m
13.4 m

7.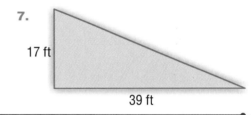
17 ft
39 ft

Apply

8. A sailmaker made two sails by dividing an 83 yd by 4 yd piece of cloth into two congruent triangles. What is the area of each sail?

9. A carpenter had a board that measured 12 feet by 4.5 feet. He cut it in half diagonally. What is the area of each piece of wood that resulted?

Review

Find the perimeter and area of each figure.

1. 25.5 ft
25.5 ft

2. 40.8 m
70 m

3.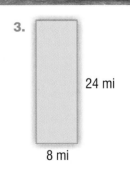
24 mi
8 mi

4.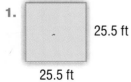
90 cm
50 cm
75 cm

5.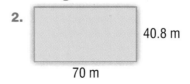
7 in.
42 in.

 Construct Meaning

Pennants for schools or teams are made in the shape of a triangle. Is the pennant shown a right triangle?

Gwen used a square centimeter grid and followed these instructions.

Draw a rectangle with the measure of the length greater than that of the width. Make a triangle without any right angles inside your rectangle. Make the base of your triangle the length of the rectangle, and place its opposite vertex on the parallel side.

w = 4 cm

Shade the triangle. How do the base and height of the triangle relate to the length and width of the rectangle?

l = 7 cm

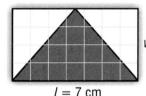

Cut your rectangle from the grid, then cut and remove your shaded triangle and the two unmarked triangles. Will the unmarked triangles fit exactly on the shaded triangle?
What does that tell you about the relationship between the area of the rectangle and the shaded triangle?

h = 4 cm

b = 7 cm

The area of any triangle may be found using the formula:
$$A = \frac{1}{2} \times base \times height$$
$$A = \frac{1}{2} \times b \times h$$

Gwen found the area for her triangle by using the formula.

Using a piece of square centimeter grid paper, draw a rectangle and follow the directions given above. Find the area of your shaded triangle.

$A = \frac{1}{2} \times b \times h$

$A = \frac{1}{2} \times 7 \text{ cm} \times 4 \text{ cm}$

$A = \frac{1}{2} \times 28 \text{ cm}^2$

$A = 14 \text{ cm}^2$

 Check Understanding

Write *true* or *false* for each statement and explain why.

a. A triangle with a base of 24 in. and a height of 13 in. has an area of 312 square inches.

b. Triangles having the same area are congruent triangles.

c. The formula for finding the area of a right triangle is the same as the formula for finding the area of any triangle.

Practice

Find b, h, and A for each triangle. Each ☐ = 1 square unit.

1.
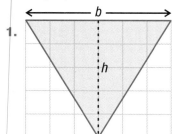

2.

3.

Use the formula to find the area of the object. Label your answer.

4.

$h = 15$ in.
8 in.

5.
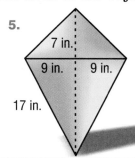
7 in.
9 in. 9 in.
17 in.

6.
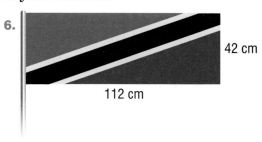
42 cm
112 cm

Apply

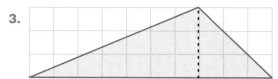

7. The triangular face of a small model of a pyramid has an area of 3 in.^{2} The measures of the base and height are whole numbers greater than 1 inch. What are the numbers that name the base and height of the triangular face?

8. How does the product of the base and height ($b \times h$) of a triangle relate to the area of the same triangle?

9. Ron drew three triangles that were not congruent. Each triangle had an area of 12 cm^2 and had a base and height that were whole numbers greater than one. The table shows the base and height of one of his triangles. Write the numbers that are needed to complete the information in the table Ron has made.

	b	h	A
Triangle 1	6 cm	4 cm	12 cm^2
Triangle 2			12 cm^2
Triangle 3			12 cm^2

Review

1. A rectangle is four times as long as it is wide. If $w = 5.2$ ft, what is the area of the rectangle?

2. Write the formula used to find the circumference of a circle.

Lesson 150

Construct Meaning

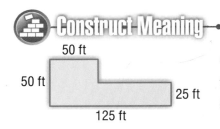

The Garner family is planning to purchase sod to cover their backyard with grass. The yard is an irregular shape as shown. How can the area of the yard be calculated?

Mr. Garner thought of the yard as two rectangles.

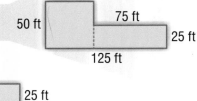

His son, Brian, thought of the yard as two different rectangles.

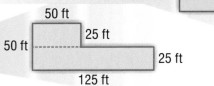

Both of them used the formula $A = l \times w$ to find the area of each rectangle, then added the two numbers for the total area.

Mr. Garner's calculations
50 ft × 50 ft = 2,500 ft^2
75 ft × 25 ft = 1,875 ft^2

  2,500 ft^2
+ 1,875 ft^2
  4,375 ft^2 total area

Brian's calculations
50 ft × 25 ft = ▦ ft^2
125 ft × 25 ft = ▦ ft^2
                    ▦ ft^2
+   ▦ ft^2
                    ▦ ft^2 total area

Mr. Garner and Brian used the same method for finding the area.
- Mentally break the irregular figure into shapes.
- Use a known formula to find the area of each shape.
- Find the sum of the individual areas.

Find the total area of the yard shown here.

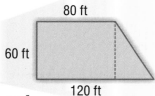

Area of a rectangle = $l \times w$
$A = 80 \text{ ft} \times 60 \text{ ft} = $ ▦ ft^2

Area of a triangle = $\frac{1}{2} \times b \times h$
How can you find b for the triangle?
$A = \frac{1}{2} \times 40 \text{ ft} \times 60 \text{ ft} = \frac{1}{2} \times 2{,}400 \text{ ft} = $ ▦ ft^2

Add the area of the rectangle and the triangle to find out the total area of the yard.

Check Understanding

a. List the steps explaining one way to find the area of an irregular figure.

b. Find the total area of the shape.

c. In the example above, why did Mr. Garner and his son arrive at the same answer?

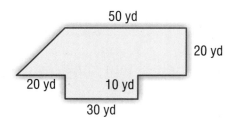

Mathematics Grade 5

Practice

Find the area of each figure.

1.
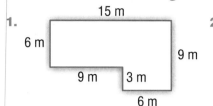

2.
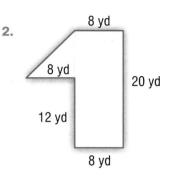

3.
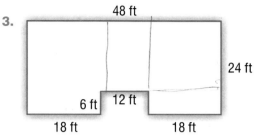

4.
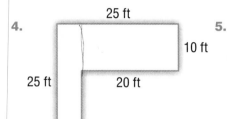

5.
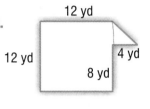

6.
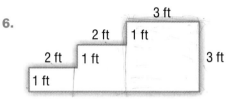

Apply

7. Mrs. Carroll is going to buy wallpaper for one wall in her dining room. The dimensions of the wall are shown, including the window. What is the area that will be covered with wallpaper?

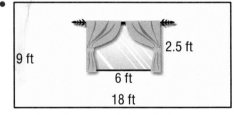

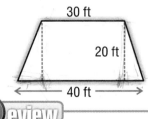

8. The students at Canaan Academy will paint one side of a wall separating two areas of their playground. The wall has the shape and dimensions shown. If one gallon of paint covers 300 square feet, how many one-gallon cans of paint should be purchased?

Review

1. Name each ordered pair for point *A* through point *H* on the grid.

2. List three points that would result in a diagonal line if they were connected.

3. If each square of the grid represents 1 cm^2, find the area and perimeter of the figure that results from connecting points *A*, *B*, *C*, and *D*.

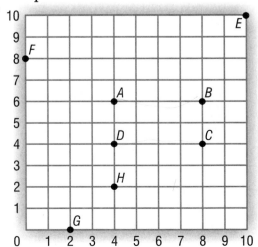

Construct Meaning

To find the area of a rectangle you must know its length and width. To determine the surface area of a rectangular prism, you need to know the length and width of each face. The **surface area** of a solid figure is the sum of the areas of all the faces.

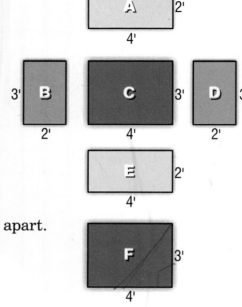

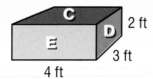

Imagine that this rectangular prism has been taken apart.

To find the surface area of the rectangular prism, find the area of each rectangle. Then find the sum of all the areas. Complete the table.

Face	Length	Width	Area
A	4 ft	2 ft	8 ft²
B	3 ft	2 ft	
C	4 ft	3 ft	
D	3 ft	2 ft	
E	4 ft	2 ft	
F	4 ft	3 ft	

Add the figures in the last column of the table to find the surface area of the rectangular prism.

Check Understanding

a. What do you notice about the area of opposite faces of a rectangular prism?

b. Is there a more efficient way than the method used above to find the surface area of a rectangular prism?

c. Explain the most efficient method of finding the surface area of a cube.

Practice

Find the surface area of each box.

1.

7 cm
7 cm
20 cm

2.
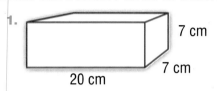
12 ft
7 ft
9 ft

3.
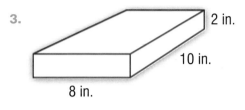
2 in.
10 in.
8 in.

Find the surface area of each object.

4. a toy box
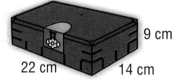
22 in.
34 in.   18 in.

5. a shoebox
5 in.
11 in.
6 in.

6. a jewelry box
9 cm
22 cm   14 cm

Apply

7. Miriam is wrapping three boxes like the one shown in problem 3 above. What is the total surface area to be covered?

8. The package of wrapping paper Miriam bought will cover five square feet. Does she have enough paper to wrap the three boxes? (144 square inches = 1 square foot)

9. Mrs. Ramirez used wallpaper to decorate a box shaped like a cube. She did not cover the top of the box because she planned to remove it. The dimensions of the box were 8 in. by 8 in. by 8 in. What was the total surface area she covered with wallpaper?

Review

Find the perimeter or circumference for each figure.

1. an equilateral triangle, $s = 13.9$ in.

2. a circle, $d = 2.1$ cm

3. a square, $s = 8.5$ yd

4. a rectangle, $l = 5.8$ mi, $w = 4.6$ mi

5. a circle, $r = 9$ mm

Construct Meaning

Volume is the measure of the amount of space within a solid figure or object.

Phil and Taryn built a rectangular prism with one-inch cubes. They found the volume by counting all of the cubes that made up the space of the prism.

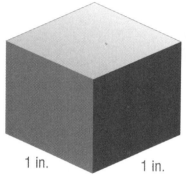

1 in.

1 in.   1 in.

Each cube of the prism measures 1 inch by 1 inch by 1 inch. It is called 1 cubic inch, 1 cu in., or 1 in^3.

Here is a drawing of the prism the students built.

Phil counted the six cubes in the top layer. Taryn said, "There are two layers, and $6 \times 2 = 12$ cubes. If each cube measures one cubic inch, the volume is 12 cubic inches." They checked their answer by counting all the cubes in their prism.

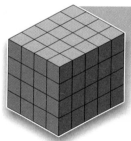

After building a figure like the one shown, Phil said, "We do not have to count every cube in the top layer. There is a faster way to determine the number of cubes in the layer."
What did he mean?

> Find the volume of the new prism.
>> How many cubes are in one layer?
>> How many layers are there?
>> Multiply and express the volume in cubic inches.

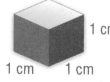

1 cm

1 cm   1 cm

If the students had used cubes with each edge measuring one centimeter, they would have found the volume in cubic centimeters. Each cube is 1 cubic centimeter, or 1 cu cm, or 1 cm^3.

Check Understanding

a. What is the difference between volume and area?

b. Which is larger, a rectangular prism with a volume of 31 cm^3 or a cube with a volume of 31 in.^{3}?

Count the cubes to determine the volume. Label your answer. 1 cube = 1 cm³

1.

2.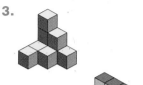

3.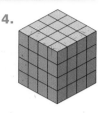

4.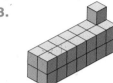

5.

6.

7.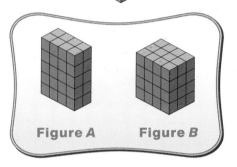

8.

9. If you looked quickly at the two figures here, which would you guess had the greater volume? Why?

10. Count the cubes and compare the volume of Figure *A* with the volume of Figure *B*. (Use cubic inches as the unit of measure.)

Figure *A*   Figure *B*

11. Joel used 20 cubes to construct solid figures. He made a figure that was one layer of 20 cubes and another figure that was two layers of ten cubes. Which figure had the greater volume?

12. Name three different ways you could use cubes in three layers to make a rectangular prism having a volume of 36 cubic units. Building a model may help.

13. How many centimeter cubes do you need to build a 4 cm × 4 cm × 4 cm cube?

Find the surface area for each figure.

1.  1 ft 4 ft 2 ft

2. 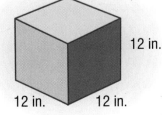 12 in. 12 in. 12 in.

3. 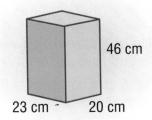 46 cm 23 cm 20 cm

Lesson 153

Construct Meaning

Jacob is going to live and work with Christians in Africa. He will leave many personal belongings in storage. To select the box with the greatest volume for packing, he will need to find the exact number of cubic units each box will hold.

Use the formula for finding the volume of a rectangular prism.

Volume = length × width × height
$$V = l \times w \times h$$

Box 1

$V = 20$ in. $\times$ 8 in. $\times$ 8 in.
$V = 20$ in. $\times$ 64 in.
$V =$ ▒ in.^{3}

Box 2

$V = 18$ in. $\times$ 13 in. $\times$ 10 in.
$V = 18$ in. $\times$ 130 in.
$V =$ ▒ in.^{3}

Box 3

$V = 19$ in. $\times$ 8 in. $\times$ 10 in.
$V = 19$ in. $\times$ 80 in.
$V =$ ▒ in.^{3}

Which box has the greatest volume?

16 cm
14 cm   6 cm

Find V for the rectangular prism shown here.

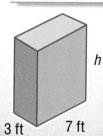

h
3 ft   7 ft

If you know the length, width, and volume of a rectangular prism, you can find its height.

$V = 189$ ft^3

$V = l \times w \times h$
189 ft^3 = 7 ft $\times$ 3 ft $\times h$
189 ft^3 = 21 ft^2 $\times h$
189 ft^3 $\div$ 21 ft^2 = h
9 ft = h

The height is 9 feet.

Check Understanding

a. Will the measure of the volume change if the length, width, and height are multiplied in a different order? Why or why not?

b. To find h in the example above, we divided the volume by the product of what two measurements?

c. If l is the missing measurement, the volume will be divided by the product of what two measurements?

328

Mathematics Grade 5

Practice

Find the volume of each object.

1.
4 ft
2 ft
3 ft

2.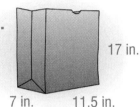
17 in.
7 in.   11.5 in.

3.
35 cm
16 cm   40 cm

Find the volume of each rectangular prism with the given dimensions.

4. 6 yd × 7 yd × 4 yd

5. 13 cm × 10 cm × 8 cm

6. 12 ft × 24 ft × 6 ft

7. 30 in. × 15 in. × 9 in.

Find the missing measurement.

8. l = 11 m
   w = 5 m
   h = 6 m
   V = ▨

9. l = 7 in.
   w = 7 in.
   h = ▨
   V = 343 in.³

10. l = ▨
    w = 15 cm
    h = 10 cm
    V = 3,150 cm³

Apply

11. A concrete patio will be 8 ft by 12 ft by $\frac{1}{2}$ ft. If forty-five cubic feet of concrete has been ordered, will there be enough to complete the patio?

12. Identify an object in your classroom that has a volume of about one cubic inch, another with a volume of about one cubic foot, and another with a volume of about one cubic yard.

13. Corbin wanted to see if doubling the measure of the length, width, and height of a rectangular prism would double its volume. After he worked with many sets of dimensions, he found a pattern in the way the volume changed when he doubled the measure of l, w, and h. Identify the pattern shown by three of his work samples.

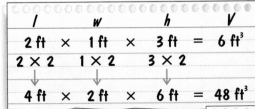

l	w	h	V
2 ft ×	1 ft ×	3 ft =	6 ft³
2 × 2	1 × 2	3 × 2	
4 ft ×	2 ft ×	6 ft =	48 ft³

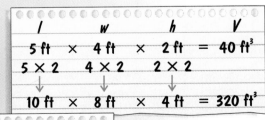

l	w	h	V
5 ft ×	4 ft ×	2 ft =	40 ft³
5 × 2	4 × 2	2 × 2	
10 ft ×	8 ft ×	4 ft =	320 ft³

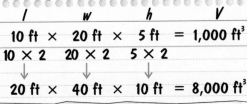

l	w	h	V
10 ft ×	20 ft ×	5 ft =	1,000 ft³
10 × 2	20 × 2	5 × 2	
20 ft ×	40 ft ×	10 ft =	8,000 ft³

Construct Meaning

Mr. Taylor planned to update the family room of his home. He will cover the floor with new tile and carpet and put new molding around the perimeter of the room.

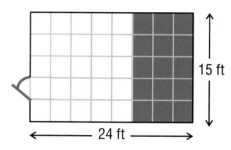

15 ft

24 ft

He drew a sketch of the floor on grid paper with the side of each square representing three feet. The area to be carpeted was shaded. Mr. Taylor will use the formulas to find out how much molding, tile, and carpet to buy.

Formulas

Area of a rectangle $A = l \times w$

Perimeter of a rectangle $P = 2l + 2w$

Perimeter of a square $P = 4s$

Circumference of a circle $C = \pi d$

Area of a triangle $A = \frac{1}{2} \times b \times h$

Volume of a rectangular prism $V = l \times w \times h$

Mr. Taylor considered the shape and dimensions of the room before choosing each formula.

He needs to know the area for the tile.

$A = l \times w$
$A = (24\text{ ft} - 9\text{ ft}) \times 15\text{ ft}$
$A = 15\text{ ft} \times 15\text{ ft}$
$A = \text{ft}^2$

He needs to know the perimeter for the molding.

$P = 2l + 2w$
$P = (2 \times 24\text{ ft}) + (2 \times 15\text{ ft})$
$P = 48\text{ ft} + 30\text{ ft}$
$P = \text{ft}$

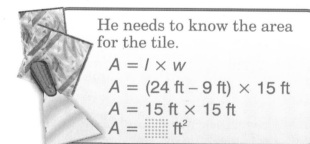

What adjustment is needed to determine the amount of molding to purchase?

Check Understanding

a. Use the appropriate formula to determine the amount of carpet needed for the shaded area of Mr. Taylor's family room.

b. If you needed to know how many 8 in. × 8 in. × $\frac{1}{4}$ in. tiles would fit into a 16 in. × 8 in. × 12 in. carton, which formula would you use?

c. Use this formula to find the number of tiles.

d. Visualize the number of tiles that will fit in one layer.

e. How many layers of tiles will fit in the carton?

Practice

1. Kamie's Sunday school class decided to make picture puzzles for the younger children at church. Kamie made her puzzle on a piece of 10 inch × 8 inch cardboard. She wanted to know the area of the puzzle to determine the size of the picture needed to cover it. What is the area of the puzzle?

2. Jim made a puzzle like the one shown. What is the area of his puzzle?

3. Some of the puzzles were placed into boxes that measured 12 inches × 9 inches × 2 inches. The children wrapped these boxes for gifts to be sent to an orphanage. How many wrapped boxes will fit into a mailing carton that measures 2 feet × 1 foot × 9 inches?

20 cm

30 cm

4. A group of parents at Kamie's church are planning to fence the circular play area behind the building. If the diameter of the area is 18 feet, how many feet of fence will be needed? (Round your answer to the nearest whole number.)

5. A porch on a house measures 5 feet by 10 feet. If the homeowners double the length and width of the porch, what will be the area of the new porch?

6. How many times greater is the area of the new porch than that of the old porch on the house?

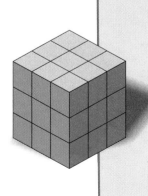

7. Seth built a cube like the one shown to teach his little sister about surface area and volume. What is the volume of his cube?

8. What is the total surface area of Seth's cube?

9. What will be the volume of the solid if Seth adds one additional layer?

10. Find the surface area if the solid has the additional layer.

Lesson 155

Around the World

Find the perimeter of each figure. Label your answer.

1.
s = 2.7 in.

2.
5.4 ft
3.4 ft

3.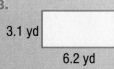
3.1 yd
6.2 yd

4.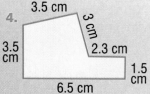
3.5 cm
3 cm
3.5 cm
2.3 cm
6.5 cm
1.5 cm

Find the circumference of each circle. Round the answer to the nearest tenth.

5.
18 m

6. 2.3 cm

7.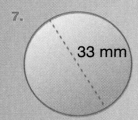
33 mm

8. 1.5 yd

Name the point for each ordered pair.

9. (7,2) 10. (1,6) 11. (5,3) 12. (2,1)

Name the ordered pair for each point.

13. E 14. F 15. A 16. H

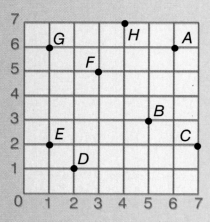

Find the area of each outlined figure using the measurements given.

17.
2 ft
4 ft

18.
6 in.
6 in.

19.
7 ft
3 ft

332

Mathematics Grade 5

Find the area of each figure.

20.
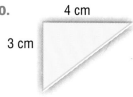
4 cm
3 cm

21.
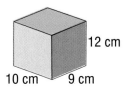
40 ft
30 ft
20 ft
25 ft

22.
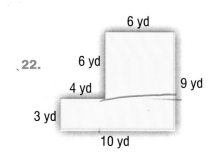
6 yd
6 yd
4 yd
9 yd
3 yd
10 yd

Find the surface area of each box.

23.

6 m
5 m
18 m

24.

12 cm
10 cm   9 cm

25.
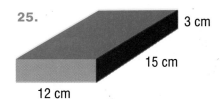
3 cm
15 cm
12 cm

Count the cubes to determine the volume. 1 cube = 1 cm³

26.
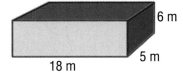

27.
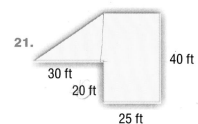

28.

Find the volume of each object.

29.

4 yd
3 yd
15 yd

30.

7 in.
6 in.   5 in.

31.

2 cm
26 cm
10 cm

Determine the volume of each rectangular prism with the given dimensions.

32. 10 yd × 11 yd × 8 yd

33. 17 cm × 14 cm × 9 cm

34. 24 ft × 36 ft × 4 ft

35. 40 in. × 25 in. × 7 in.

36. Diane used 30 cubes to build solid figures. She constructed one figure that was two layers with six cubes in each layer and another that was one layer of 18 cubes. Which solid figure has the greater volume?

Grade Five

13 Chapter

Ah, Lord GOD! Behold, You have made the heavens and the earth by Your great power and outstretched arm. There is nothing too hard for You.

 **Construct Meaning**

Three ways to collect data are surveys, questionnaires, and experiments. Three ways of organizing data are tables, charts, and graphs. Each has a different purpose.

SURVEY

Danell discovered that lights, insect repellers, fountains, and radios can be powered by solar energy. She wanted to find out which item her classmates would be most interested in purchasing.

Solar-powered items preferred by a sample of Danell's classmates	
Items	**Preferences**
Garden Water Fountain	IIII
Radical Sound Radio	IIII IIII IIII I
Super-Bright Lantern	IIII II
Mosquito-Repelling Zipper Pull	IIII IIII

Danell collected data by conducting a survey of a small group, or sample, of students at her school. The results are organized in this table.

QUESTIONNAIRE

Exaud is from Arusha, Tanzania. He was wondering about solar energy use in his town. He made a questionnaire for residents to complete.

	YES	NO	MAYBE
Do you have solar energy?	☐	☑	☐
Do you think solar energy would work in Arusha?	☑	☐	☐
Would you use it to heat water?	☐	☐	☑
Would you use it to run lights?	☑	☐	☐
If it was inexpensive, would you buy it?	☑	☐	☐

EXPERIMENT

After making a prediction about what position would be best for a solar panel on the roof of his house, Exaud placed four thermometers on the roof and monitored them during the day. He recorded the temperatures in a chart and made a line graph of Thermometer Number 3.

Thermometer				
TIME	#1	#2	#3	#4
8:00 A.M.	61°	54°	72°	60°
10:00 A.M.	75°	62°	81°	73°
12:00 P.M.	87°	76°	99°	84°
2:00 P.M.	98°	82°	110°	96°
4:00 P.M.	100°	90°	120°	101°
6:00 P.M.	95°	86°	116°	90°
8:00 P.M.	89°	80°	109°	84°

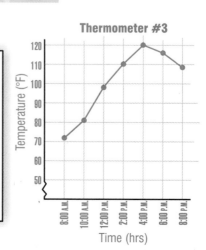

Thermometer #3

Collecting and Organizing Data

 **Check Understanding**

a. Use the data from Danell's survey to predict which item would be the most popular in other schools.

b. What would be a good title for Exaud's questionnaire?

c. Why should Exaud give his questionnaire to a random sample of people?

d. Examine the data from Exaud's experiment. Why do you think he chose Thermometer Number 3 to graph?

e. What do you think the broken line means on the temperature axis of the graph?

Practice

1. When collecting data, why would you survey only a sample of the population?

2. Organize the following data in a table: 42 girls chose red, 50 boys chose red, 62 girls chose purple, 30 boys chose purple, 10 girls chose black, 40 boys chose black, 25 girls chose yellow, and 15 boys chose yellow. What is the most popular color for girls? for boys?

3. Design a survey that determines what type of pets your classmates have. Perform the survey. Make a prediction about a larger population of fifth graders.

4. Pretend you are going to start an after-school club. Develop a five-question questionnaire that you might use.

5. What would be the best way to find answers for each of the following questions? Write *survey, questionnaire,* or *experiment.*
    a. What are your classmates' favorite subjects?
    b. What is the most efficient power source?
    c. What type of person makes the best teacher?

6. For each item, explain how you would make sure that a random survey was taken.
    a. favorite food of students in your school
    b. the most important concern for people in your community
    c. favorite place to vacation

Construct Meaning

Sandra's Sunday school class is planning a pizza party. Sandra asked her classmates what type of pizza they prefer. She organized their preferences in a frequency table, then used the data to make a bar graph. The number of times a certain item appears in a set of data is the **frequency**.

Sunday School Pizza Party		
Pizza Type	Number of Students	
Pepperoni	ʬ III	8
Veggie	II	2
Meat	I	1
Cheese	ʬ II	7
Everything	ʬ	5

Pizza Preferences of Sunday School Class

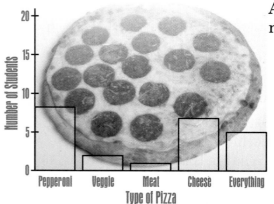

A **bar graph** uses bars to represent and compare numbers for several items.

What is the title of the bar graph?
What is presented on the vertical axis?
What interval (the space between the numbers on an axis) is used?
What is presented on the horizontal axis?
How do you read a bar that is between two numbers on a scale?

By looking at the bar graph of pizza preferences, the students determined the three most preferred pizzas to be Pepperoni, Cheese, and Everything. Sandra called Super Pizza and Pizza Bravo to find out how much each pizza costs. She made a double bar graph to show the cost comparisons. A **double bar graph** uses two sets of bars to represent and compare numbers having the same units.

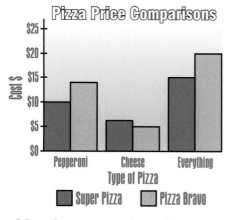

What is the title of the double bar graph?
What is represented by the blue bars? What is represented by the orange bars?
What information is presented on each axis?

Check Understanding

Use the Pizza Price Comparisons graph to answer the following questions.

a. Which pizza costs about the same at Super Pizza and Pizza Bravo?

b. Estimate which pizza place offers the more reasonable prices.

c. What is the approximate price difference for a pepperoni pizza?

d. If the students bought three "Everything" pizzas from Super Pizza instead of from Pizza Bravo, what were their total savings?

Use the double bar graph to answer the questions.

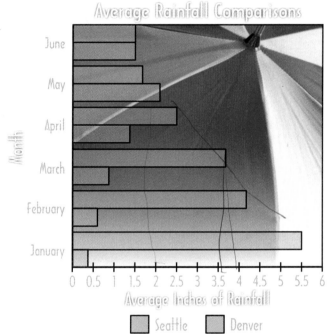

Average Rainfall Comparisons

Month

Average Inches of Rainfall

☐ Seattle ☐ Denver

1. What is the title of the graph?

2. What two cities are compared on the graph?

3. What is compared between the cities?

4. How many months are recorded?

5. Which city receives more rainfall?

6. Which city receives more rainfall in the month of May?

7. During which month do the cities receive the same amount of rainfall?

8. About how many total inches of rainfall does Seattle receive during the represented months?

9. Design a bar graph using the data from the table. Follow the steps.

- Draw and label the vertical and horizontal axes. Title the graph.

- Determine and write the intervals that best present the information.

- Draw the bars on your graph.

FAVORITE FOODS OF 5TH GRADERS	
Foods	Number of Students
Spaghetti	ᵗᴴᴸ IIII
Fish Sticks	ᵗᴴᴸ
Pizza	ᵗᴴᴸ ᵗᴴᴸ ᵗᴴᴸ
Hamburgers	ᵗᴴᴸ ᵗᴴᴸ I
Other	ᵗᴴᴸ I

Write *bar graph* or *double bar graph* to indicate how the data would best be displayed.

10.

Sugar Content of One Serving	
Apple	16g
Cherries	19g
Banana	29g
Orange	14g

11.

Average Temperature		
Month	Minneapolis	Boston
April	46°F	48°F
May	59°F	58°F
June	68°F	68°F
July	74°F	73°F

12.

Spring Valley Orchard Apple Trees	
Green	59
Yellow	72
Red	100
Red/Yellow	48

Construct Meaning

"He sends out His word and melts them; He causes His wind to blow, and the waters to flow." Psalms 147:18

Energy from water, called hydroelectric power, is an alternate energy source that can be measured in megawatts.

A **histogram** is a graph that uses bars to represent how many of a particular item are found in a given category or interval. The horizontal axis must show information that can be expressed on a continuous scale such as dollars, hours, or megawatts.

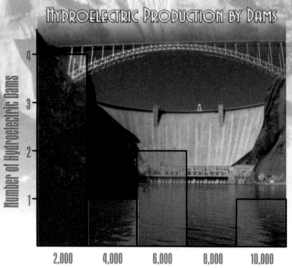

HYDROELECTRIC PRODUCTION BY DAMS

The vertical axis shows the number of items. Together they express how many of an item are in a given category.

On this histogram, the number 2,000 on the horizontal axis represents the interval of zero to 2,000.

The first bar on the histogram shows that four dams produce between zero and 2,000 megawatts.

Why is there a space between 6,001 and 8,000 megawatts?

Use the histogram to the right to answer the following questions.

What is the title?

What is the vertical axis?

What is the horizontal axis?

Which axis expresses a quantity?

Which axis shows a continuous scale?

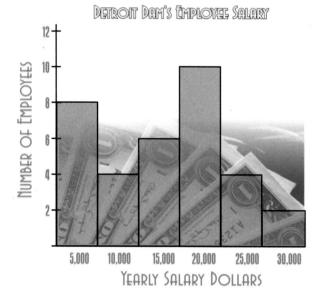

DETROIT DAM'S EMPLOYEE SALARY

Check Understanding

Use the employee salary histogram to answer the following questions.

a. How many employees earn between $15,001 and $20,000?

b. Ten employees are in which salary category?

c. How many employees are in the highest salary category?

d. What are the intervals on the horizontal axis ? vertical axis?

Practice

1. What type of information is required for the horizontal axis of a histogram?

2. Why is it important to have the interval, the scale between the numbers on an axis, equal?

3. Together, what do the horizontal and vertical axes express?

Jaciara is from Brazil. She visited the Itaipu Dam, which produces the largest amount of electric power in the world. Jaciara recorded data about the amount of water released from each turbine, and made the histogram below. Using Jaciara's Itaipu Dam histogram, answer the following questions.

4. What is the histogram telling you?

5. What is the interval on the continuous scale?

6. How many turbines operate between 2,001 and 2,500 cfs?

7. How many turbines operate between 1,001 and 2,500 cfs?

8. Are there five turbines that operate within the same category?

9. Use the data table below to make a histogram. The following statements and questions will help you get started.

The first interval in the continuous scale should start at 0 and end at 2,000. Complete the scale.

What should the vertical axis be called? Remember it is an amount or number. (Hint: See the first histogram under Construct Meaning.)

Name	Power Output (megawatts)
A. Itaipu Dam	12,600
B. Grand Coulee Dam	6,480
C. Hoover Dam	2,000
D. Dwanshak Dam	860
E. LCRA Dams	240
F. Glen Canyon Dam	104

Apply

10. Use the data collected by your teacher about the amount of time each student spends doing weekly chores.
    a. Make a data table.
    b. Choose horizontal and vertical axis scales.
    c. Make a histogram from your results.

Construct Meaning

Yoonie surveyed the students at Heritage Academy to find out how many participated in athletics. She collected the results and recorded them on a frequency table. She used the data to make a pictograph.

A **pictograph** is a graph that illustrates data by using symbols to represent numbers. The key explains what is represented by the symbols.

Students in Athletics

Sport	Number of Students	
Volleyball	|||| |||| |||| |||	18
Basketball	|||| |||| |||| ||||	20
Track	|||| |||| ||||		16
Wrestling	|||| |||| ||	12
Football	|||| |||| ||||		16
Swimming	||||		6

Number of Students in Heritage Academy Athletics

Volleyball	� � � � ⸙
Basketball	� � � � �
Track	� � ☆ ☆
Wrestling	☆ ☆ ☆
Football	☆ ☆ ☆ ☆
Swimming	☆ ⸙

Key: ☆ = 4 students   ⸙ = 2 students

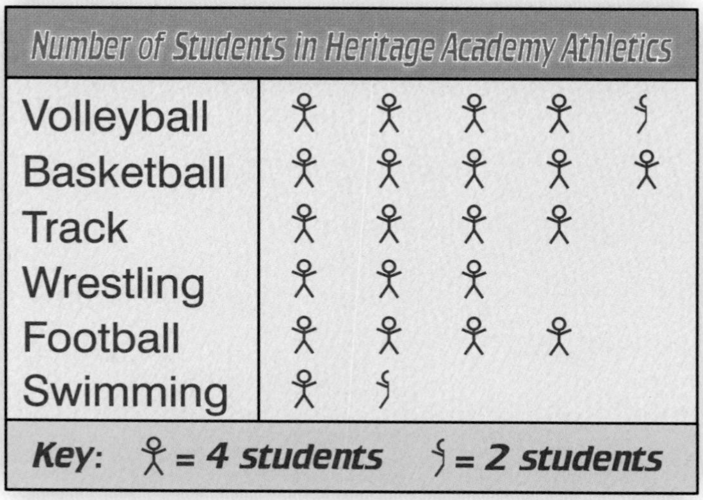

Steps for Making a Pictograph

• *Choose a title.*
• *List each item being represented.*
• *Choose a symbol.*
• *Make a key to define the symbol.*
• *Enter the data in picture form.*

How many students are represented by one ☆ ?

How many students are represented by one ⸙ ?

Check Understanding

Use the pictograph to answer each question.

a. What is the difference in number of students who participated in basketball and wrestling?

b. List the sports in order of the least to greatest number of students participating.

c. How could Yoonie show 22 students by using her symbols?

d. How could Yoonie change the key so only whole symbols would be used?

Use the pictograph to complete each problem.

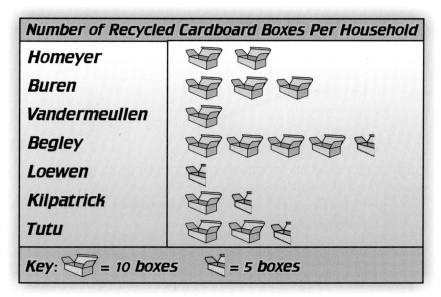

Number of Recycled Cardboard Boxes Per Household

Homeyer	
Buren	
Vandermeullen	
Begley	
Loewen	
Kilpatrick	
Tutu	

Key: = 10 boxes   = 5 boxes

Dustin surveyed people at his dad's office to see how many cardboard boxes they recycled in a month. Dustin presented his information in the pictograph.

1. What does each symbol represent?

2. What information is represented on the graph?

3. Who recycles the most cardboard boxes?

4. How many more boxes do the Burens recycle than the Kilpatricks?

5. What is the total number of boxes recycled?

6. Why might Dustin have decided to display the information as a pictograph?

7. Work backward and make the pictograph into a frequency table.

8. Use the data from this frequency table. Follow the Steps for Making a Pictograph to illustrate the data.

Dogs in the Neighborhood

Street	Number of Dogs	
Lincoln	ꟿꟿ III	8
Wallace	ꟿꟿ ꟿꟿ ꟿꟿ I	16
Zena	ꟿꟿ ꟿꟿ	10
Edgewater	III	3
Berry	ꟿꟿ ꟿꟿ II	12
Fourth	III	3

Construct Meaning

Solar heat varies with season, years, and days. All life depends on the output of the sun. Genesis 1:14–15 says, "Let there be lights in the firmament of the heavens to divide the day from the night; and let them be for signs and seasons, and for days and years; and let them be for lights in the firmament of the heavens to give light on the earth. . . ."

A **line graph** uses lines to represent increases or decreases over a period of time.

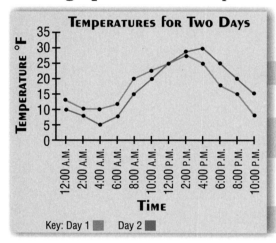

Use the graph at the left to answer the following questions.

★ What is the title of the graph?

★ What is being measured?

★ What is the interval (the space between the numbers on the scale) of the horizontal axis?

★ At 4:00 P.M., what was the temperature on Day 1? Day 2?

★ What is the general trend of the graph?

Joseph wanted to see how much the temperature in his town varied on two days. Use the data Joseph recorded to make a line graph. Plot both days' temperatures on the same graph using different colors.

TIME	Temperature °F	
	Day 1	Day 2
12:00 A.M.	35	32
2:00 A.M.	33	30
4:00 A.M.	25	29
6:00 A.M.	29	30
8:00 A.M.	35	36
10:00 A.M.	40	39
12:00 P.M.	48	45
2:00 P.M.	55	51
4:00 P.M.	60	60
6:00 P.M.	54	50
8:00 P.M.	40	42
10:00 P.M.	35	38

➡ Start by drawing the horizontal axis. What is being measured? How is it measured? What is the total interval of time? What would be the best representation of the intervals in the scale?

➡ Next, draw the vertical axis and ask the same questions as above.

➡ Beginning with the first time on Day 1, plot each data point for that day. Connect the dots with line segments. Repeat for Day 2, using a different color. Make a key to show what color represents each day.

Remember to ask yourself these questions as you make a graph.
1. What is being measured?
2. What is the interval?
3. What is the best representation of that interval?

Remember to do each step.
1. Label both axes.
2. Connect the points with line segments.
3. Title the graph.

Check Understanding

Use the graph you made to answer each question.

a. When was it 60°F on Day 2?

b. What was the greatest increase in temperature during a two-hour period on Day 2?

c. What do you think the temperature was at 11:00 A.M. on *Day 1*?

d. Was one day significantly warmer than the other?

Practice

Mr. Hausler filled his oil heater with ten gallons of oil. He started the heater and periodically checked the gauge to see how much oil remained.

Elapsed time (hours)	0	4	6	12	14	16
Remaining oil (gallons)	10	8	7	4	3	2

1. Make a line graph using Mr. Hausler's data. Label each axis and title your graph.

2. Use the graph to determine how much oil was left after 8 hours.

3. Predict how many hours the heater can run until the oil is gone.

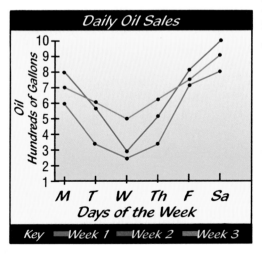

Mr. Kropf made a graph of his daily oil sales for three weeks. Use his graph to answer the questions.

4. How many more gallons of oil were sold on Monday of the second week than on Monday of the first week?

5. On which two days of the week does Mr. Kropf usually sell the most oil?

6. If Mr. Kropf decided to close his shop on one day of the week, what day would probably be best?

7. Which week had the lowest sales?

PERCENTAGE OF POWER TYPES USED

9% HYDROELECTRIC

19% NUCLEAR

72% FOSSIL FUEL

Every time you ride in a car, turn on a light, take a shower, or use the phone, power is required. The circle graph shows the types and amounts of power used in the United States.

A **circle graph** is a type of graph that compares parts of a whole. The whole circle stands for the total amount of power usage. Each section of the circle shows a percentage of the total power used. Since each section shows a percentage, or fraction, of the whole, the sum of the percentages must be 100%.

Use the circle graph above to answer the following questions.

What is the percentage of the power source used the most?

Can the sum of the percents shown in a circle graph be greater than 100%?

What percent of US power comes from hydroelectric sources?

How much greater is nuclear power usage than hydroelectric power usage?

Construct your own circle graph using these percentages: 75% fossil fuel, 20% nuclear, and 5% hydroelectric.

a. Use the given information to make a circle graph and label each section of the circle with the percent and name.

★ US POWER SOURCES ★	
POWER TYPES	% USED
Coal	52
Natural gas	15
Oil	4
Nuclear	19
Hydroelectric	9
Other (wind solar)	1

b. Do the percentages add up to 100%?

c. Which power source is used the most?

d. Which two power types, when added together, equal 28% of the power used?

1. The four countries that were the top megawatt producers of wind energy in 1999 were China, Denmark, Germany, and Spain. Of the energy produced by those four countries, China produced 4%, Denmark produced 13%, Germany produced 54%, and Spain produced 29%. Use this information to make a circle graph.

Use the graph in problem 1.

2. What country produced the greatest amount of wind energy?

3. What two countries together produced over three-fourths of the total?

4. Which country produced less than one-tenth of the total wind energy?

5. Make a circle graph using the data given below.

Manufacturing Sector Use of Energy	
Sector	% Used
Paper Products	12%
Chemical Products	25%
Petroleum & Coal Products	30%
Primary Metal Industries	11%
All Other Manufacturing	22%

6. Mr. Chang's business has $4,000 to spend on solar-powered items. The table describes how he decided to budget his money. Using the data, make a circle graph and answer the questions.

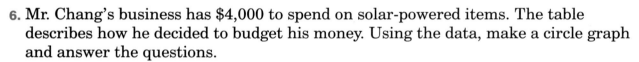

Solar Budget	
Item	% of Budget
Small Solar Toy Cars	14%
One Solar Panel	25%
Solar Water Heater	38%
Portable Solar Battery	23%

7. How much money will be spent on the solar toy cars?

8. One-fourth of the budget will be spent on what item?

9. During a 24-hour day, Chiyoko recorded the energy certain appliances consumed. Use the data given to make a circle graph of the percent of energy used by each appliance.

10. What was the greatest energy consumer?

11. What consumed the least amount of energy?

Energy Consumption	
Appliance	Kilowatt hours
Lighting	4
Heater	2
Clothes Dryer	6
Power Tools	1
Oven	10
Coffee Maker	1
Microwave	1

Lesson 162

Construct Meaning

Some day you may have an opportunity to travel the world. In traveling, you will encounter problems that will require you to use many skills. Using graphs is a good way to compare many types of data. But sometimes graphs can be misleading and confusing. When solving any problem, make sure you have all the information before you draw a conclusion.

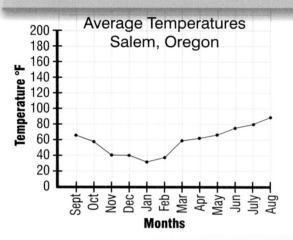

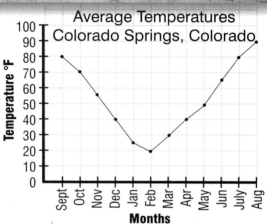

● The titles at the top and the labels at the bottom tell you that both line graphs show average temperature for a one-year period. The graph on the left shows average temperatures for Salem, Oregon. The graph on the right shows average temperatures for Colorado Springs, Colorado.

● The labels at the left side of each graph mark the temperature in degrees Fahrenheit. The intervals are marked in 20°F units on the graph at the left and 10°F units on the graph at the right.

● Critically compare the information in these graphs.

   Is the information on both graphs presented the same way?
   What is the general trend of each graph?
   Closely compare the scales of the vertical axes. What is different about them?
   Does the scale on the axis affect how the line (connecting the data points) on the graph looks?

Check Understanding

a. In general, does Salem have lower temperatures than Colorado Springs?

b. In the month of April, what is the average temperature in Colorado Springs?

348

Mathematics Grade 5

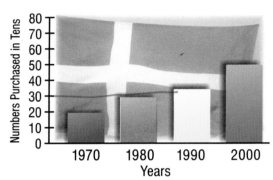

**Denmark
Solar Panels Purchased**

Numbers Purchased in Tens

80
70
60
50
40
30
20
10
0

1970   1980   1990   2000
Years

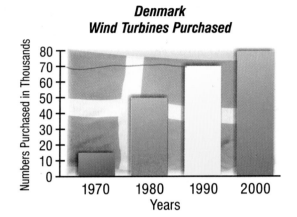

**Denmark
Wind Turbines Purchased**

Numbers Purchased in Thousands

80
70
60
50
40
30
20
10
0

1970   1980   1990   2000
Years

Use the bar graphs above to answer the following questions.

1. In 1970, did Denmark purchase more solar panels or wind turbines?

2. Which energy product shows the greatest change between 1990 and 2000?

3. How many more wind turbines were purchased in 1990 than solar panels?

4. Did the number of wind turbines purchased in 1980 equal the number of solar panels purchased in 2000? Explain your answer.

5. In which years did Denmark purchase more than 40,000 wind turbines?

6. In which years did Denmark purchase more than 40,000 solar panels?

7. In which years did Denmark purchase more solar panels than wind turbines?

8. Collect a data set of your own. Make a table that will contain different hair colors in your class and tally how many students fit in each category. Using your data, draw the best type of graph that will fit your data. Explain why you chose that graph type. Do not forget to title and label your graph.

Construct Meaning

Statistics is a branch of mathematics that deals with collecting, organizing, and analyzing data. Candy-coated chocolates are a perfect tool for understanding statistics.

FREQUENCY TABLE

| | BAG 1 | | | BAG 2 | | | |
Color	Tally	Sub total	Color	Tally	Sub total	Total/ Frequency
Purple	III	3	Purple	II	2	5
Green	ʕʜʯ	5	Green	ʕʜʯ III	8	13
Yellow	ʕʜʯ I	6	Yellow	ʕʜʯ	5	11
Red	ʕʜʯ	5	Red	IIII	4	9
Brown	ʕʜʯ ʕʜʯ	10	Brown	ʕʜʯ ʕʜʯ II	12	22

To collect data about the color of candies, count the colors and tally the results. The table shows the results of counting the contents of two bags of candy. The Total/Frequency column shows how many or how often each color was found.

A **line plot** is a graph that uses an × to represent a number. This line plot has two axes with color along the horizontal axis and frequency along the vertical axis. The × represents one candy of a certain color. The number of ×s in each color column should equal the number in the Total column in the table. There are three ways to analyze the data.

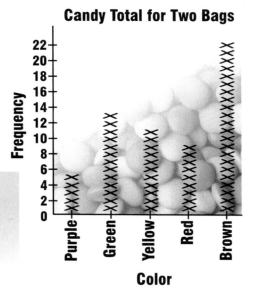

Candy Total for Two Bags

Median: the middle number in a set of data.

> To find the median, put the numbers found in the Total column on the table above into numerical order.

5, 9, 11, 13, 22   Median 11

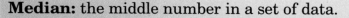

Mean: the average of a set of data.

> What is the mean number of candies per bag? Add all the numbers in the Total column and divide by two, because two bags of candy were counted.

Mean 30 candies per bag

Mode: the number that occurs most often in a set of data.

> To find the mode, look in the Total column or on the line plot. The column with the highest frequency is the mode.

Mode brown

Check Understanding

a. Find the mean number of each candy color per bag, using the table on the previous page.

b. What is the median of 50, 75, 100, 101, 115?

c. Could there ever be more than one mode?

Practice

1. Zaburi recorded the following wind speeds (mph) at hourly intervals during a day.

10, 10, 5, 25, 10, 20, 30, 10, 35, 35, 5, 50

a. Make a line plot with the given information.

b. Calculate the mean wind speed for the day, rounded to the nearest whole number.

c. What is the mode?

Use a Calculator

2. Fatima recorded the daily high temperatures (°F) each day of her family vacation as follows: 60, 64, 70, 70, 60, 60, 80, 80, 78, 80, 80, 78, 72.

a. Make a frequency table tallying the data above.

b. Draw a line plot.

c. Find the mode.

d. Find the median.

e. Use a calculator to find the mean. Round to the nearest whole number.

3. What do you think would happen to the mean in problem 2 if one of the recorded temperatures was 35°F?

4. Write a definition of each term.

a. mean

b. mode

c. median

 **Construct Meaning**

The posse caught up with the <u>mean</u> bank robber while riding a <u>median</u>-sized horse on the open <u>range</u> and <u>mode</u> him down.

Sentences with play-on-words often have little to do with the actual <u>meaning</u> of the word! Mathematical terminology <u>ranges</u> from simple to complex. In the previous lesson, mean, median, and mode were defined and applied in statistics. **Range** is the difference between the greatest and least numbers in a set of numerical data.

In the southwestern United States, there are vast areas of land that are used to raise and herd cattle. Often these areas are called <u>range</u>lands, and it is here that temperatures can become extremely hot.

When finding the range, subtract the lowest temperature from the highest temperature.

80°F 95°F 62°F 101°F 95°F   101°F − 62°F = 39°F

 If there are two middle numbers, the median is the mean of the two middle numbers. Find the median after arranging the numbers in order.

84°F 86°F 90°F 95°F 97°F 99°F   (90°F + 95°F) ÷ 2 = 185°F ÷ 2 = 92.5°F

The mode is the number that appears the most often in a set of data. Sometimes no one number appears more often, in which case there is no mode.

120°F 113°F 116°F 118°F 110°F

 Check Understanding

a. What is the difference between median and mode?

b. How do the mean and the median differ from each other?

c. Using counters or cubes, make one stack each of 2, 5, 3, 6, and 10. Arrange the stacks from tallest to shortest and find the range, median, and mode.

d.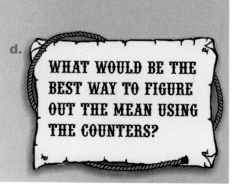

WHAT WOULD BE THE BEST WAY TO FIGURE OUT THE MEAN USING THE COUNTERS?

pply

1. During training, a horse ran at several different speeds. These speeds were recorded in the data set below. Find the range, median, mode, and mean.

   16 mph   21 mph   40 mph   18 mph   32 mph   39 mph   2 mph

2. Zookeeper Larry noted the speed of some of the fastest animals. Find the range, median, mode, and mean. Round to the nearest tenth.

Grant's gazelle	47 mph	Pronghorn antelope	55 mph
Brown hare	45 mph	Springbok	50 mph
Mongolian gazelle	50 mph	Cheetah	65 mph
Horse	43 mph	Thompson's gazelle	47 mph
Red deer	42 mph	Greyhound	42 mph

Bank tellers have different amounts of change at their stations during a day. Copy and complete the table below.

	Number of Quarters	Range	Median	Mode	Mean
3.	53 64 100 24 73 89 24				
4.	40 44 41 49 40 40 40				
5.	70 72 70 81 83 70 86				

6. Brandon owns a horse farm where he breeds horses. For his records he needs to know the range, median, mean, and mode of the height of the horses. Use the data below to find the value of each term.

   50 in. 68 in. 35 in. 42 in. 30 in. 50 in.
   62 in. 30 in. 50 in. 50 in. 61 in.

7. In order to make the range 25, change one number in the data set.
   17 25 5 20 29 7 13

8. Estimate to determine which set of data has the greater mean. Write *a* or *b*.
   a. 90 76 45 57 80 81   b. 80 92 121 55 43 85

9. In order to make the mode 15, change one number in the data set.
   10 21 15 31 6 29

 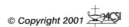

Construct Meaning

Job and his family lived prosperously in the land of Uz. He was a blameless, upright man who feared God and shunned evil. Through several circumstances he lost all his flocks, his children died, and his health failed. But Job remained faithful to God in the midst of the hardships. Because of this, the Lord blessed the latter days of Job more than his first by giving him a greater amount than he had before.

A double bar graph of Job's herds was made using the numbers listed in Job 1:3 and Job 42:12.

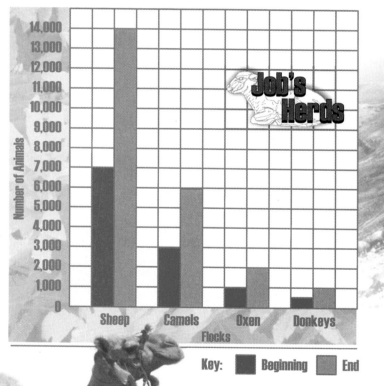

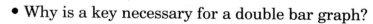

- Why is a key necessary for a double bar graph?

- Job began with the greatest number of which animal?

- How many more camels than donkeys did Job have at the end?

- Did Job have more oxen or donkeys at the beginning?

 **Check Understanding**

Use the double bar graph of Job's herds to answer the following questions.

a. Find the difference between the beginning numbers and the end numbers for each type of animal.

b. What pattern do you notice when comparing the beginning and end herd numbers?

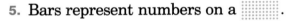 **Practice**

Rancher Tobias has many herds of sheep. He has listed the numbers in each herd.

100   160   40   240   120   150   240   200   165   90

1. Find the range.
2. Find the mode.
3. Find the mean.
4. Find the median.

5. Bars represent numbers on a ▦ .

6. Increases or decreases over time are graphed on a ▦ .

7. Symbols represent numbers on a ▦ .

8. Parts of a whole are shown on a ▦ .

WORD BANK

line graph
circle graph
bar graph
pictograph

9. Anthia gives her horse a type of feed that contains 50% alfalfa, 15% barley, 15% oats, 10% corn, 5% molasses, and 5% soybeans. Make a circle graph to show the percentages.

Days of Sunshine

Month	Jan.	Feb	Mar.	Apr.	May	June	July
Number of Days	2	2	10	12	9	26	22

10. Use the table to make a pictograph.

11. Use the table to make a line graph.

 Apply

Sonja took a survey in her class at school. She asked her classmates what type of transportation they used in order to get to school. She found that 7 students came by car, 9 by bus, 4 rode bicycles, and 6 walked.

12. Make a frequency table using Sonja's data.

13. Make a line plot using the information from the frequency table.

Construct Meaning

If the earth was produced by chance, how many different factors would be involved? Thickness of the earth's crust, the earth's tilt on its axis, and the distance from the sun are just a few of the factors that would have to be considered. God in His wisdom figured out all the factors necessary for life on Earth, not by chance, but by design.

The likelihood that a given event will occur is called **probability**. Probability is a ratio and can be expressed in several ways: $\frac{1}{100}$, 1:100, 1 chance in 10^2.

For example, there are two possible outcomes when you toss a coin: heads and tails. There is one chance in two of tossing tails. It is equally likely that the coin will show heads (H) as it will show tails (T). The probability can be written as a fraction.

$$P\text{(tails)} = \frac{\textbf{Number of Favorable Outcomes (tails)}}{\textbf{Number of Possible Outcomes (tails, heads)}} = \frac{1}{2}$$

We write, $P(T) = \frac{1}{2}$. P represents probability of a certain outcome (T), tails.

The probability of tails as an outcome is one-half or one out of two.

Answer the following questions about the spinner.

Are the sections equivalent?
What are the possible outcomes when spinning the spinner?
How many possible outcomes are there?
What is the probability of the spinner landing on blue?

$$P\text{(blue)} = \frac{\text{Favorable Outcomes (blue)}}{\text{Possible Outcomes (blue, purple, orange, purple)}} = \frac{}{}$$

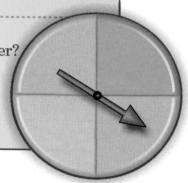

Check Understanding

a. On what color will the spinner probably land the most often? Why?

b. $P\text{(purple)} = \dfrac{\text{Favorable Outcomes (purple, purple)}}{\text{Possible Outcomes (blue, purple, orange, purple)}} = \frac{}{}$

c. $P\text{(orange)} = \dfrac{\text{Favorable Outcomes (orange)}}{\text{Possible Outcomes (blue, purple, orange, purple)}} = \frac{}{}$

d. Use a proportion to make a prediction. If you spin the spinner sixteen times, how many times do you calculate it will land on purple? orange? blue?

Matt enjoys playing *Rock, Paper, Scissors*. There are three possible hand formations for playing the game: two fingers out represents scissors, a fist represents a rock, and a flat hand (fingers extended) represents paper. Suppose there are never any ties.

1. How many possible outcomes are there?

2. Find each probability.
   a. $P(\text{rock}) = $ b. $P(\text{paper}) = $ c. $P(\text{scissors}) = $

3. If thirty rounds are played, how many times would you predict scissors to win? Use a proportion. How many times do you think rock would win? Paper?

4. Make a tally table and play thirty rounds of *Rock, Paper, Scissors*. Record the winning hand formation for each round. Total the number of wins for each. Compare actual outcomes for scissors to your predicted outcome in problem 3. Was it greater than, less than, or equal to the prediction? Explain why.

Lisa and Michael have been married three years and are expecting their first child. Find the following probabilities.

5. $P(\text{boy}) = $ 6. $P(\text{girl}) = $

7. What will be the probability of having a boy as their third child?

Michaela has a regular six-sided number cube numbered one through six.

8. What are the possible outcomes when she rolls the cube?

9. How many possible outcomes are there?

10. What is the probability of rolling a four, $P(4)$?

11. What is the probability of rolling an odd number, $P(\text{odd})$?

12. If she rolled the cube ten times, what is $P(2)$?

Genetically, Lisa and Michael's child is more likely to have brown eyes than blue. This probability is represented on the spinner. Find the probability for each eye color.

13. $P(\text{brown}) = $

14. $P(\text{blue}) = $

 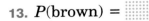

Construct Meaning

"There is a lad here who has five barley loaves and two small fish, but what are they among so many? . . . So when they were filled, He said to His disciples, 'Gather up the fragments that remain, so that nothing is lost.'" John 6:9,12

If the lad had brought the five barley loaves and two small fish to the disciples in a bag, its contents would be unknown. If one item was randomly taken from the bag, what is the probability that it would be a loaf?

$$P(\text{loaf}) = \frac{\text{Favorable outcomes (loaves)}}{\text{Possible Outcomes (loaf, loaf, loaf, loaf, loaf, fish, fish)}} = \frac{5}{7}, \ P(\text{loaf}) = \frac{5}{7}$$

What is the probability that it would be cheese?

$$P(\text{cheese}) = \frac{\text{Favorable outcomes (cheese)}}{\text{Possible Outcomes}} = \frac{0}{7}, \ P(\text{cheese}) = 0$$

> When an event is impossible, the probability is zero.

What is the probability that the item is food?

$$P(\text{food}) = \frac{\text{Favorable outcomes (food)}}{\text{Possible Outcomes}} = \frac{7}{7} = 1, \ P(\text{food}) = 1$$

Since all the items are food, it is certain that the item chosen will be food.

> When an event is certain, the probability is one.

The closer the probability is to one, the more likely it is the event will happen.

Which probability in each pair represents an event more likely to occur?

$\frac{1}{8}$ or $\frac{1}{2}$ 0 or 1 $\frac{5}{16}$ or $\frac{3}{4}$

Check Understanding

Possible Outcomes	
Coin 1	Coin 2
H	H
H	T
T	H
T	T

If two coins are flipped at the same time, there are four different possibilities for combinations of heads and tails as listed below.

a. What is the probability that both coins will be heads?
b. What is the probability that both coins will be tails?
c. What is the probability that the coins will be different?

A dime, a nickel, and a penny are all flipped at the same time. The possible outcomes are listed below.

Possible Outcomes		
dime	**nickel**	**penny**
H	H	H
H	H	T
H	T	H
H	T	T
T	H	H
T	H	T
T	T	H
T	T	T

1. What is the probability that all three coins will show the same side?

2. What is the probability that the dime will be heads?

3. What is the probability that all three coins will show different sides?

4. What is the probability that the dime and the nickel will both be tails?

5. What is the probability that all three coins will be heads?

6. Predict how many times all three coins will be heads for 24 tosses.

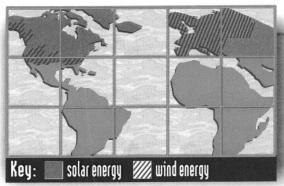

Key: ☐ solar energy ▨ wind energy

Alex had a world map showing areas where solar energy and wind energy are used. He made a game by cutting the map into 15 pieces and shuffling them.

7. If Kimberly draws one card, what is the probability that her card will be entirely water?

8. What is the probability that she would draw a card that shows wind energy use?

9. What is the probability that she would draw a card that shows solar energy use?

10. What would be the probability of choosing a card that shows <u>either</u> wind energy or solar energy?

Solar Strategies

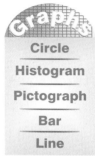

Graph
Circle
Histogram
Pictograph
Bar
Line

Choose the type of graph that would best represent the given information.

1. Norwegian Energy Council financial budget.
2. Classmates' favorite colors of bicycles.
3. Solar energy output over five years.
4. Salaries earned by one hundred employees.
5. Comparing the cost of different types of wind turbines.

A ranch has a holding tank to preserve water in case of a drought. Exposure to the hot sun causes the water to evaporate into the air, decreasing the amount of water in the tank. Make a line graph using the given data.

Time	Water Level
8:30 A.M.	140 cm
10:30 A.M.	140 cm
12:30 P.M.	139 cm
2:30 P.M.	125 cm
4:30 P.M.	112 cm
6:30 P.M.	110 cm
8:30 P.M.	109 cm
10:30 P.M.	109 cm
12:30 A.M.	109 cm

6. What was the total decrease in water level?
7. During which two-hour interval was the water loss the greatest?
8. What could be done to prevent this water loss?
9. Make a prediction about the water level at 2:30 A.M.

Complete each sentence.

10. The number that occurs the most often in a set of data is the ⬚.
11. The middle number in a set of data is the ⬚.
12. The average of the numbers in a set of data is the ⬚.
13. The difference between the largest and smallest numbers in a set of data is the ⬚.

Use the data to find the range, mode, median, and mean.

14. 39 35 16 51 23 16
15. 101 200 243 212 189
16. 10 2 12 4 15 4 16
17. 20 8 32 20 10

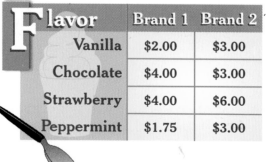

Flavor	Brand 1	Brand 2
Vanilla	$2.00	$3.00
Chocolate	$4.00	$3.00
Strawberry	$4.00	$6.00
Peppermint	$1.75	$3.00

18. Use the table at the left to make a double bar graph.
19. Which brand is usually more expensive?
20. How much does Brand 2 strawberry cost?
21. What is the least expensive brand and flavor?
22. How much more is Brand 2 strawberry than Brand 1 peppermint?

Claire and her mother purchased fruit to make fruit baskets for elderly people in their church. Use the circle graph to answer the following questions.

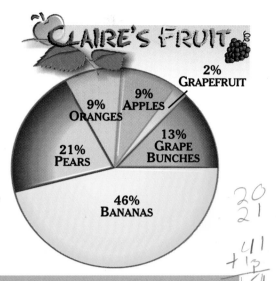

23. Do the percentages add up to 100%?

24. What percentage of the fruit requires peeling before eating?

25. Was the amount of apples and oranges together greater than or less than the amount of pears?

26. Which fruit category represents about one half of the total fruit?

27. What two fruits have equal amounts?

Complete each problem about the spinner on the left.

28. How many possible outcomes are there?

29. $P(7) =$

30. $P(4) =$

31. P(even number) =

32. P(odd number) =

These letter tiles are hidden in a bag.

R S A T P A U R R L L O

33. If one tile is drawn, how many possible outcomes are there?

34. $P(a) =$

35. $P(t) =$

36. $P(r) =$

37. P(vowel) =

Samantha tallied the different colors of candies in one bag of her favorite candy. She made a line plot of the results. Use her line plot to answer the following questions.

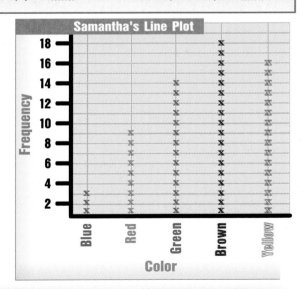

38. What color of candy has the highest frequency?

39. What color of candy occurs the least?

40. How many more yellow candies are there than red?

"I am the light of the world. He who follows Me shall not walk in darkness, but have the light of life." John 8:12

Grade Five

14

Chapter

Lessons 169–176

Go therefore and make disciples of all the nations, . . . and lo, I am with you always, *even* to the end of the age.

Matthew 28:19a, 20b

Construct Meaning

"I went two steps forward, but took three steps back," is an expression used when someone is frustrated by a lack of progress. An example of the statement would be moving ahead two squares when playing a board game, but then drawing a card telling you to move three squares back.

The distance of moving two steps forward and three steps backward may be expressed using **positive numbers** and **negative numbers**.

The two steps forward can be written +2 and read as positive 2. Three steps backward would be –3, which is read as negative 3. The numbers +2 and –3 are called **integers**.

Integers include:
all the positive whole numbers   +1, +2, +3 . . .
all the negative whole numbers   –1, –2, –3 . . .
and zero.

Integers may be shown on a number line.

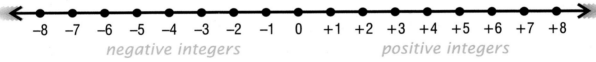

–8 –7 –6 –5 –4 –3 –2 –1   0   +1 +2 +3 +4 +5 +6 +7 +8

negative integers   *positive integers*

Zero is considered neither positive nor negative.

–4 is four units to the left of 0. +4 is four units to the right of 0. –4 and +4 are **opposite numbers** because they are on opposite sides of zero but are the same distance from zero.

A thermometer has a scale showing positive and negative integers. 10° above zero may be expressed as +10° or as 10°. 10° below zero would be –10°.

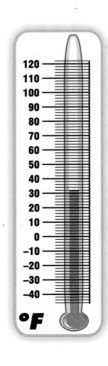

120
110
100
90
80
70
60
50
40
30
20
10
0
–10
–20
–30
–40
°F

Check Understanding

Write the integer and its opposite.

a. a profit of $6.00

b. a ten point penalty

c. an eight point loss

d. a debt of $15.00

e. the freezing point of water on a Fahrenheit thermometer

Copy and complete each sentence.

1. ░░░░░ include all of the positive and negative whole numbers and zero.

2. ░░░░░ is neither positive nor negative.

3. –9 is nine units to the ░░░░ of zero on a number line.

4. +8 and –8 are ░░░░ integers.

Example:

3 feet upward is +3.
3 feet downward is –3.

Write the opposite in words using the opposite integer.

5. 15 miles north is +15.

6. 9 steps backward is –9.

7. $20 loss is –20.

8. A ten-foot fall is –10.

9. 3 hours after shuttle liftoff is +3.

Apply

10. The summit of Mount Everest, which is the highest point on Earth, rises to 29,028 feet above sea level. The shoreline of the Dead Sea is the lowest place on Earth and is 1,312 feet below sea level. If sea level is considered to be zero, how can you express the highest and lowest points on Earth as integers?

11. Name two integers that are one hundred units from zero.

12. Identify the least positive integer and the greatest negative integer.

13. Explain why you agree with this statement: The integer that indicates freezing on a Celsius thermometer is neither positive nor negative.

14. How many degrees separate –2°F from the freezing point of water shown on a Fahrenheit thermometer?

15. Naomi and Ken were playing a game on a number line marked with positive and negative integers. Ken placed his game piece on –3. Naomi's game piece was 9 units to the right of Ken's. Where was Naomi's game piece?

Construct Meaning

On a January morning, it may be ten degrees Fahrenheit in Gunnison, Colorado; five degrees below zero in Fairbanks, Alaska; and two degrees below zero in Yellowstone Park.

Which of the three temperatures is a positive integer?

Identify the two temperatures that are negative integers.

State the warmest and coldest temperatures of the three.

Use a number line to compare integers.

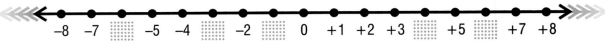

−10 −9 −8 −7 −6 −5 −4 −3 −2 −1 0 +1 +2 +3 +4 +5 +6 +7 +8 +9 +10

Compare +3 and −5.   *Compare −2 and −5.*
+3 > −5   *−2 > −5*

As you move to the right on the number line, the integers become greater.

Compare +1 and −7.   *Compare −1 and −7.*
−7 < +1   *−7 < −1*

−7 is to the left of +7 and −1, so it is less than both of those integers.

To order a set of integers: • *Compare them two at a time.* • *Remember that the greater integer is farther to the right on the number line.*

Order +4, −4, −3, and +6 from the greatest to least.

$$+6 > +4 \qquad +4 > -3$$
$$-3 > -4$$

The order is +6, +4, −3, −4.

Identify the missing integers on the number line, naming them in order from least to greatest. Now name them from greatest to least.

−8 −7 ▦ −5 −4 ▦ −2 ▦ 0 +1 +2 +3 ▦ +5 ▦ +7 +8

Check Understanding

Use > or < to compare the integers.

a. +3 ▦ +7   b. +5 ▦ −1   c. −7 ▦ −2   d. −4 ▦ 0

Write in order from greatest to least.

e. +2 −8 −6 0   f. +4 +1 2 −1

 ractice

Write *true* or *false* for each statement.

1. Of two negative integers, the greater one is located closer to zero on a number line.

2. The integers on a number line become greater as you move to the right.

3. Of two positive integers, the greater one is located closer to zero on a number line.

Use > or < to compare the integers.

4. +2 ⬚ +10   5. +5 ⬚ −5   6. −1 ⬚ 0   7. +3 ⬚ −4

8. −9 ⬚ −10   9. −5 ⬚ −2   10. +6 ⬚ −12   11. −3 ⬚ +3

12. 0 ⬚ −6   13. −8 ⬚ −6   14. +5 ⬚ −7   15. −2 ⬚ −1

Identify the missing numbers from each pattern. Write *greatest to least* or *least to greatest* to tell the order of the integers in the pattern.

16. +2   +1   0   ⬚   −2   ⬚

17. −3   −4   ⬚   −6   ⬚   −8

18. −15   −10   ⬚   0   +5   ⬚

19. +16   +8   ⬚   −8   ⬚   −24

Dunes of Death Valley

20. Which location is closer to sea level, China's Turfan Depression at 505 feet below sea level, or America's Death Valley, which is 282 feet below sea level?

Continent	High Temperature	Low Temperature
Africa	136°F	−9°F
Antarctica	58°F	−129°F
Asia	129°F	−94°F
North America	134°F	−81°F

21. The chart shows extreme temperatures (rounded to whole numbers) that have been recorded on four of the world's seven continents. Order all eight temperatures from least to greatest.

Construct Meaning

Olga and Kenji played a game that involved the gain and loss of points. They used positive and negative integers to keep track of their individual scores.

Olga's Scorecard

POSITIVE	NEGATIVE
+5	−2

Olga made five points on her first turn, but lost two points in the next round. What is her score?

Begin at +5 on the number line.
Move back two numbers.
Her score is +3.

The scorecard shows that Kenji lost points on his first two turns. What is his score?

Begin at −3 on the number line.
Move back five numbers.
His score is −8.

Kenji's Scorecard

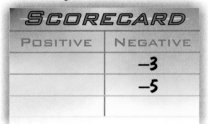

POSITIVE	NEGATIVE
	−3
	−5

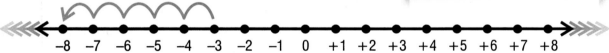

How much greater is Olga's score? Use a number line to compare.

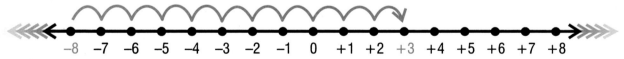

Count forward from Kenji's score to Olga's score.

Olga is ahead by ░░ points.

Check Understanding

a. If Kenji's score is −8, how many points does he need to have a total score that is a positive integer?

b. If Olga's score for her third turn is −3, will her total score be a positive or negative integer?

c. Explain why you agree or disagree with this statement:
   If your score is a negative integer, you must gain a number of points greater than the opposite of that integer to move to the right of zero.

pply

1. Leilani is playing a game on a number line. The game requires using the numbers from two cubes, one marked with positive integers and one with negative integers, to move along the number line. If she begins at 0 and gets the numbers −4 and +6, where will she land?

2. On her next turn, Leilani's numbers were +5 and −5. Where will she place her marker?

3. Mountain climbers experience a variety of weather conditions. If the high temperature on the mountain was 12°F and the low temperature that night was −13°F, what was the difference between the two temperatures?

4. If it was −2°F at 6:00 P.M., and the temperature dropped 14 degrees in the next six hours, what was the temperature at midnight?

The elevation of a location tells how far it is above or below sea level. The surface of the Dead Sea is about 1,300 feet below sea level. Other than simple organisms, no plant or animal life is found there.

Begin at the Dead Sea, and "take a tour" of the Holy Land.

5. To visit the caves where the Dead Sea Scrolls were found, travel to Qumran, which is about 100 feet above the Dead Sea. What is the approximate elevation of Qumran?

6. Travel on to Engedi, a beautiful oasis about 650 feet above the Dead Sea. It was here that David found refuge from Saul as described in I Samuel 23:29. Engedi was also the location where David spared Saul's life, as told in I Samuel 24. What is the approximate elevation of Engedi?

7. Go on to the Judean Hills to visit Bethlehem, which has an elevation of 2,500 feet above sea level. Bethlehem, the birthplace of Christ, was also the birthplace of David, who tended his father's sheep on the nearby hills. What is the approximate difference between the elevation of the Dead Sea and the city of Bethlehem?

Lesson 172

Name the place value of the underlined digit.

1. 95.3<u>9</u>2
2. 0.5<u>46</u>
3. 845,<u>7</u>11
4. <u>4</u>6,929

Round to the nearest place value given.

5. thousandths: 64.0742
6. thousands: 31,688

7. ten thousands: 12,812
8. millions: 727,035,305

Estimate the sum by rounding to the nearest whole number before adding.

9. 10.5
   +30.4

10. 61.71
    +19.68

11. 755.08
    +101.39

12. 0.60
    +52.22

Estimate the difference by rounding to the nearest ten before subtracting.

13. $258.52
    − 49.99

14. 873.618
    − 122.036

15. 95.455
    − 9.700

Write in order from least to greatest.

16. 12.632   12.063   12.620   12.263

17. 2,010,000   2,100,000   2,000,100

Write the number in word form.

18. 0.931
19. 22,413
20. 19,988,001

Write the number in expanded form.

21. 608.15
22. 2,826

23. 16,510

Australia

England

United States of America

China

370

Tanzania

Solve.

24. $12.43
    + 76.89

25. 64.72
    − 26.931

26. 2,848 + 5,620 + 8,012

27. $r + 25 = 172$

28. $a - 33.20 = 70.80$

29. $z - 305 = 66.16$

30. $194 + n = 231$

31. $w - 49 = 685$

32. $781.04 - 59.55 = b$

Write an equivalent decimal for each number.

33. 8.9

34. 13.600

35. 84.10

36. 428.21

Write each number in standard form.

37. fifty-five million, six hundred eighty thousand, three hundred

38. eight hundred forty-two million, four hundred ten thousand, two hundred fifty

39. 900,000 + 80,000 + 2,000 + 200 + 50 + 6

40. 2,000,000 + 500,000 + 60,000 + 9,000 + 800 + 1

French Alps

France

"But you shall receive power when the Holy Spirit has come upon you; and you shall be witnesses to Me in Jerusalem, and in all Judea and Samaria, and to the end of the earth."
Acts 1:8

Thailand

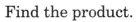

Find the product.

1. 66
    × 4

2. 824
    × 76

3. 307
    ×185

4. 5,280
    ×   93

5. 589
    × 30

6. 4,762
    ×   909

7. 73
    × 73

8. 175
    ×500

Find the quotient.

9. 6)366   10. 7)500̅ᴿ   11. 52)28,560̅ᴿ   12. 18)5,400

13. 42)1,514̅ᴿ   14. 69)1,725   15. 15)175̅ᴿ   16. 24)365̅ᴿ

Find the Least Common Multiple for each pair.

17. 5 and 8   18. 3 and 4   19. 7 and 2   20. 6 and 9

Find the equivalent equation.

21. 18 × (51 + 49) =

   a. (18 + 51) × 49
   b. (18 × 51) × (18 × 49)
   c. (18 × 51) + (18 × 49)

22. 62 × (225 × 9) =

   a. (62 + 225) × 9
   b. (62 × 225) × 9
   c. 62 × (225 + 9)

Find the average for each set of numbers.

23. 22   38   12   42   26

24. 115   120   110   100   125

25. 62   56   40   48   54

26. 1,000   1,500   950   2,050

Estimate the product by rounding both factors to the greatest place value.

27. 565	28. 1,100	29. 144
× 72	× 39	× 12

Find the greatest common factor for each pair.

30. 10 and 20   31. 9 and 21   32. 12 and 16

Select the estimated product using front-end digits.

33. 505 × 41

    a. 20,000
    b. 25,000
    c. 2,000

34. 925 × 12

    a. 9,000
    b. 10,000
    c. 20,000

35. 2,100 × 11

    a. 40,000
    b. 20,000
    c. 30,000

Use mental math to find the product.

36. 900 × 100   37. 5,000 × 80   38. 60 × 300   39. 2,500 × 10

40. Copy the lattice and fill in the missing numbers. Use the lattice to find the product of 486 × 124.

"I will praise You, for I am fearfully *and* wonderfully made; marvelous are Your works, And *that* my soul knows very well." Psalm 139:14

Caribbean bongos

Write the letter of the best answer.

1. A solid figure with flat faces
   - a. angle
   - b. polyhedron
   - c. polygon
   - d. hexagon

2. An exact location in space
   - a. line
   - b. degree
   - c. edge
   - d. point

3. An angle greater than 90°, but less than 180°
   - a. right
   - b. obtuse
   - c. acute
   - d. reflex

4. A tool used to measure angles
   - a. compass
   - b. ruler
   - c. protractor
   - d. level

5. An infinite set of points going in both directions
   - a. line
   - b. ray
   - c. polygon
   - d. figure

6. A closed, plane figure having all points an equal distance from the center
   - a. polygon
   - b. line
   - c. rectangle
   - d. circle

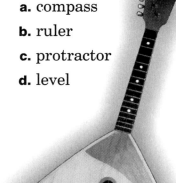

Russian balalaika

7. A polygon having all sides equal in length and all angles equal in measure
   - a. congruent polygon
   - b. regular polygon
   - c. similar polygon
   - d. right triangle

Divide.

8. $4\overline{)6.024}$

9. $3\overline{)12.78}$

10. $25\overline{)75.50}$

11. $8\overline{)0.08}$

12. $15\overline{)42.30}$

13. $12\overline{)13.68}$

14. $8\overline{)\$95.20}$

15. $100\overline{)8.8}$

16. $5\overline{)\$2.50}$

17. $18\overline{)30.96}$

Write the letter of the equation that matches the given answer.

18. Answer: 0.155
    - a. $15.5 \div 10 = n$
    - b. $15.5 \div 100 = n$
    - c. $15.5 \div 1,000 = n$

19. Answer: 0.2983
    - a. $298.3 \div 10 = n$
    - b. $298.3 \div 100 = n$
    - c. $298.3 \div 1,000 = n$

20. Answer: 7.627
    - a. $76.27 \div 10 = n$
    - b. $76.27 \div 100 = n$
    - c. $76.27 \div 1,000 = n$

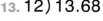

Scottish bagpipes

gongs, Indonesia

Write *true* or *false*.

21. A rectangular prism is a polygon.

22. A square pyramid may be congruent to a triangular pyramid.

23. A right triangle has only one set of perpendicular lines.

24. A regular hexagon has six congruent sides and six congruent angles.

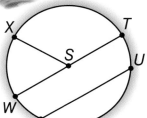

25. Name the circle.

26. Name the diameter shown.

27. ∠*XST* is a(n) .... angle.

28. ∠*WSX* is a(n) .... angle.

29. ∠*WST* is a(n) .... angle.

30. $\overline{VU}$ is a ....

31. $\overline{ST}$ is a ....

Find the product.

32.	33.	34.	35.	36.
0.7	5.064	9.21	50.25	2.767
× 9	× 8	× 2	× 4	× 0.75

37. 338 × 5.5   38. 16.08 × 70.41   39. 0.004 × 66

Italian ocarina

40. Complete the pattern.

$$1 \times \$0.75 = \$0.75$$
$$10 \times \$0.75 = \$7.50$$
$$100 \times \$0.75 = \text{........}$$
$$1{,}000 \times \$0.75 = \text{........}$$

pipe organ, Canada

"Praise Him with the sound of the trumpet;
Praise Him with the lute and harp!
Praise Him with the timbrel and dance;
Praise Him with stringed instruments and flutes!
Praise Him with loud cymbals;
Praise Him with clashing cymbals!
Let everything that has breath praise the LORD.
Praise the LORD!" Psalm 150:3–6

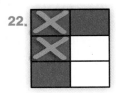

The Netherlands

Write the missing number of the equivalent fraction.

1. $\frac{3}{4} = \frac{}{12}$ 2. $\frac{5}{8} = \frac{}{16}$ 3. $\frac{2}{3} = \frac{}{9}$ 4. $\frac{4}{5} = \frac{}{20}$

List all the factors of each number. Write *prime* or *composite*.

5. 24   6. 19   7. 32   8. 15

List the common factors. Circle the GCF.

9. 6 and 18   10. 9 and 12   11. 7 and 35   12. 18 and 24

Write in order from least to greatest.

13. $\frac{5}{9}$ $\frac{1}{3}$ $\frac{5}{6}$ 14. $\frac{1}{2}$ $\frac{2}{3}$ $\frac{1}{4}$ 15. $\frac{3}{8}$ $\frac{5}{16}$ $\frac{3}{4}$ 16. $\frac{1}{3}$ $\frac{1}{5}$ $\frac{4}{15}$

Rename as a mixed number.

17. $\frac{11}{3}$ 18. $\frac{37}{6}$ 19. $\frac{23}{5}$ 20. $\frac{21}{8}$

Write the equation shown by the fraction models.
Write the answer in simplest form.

21.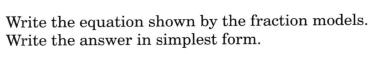

22.

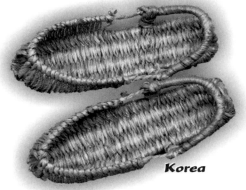

Korea

Turkey

Japan

Add or subtract the fractions using the LCD. Write the answer in simplest form.

23. $\frac{1}{2}$
$+\frac{3}{8}$

24. $\frac{11}{14}$
$-\frac{5}{7}$

25. $\frac{12}{15}$
$-\frac{2}{5}$

26. $\frac{2}{3}$
$+\frac{3}{4}$

27. $6\frac{1}{3}$
$+9\frac{1}{2}$

28. $10\frac{7}{10}$
$-5\frac{1}{4}$

29. $12\frac{1}{4}$
$-6\frac{3}{8}$

30. $10\frac{9}{10}$
$+4\frac{3}{5}$

Multiply. Write the product in simplest form.

31. $\frac{3}{5} \times \frac{1}{2}$ 32. $\frac{2}{3} \times \frac{3}{4}$ 33. $\frac{4}{9} \times \frac{2}{3}$ 34. $\frac{1}{8} \times \frac{4}{10}$

Write the letter of the correct answer.

35. $5\frac{1}{2} \times 4\frac{1}{4}$ **a.** $20\frac{3}{8}$ **b.** $23\frac{1}{8}$ **c.** $23\frac{3}{4}$ **d.** $23\frac{3}{8}$

36. $12\frac{1}{3} \times \frac{1}{5}$ **a.** $2\frac{9}{15}$ **b.** $3\frac{1}{15}$ **c.** $2\frac{1}{2}$ **d.** $2\frac{7}{15}$

37. $\frac{1}{2} \div \frac{1}{4}$ **a.** 4 **b.** $\frac{1}{4}$ **c.** 2 **d.** $\frac{1}{2}$

38. $3 \div \frac{1}{6}$ **a.** 18 **b.** 12 **c.** $\frac{1}{2}$ **d.** 15

India

Round each number to the nearest whole number to estimate the product.

39. $9\frac{1}{3} \times 7\frac{3}{4}$ 40. $12\frac{5}{6} \times 10\frac{2}{5}$

"How beautiful upon the mountains
Are the feet of him who brings good news,
Who proclaims peace,
Who brings glad tidings of good *things*,
Who proclaims salvation,
Who says to Zion,
'Your God reigns!'" Isaiah 52:7

United States

Japan

Find the missing number in each proportion.

1. $\dfrac{10}{15} = \dfrac{n}{60}$

2. $\dfrac{2}{5} = \dfrac{12}{n}$

3. $\dfrac{9}{n} = \dfrac{3}{9}$

Write each ratio two different ways.

4. 2:3

5. 8 to 10

6. $\dfrac{4}{7}$

Write each ratio as a percent.

7. 52:100

8. $\dfrac{23}{100}$

9. 65:100

10. $\dfrac{5}{100}$

11. 144:100

Write each percent as a fraction in simplest form.

12. 25%

13. 62%

14. 75%

15. 33%

16. 80%

17. Lynelle reported that when the sale began, there were 275 pairs of shoes on the clearance racks. 36% have now been sold. How many pairs are left?

Complete each equation.

18. 144 fl oz = ▦ c

19. 4 gal = ▦ qt

20. 12 c = ▦ pt

21. 6 yd 4 ft = ▦ ft

22. 2 mi = ▦ ft

23. 6 mi = ▦ yd

24. 4 dm = ▦ cm

25. 200 cm = ▦ m

26. 10 m = ▦ cm

27. 6,400 m = ▦ km

28. 4 g = ▦ mg

29. 1,000 mg = ▦ g

Write each measurement in pounds.

30. 496 oz

31. 48 oz

32. 100 oz

Yemen

Ireland

Find the perimeter of each figure. Label your answer.

33.
6.2 ft 6.2 ft
6.2 ft

34.
2 cm
4 cm

35.
s = 1.8 in.

Canada

Find the circumference of each circle. Round the answer to the nearest tenth.

36. 2.2 cm

37. 13 mm

38. 3 in.

39. 12 m

Find the area of each figure.

40.
5 cm
12 cm

41.
6 ft
6 ft
10 ft
8 ft

Determine the volume if 1 cube = 1 ft³.

42.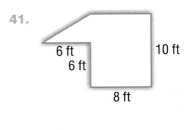

43.

44.

The Netherlands

Find the volume of each object.

45.
9.1 m
1 m
7 m

46.
6 yd
5 yd   7 yd

47.
12 in.
2 in.
2 in.

"But as for me and my house, we will serve the LORD." Joshua 24:15b

England

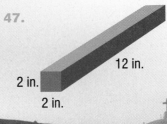

Greece

Table of Measures

Customary Units

Temperature

32°Fahrenheit (F) – water freezes

212°Fahrenheit (F) – water boils

98.6°Fahrenheit (F) – normal body temperature

Length

12 inches (in.) = 1 foot (ft)

$\left.\begin{array}{l}\text{3 feet}\\\text{36 inches}\end{array}\right\}$ = 1 yard (yd)

$\left.\begin{array}{l}\text{5,280 feet}\\\text{1,760 yards}\end{array}\right\}$ = 1 mile (mi)

Weight

16 ounces (oz) = 1 pound (lb)

2,000 pounds = 1 ton (T)

Capacity

3 teaspoon (tsp) = 1 tablespoon (tbsp)

8 fluid ounces (fl oz) = 1 cup (c)

2 cups = 1 pint (pt)

2 pints = 1 quart (qt)

4 quarts = 1 gallon (gal)

Metric Units

Temperature

0°Celsius (C) – water freezes

100°Celsius (C) – water boils

37°Celsius (C) – normal body temperature

Length

10 millimeters (mm) = 1 centimeter (cm)

10 centimeters = 1 decimeter (dm)

$\left.\begin{array}{l}\text{100 centimeters}\\\text{10 decimeters}\end{array}\right\}$ = 1 meter (m)

1,000 meters = 1 kilometer (km)

Mass

1,000 milligrams (mg) = 1 gram (g)

1,000 grams = 1 kilogram (kg)

Capacity

1,000 milliliters (mL) = 1 liter (L)

Units of Time

60 seconds (sec) = 1 minute (min)

60 minutes = 1 hour (hr)

24 hours = 1 day (d)

7 days = 1 week (wk)

about 4 weeks = 1 month (mo)

$\left.\begin{array}{l}\text{365 days}\\\text{52 weeks}\\\text{12 months}\end{array}\right\}$ = 1 year (yr)

366 days = 1 leap year

10 years = 1 decade

100 years = 1 century

1,000 years = 1 millennium

Formulas

Perimeter of a rectangle $P = 2l + 2w$

Perimeter of a square $P = 4s$

Circumference of a circle $C = \pi d$

Area of a rectangle $A = l \times w$

Area of a triangle $A = \frac{1}{2} \times b \times h$

Volume of a rectangular prism $V = l \times w \times h$

Symbols

<	is less than	$\bullet A$	point A	$\parallel$	is parallel to
>	is greater than	$\overleftrightarrow{AB}$	line AB	$\perp$	is perpendicular to
=	is equal to	$\overline{AB}$	line segment AB	$\cong$	is congruent to
$\neq$	is not equal to	$\overrightarrow{AB}$	ray AB	(2,3)	ordered pair 2,3
$\approx$	is approximately equal to	$\angle ABC$	angle ABC	10^4	ten to the fourth power
°	degree	$\triangle ABC$	triangle ABC	1:3	ratio of 1 to 3
%	percent	π	pi ($\pi \approx 3.14$)	$\frac{3}{4}$	three-fourths

A

Acute angle An angle measuring less than 90°. (p. 154)

J
45°
K — L

Acute triangle A triangle having three acute angles. (p. 160)

Addition The mathematical operation that combines two or more addends to obtain a sum. (p. 38)

```
 29 ← addend
+48 ← addend
 77 ← sum
```

A.M. *Ante meridiem*. The time period beginning at midnight and continuing until noon. (p. 294)

Angle An angle is formed by two rays with the same endpoint. (p. 154) ∠*ABC* or ∠*B*

A
C
B

Area The number of square units that cover a surface. (p. 310)

Associative (Grouping) Property of Addition Addends can be grouped differently without changing the sum. (p. 38) **(7 + 3) + 2 = 7 + (3 + 2)**

Associative (Grouping) Property of Multiplication The grouping of factors may change without changing the product. (p. 56) **(6 × 5) × 2 = 6 × (5 × 2)**

Asymmetry No lines of symmetry exist. (p. 174)

Average The number obtained by dividing the sum of a set of numbers by the number of addends. Also called the *mean*. (p. 98)

B

Bar graph Uses horizontal or vertical bars to represent and compare information. (p. 338)

Base A side of a polygon or a face of a solid figure. (p. 166)

Base number The number used as a repeated factor. (p. 80)

C

Capacity The amount a container can hold when it is filled. (p. 290)

Centimeter (cm) A metric unit of length. 100 centimeters equal 1 meter. (p. 298)

Chord A line segment with both endpoints on the circle. (p. 172)

A
B   C

Circle A closed plane figure with all points an equal distance from the center. (p. 172)

Circle graph A circle divided into sections comparing parts to the whole. (p. 346)

Circumference The distance around a circle. (p. 314)

Common factor A factor shared by two or more numbers. (p. 62)

Common multiples Multiples that are shared by two or more numbers. (p. 60)

Commutative (Order) Property of Addition Rearranging the order of addends does not change the sum. (p. 38) **4 + 8 + 5 = 8 + 4 + 5**

Commutative (Order) Property of Multiplication Changing the order of the factors does not change the product. (p. 56) $6 \times 9 = 9 \times 6$

Compass A tool used to draw a circle. (p. 172)

Compatible numbers Numbers that can be computed mentally and are near the numbers in a problem. (p. 94)

Composite number A whole number that has more than two factors. (p. 190)
12 is a composite number. Its factors are 1, 2, 3, 4, 6, and 12.

Cone A solid figure with a circular base and one vertex. (p. 168)

Congruent figures Figures that have the same shape and size. (p.178)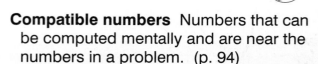
$\triangle ABC \cong \triangle XYZ$

Coordinates The numbers of an ordered pair used to locate a point on a grid. (p. 316)

Cross products Using two equal ratios, multiply each numerator by the denominator of the other ratio. (p. 264)

Cube A solid figure with six congruent square faces. (p. 168)

Cup (c) A customary unit for measuring capacity. 8 fluid ounces equal 1 cup. (p. 290)

Customary system The measurement system used primarily in the United States. (p. 288)

Cylinder A solid figure with two congruent circular bases that are parallel. (p. 168)

D

Data Individual facts or items of information. (p. 336)

Decimal A number that uses a decimal point and place value to show tenths, hundredths, thousandths, and so on. (p. 12)

Decimeter (dm) A metric unit of length. 10 decimeters equal 1 meter. (p. 298)

Degree (°) The unit used to measure an angle or temperature, shown by the symbol °. (p. 154, 296)

Degree Celsius (°C) The metric unit for measuring temperature. (p. 296)

Degree Fahrenheit (°F) The customary unit for measuring temperature. (p. 296)

Denominator The number below the line in a fraction that tells the total number of equal parts in a whole. (p. 184) $\frac{3}{4}$ ← denominator

Diameter A line segment crossing the center of a circle and having both endpoints on the circle. (p. 172) M ⊙ N

Digit A symbol used for writing numbers: 0, 1, 2, 3, 4, 5, 6, 7, 8, and 9. (p. 2)

Distributive Property The product remains the same whether the factor is multiplied by the sum of the addends or by each addend. (p. 56)

Dividend The number that is divided. (p. 90)

Divisible A number is divisible by another number if it can be divided by that number with no remainder. (p. 88)

Division The mathematical operation that separates a number into equal groups or an equal number of groups. (p. 88)

quotient
3 R1
divisor 5) 16 dividend
−15
1 remainder

Divisor The number that divides the dividend. (p. 90)

Double bar graph A bar graph that uses two sets of bars to represent and compare numbers having the same units. (p. 338)

E

Edge A line segment where two faces of a polyhedron intersect. (p. 168)

EDGES

Endpoint The point at the end of a line segment or ray. (p. 152)

Equal ratio Ratios that give the same comparison. (p. 262)

Equation A number sentence written with an equal sign. (p. 32)

Equilateral triangle A triangle with three sides of equal length. (p. 160)

Equivalent decimals Different names for the same number. (p. 44) 0.2 0.20 0.200

Equivalent fractions Fractions that name the same amount or number. (p. 186) $\frac{1}{2} = \frac{2}{4}$

Estimate An answer that is close to the exact answer. (p. 26)

Expanded form A way to write a number to show the value of each digit. (p. 2) 1,000 + 300 + 80 + 6

Exponent Tells the number of times the base number is used as a factor. (p. 80)

F

Face A flat surface of a solid figure. (p. 168)

FACES

Factor A number multiplied by another number to find a product. (p. 56) 8 × 4 =32 ↑ ↑ factor

Flip (*See* Reflection.)

Fluid ounce (fl oz) A customary unit of capacity. 8 fluid ounces equal 1 cup. (p. 290)

Foot (ft) A customary unit of length. 12 inches equal 1 foot. (p. 288)

Fraction A number that names part of a whole or part of a group. (p. 184)

Frequency The number of times a certain item appears in a set of data. (p. 338)

Front-end digit The digit in the greatest place value. (p. 28)

G

Gallon (gal) A customary unit of capacity. 4 quarts equal 1 gallon. (p. 290)

Geometry The branch of mathematics that identifies and studies lines, shapes, and figures. (p. 152)

Gram (g) A metric unit of mass. 1,000 milligrams equal 1 gram. (p. 302)

Graph A drawing that includes a title, axis headings, and increments to show and compare information. (p. 336)

Greater than The symbol > used to compare one number with another. The greater number is written before the symbol. (p. 6) **57 > 52**

Greatest common factor (GCF) The largest common factor of two or more numbers. (p. 62) **2 is the greatest common factor of 4 and 10.**

Grouping Property of Addition (*See* Associative [Grouping] Property of Addition.)

Grouping Property of Multiplication (*See* Commutative [Order] Property of Multiplication.)

Hexagon A polygon having six sides. (p. 170)

Histogram A graph that uses bars to represent how many of a particular item are found in a given category or interval. (p. 340)

Improper fraction A fraction that has a numerator greater than or equal to $\frac{5}{4}$ the denominator. (p. 200)

Inch (in.) The smallest customary unit of length. 12 inches equal 1 foot. (p. 288)

Inequality A number sentence written with > , < , or ≠ symbol. (p.263)

Integers Positive and negative whole numbers and zero. (p. 364)

Interest Money paid to borrow money or money earned by investing money. (p. 283)

Intersecting lines Lines which cross each other, meeting at a common point. (p. 152)

Interval The number of units between the lines on the scale of a graph. (p. 344)

Inverse operation The opposite, or inverse, operation of subtraction is addition. (p. 30) The inverse operation of division is multiplication. (p. 142)

Isosceles triangle A triangle with at least two sides of equal length. (p. 160)

Kilogram (kg) A metric unit of mass. 1,000 grams equal 1 kilogram. (p. 302)

Kilometer (km) A metric unit of length. 1,000 meters equal 1 kilometer. (p. 298)

Least common denominator (LCD) The smallest common multiple of two or more denominators. (p. 220)

Least common multiple (LCM) The smallest common multiple of two or more numbers. (p. 60)

Less than The symbol < used to compare one number with another. The lesser number is written before the symbol. (p. 16) **52 < 57**

Line A straight path that continues without end in both directions. (p. 152)

Line graph Uses lines to represent increases or decreases over a period of time. (p. 344)

Line of symmetry A line (or fold) that divides a figure into congruent halves. (p. 174)

Line plot A graph that uses an × to represent a quantity and show comparisons. (p. 350)

Line segment Part of a line between two endpoints. (p. 152)

Liter (L) A metric unit of capacity. 1,000 milliliters equal 1 liter. (p. 300)

Mass Mass is a measure of how much matter there is in an object. (p. 302)

Mean The number obtained by dividing the sum of a set of numbers by the number of addends. Also called the *average*. (p. 98)

Median The middle number in a set of ordered data. (p. 350) **5, 9, 11, 13, 22**
Median: 11

Meter (m) The basic unit of length in the metric system. 100 centimeters equal 1 meter. (p. 298)

Metric system An international measurement system used by most nations of the world. (p. 298)

Mile (mi) A customary unit of length. 5,280 feet equal 1 mile. (p. 288)

Milligram (mg) A metric unit of mass. 1,000 milligrams equal 1 gram. (p. 302)

Milliliter (mL) A metric unit of capacity. 1,000 milliliters equal 1 liter. (p. 300)

Millimeter (mm) A metric unit of length. 10 millimeters equal 1 centimeter. (p. 298)

Mixed number A number that has a whole number and a fraction. (p. 200) $2\frac{3}{8}$

Mode The number that occurs most often in a set of data. (p. 350)

Multiple A multiple is the product of a select number and another whole number. (p. 58) **Multiples of 8 (8 × 1, 8 × 2, 8 × 3, etc.) are 8, 16, 24, etc.**

Multiplication Multiplication is the mathematical operation that combines groups of equal size a certain number of times resulting in a product. (p. 56)

8 ← factor
× 9 ← factor
72 ← product

Multiplication Identity Property of One If one factor is 1, the product will be the other factor. (p. 56) **1 × 57 = 57**

Negative number A number that is less than zero. (p. 364)

Number line A line that shows numbers in order. (p. 8)

Numerator The number above the line in a fraction that tells the number of equal parts being considered. (p. 184)

$\frac{4}{9}$ ←numerator

Obtuse angle An angle measuring greater than 90° but less than 180°. (p. 154)

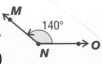

Obtuse triangle A triangle having one angle greater than 90°. (p. 160)

Octagon A polygon having eight sides. (p. 170)

Opposite numbers Numbers that are on opposite sides of zero and are equal distance from zero. (p. 364)

Order Property of Addition (*See* Commutative [Order] Property of Addition.)

Order Property of Multiplication (*See* Commutative [Order] Property of Multiplication.)

Ordered pair The numbers used to locate a point on a grid. (p. 316)

Ounce (oz) A customary unit of weight. 16 ounces equal 1 pound. (p. 292)

Outcome A possible result in a probability event. (p. 356)

Parallel lines Lines in the same plane which do not intersect. (p. 152)

Parallelogram A quadrilateral having opposite sides that are parallel. The opposite sides are congruent, or same length. (p. 166)

Pentagon A polygon having five sides. (p. 170)

Pentomino Five equal squares arranged so that at least one whole side of each square is touching a whole side of another square. (p. 156)

Percent (%) Percent means per one hundred. (p. 270)

Perimeter The distance around a figure. (p. 312)

Period A group of three digits separated by a comma. Ones, thousands, and millions are periods. (p. 2)

Perpendicular lines Intersecting lines that form right angles. (p. 152)

Pi (π) The ratio of the circumference of a circle to its diameter. (p. 314) π ≈ **3.14.**

Pictograph A graph that illustrates data by using symbols to represent numbers. (p. 342)

Pint (pt) A customary unit of capacity. 2 cups equal 1 pint. (p. 290)

Plane A flat surface that extends without

end in all directions. (p. 152)

Plane figure A figure that lies on a flat surface. (p. 160)

P.M. *Post meridiem*. The time period beginning at noon and continuing until midnight. (p. 294)

Point A fixed location in space. (p. 152)

•*A*

Polygon A polygon is a closed plane figure formed by line segments. (p. 164)

Polyhedron A solid figure having only flat surfaces called faces. (p. 168)

Positive number A number that is greater than zero. (p. 364)

Pound (lb) A customary unit of weight. 16 ounces equal 1 pound. (p. 292)

Prime factorization Factoring a number until all the numbers are prime. (p. 190)

Prime number A whole number that has exactly two factors, 1 and the number itself. (p. 190) **2, 3, 5, 7, and 11 are prime numbers.**

Prism A prism is a polyhedron with two parallel congruent bases and rectangular sides. (p. 168)

Probability The likelihood that a given event will occur. (p. 356)

$$\text{Probability} = \frac{\text{Number of Favorable Outcomes}}{\text{Number of Possible Outcomes}}$$

Product The result of multiplying two or more factors. (p. 56)

Proportion An equation that shows that two ratios are equal. (p. 264)

Protractor An instrument that is used for constructing and measuring angles. (p. 158)

Pyramid A solid figure with a polygon base having triangular faces that meet at a common vertex. (p. 168)

triangular
square
rectangular

Q

Quadrilateral A polygon with four sides. (p. 166)

Quart (qt) A customary unit of capacity. 2 pints equal 1 quart. (p. 290)

Quotient The result of dividing one number by another. (p. 90)

R

Radius A line segment from the center to a point on the circle. (p. 172)

Range The difference between the greatest number and the least number in a set of numerical data. (p. 98)

Ratio A ratio compares two numbers. (p. 260) $\frac{10}{100}$; 10 to 100; 10:100

Ratio table Shows a series of equal ratios. (p. 262)

miles	3	6	9
minutes	1	2	3

Ray Part of a line that has one endpoint and goes on without end in one direction. (p. 152)

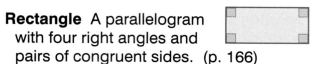

Grade Five

Rectangle A parallelogram with four right angles and pairs of congruent sides. (p. 166)

Rectangular Prism A solid figure having six rectangular faces. (p. 168)

Reflection A move that turns the figure over on a line of symmetry. Also called a *flip*. (p. 176)

Regular polygon Has sides that are equal in length and angles that are equal in size. (p. 164)

Remainder The number that is left over after dividing and is smaller than the divisor. (p. 92)

Rhombus A parallelogram having all sides congruent. (p. 166)

Right angle An angle measuring 90°. (p. 154)

Right triangle A triangle having one 90° angle. (p. 160)

Roman numerals An ancient Roman system for writing numbers. (p. 21)

Rotation A rotation moves the figure around a fixed point. Also called a *turn*. (p. 157)

Rounded number A number expressed to a specific nearest place value. (p. 8) 439 rounded to the nearest hundred is 400.

Sales tax A tax imposed on the cost of

goods or services and is computed as a percentage of the total sales price. (p. 282)

Scale (1) A scale on a map shows the relationship between a unit of distance on the map and a unit of ground distance. (p. 232) (2) Numbers along the side or bottom of a graph. (p. 338)

Scale drawing A scale drawing represents what is actual by showing a proportional drawing. (p. 268)

Scalene triangle A triangle having three unequal sides. (p. 160)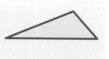

Similar figures Figures that have the same shape but may not have the same size. (p. 178)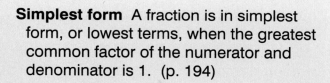

Simplest form A fraction is in simplest form, or lowest terms, when the greatest common factor of the numerator and denominator is 1. (p. 194)

Slide (*See* Translation.)

Solid figure A solid figure has length, width, and height and takes up space. (p. 168)

Sphere A solid figure with all points the same distance from the center. (p. 168)

Square A rectangle having four congruent sides. (p. 166)

Standard form The usual way to write a number using digits. (p. 2) 1,386

Statistics A branch of mathematics that deals with collecting, organizing, and analyzing data. (p. 350)

Straight angle An angle of 180°. (p. 154)

Subtraction The mathematical operation that finds a difference between two numbers. (p. 28)

83 ← minuend
− 27 ← subtrahend
56 ← difference

Surface area The sum of the areas of all the faces of a solid figure. (p. 324)

Symmetry At least one line of symmetry can be drawn in a figure. Symmetrical halves appear as mirror images. (p. 174)

Tablespoon (tbsp) A customary unit of capacity. 3 teaspoons equal 1 tablespoon. (p. 290)

Ton (T) A customary unit of weight. 2,000 pounds equal 1 ton. (p. 292)

Transformation A change in the location or position of a figure, but not in its size or shape. (p. 176)

Translation A translation moves the figure in a straight line, changing its location, but not its position. Also called a *slide*. (p. 176)

Trapezoid A quadrilateral with only two opposite sides parallel. (p. 166)

Triangle A polygon having three sides. (p. 160)

Triangular prism A solid figure having two triangular bases and rectangular sides. (p. 168)

Turn (*See* Rotation.)

Vertex (plural, vertices) (1) The endpoint at which two rays intersect. (2) The point at which two sides of a polygon intersect. (3) The point where edges meet on a solid figure. (p. 154)

(1) (2) (3)

Volume Volume is the measure of the amount of space within a solid figure or object. It is expressed in cubic units. (p. 326)

Whole number Any of the numbers 0, 1, 2, 3, and so on. (p. 2)

Word form A way to write a number using words. (p. 2) **two hundred sixty-four**

Yard (yd) A customary unit of length. 3 feet or 36 inches equal 1 yard. (p. 288)

Zero Property of Addition When zero is added to any addend, the sum is the other addend. (p. 38)

Zero Property of Multiplication Multiplying any factor by 0 results in a product of zero. (p. 56)

Index

Grade Five

Q

Grade Five